BRITISH POLITICAL SOCIOLOGY YEARBOOK

Elites in Western Democracy

VOLUME 1

Elites in Western Democracy

EDITED BY IVOR CREWE

A HALSTED PRESS BOOK

JOHN WILEY & SONS

New York — Toronto

First published 1974
© 1974 by Croom Helm Ltd

Published in the USA and Canada by Halsted Press,
a Division of John Wiley and Sons, Inc., New York.

ISBN: 0–470–18685–2

Library of Congress Catalog Card Number: 73-9248

75-302714

Printed in Great Britain

CONTENTS

5

PREFACE

The purpose of the *British Political Sociology Yearbook* is to strengthen the state of political sociology *in* Britain by gathering together original work on the political sociology *of* Britain. The original inspiration for the book came from David Martin's *Yearbook of the Sociology of Religion in Britain*. It occurred to me that although over the last decade the curriculum in university and college departments of politics throughout Britain had undergone a 'sociological revolution', as an organised academic activity British political sociology, like the sociology of religion, could hardly be said to exist. The subject lacked the two main requisites of a healthy discipline: a specialised journal and regular conferences and workshops. A regular medium of communication amongst political sociologists seemed clearly overdue.

This *Yearbook* takes political sociology to be concerned with the attempt to describe and explain political phenomena through the use of sociological concepts and theories. What distinguishes political sociology from other branches of the social sciences is not its method of collecting and analysing data, nor its substantive content, but the particular set of concepts, and of theories composed of such concepts, that it adopts for understanding politics.

This is the first of what will be an annual series. Each volume will contain hitherto unpublished papers on a single but broadly conceived theme. Next year's volume will be devoted to the political sociology of race in contemporary Britain, and subsequent issues are expected to cover politics and social stratification, political ideology and culture, and community power. The intention is to give each issue a similar structure. Each will contain discussions of fresh empirical research, innovations of method and developments in concepts and theory, as well as critiques of past work. And as befits a yearbook, each volume will contain a bibliography, notes on current research and a report on 'the state of the discipline' appropriate to that year's theme. For this first volume it was naturally necessary to commission all the papers; but unprompted contributions to next year's issue on race and politics in Britain will be most welcome.

I.M.C.

ACKNOWLEDGEMENTS

Michael Hill of the London School of Economics gave me valuable advice at the start of this project; and David Croom was always more patient and encouraging than I had the right to expect.

I owe a special debt of gratitude to Tony Fox for helping me in various ways, but especially in the preparation of the bibliography.

1. Introduction:
Studying Elites in Britain

IVOR CREWE

The first volume of the *Yearbook* is about elites, especially elites in Britain, for two reasons. Firstly, the subject clearly lies in the mainstream of political sociology, however defined. Few of those prepared to label themselves political sociologists, whatever their institutional or political affiliations, would deny the importance of studying elites, and almost all political sociology courses offered in British universities include the topic in their syllabi. The classical elite theorists – Pareto, Mosca and Michels – are traditionally accorded a place in the pantheon of the discipline's founding fathers; and the topic is typically approached in a way that emphasises what many consider to be the discipline's distinctive concern (linking social structures with political regimes) and what others mistakenly assume to be its distinctive method (positivist and quantitative). Only orthodox Marxists denigrate the study of elites, claiming that the concept is an ideological tool of bourgeois social science (Poulantzas, 1969), but they are prone to concern themselves with the identical area, whilst substituting their own vocabulary. The fashionable Marxist term for elite at present appears to be 'class fraction'.

Secondly, this is an appropriate time to assess the state of British elite studies. Creative work on British elites seems to come in waves at the rate of about one per decade. In the mid-1950s a flurry of books appeared which served as models for years to come: R. T. McKenzie's analysis of oligarchy in the Labour and Conservative Parties (1955), still authoritative, but in need of updating since its last revision (1964); Kelsall's scholarly research on recruitment to the senior Civil Service (1955); and two pioneering works on British industrialists and managers by Copeman (1955) and the Acton Trust Society (1956). A second wave appeared in the early 1960s with the publication of Guttsman's painstaking analysis of *The British Political Elite* (1963), also badly in need of updating, and Sampson's impressionistic but stimulating *Anatomy of Britain*

(1962, 1971). At about this time the ascriptive, high status backgrounds of British cabinet ministers, civil servants and boardroom directors were increasingly condemned as 'amateur' and held responsible for (among other economic ills) low productivity, falling exports and poor industrial relations (Sampson, 1962; *Encounter*, 1962). A subject of national concern, it provoked research into elites which was reported in subsequent years (e.g. the Fulton Report on the Civil Service, Vol. 1 and 3 (1)). It was also in this period that English translations of the classic works on elites reappeared in convenient form; Michels' *Political Parties* (1959), selections from Pareto's writings (Pareto, 1959; Finer, 1966) and the whole of Mosca's *The Ruling Class* were again in print for the first time since the war; and were the subject of important critiques, from differing political standpoints, by Keller (1963) and Bottomore (1964).

Further work has, of course, been published since the early 1960s, of which that by Miliband (1969), Nichols (1969) and Johnson (1973) is clearly important; but the rate of progress has been modest. Extensions to our knowledge have been minor, methodological innovations few, and developments in elite theory almost nil. The major controversies (ruling class *v.* power elite; elitism *v.* pluralism; reputational *v.* decision-making approaches) have become stale. There is currently a renewal of interest in British elites, however, which seems likely to produce some of the advances that were lacking over the last decade, and on which we already have preliminary reports (Headey, 1970; Rose, 1971; Giddens, 1972; Putnam, 1973; and Morris and Newton, 1969 onwards). The SSRC has sponsored community studies in Birmingham, Liverpool, Aberdeen, Salford, Southampton, Dundee, Ashford, Glasgow and Sheffield; the last has already been published (Hampton, 1971). Although each study is entirely independent, and some like Hampton's focus on participation rather than power or decision-making, they will clearly provide for the first time the necessary comparative basis for testing theories about elites in local communities. The SSRC has also funded Cambridge University's project on 'Elites in the Class Structure', of which Stanworth's contribution to this volume is a product. This has collected substantially more data on the origins, circulation and connections of a greater variety of elites than has ever been collected before, and especially on economic elites. Further forbidden territory has been entered by Headey, whose interview study of cabinet ministers will appear shortly, and by Putnam and his associates at the University of Michigan, who are engaged on a comparative interview survey of senior civil servants in British and other Western democracies.

All these studies use conventional methods to add to our knowledge. Others are applying new techniques of analysis to conventional concerns. Two important examples of such innovation are included in this volume. Budge and Farlie employ the PYRA computer programme to produce 'likelihood vectors' for each elite member and thus are able to examine the customary assumptions about the influence of social background on elite values with a rigour that such assumptions have always required yet have previously forgone. And Wakeford *et al.* adopt, for the first time, a variety of cluster analysis to trace the interconnections amongst various contemporary elite groups in Britain. The pace of theoretical and conceptual advance also appears to be quickening. Parry and Morriss, both of whom have written on power and elites elsewhere (Parry, 1966 and 1969; Morriss, 1972) contribute to the *Yearbook* an elaboration of the concept of non-decision which manages to provide an empirical basis for locating its existence and to avoid the usual ideological polemics. And Hennessey and Wellhofer in this volume show how alternative explanations to those of Michels for the behaviour of party elites can be derived from the 'rational-choice' concepts and hypotheses contained in Hirschman's *Exit, Voice and Loyalty*, the latest substantial contribution to the recent revival of political economy.

Definitions

But whatever current and future work on British elites turns up, past studies of British elites reveal a noticeably uniform and conventional approach. There can be said to be a distinctive (but not necessarily distinguished) tradition of British elite studies. Its first major feature is negative – the absence of the kind of acrimonious debate on terms, with its implications for democratic theory, that has occurred between 'elitists' and 'pluralists' in the United States and (further back in time) between Marxists and 'elitists' on the European Continent (European elitists being ideologically distant but analytically close to their namesakes in the United States). Social science in Britain has suffered the same semantic confusion in the area of elite studies as it has elsewhere, being littered with the inconsistent and ambiguous use of such terms as power elite, ruling class, polyarchy, political class, political elite and governing class. But these concepts have been confined to the theoretical literature

11

or to work on foreign elites and hardly ever applied to Britain (for a rare exception, see Aaronovitch, 1961). The only specifically British contribution to these labels has been the peculiarly unhelpful notion of 'The Establishment' on the existence of which, like the Marxist 'ruling' class, many more have been convinced than convincing, and on the definition of which there has been even less clarity. Blondel (1963) makes the most sustained attempt at a definition but does not resolve its precise terms of membership, social or ideological.

Giddens (1972) has recently cleared much of the fog by suggesting four dimensions on which elites can usefully be described: (i) the openness or closedness, in socio-economic terms, of their recruitment; (ii) the high or low degree of their integration, both 'social' and 'moral'; (iii) the 'broad' or 'restricted' scope of issues over which the elite has influence; and (iv) the degree to which the elite shares power with the non-elite. On this basis a 'ruling class' is defined as having closed recruitment and a monopoly of power, but somewhat surprisingly Giddens does not specify that it must have a high degree of integration or exercise power over a broad range of issues. A 'power elite' is openly recruited but highly integrated and monopolises power, but again somewhat unexpectedly, over only a narrow range of issues. 'Leadership groups' describes a situation in which elites are openly recruited, possess low integration and are forced to share their power with non-elite groups. But again, Giddens leaves the question of the range of issues over which each has influence quite open, thus defining the situation slightly differently from Dahl's 'polyarchy' with which it otherwise has close affinity (Dahl, 1971). Naturally, these are all regarded as ideal-type constructions to which any actual pattern of elite formation and power will only approximate; but for precisely that reason it is surprising that Giddens should have unnecessarily added to the confusion in this area by failing to construct purer ideal-types. Nonetheless, the criteria are simple, clear and amenable to ordinal measurement, and as such must count as a considerable improvement upon previous discussions.

THE BRITISH TRADITION OF ELITE STUDIES

Disputes over definitions and terms rarely figure in British elite studies, and those employed are uniform and consistent. This can be attributed to the monotony in British approaches to such studies, which might be unkindly summarised as follows: (1) Make no attempt to analyse the whole of the British elite structure; study only one elite group at a time. (2) Select the single elite group on grounds of accessibility of data and the clarity of its boundaries rather than its importance within the power structure of Britain. (3) Focus on the elite group's collective biography - on who they are (or more likely, *were*), not what they believe (ideology) or what they do (roles). (4) Exclusively focus on its economic, educational and demographic origins. Thus the typical conception of an elite group for British social scientists consists of the incumbents of the top echelons of clearly structured and bounded social organisations which appear to possess manifest power or prestige; and the customary way of understanding its nature is to analyse its social origins. Thus the British elite structure as a whole is assumed to consist of a simple aggregation of the social background of each component elite group. This approach seems at least to have the saving virtue of clearly and simply operationalising the study of elites.

This is a caricature of British elite studies, but not an unreasonable one. A glance at the bibliography that concludes this volume reveals a wealth of bibliographical material on select elite groups, but a dearth of any other kind of study. Even in the area of collective biography there remain large gaps in our knowledge, and short-comings in the way the material has been compiled and in the uses to which it has been put; but it does constitute the strength or weakness, according to one's point of view, of the British tradition of elite studies.

Let us therefore examine this tradition in more detail. Its first feature is the absence of a specifically British equivalent to C. Wright Mill's *The Power Elite* or Rose's *The Power Structure*, where the attempt is made to analyse the overall distribution of power in the United States. Nicholson's *The System* and Sampson's various 'anatomies' of Britain are tendentious and impressionistic. Both succumb to the journalist's weakness for confusing the new and distinctive with the norm. Thus Sampson describes the 1970s as the 'apotheosis of the clever grammar school boy' without any evidence that extends beyond the life histories of Heath, Wilson and a few other men of prominence. Stronger candidates are Guttsman's *The British Political Elite* and Miliband's *The State in Capitalist Society*; but the former really consists of an analysis of certain *elite groups*, especially MPs, and makes little attempt to delineate *the* British elite, whereas the latter, which does make the attempt, is closer to speculative theory than empirical analysis, as I argue at greater length in a later section of this Introduction. So far no sustained empirical analysis of the British power structure has appeared.

Particularism

To assume that *the* British elite is somehow composed of all the separate elite groups added together only begs many of the most important questions about a society's structure of power. It takes for granted, for instance, the hotly disputed thesis that contemporary Western society consists of a proliferation of functionally specific and strategic elites, each with roughly equal power (see Kornhauser, 1961; Keller, 1963; A. Rose, 1967). It therefore avoids the crucial task of arranging the set of elite groups into a hierarchy of power. Nobody has yet made a rigorous and sustained empirical attempt to rank the power of British elite groups over a *single* issue-area, let alone all. Instead, one of two convenient but unsatisfactory solutions has been adopted: the first includes in the power structure all groups with an 'obvious' claim to power or prestige and for which information exists, according each equal weight (see Guttsman, 1963; and Wakeford *et al.* in this volume). The second simply asserts that some groups, or more often just one, are 'obviously' the most powerful, without substantiating evidence (see Westergaard, 1965; Worsley, 1964; Miliband, 1969). Apart from the fallacy of its initial assumption, the weakness of the first strategy is that it tends to include elites who have lost most of the influence they undoubtedly possessed in the past, such as the Lords, the Church and the military, but which nobody has had the courage to drop. Moreover it is prone to select what seems an equal proportion from the hierarchy of each elite group as members of *the* elite. Thus if high court judges, junior ministers, permanent secretaries and Governors of the Bank of England are deemed of equivalent rank within their 'sectors' all are counted as part of *the* elite, since each sector has already been presumed to be of equal importance. But it might be more realistic, for example, to omit junior ministers and high court judges altogether, yet delve further down the Civil Service and Bank of England hierarchies. And whether reliable comparisons of ranks across elite groups can be made in the first place may also be doubted, as Colin Bell argues in this *Yearbook*. The danger of the second strategy, as I try to show in more detail later, is that tautology and dubious inference creep into the tortured attempts to reduce ultimate power to one or a few elite groups (invariably capitalists). Both approaches suffer from trying to make reliable statements about elites without first formulating a satisfactory theory of power: one dispenses with any theory at all, whereas the other is so convinced it possesses the correct theory that it sees no need to substantiate it.

A possible reason for the failure of British social scientists so far to study *the* elite is that from the evidence accumulated on separate elite groups there really appears no need. Since cabinet ministers, permanent secretaries, high ranking officers, judges, the chairmen of large public companies, nationalised industries and royal commissions, the governors of the BBC and the Bank of England, and indeed members of every other elite group except the Trade Unions and, decreasingly, the Labour Party, are remarkably likely to have come from upper-class or upper-middle-class families, public boarding schools and/or Oxford and Cambridge, it is natural to conclude that a small, economically and educationally privileged group of high traditional status possess a pervasive and decisive influence in British affairs; and that no more need be done or said. But to establish the common but unrepresentative social antecedents of British elite groups is only part of the story. It does not show that these groups possess Meisel's three 'C's - consciousness, conspiracy or coherence – which form the necessary conditions for something akin to a 'ruling class' or 'power elite' to be said to exist. What may be said, then, of the connections and communities of interest among British elite groups? Nettl (1965, 1967) is only one of a number who have argued that power in Britain is not defined by or dependent upon incumbency of the highest echelons of powerful institutions to the same extent as in the United States with its 'legal/constitutional' political culture, but is instead exercised by small groups of men who occupy numerous elite positions and move frequently and easily between them. A partisan but acute portrait of one such man, Lord Radcliffe, has been provided by Thompson (1970). Power in Britain is lubricated by a political culture which expects and values the role-playing and personal management of role conflicts which are necessarily required by the transfer and multiple occupancy of elite positions among a small number of men.

But, again, there is far less reliable evidence for Britain than one might at first imagine. Sampson (1962, 1971) has traced the tentacles of power and influence of a few large aristocratic families, such as the Salisbury and Devonshire dynasties; Lupton and Wilson (1959) and Aaronovitch (1961) establish the networks of interests that exist within the City and between the City, the upper classes and Conservative Party; and Roth (1963, 1965, 1967, 1972) has compiled a series of

15

invaluable registers on MPs' financial interests. But after that one is quickly reduced to *Private Eye*. There is simply no equivalent of Domhoff's detective work on the connections between American elites. Wakeford *et al.*'s paper in this volume is a preliminary attempt to make amends.

Establishing the precise pattern of connections between elite groups is clearly important, since it is quite possible for all elites to be largely drawn from a similarly privileged economic and educational background and yet differ in their degree and scope of integration with each other. Wakeford *et al.* in this volume show, for example, how the Civil Service and universities are relatively insulated from other elites. But by relying on the information in *Who's Who* the authors are mainly concerned with connections of kinship and marriage. Ideally, what is required is a survey of connections of all kinds – associates, friendship networks, membership of clubs and societies, and above all, mobility within, and multiple occupancy of, elite positions.

Yet even if such an ambitious project were undertaken, it would tell us little about the relative influence of each elite group or member without a simultaneous empirical investigation into the political consequences of such connections. The establishment of inter-elite links has generally been thought sufficient by itself, their political implications being taken for granted. But these implications can be contradictory. Thus political sociologists argue both that the existence of connections gives an elite group special advantages (information, access, control, tacit influence) and that the relative absence of connections, as in the case of the Civil Service, signifies the inward-looking *esprit de corps* which also makes for collective power. Nettl suggests, most unfashionably, that the extensive connections between business and other elite groups is only a desperate response to their impotence and lack of identity or confidence in the face of the Civil Service. Evidence of inter-elite connections is interesting but its significance is not obvious; it may denote the possession or absence of power just as insulation from other elites may reflect the lack of any need (Civil Service?) as much as the lack of opportunity (Trade Unions?). Once again, studies of elites cannot lead to a theory of power; they need such a theory before they can profitably begin.

The Visibility of Elites

The second typical characteristic of British elite studies also reveals a timidity of academic enterprise, namely a reliance on easily available information on 'obvious' elites made visible by their concrete social organisation. The main difficulty with this approach is that not all elites are embedded in tangible organisations with identifiable staffs, functions, buildings, etc., and not all power is exercised by men belonging to such elites. This is not a preamble to a conspiracy theory, but a reminder of the number of important decisions that are 'made' by informal or *ad hoc* bodies – inter-departmental committees, Whitehall advisory committees, and specially commissioned tribunals or investigatory committees – which are rarely defined as part of an elite group. In the last few years the Government has appointed small investigatory committees and enquiries into such delicate areas as the Derry 'massacres', the miners' strike, the employment conditions on the docks, the security implications of the Lambton affair and the rapid rise in beef prices. The membership and supporting staff of these temporary, informal and sometimes secret bodies is not conveniently recorded (although not impossible to discover) yet in their conciliatory role as 'trouble-shooters' they are clearly important. The Government (i.e. ministers and senior civil servants) enjoys an increasing patronage of such 'conflict-managing' positions and yet we know nothing of the considerations that enter their recruitment and the kind of pressures to which they are subject. Another, growing, 'unofficial' elite is composed of the Civil Service 'irregulars' (Brittan, in Rose, 1969) – the academics and industrialists brought in as short-term top-level advisers especially at the beginning of incoming Governments. The extent of their influence has been questioned (Brittan, 1967; Gunn, 1972) but further substantial research on their role is clearly required. Here therefore are two unchartered areas for future elite studies.

A slightly different and less excusable weakness in the present state of studies is the neglect of powerful groups for which reliable information exists but which have so far failed to be labelled as elites. Examples include the research foundations, which help define legitimate areas of enquiry (see Hart, 1972); the established research institutes which set the climate of opinion amongst other elite groups; the leadership and professional staff of the powerful interest groups (strangely neglected by conventional pressure group studies); and the personnel of such quasi-Governmental bodies as the Monopolies Commission, Pay Board, Independent Broad-casting Authority or University Grants Committee. Work on the

17

composition, ideology and roles of the proliferation of semi-autonomous bodies lying in the penumbra of Government is particularly urgent. Other elite groups that had long been neglected, however, have recently been surveyed. Tunstall's account (1969) of lobby-correspondents tells us much more besides by capturing the precarious balance of tacit agreements by which two elite groups with conflicting interests and sufficient power to hurt the other manage to co-operate; and Collission and Millen (1969) have provided a straightforward account of university chancellors and college principals which now needs to be supplemented with research into their relations with the Government and UGC.

Even the studies of 'obvious' elites are surprisingly patchy: whilst analyses of MPs (Guttsman, 1963 and this volume; Johnson, 1973) and of senior civil servants (Kelsall, 1955; Dodd, 1967; Halsey and Crewe, 1969) are plentiful, there is next to nothing on the judiciary (but see Goldstein-Jackson, 1970) or on the directors and senior managers of Britain's leading public companies (but see Institute of Directors, 1959, 1965, 1966 for skeletal biographical details). The less important bishopry and officer corps, however, have been well researched by Morgan (1969) and Otley (1968, 1970).

Circulation of Elites

In addition, Britain lacks a satisfactory theory of the circulation of its elite, in Pareto's sense of the rise and fall of different social groups to and from power. This is partly due to the general poverty of theory in this area, but also a reflection of the British tradition's suspicion of macro-theory. Pareto suggested a psychological explanation in which elites declined through the preservation of elite positions for decadent descendants who lacked the necessary degree of force or guile to maintain power, and who were superseded by counter-elites who did possess these prerequisites. But Pareto fails to answer the crucial question of why some social groups rather than others happen to possess these prerequisites at particular times. The one theory that does appear to supply an answer is the economic functionalism of Marx, and St Simon before him, and most explanations of elite circulation in this century are updated revisions. The 'owners' of the scarcest factor of production are assumed to constitute the most powerful group in society; as the technological and organisational basis of the economy changes, the scarce factors of production shift and their 'owners' are described as the emerging elite. Hence Veblen (1921) saw engineers, Burnham (1941) saw

18

managers and administrators and Galbraith (1967) a 'techno-structure' as the elites of the future, all on the same grounds of their indispensability for the expansion of production levels and thus their inevitable accumulation of power and privilege.

All these theories assume the primacy of economic indispensability but fail to distinguish between the two forms of power that it generates, *market* power and *strategic* power. The first refers to scarcity of supply which in a market-based economy inevitably allocates high rewards to each *individual* member of the indispensable 'group'. The second refers to the power the group could exercise if it acted collectively, e.g. by withdrawing from the production process, deliberately restricting supply, or by extracting rewards even higher than the free market would pay. The first involves subserviency to market forces and provides largely material rewards to the indivi-dual; the second involves domination over market forces and provides power, and *therefore* material rewards, but to the individual only as a member of a collectivity. It is the exploitation of strategic power that largely determines whether the functionally indispensable become an elite-group, i.e. whether there is a circulation of elites. By neglecting the distinction between market and strategic power, the economic functionalists fail to focus on the factors that deter-mine whether managers and technocrats form a group rather than mere aggregate, or to use Marx's celebrated distinction, a 'class *for* itself' as opposed to a 'class *in* itself'. Olsen (1965) uses a rational-choice approach to explain why the group interest is not always reached by aggregating the interest of each of its members, i.e. why the rational strategy of an egotistical manager or technocrat would be to exploit his market power only. Unfortunately the empirical sociology of managers and technocrats in Britain has been content so far to demonstrate rather than explain why they do not constitute a 'class for itself' (Miliband, 1968, 1969; Nichols, 1969). Meanwhile impressionistic speculation on emerging elites in Britain continues to commit the fallacies of the economic functionalist: a recent example is the envisaged rise of the 'datacrat' in 'post-industrial' societies (see Bell, 1967; Johnson, 1969).

Not all theories of elite circulation are of this variety, however; Weber, Lenin and Michels in different ways all recognised the 'autonomy of the political realm', i.e. the independent power held by the leaders of political and administrative organisations, and reference is made to such assumptions by those who regard the Civil Service and/or Cabinet as clearly supreme in the British power structure (see Nettl, 1965; McKenzie, 1955). And Lasswell (1951, 1952) formulated a theory of elite circulation based on 'political-functionalism', that is the changing requirements of the polity, such as the emerging need for 'agitators', 'ideologists' and 'coercers'; but nobody has tried to apply this schema to Britain, as C. Wright Mills (1956) did, somewhat perfunctionarily, to the United States.

Elite Recruitment and the Social Background Approach

The British tradition regards the study of elites as an exercise in social arithmetic. The overwhelming emphasis on elites' recruitment patterns to the almost complete exclusion of their ideology, performance, power, or relations with other elites exists for a number of reasons. Firstly, it is easy. All one need do is install oneself in the university library, and carefully record the biographical details of one's selected group of university registrars, judges, bishops, Fellows of the Royal Society or whoever from the *Dictionary of National Biography* or *Who's Who*; and if this proves tedious, a research assistant can always be found. Hacker (1959) has mischievously suggested that British social scientists generally prefer, compared with their American counterparts, to conduct their research off the streets and within the cosy confines of the library. Secondly, it is often fun. The personal life histories of the nation's good and great has always fascinated the mass public, and academics can hardly be expected to be exempt from this harmless form of voyeurism. Thirdly, as Lockwood (1964) points out, although we commonly refer to the 'distribution' of power, it is not distributed in the same observable and measurable way as wealth or even occupational prestige. It is complex, diffuse and to the extent that 'anticipated reactions', 'non-decision making' and 'manipulated consensus' occur, invisible (Bachrach and Baratz, 1962, 1963). But the collective biography of an elite group can be quantified and has the feel of concreteness (one either did or did not go to boarding school); thus social arithmetic allows for some comparison between elites, societies and periods of time.

But the major reason for focusing on the social antecedents of elite personnel is the implicit assumption that if we know who they are, and were, and how they came to be such, then we already have a reliable guide to what they believe and do. Some express this conviction with more caution and sophistication than others. Miliband (1969), for example, talks of the importance of class origins for the 'field of consciousness', and the 'inarticulated major

20

premises' of elites and uses the lame, negative argument that it is unlikely that class background does not have some effect. But none doubt that social origins *are* important, justifying their focus by arguing that social background is a useful indicator of the following characteristics of an elite: (1) its cohesion (2) its self-interest (3) its values (4) its representativeness of the general public (or special publics with which it deals), and therefore (5) its responsiveness to the needs and demands of the general public (6) its performance – usually in terms of efficiency and professionalism and (7) the 'smoothness' of its relationships with other elites. Why, therefore, conduct separate studies into elite solidarity, ideology or performance when an analysis of recruitment will do?

These assumptions have rarely been put to rigorous empirical test, but what little evidence exists questions their validity. Edinger and Searing's (1967) well-known test of the relationship between the social background and policy preferences of French and German elites showed that the strongest predictors of preferences varied both between countries and policies, but that they were generally aspects of the elite's political rather than social background, and referred to adult and not childhood or adolescent experiences. In this volume Budge and Farlie repeat this kind of analysis for local and national political elites in Britain and elsewhere and reach similar conclusions. Indeed, the one conventional background variable which did affect elite attitudes was not class or education, but religion among Belfast councillors. Moreover, casual observation of the complexity of the relationship between class origins and political beliefs – from the typically bourgeois background of revolutionary leaders to the tendency for working-class legislators to become rapidly more conservative – suggests that simple assumptions about the importance of class origins are unwarranted.

Considerably more evidence is required, however, before dismissing the social background approach out of hand. Not all the assumptions that lie behind it have been tested, and some, like the postulated connection between homogeneous origins and group cohesion (especially loyalty and co-operation) are more plausible than the one tested by Budge and Farlie. Their analysis, moreover, will be criticised by some for excluding 'fundamental' policies and for using social background categories that were not designed to tap the disproportionate influence that can be exercised by, for example, the products of a few exclusive schools or select families. And Miliband's argument that social class origins negatively shape the mental universe of elites so as to exclude their giving serious consideration to radically alternative futures, could still be upheld.

Nevertheless, the social background approach is disappointing to political scientists, and much more attractive to sociologists and social historians. It tells us more about society than polity, about the distribution of life-chances and the structure of social mobility in a society than about the values, interests or performance of its political leaders. It treats power as one dimension of social stratification and political elites as a highly privileged and prestigious stratum. So long as these sociological concerns are accepted as a legitimate area of interest for political sociologists the social background approach to the study of elites will continue to be useful and fascinating. Two such studies might be cited as testimony.

One is Johnson's conventional but highly imaginative analysis of the background of Labour and Conservative MPs between 1955–70 (1973). He demonstrates, for example, that Labour MPs have a higher status background than the general public, that this is even more true of Labour cabinets, and that the social distance between the PLP and the electorate has steadily grown wider. None of this comes as a great surprise. But Johnson also shows why this has happened. To become a cabinet minister an MP must first serve a long apprenticeship as backbencher, PPS, junior minister or Opposition spokesman, generally lasting at least fifteen years. Moreover, few cabinet ministers are first appointed over the age of fifty-five. These two constraints entail that most Labour cabinet ministers are appointed from those who first entered the Commons under the age of forty representing safe seats. Since many of the safest Labour seats are sponsored by Trade Unions, one might imagine that these constraints favour the appointment of young, bright working-class MPs to future cabinets. But no; for even if working-class candidates are nominated they are unlikely to be young, for two reasons. One is that for a working-class man or woman to become prominent enough for nomination and selection as candidate they generally need to work their way up the local Trade Union or, perhaps, Co-operative Society hierarchy, which takes many years. The second is that in solidly working-class communities age is one of the few sources of social differentiation and prestige and is an important factor, therefore, in awarding a 'local' the 'prize' of a safe seat in Parliament. Moreover, a growing number of Trade Union-sponsored safe seats have selected young middle-class outsiders as candidates (often in order to conciliate feuding local factions) who, given

22

natural longevity, stand a better than evens chance of obtaining some Government post in their parliamentary career (see also Rose, 1971). If these trends continue, Johnson concludes, there will soon be a reversion to a Victorian system of two upper-middle-class parties and the working-class MP 'will become as extinct as the buffalo in the next generation'.

Secondly, consider the series of research reports on recruitment to the Administrative Class written by various hands for the Fulton Committee on the Civil Service in the late 1960s (see Report on the Civil Service, 1968). They found that the main trend in the recruitment of direct entrants to the administrative class since the war had in fact been contrary to what was usually assumed: it was *not* moving towards a steadily widening social background but was continuing to consist of remarkably high proportions of upper-middle-class, traditional arts graduates educated at public boarding schools and Oxford or Cambridge. This was despite the 1944 Education Act and university maintenance grant system which had produced an increase in the proportion of working-class boys at LEA grammar schools and university, and despite the expansion of redbrick universities and of interest in the natural and social sciences, which had led to both Oxbridge students and traditional arts students constituting a falling proportion of the total student body. How had this come about? Research revealed a number of alternative reasons to the conventional charge of snobbish bias. One was that a process of self-selection was operating. Such was the Civil Service Commissioners' reputation for admitting traditional arts graduates from Oxbridge that intelligent graduates with different educational backgrounds felt discouraged from applying. This was reinforced by the nature of the Commissioners' 'recruitment drive' which took the form of sending young principals to their *alma mater*! Secondly, a number of changes in the social composition, intellectual tastes and opportunities of students—the dwindling interest in classics and growing popularity of the natural and applied sciences, the rising proportion of women students, and the expansion of student numbers outside Oxbridge—all served to concentrate more intelligent, male, traditional arts students in Oxford and Cambridge than ever before. Few women, or natural or social scientists thought it worthwhile to apply to the administrative class, for reasons already stated; moreover, since the Commissioners confined their duties to impartial selection from whatever field of candidates presented itself, and did not feel obliged to shape the composition of that field,

23

Oxford and Cambridge not surprisingly maintained its 'over-representation'. And thirdly, there *did* appear to be a residue of social bias in selection procedures: for example, about one in eight direct entrants possessed only lower second- or third-class degrees, and they came very largely from public boarding schools and Oxbridge; whereas among the one in every two candidates with first-class degrees who were rejected, disproportionately high numbers came from LEA grammar schools and the provincial redbrick universities.

The preceding two paragraphs reveal only a tiny fraction of what now exists on the recruitment of civil servants and MPs; and there are numerous other titbits of information to be gleaned from other studies. It is fascinating, for instance, that until only very recently there was not a single senior army officer, Anglican bishop or high court judge who had a manual worker as father (see Otley, 1970; Morgan, 1969; and Goldstein-Jackson, 1970); or that as the ecclesiastical bench and officers' mess have become a diminishing attraction to the upper class since the war, due, perhaps, to their declining importance and prestige in British society, so these two elite groups have increasingly resembled a caste, recruiting not from the working or lower middle classes, but from the sons of clergymen and army officers. Yet all this material is only useful and interesting if the social origins of elite groups are considered intrinsically important in the first place, as they are to sociologists but not political scientists.

Improving the Social Background Approach

On the presumption that the conventional social background study will continue unabated, this might be an appropriate place to suggest ways in which it might be improved. One area ripe for reform is the set of Tired Old Variables upon which researchers continue to rely. 'Class origins', for example, normally refers to father's occupation, but the latter is rarely standardised by comparing fathers of a similar age, or checked against the possibility that the father was occupationally mobile during the respondent's lifetime. It is highly likely that the proportion of elite members recorded as 'of working-class origin' has been badly exaggerated by underestimating the number of their fathers who achieved an upward 'career' mobility (not to mention the number who exaggerate their proletarian origins: see Blake, in Rose (1966) on Mr Wilson's childhood). Kelsall (1972) found that a substantial proportion of 'working-class' students had upwardly mobile fathers (and also middle-class grandparents) and concluded that many would be more accurately described as emanating from a 'submerged' middle class. And since a person's class origin, especially if he belongs to an elite, may well have shaped only the first two decades of his life, it would seem more sensible to pay greater attention to the economic and social circumstances more immediately prior to his joining the elite. How meaningful, for instance, is it to categorise Mr Roy Jenkins as 'working class' or Mr Tony Benn as 'upper class'?

More imagination could be applied to the task of adding to the familiar list of background variables. The concept of 'generation' is one possibility. It could be alternatively defined as time of entry into the elite, or, following Butler and Stokes (1969), the period that most decisively shaped a person's political consciousness. There already exists scattered evidence on the importance of elite 'generations'. Johnson (1973) has traced how the changes of government in 1951 and 1964 brought with them a new wave of MPs with a different social composition from their predecessors, and, impression has it, different values. Alt (1974) cites the same two years as ushering in a new generation of cabinet ministers. And Putnam (1973) tentatively suggests on the basis of an attitude survey that the youngest generation in the Higher Civil Service have a distinctive conception of their role which emphasises 'problem-solving' and a 'specific issue-orientation' rather than sound administration and disdain for politics.

A second area fit for investigation is the conventional distinction between ascriptive and achieved status. It has implicitly become a synonym for 'bad thing/good thing' in researchers' evaluation of elite recruitment, but how sensible this is will not be discussed here. One weakness of the distinction is that it makes more conceptual than empirical sense, since achieved statuses like a university education are well known to be aided by ascriptive advantages such as the possession of middle-class parents. Another is that high ascriptive status amongst those who share a common high achieved status is often the real but unnoticed source of entry into an elite. Here, for example, is Lord Rothschild describing how he chose his team for the CPRS 'think-tank':

> . . . we looked around. I sometimes go to the Barbados, and since Dick Ross [already appointed to the CPRS] told me he knew a very good man on one of these sugar boards called Hector Hawkins, I made it my business to have a rum punch with

him — perhaps two — and I thought Hector was very nice and very good . . . Well, then Peter Bowcock was recommended to me by Lord Jellicoe. Kate Mortimer I knew because she was a contemporary of my daughter Emma's at Oxford, so I knew her quite well . . . I think I got hold of William Plowden because his father's rather a friend of mine and I asked his father if he might like it. I knew quite a lot about William because I knew him from his Cambridge days. I'm afraid that the selection might be considered rather random. [*Interviewer:* or rather personal?] Personal perhaps except some of them were very strongly recommended by departments. [Fox, 1973.]

If the places in an elite group are small compared to the pool of talent available, and if it controls its own recruitment, the ascriptive/achievement distinction may break down in reality.

Giddens (1972) has pointed out that British elite studies tend to emphasise the rate and composition of recruits to the neglect of the *avenues* by which they have arrived. A particular channel of mobility (e.g. Oxbridge) may tell us considerably more about the recruits than the wider social category (e.g. 'university education') to which it belongs. Giddens emphasises the importance of 'switchboard' institutions which direct individuals, regardless of their earlier background, towards certain elite groups and which function to socialise potential recruits into the skills and values which will subsequently be required. The importance of Oxbridge for entering the Administrative Class, of the military public schools for becoming a senior officer, of a select few theological colleges for achieving ecclesiastical emmence and of a long career in a major trade union for a worker aspiring to a place on the Labour backbenches, are all well-known examples.

More studies of these servicing institutions are therefore needed if we are to understand fully the nature of elite recruitment in Britain. The values they propagate and changes in the size, success and composition of their intake need investigation. The latter in particular tends to be ignored. It seems clear, for example, from the research reports for the Fulton Committee that the small increase of working-class recruits was entirely due to the slowly widening social background of Oxbridge graduates. Indeed, it was also evident that almost no working-class recruit escaped the socialisation into 'traditional values' of *either* Oxbridge *or* a public school *or* a classical education (see Dodd, 1967; and Halsey and Crewe, 1969). There exist a few interesting studies of British boarding schools (Wakeford, 1969; Weinberg, 1967; and Wilkinson, 1964) of which the last has useful statistics. Otley (1965) suggests that the spartan conditions, male segregation, compulsory corps and ritual surrounding ex-pupils killed in battle all serve to ease and encourage a progression from boarding school to military academy and a senior commission; and Wilkinson (1964) has described how the late nineteenth-century public school inculcated values appropriate for the future rulers of the Empire. But Oxford and Cambridge have probably become more important as switchboard institutions since the war and they have yet to be blessed with a reputable sociological analysis of their servicing functions.

Finally, one methodological improvement to the social background approach should be mentioned briefly. The normal procedure is to count each current member of one's selected elite group as of equal weight in any description of or inference from the social composition of the group. But some have been members of an elite much longer than others, and if we are to assume some relationship between the social composition and values of an institution it is reasonable to expect that the longest-serving members should be weighted proportionately, so that our basic unit of analysis becomes man-years. Vic Hanby's analysis of the Labour NEC in this *Yearbook* is one of the first to adopt this obvious tactic.

Other Aspects of Elite Recruitment

The British tradition of elite studies is so preoccupied with the social background of recruits that it tends to neglect other aspects of elite recruitment. The *process* of recruitment is itself a social institution, but one that is rarely examined in depth. Detailed accounts of the official procedures and criteria for Civil Service recruitment are available and statistical analyses of the outcomes of different methods exist (Report of the Method II System of Selection, 1969). And Rush (1969) and Paterson (1967) have given inside reports on the ways and means of the constituency parties' selection conferences. But an increasing proportion of elite recruitment is in the patronage of cabinet ministers and their senior civil servants. What considerations enter the selection of royal commissions, members of tribunals, magistrates and the chairmen of the proliferating quasi-independent boards and committees? What is the balance of influence between the Civil Service and nominating institution, and the balance between 'political' and 'efficiency' considerations? What must candidates for

27

such posts do to make themselves visible to the selectors in the first place? These and numerous other questions remain unanswered for the moment.

Elite recruitment is also subject to variations of turnover, level of entry, patterns of promotion and autonomy of control, all of which can have political implications quite independent of social composition. One ideal type to which both the Higher Civil Service and the armed forces approximate might be characterised as having (i) low turnover and steady, incremental rates of renewal, (ii) entry confined to the bottom ranks, (iii) slow, incremental, and predictable patterns of promotion and (iv) autonomy over selection and promotion (usually within an externally imposed framework of rules). The polar opposite is perhaps most closely resembled by the British cabinet which is subject to rapid and dramatic turnover (due to resignation, reshuffles, electoral defeat), some lateral entry and meteoric promotion (usually at the beginning of a change of government) and, despite the Prime Minister's formal powers of hiring and firing, to considerable constraints in recruitment (Rose, 1971). These varieties of recruitment patterns could clearly be significant for relationships between elites, as Weber partially recognised when he contrasted the professionalism of bureaucracies with the 'dilletantism' of politicians (Gerth and Mills, 1948). King (1966) and Herman (1974) have both shown that *ministerial* turnover in Britain is peculiarly high compared with other Western democracies (in contrast to turnover of *governments*) and this must weaken the minister's position *vis-à-vis* his senior civil servants. Similarly Nettl (1965) suggests that the bureaucratic structure and clear social identity of the Civil Service allows it to 'create consensus' and dominate business.

Elite Socialisation

New entrants to an elite group inevitably undergo a process of socialisation. Elites need to maintain a cohesion and a set of established norms for dealing with the public and other elite groups, as well as a *modus vivendi* in their internal relations, and so new members must be inculcated into a departmental or regimental tradition, the parliamentary 'rules of the game', the 'way things are done'. Critical observers like Miliband (1969) lay stress on the power of the socialisation process (or of 'anticipatory socialisation' in servicing institutions) to detach lower-class recruits from the values and interests of their class of origin. It is well known that the fiery radicalism of young Labour MPs can be relied upon to turn into a cosy attachment to Parliamentary procedure after ten or so years; what is not known is how exactly this happens. The British tradition of elite studies has paid some attention to the *childhood* socialisation of elite groups, especially in boarding schools, but has completely ignored *adult* socialisation. Unfortunately this volume fails to include any such study but this simply reflects the absence of serious research in this area. The only project on adult elite socialisation known to this author is an extensive interview study of MPs by Donald Searing of the University of North Carolina on which nothing has yet been reported. Otherwise we have to rely on the memoirs and biographies of prominent men and such occasional pieces as Bottomore's (1964) on the Civil Service and Barnett (1967) on military officers.

Elite Ideology

If we are unaware of the *process* of elite socialisation, we are equally ignorant of the *substance* of that socialisation. Next to nothing is known of the general values and specific beliefs held by elite groups in Britain. Yet this is clearly a crucial area of enquiry. Conservatives insist that to establish the existence of a power elite or ruling class it must be shown to conform to Meisel's three 'C's — consciousness, cohesiveness and conspiracy. It must be shown to think of itself *as* an elite, as a powerful, privileged community which deliberately uses its advantages to pursue its own interests which it knows to be to the detriment of the public at large. Thoenies (1966) is less stringent, conceding that elite and non-elite can share the same values and interests, but argues that to be deemed an elite a group must possess not only power and wealth but an Idea (God, Nation, Science) to which it sees itself in service on behalf of society as a whole. Elites must regard themselves as 'guardians of a mission'. Radicals are equally interested in elite ideology, although for different reasons. Marxist and radical scholars have increasingly resorted to such 'superstructural' notions as 'cultural hegemony' (Anderson, 1964; Miliband, 1969) or the 'powers of legitimation' to explain how elites maintain power over a long period. Conservatives are interested in whether and how elites legitimate their position to themselves; radicals are concerned with how elites legitimate their position to others.

But however we define elite ideology, there are precious few studies of it in contemporary Britain. Guttsman (1969) has collected an anthology of elite self-justification but it refers mainly to the nineteenth century. Otherwise we are forced to rely on insight rather than evidence. Miliband (1969), for example, suggests that the interests of large capital have managed to retain dominance in modern Britain by persuading the general public (and less powerful groups like civil servants) to identify the national interest with those of the City and big business. This seems highly plausible. But does either big business, the Civil Service or the mass public in fact make such an identification? If so, how 'sincere' is big business, and why has it been so easy to persuade the general public? Hard evidence is thin on the ground. At a more mundane level, it would be interesting to discover what knowledge, prejudices and images elite groups have of each other and of the general public. How is the electorate perceived by politicians, politicians by civil servants and civil servants by leading businessmen; and why and how have these perceptions arisen?

The few studies that exist on the ideology of British elites deserve mention. One is Colin Crouch's examination of the Reports of the National Board for Prices and Incomes, which was set up to deal with pay claims and price-fixing on the basis of 'fair' and objective criteria. Attitudes towards inequality are a crucial component of any ideology, and these Reports reveal what the Labour Government and the administrative elite that served it defined as fair inequality, and why it arrived at this particular conception of fairness. Crouch shows how the NBPI's notion of justifiable inequality was that of the administrator and 'organisation man' rather than of the entrepreneur, with an emphasis on rewards for skill, expertise and responsibility rather than on risk-taking or initiative. He shows how the Board held a coherent model of an ideal social structure in their minds, and how this differed from the ones presumably held by socialists, trade union leaders, or independent businessmen.

The Reports contained the substantive and specific beliefs of an elite. Clements' (1969) neglected study of local 'Notables' in Bristol provides a vivid picture of a different aspect of an elite's ideology — its attitude towards the use of power and styles of decision-making. Clements found, as had earlier investigators of other communities (Birch, 1959; Lee, 1963; Jones, 1969), a steady decline in the number of economic and social 'Notables' serving on the local council, although their voluntary work in other areas of community life remained substantial. To discover the reason Clements interviewed all of Bristol's 'Notables' and detected a distinct disdain for council work, ordinary local councillors, democratic processes and party politics generally. Council procedures were regarded as inefficient, laborious and cumbersome; councillors were petty, incompetent and 'on the make'; party politics was trivial, dishonest and meaningless; party discipline was intolerable, and local democracy generally was regarded as, at best, necessary but unpalatable. Clements attributed the source of these views to the roles and relationships of authority typically enjoyed by the Notables outside the sphere of local politics. The member of a Board of Directors is accustomed to deference from his colleagues, not equality or competition; to individual and not collective decision-making; to unquestioned authority rather than the need to persuade; to clear criteria for satisfactory performance rather than a plurality of aims, and to being sought after rather than seeking. All these expectations are fulfilled in such voluntary work as organising a community appeal or serving as the Chairman of hospital or school governors; but they have no place in Council or party politics. Thus politics itself is suspect, being regarded as inefficient and unnecessarily divisive.

One might have expected the same scepticism for democratic politics from the Higher Civil Service, but Putnam's comparative interview study (1973) of British, German and Italian civil servants shows the opposite to be the case. The British respondents were the only ones to obtain a high score on Putnam's 'Index for Tolerance of Politics' scale, which attempted to tap their sympathy towards Parliamentary interference, trust in politicians' motives, and acceptance of political as opposed to technical considerations in administrative decisions. They also secured the highest score on his 'Index of Programmatic Commitment' which was intended to measure commitment to a role of implementing political ideals and programmes, as opposed to the 'classical' bureaucratic preference for 'pure' and 'neutral' administration. Other bits of scattered evidence (see, for instance, Chapman, 1970 on the high proportion of Labour supporters among principals in 1964) contribute to a picture of the Higher Civil Service in Britain somewhat removed from the antipolitical conservative force portrayed by Miliband (1969).

Elite Roles

So far we have avoided discussion of the most crucial aspect of elites — what they actually do. Neither knowing who they are or what they believe is necessarily a good guide. Again, both conservative and radical observers are interested in what elites do, but for different reasons. The conservative accepts the existence of elites as necessary and desirable, but is concerned with their quality, both moral and technical. He is interested in their training and fitness for leadership.

The radical regards the existence of elites as unacceptable and is therefore concerned with the ways they use their advantages to manipulate and maintain domination over the general public. Neither interest will find much satisfaction from the present state of literature on British elites. The most reliable studies would need to be undertaken by a participant-observer, which is clearly near impossible for most national elites, even if subterfuge or disloyalty is contemplated (see McGinniss, 1970). It is more feasible at the local level, as Dennis' two studies (1971, 1972) of 'elitist' policy-making by housing officials demonstrate. Otherwise one must rely on the inevitably distorted and 'untrained' memories of ex-members, or the accounts of participants who are hardly neutral. Within these constraints their reports can be most informative (see, for example, Dale, 1941; and Strang, in Rose, 1969, on the Civil Service; and Marples in Rose, 1969 and Castle, 1973, on being a cabinet minister). What the directors of major public companies, the leading merchant bankers, the chairmen of the nationalised industries and other members of the economic elite actually do may be known to management-consultants but remains almost a total mystery to the outside academic observer.

The one light in this area of darkness is Headey's interview study of cabinet ministers and his analysis of the factors that determine their effectiveness (Headey, 1970, 1974). He shows first, from an analysis of their diaries, the sheer lack of time available to ministers for consideration of policy and planning (about fifteen hours, usually late in the day, out of a sixty-hour working week) as a result of increasing demands made by the Commons, the cabinet and cabinet committees, formal receptions, visits and inspections, the local constituency and by deputations. Despite the enormous increase in the number and complexity of policy decisions facing a minister, he has probably less time than his predecessors a century ago to deal with them. To be in any sense effective, therefore, a minister must opt for one of three roles: the 'key issues minister' who 'devotes as much of his own time as possible to formulating policy in relation to those issues'; the 'executive minister' who is particularly good at getting decisions which have been agreed by the Department'; and the 'ambassador' who sells his Department's policies or services to outsiders. Each of these roles require special personal and political qualities. The first demands the ability to delegate, to master a voluminous pile of memoranda, to explore alternative options and generally be an imaginative administrator. The second requires an ability to win face-to-face conflicts, and to master committee tactics and procedures. The third demands a flair for publicity. But whatever the role adopted, some qualities and conditions will always be necessary to be successful, such as executive ability, the capacity to defend oneself in the Chamber and Lobby, and time to become thoroughly familiar with the Department's work.

As Headey and Rose (1971) point out, however, the typical background and conditions of tenure of a minister in Britain hardly fit him for his job. The high rate of mobility and consequent insecurity amongst ministers gives them neither the time nor incentive to master the details of their Department's concerns, and renders them unnecessarily dependent on their permanent secretaries. The convention that Ministers be MPs and, moreover, serve a Parliamentary apprenticeship of about fifteen years, fits them well for one function, that of representing the Department in Parliament and to other Departments and the outside world, but is no training at all for the 'key issues' role which demands detailed administrative and substantive knowledge and imaginative administrative abilities. Backbenchers have almost no administrative duties or experience, given their non-executive role in Parliament and the need to enter Parliament under the age of 40 in order to become a minister.

The Distribution of Power

What is noticeable about the last piece of analysis is that it makes assumptions about the nature of power which are unobjectionable to political scientists but quite alien to the contemporary sociologist. It ignores the cultural and economic constraints on ministerial effectiveness, stressing personal and purely political determinants instead; and it is couched within an entirely political framework which assumes that *political* power is ultimately supreme. Yet it would hardly occur to a sociologist to look to the practices and procedures of Parliament for an explanation of the relative inability of a political elite to exercise effective power. Worsley (1964) distinguishes between Politics I — 'the exercise of constraint in any relationship' — and Politics II — 'the specialised machinery of government together with the administrative apparatus of state and party organisation'. This is typical of the sociologist's sensitivity to the informal and pervasive nature of power, to its existence in institutions and relationships that are not confined to what is formally and overtly political. Indeed, it is typical of his suspicion that effective power does not reside in officially political relationships at all; that political power competes for effectiveness with cultural and economic power, and often loses.

No satisfactory theory of elites is possible without a prior theory of power. We normally require a conception of power to decide who or what can count as an elite (the exception occurs where 'elite' is given the literal but peculiar meaning of 'the best') and which elites are more 'important' than others. But in addition we cannot assess the significance of any of the 'facts' we possess about elites without a prior theory of power. It is only worthwhile investigating the social origins of an elite group if we already possess evidence (or wish to tests hypotheses) on the importance of social background for the exercise of power. Otherwise we might as well investigate any of the infinite amount of information that could be discovered about our elite group, such as the colour of their hair or the size of their socks. Indeed, to consider anything a fact necessarily requires a preceding concept, and to consider something a significant fact, necessarily requires a preceding theoretical assumption. Moreover, a concept does not exist in isolation: to be given a substantive definition, further concepts must be created. The notion of a ruling class, for example, cannot be given meaning without the additional notion of an exploited class.

The concept, distribution and method of locating power in Western democracies has been subject to acrimonious and celebrated dispute since the 1950s. The terms of the debate will be familiar to most readers. Those who have investigated a society's or community's distribution of power by indentifying 'key issues' and tracing the people directly associated with their generation and outcome invariably fail to find anything resembling a ruling class, power elite, or even dominant group. Instead they generally conclude that power is fragmented amongst a number of competing elite groups (including representatives of the non-privileged and non-prestigious), none of which possess more than temporary ascendancy in more than one 'issue-area'. Lower class groups and the mass electorate generally have some degree of influence, therefore, because they have access to political institutions (parties, elections, etc.) which have the capacity to override economic and cultural power. This is the political scientist's approach, the best-known example being Dahl's *Who Governs?* (1964). Yet radically different pictures of the same or very similar societies have been painted by those (usually sociologists) operating with alternative concepts and methods of locating power. The 'social background approach', which infers the distribution of power amongst social groups from the social origins and affiliations of those occupying elite posts, normally concludes that power is

34

concentrated amongst the economically dominant (Guttsman, 1963; Domhoff, 1967). This is the British tradition of elite studies and has been commented upon at length in this Introduction. The 'reputational approach' which identifies the most powerful in a community on the basis of judgements made by prominent and informed members of that community, is equally prone to arrive at the same elitist conclusion (Hunter, 1953). Both kinds of study are somewhat out of date, however; and now that more recent investigations have revealed a slight decomposition in the social and economic homogeneity of elite backgrounds, those who remain sceptical that a ruling class or power elite is (or is in the process of) disappearing have become increasingly aware of the less tangible and obvious aspects of power, of what Bachrach and Baratz (1962, 1963) call the 'invisible face of power'. Such concepts as 'anticipated reactions', 'manipulated consensus', 'cultural power' and 'non-decisions' have been invoked to show that the distribution of power cannot be measured by studying the conspicuous manifestations of power alone, convenient though it may be to do so. It is worth noting that there is no *logical* relationship between these concepts and the elitist verdict that, in fact, regularly follows their adoption.

This is not the place to discuss the controversy in further detail. Adequate summaries of the voluminous literature can be found in Bell and Newby (1972) and Wolfinger (1971). But it is appropriate to examine briefly the relationship of this controversy to studies on Britain. What is immediately striking about the literature on the debate is its almost exclusive reference to the United States. It is astonishing to have to record that with the exception of some unpublished doctoral theses (e.g. Green, 1968) there exist no studies of community power in Britain. There are numerous 'community studies' by anthropologically inclined sociologists which tend to focus on kinship behaviour, the management of social conflict and interpersonal aspects of social stratification (see Frankenburg, 1966, and Bell and Newby, 1971, for summaries). And there are a number of 'constituency studies' by political scientists which are largely concerned with the formal political processes and institutions of the locality (Bealey *et al.*, 1965; Jones, 1969; and Hampton, 1970). The nearest to a community power study is Stacey on Banbury (1960) and Birch on Glossop (1959). But both involved a social background approach to questions of power, paid more attention to other issues, and are by now badly out of date (although a report on Banbury revisited is forthcoming). The reputational approach has rarely been adopted for Britain: Sampson's unsystematic attempts (1962, 1971) and Miller's comparative study of Seattle and Bristol (1958, 1959) are the exceptions. And Dahl's 'decision-making' approach has never been applied to any local British community and only once to an issue — the 1958 Bank rate leak and subsequent tribunal — which revealed a dense network of connections between the City, aristocracy and Conservative Party. The one decision-making analysis of the national political system is a careful and ingenious paper by Hewitt (1973) which arrives at pluralist conclusions.

Conspicuous by its absence so far has been any reference to Miliband's widely read and important contribution, *The State in Capitalist Society*. Miliband combines a 'social background' approach with frequent reminders of the 'invisible face of power' to conclude that

> the most important fact about advanced capitalist societies . . . is the continued existence in them of private and ever more concentrated economic power. As a result of that power, the men — owners and controllers — in whose hands it lies enjoy a massive preponderance in society, in the political system, and in the determination of the state's policies and actions.

No British Dahl has yet emerged to contest this assertion. The only criticism it has received has ironically come from the Left by Poulantzas (1969) who agrees with the conclusion but objects to the way in which it was reached. Poulantzas criticises Miliband for 'attacking bourgeois ideologies of the State whilst placing himself on their terrain' and for not appreciating that 'it is never possible simply to oppose "concrete facts" to concepts' which 'must be attacked by other parallel concepts situated in a different problematic'. As a consequence Miliband risks being 'unconsciously and surreptitiously contaminated by the very epistomological principles of the adversary'. One instance of this happening is Miliband's reduction of social classes and groups, of the state, and of the relationship between the two, to inter-personal relationships of individuals. For social classes and the state are 'objective structures', and their relations are 'an objective system of regular connections, whose agents, "men", are in the words of Marx, "bearers" of it — *träger*.' Thus 'the relation between the bourgeois class and the State is an *objective* relation'. Whether the bourgeoisie directly mans the apparatus of the state is irrelevant, for the role of the state cannot be reduced to the conduct and 'behaviour' of members of the state apparatus. Indeed, 'the

36

capitalist state best serves the interests of the capitalist class only when members of this class do not participate directly in the State apparatus, that is to say when the *ruling class* is not the *politically governing class*'. Miliband is guilty of avoiding 'the necessary preliminary of a critique of the ideological notion of elite in the light of the scientific concepts of Marxist theory'.

Poulantzas clearly raises crucial issues. He reminds us that our choice of concepts inevitably determines our notion of what constitutes 'facts' and necessarily presupposes a prior view of the totality of a society's structure. He thereby resurrects the question of whether classes or elites are 'people' or objective categories, and whether power should be regarded as the property of people and groups, or of objective relationships. Yet Poulantzas' critique is fundamentally unsatisfactory. One sympathises with Dr Johnson, who on being told by Boswell that it was impossible to refute Bishop Berkeley's proof of the non-existence of matter, struck 'his foot with mightly force against a large stone, till he rebounded from it, and answered, "I refute it *thus*"' (Boswell's *Diary*, 6 August 1763). 'To provide a singularly clear example of a claim true by definition, and which cannot be refuted' is not, as Urry claims in his and Wakeford's Introduction to their *Power in Britain*, 'particularly interesting'. It is particularly *un*interesting, so long as one man's science continues to be another man's ideology. The claim that Marx's analysis (in its Althusserian interpretation) is scientific, whereas pluralist concepts are ideological, without telling us what makes them so is amusingly reminiscent of Pareto's insistence sixty years ago that he was scientific and Marxism was a mere 'derivation'. The opposition of two sets of epistomological principles may provide peculiarly coherent theories of power in capitalist society, but if they lead to radically opposite conclusions, it is not unreasonable to ask which is right (or at least the preferable); and no amount of calling one scientific and the other ideological provides a satisfactory answer.

The irony of Poulantzas' objections is that Miliband does not, in fact, 'place himself on the terrain' of his bourgeois adversaries, and does not rely on a reduction of social classes and their relation to the state to inter-personal relationships between individuals. On the contrary, careful reading shows that his attack on pluralism essentially depends upon opposing concrete facts with 'parallel concepts situated in a different problematic', even if this is less brazenly done than Poulantzas would like. For where an analysis of the social origins and affiliations of those staffing or benefiting from the state apparatus

37

fails to reveal the manifest existence of a ruling capitalist class, Miliband resorts to a set of non-positivist procedures and non-refutable arguments for establishing its existence. For example, if the 'ruling class' appears to be divided (as on the Common Market, incomes policy, race relations policy, and industrial subsidies, to name but a few at present) such issues are dismissed as 'not fundamental'. The criteria that render an issue 'fundamental' are never specified, although it can be inferred that the preservation of the ruling class and of private property would count. (The former is, of course, a tautological argument, for it assumes what is in question, namely the existence of a ruling class.) If the 'ruling class' appear to accede against its obvious wishes and interests to working-class demands (New Deal, Welfare State), this is relegated to the status of a 'tactical concession'. Again, the concessions are said to be either on non-fundamental issues or in order to preserve the position and privileges of the ruling class. How tactical concessions are to be distinguished from democratic responsiveness is never made clear. If members or representatives of the working class appear to gain access to the state, this is discounted by emphasising the 'anticipatory socialisation' that the upwardly mobile undergo in a society of 'sponsored mobility' and the isolated, minority position of Trade Unions, the Labour Party, ex-working class civil servants, etc. amongst the members and agents of the capitalist class. Thus the growing integration of big business and the state is cited as *prima facie* evidence for the state's subordination to big business, whereas the growing integration of trade unions and the state is cited as *prima facie* evidence for the subordination of trade unions to the state. If there appears to be an acceptance by the non-elite of the *status quo* this is interpreted as 'prudential' rather than 'normative', or the consequence of 'manipulated consensus', or the cultural hegemony of the ruling class.

It goes without saying that each of these arguments is highly plausible on occasion and that it is not impossible that they were always valid whenever used by Miliband. Elites *do* deliberately make what they regard as tactical concessions; do try to organise 'public opinion' in their favour; do promote and reward the most 'respectable' members of the non-elite; and do deflect embarrassing issues from the political arena. Not a year passes without revelation of some major illegal conspiracy perpetrated against the public by large capitalism in its own interests. But to assert rather than demonstrate the truth of these arguments is insufficient and too easy. Moreover the frequent use of such escape clauses only renders the existence of a

38

ruling class less convincing. For example, if the ruling class does possess the cultural hegemony so frequently attributed to it of late, it is difficult to understand why any 'issue', fundamental or not, ever arises; why *any* concessions need to be made, and why conspiracies should ever be necessary. To the extent that an elite's ability to manipulate consciousness is limited – and resort to the notions of 'concession' and 'non-fundamental issues' imply it is – an analysis is required of who or what has the power to *keep* it limited.

The objection to Miliband's analysis is therefore that whenever the evidence for a ruling capitalist class gets thin, he resorts to intellectual sleights of hand which render the thesis unamenable to empirical refutation. It fails to specify what would count against his thesis. Miliband's position might be defended, however, by citing Lockwood's (1964) argument that if a small group can permanently maintain its marked privileges despite the growth of institutions formally intended to challenge them, this constitutes significant evidence about the true locus of power. The fact that the rich, like the poor, are always among us, despite the welfare state, nationalised industries, progressive taxation, universal suffrage, Trade Unions and the Labour Party, is strong evidence that the rich possess decisive power. Thus what Miliband would presumably accept as a refutation of his conclusions is the equalisation of wealth or wholesale abolition of property in Britain or any other advanced capitalist society.

The equation of 'who has power' with 'who benefits' takes two forms with very different theoretical implications. The first bears a close affinity to Poulantzas' severely structural concept of the ruling class as an objective social category, the members of which are agents rather than controllers of the 'system'. Being almost as helplessly subject to the 'system's' inexorable processes as the exploited classes, their privileged position cannot be attributed to any deliberate action on their part. Thus their motives and intentions are irrelevant to the concept of a ruling class. They do not 'possess' power which they deliberately exert to further their own interests; rather they inevitably benefit from the power that resides in social relationships in which they are necessarily involved. The very term 'they' is misleading, moreover, because it suggests that the ruling class consists of an identifiable group of persons, when it in fact refers to an objective social category, e.g. owners of land or owners of finance-capital. The weakness of this concept of ruling class is that its gain in logical coherence is at the expense of the connotations normally associated

39

with the term. The condition of using the 'powerful' or 'ruling class' in this sense is that it must be divorced from any implication of manipulation, exploitation or the purposeful pursuit of self-interest, unless these terms are in turn redefined as purely objective relationships emptied of their conventional moral and deliberative content.

The second form of the equation is closer to customary meaning but logically less sound. Here the implicit assumption is that all beneficial consequences were intended, and in the teeth of opposition. The extent of the power of those 'who benefit' is indicated by their success. Whereas intentions were irrelevant in the first sense of the equation, they are central to its second sense. Thus the post-war Labour Government's nationalisation programme is dismissed as evidence against the thesis of a ruling capitalist class by Miliband on the grounds that the original private owners received generous compensation, positions on the new Boards, and a convenient solution to what was often a loss-making concern. In the final reckoning they gained rather than lost. But to imply the existence of a ruling capitalist class on this basis is fallacious. For if the proposals were so favourable to the owners' interests it is odd that they opposed them so passionately; which they did, of course, because they were unaware of their future benefits *at that time*.

The benefits that some enjoy, moreover, may be a better reflection of others' indifference than their own power. The stability of wealth disparities in Britain this century could be as plausibly attributed to public acceptance and weak opposition as to the power of the wealthy. Defenders of the equation deny any distinction between the two, of course, arguing that the power of the wealthy consists of instilling public acceptance and keeping opposition weak. The ruling class has the capacity to prevent effective challenge by their cultural power to create their own public legitimacy, by their ability to deflect potential conflict from the political sphere, and by the 'power of power', that is their very reputation for possessing power which by a process of anticipated reactions forestalls serious challenge from the less privileged. Thus the absence of a successful socialist revolution in advanced capitalist society is taken as the most important evidence for the existence of 'invisible power', and is the most crucial of all 'non-issues'. There are two objections to this negative proof of a capitalist ruling class. Firstly, the attempt to identify the powerful on the basis of what has failed to occur faces the difficulty that an infinity of non-occurrences 'exists'. For example, the persistent failure of fascists to seize power in Britain has probably benefited Jews, Blacks and Com-

40

munists more than any others, but few would seriously suggest that any or all of these groups formed a ruling class.

Nowadays it is customary to regard the pluralist-elitist debate as incapable of empirical resolution, as an essentially epistomological dispute about the nature of power. The varieties of 'invisible power' obviously represent everyday reality yet are open to the fallacy of infinite regress, to impossibility of disproof. Conspiracies are revealed too frequently to be omitted from any account of power but not so prevalent as to deserve the central role. Logically, if all power were conspiratorial, this discussion would be impossible. But since it is both necessary yet impossible by the very nature of conspiracy to know when and where they are occurring, an empirically objective description of the distribution and uses of power is impossible. Similarly reactions are 'anticipated' all the time but as it is a way of exercising power that emits no 'signals' and as it allows the wielder of power to do so quite unconsciously, it is inaccessible to empirical research.

This view may be too pessimistic. Reactions are not anticipated randomly but only on the basis of some actor's reputation for power. As Merelman observes (1968), that reputation must be based on the *actual* public exercise of power against opposition in the past, and this is amenable to investigation. Similarly, issues can only be prevented from becoming political by *some* action or communication by the postulated elite; and public consensus can only be moulded and changed by extensive and long-term action by the postulated elite. It is not too cynical to suggest that it suits both elitists and pluralists to believe that 'invisible power' really is invisible and cannot be investigated. Pluralists find it convenient to discard such embarrassing ideas by such a charge; elitists fear the need to qualify their neat but over-simplified models. It should not be beyond the bounds of social science's capabilities to operationalise and measure the exercise of invisible power in years to come.

NEW APPROACHES TO ELITE STUDIES

A major purpose of this Introduction has been to chart the substantial gaps in our knowledge of British elites. Some of these gaps result from a modesty and cautiousness of approach, and some attention should therefore be devoted to the fresh orientations that one might hopefully expect from British elite studies in the future.

The most obvious is the need for systematic comparative research. There are technical obstacles connected with the difficulty of estab-

41

lishing equivalences of function and rank between countries. On most of the Continent there is no exact equivalent of an Opposition front bench or life peer. Furthermore an elite group in one country (e.g. scientists or leading businessmen in Portugal) might be too insignificant on an international scale to compare against the same elite groups in another, e.g. West Germany. But these are minor problems, especially if comparisons are confined to Western democracies with a similar level of socio-economic development. Without such studies one cannot place findings on Britain in a proper perspective. It becomes impossible to know whether a feature of British elites is typical of all Western democracies, or of only some, or is unique. The social 'exclusiveness' of the British senior Civil Service takes on a different colouring if it can be shown that it is less marked than among the major European powers (Subranamiam, 1967) and the well-recorded *embourgeoisement* of the Parliamentary Labour Party carries slightly less significance if it can be shown that almost all Social Democratic and Communist Parties on the Continent have undergone the same mutation, to the extent that the PLP contains a *higher* than average proportion of ex-manual workers (see the various chapters in Linz and Doggan, forthcoming; and Guttsman in this volume). Moreover, without comparative analysis it is impossible to formulate general empirical theories about elites of any rigour, especially theories which contain *national-scale* variables. If one's hypothesis, for example, is that extensions of the suffrage generally take two generations to be translated, in terms of social composition, at the elite level (Johnson, 1973; Guttsman, 1963), or that single-seat, simple plurality, electoral systems create a faster turnover of legislative elites than proportional representation, or that war results in greater changes in elite social composition than any other observable 'event', then only a comparative study will tell. This volume includes two comparative studies, by Budge, Farlie and Guttsman, which almost doubles the number of published comparative studies on British elites! Linz and Doggan's important multi-national study of legislators (forthcoming) unfortunately excludes Britain; thus apart from Putnam's (1971) study of the values held by British and Italian MPs and Herman's work on ministerial turnover (1974), only senior civil servants have been subject to comparative scrutiny (Subranamiam, 1967; Crewe and Halsey, 1969; and Putnam, 1973).

Secondly, elites need to be interviewed. The best way of finding out about people is talking to them. It cannot guarantee to secure the truth, especially from people well practised in the arts of discretion, but it is surely superior to any alternative way of discovering what they believe and do. Content analysis of an elite's written output is an even less reliable guide to their real views, although as Crouch shows in this volume, it may provide a valuable indication of the views with which they wish to be associated in public. Personal access to elites is always difficult, especially in the political and cultural conditions of Britain. The habit of secrecy among the powerful in Britain – and its passive acceptance by the public – is far stronger than in the United States (Shils, 1956). Discovering who sits on cabinet committees in Britain is a major problem, for example (*The Times*, 1973). Britain lacks America's populist, muckraking tradition which encourages researchers to ask, as well as the ethos of 'citizenship training in democracy' which encourages the powerful to answer. Nevertheless, the problems of talking to elites are not insuperable as earlier references to small interview surveys of civil servants, cabinet ministers and local 'Notables' reveal. The very recent major breakthroughs by Putnam on civil servants and Searing on MPs' socialisation suggests that interview studies of elites should develop rapidly in the near future. Not for the first time in the sociology of British politics, native social scientists will be indebted to the adventurous trail-blazing of American visitors.

Finally, a plea should be entered for the construction and testing of *theories* about elites. The distinctive British contribution to elite studies reflects a general tradition in British sociology which is better known for its focus on the conditions of life at the other end of the social scale. Like the late nineteenth-century 'social investigatory' school of Booth, the Rowntrees and Webbs (see Abrams, 1968), the best of British elite studies is positivist, descriptive, meticulous, a tribute to historical scholarship, packed with information intended to appeal to an innate sense of injustice, but essentially lacking any broad dynamic theory that explains the existence of the facts so vividly described. British studies have produced an impressive output of information on elites, especially their social background, which has formed the basis of acute and imaginative speculation at best (Miliband, 1969) and plain sloppy inference at worst, but rarely that of rigorous theory-testing. The only empirical theories that British elite studies could be said to have tested have been ones of representation and equality, of democracy and social mobility, but not of elites. Showing 'how unfair it all is' is doubtless important and interesting, but does not explain why the unfairness arises in the first place, how it is maintained, and what impact it has for society and polity. What is now required is a systematic use of the material at our disposal to explore the ungrounded assumptions that abound on the subject of elites. What difference, if any, do distant social antecedents in fact make to the beliefs and actions of elite groups? Does a specialist rather than generalist education and training really produce 'better' or even different decisions from civil servants? Where big business and the government conflict, which side normally 'wins'? Needed also are theories that exploit the longitudinal nature of much of the data on British elites.

The lack of any satisfactory explanation for the circulation of elites has already been mentioned. The work of Rokkan and Lipset (1967) on the inter-relationships between socio-economic development and party systems in Western Europe over the last two centuries suggests that a similar effort devoted to the impact on elite formation of changes in social structure would be fruitful. Why and how has the industrialisation of nineteenth- and twentieth-century Europe differed in the extent and pace with which this has been translated at elite level? And what have been the consequences for the nature and stability of each country's political system? (see Barrington Moore, 1965, and Bendix, 1964, for some stimulating ideas).

There are theories to be generated and tested, moreover, which do not focus on social composition as either *explicans* or *explicandum*. The means used by elites to maintain their power and privileges has yet to be thoroughly explored. Under what conditions and with what consequences for themselves and society at large do different elite groups resort to coercion or concessions, exclusion or absorption, co-operation or conflict with other elite groups? Why does their 'political formula', the form taken by their legitimating ideology, change over different periods? Pluralists and elitists engage in acrimonious controversy over the structure of inter-elite relations existing at one particular time in one particular society; but neither side has attempted the comparative analysis required for a thorough investigation of why a traditional ruling class does or does not fragment into competing elite groups in a liberal democracy. Pessimists would maintain that whilst disagreement over the nature and methods of locating power exist, little theoretical progress can be made. Optimists regard the area of elite studies as one in which theories in search of facts and facts in search of theories abound, waiting to be matched up by diligent and skilful social scientists. This volume is a preliminary foray in that direction.

44

REFERENCES

Aaronovitch, S., *The Ruling Class: A Study of British Finance Capital*, Lawrence & Wishart, London, 1961.

Abrams, P., *The Origins of British Sociology 1824–1914*, University of Chicago Press, Chicago, 1968.

Acton Society Trust, *Management Succession*, Acton Society Trust, London, 1956.

Alt, J., 'Continuity, Turnover, and Experience in the British Cabinet, 1868–1970', in Alt, J. and Herman, V. (eds.), *Cabinet Studies*, Macmillan, London, 1974.

Anderson, P., 'Origins of the Present Crisis', *New Left Review*, No. 23, January–February 1964, pp. 26–53.

Bachrach, P. and Baratz, M. S., (a) 'Two Faces of Power', *American Political Science Review*, vol. 56, No. 4, December 1962, pp. 947–52.

—— (b) 'Decisions and Non-decisions: an Analytical Framework', *American Political Science Review*, vol. 57, No. 3, September 1963, pp. 632–42.

Barnett, C., 'The Education of Military Elites', *Journal of Contemporary History*, vol. 2, No. 3, July 1967, pp. 15–36.

Bealey, F. *et al.*, *Constituency Politics*, Faber & Faber, London, 1965.

Bell, C. and Newby, H., *Community Studies*, George Allen & Unwin, London, 1971.

Bell, D., 'Notes on the Post-Industrial Society', *The Public Interest*, No. 6, Winter 1967, pp. 24–35; and No. 7, Spring 1967, pp. 102–17.

Bendix, R., *Nation-Building and Citizenship*, Wiley, New York, 1964.

Birch, A. H., *Small Town Politics*, Oxford University Press, Oxford, 1959.

Bishop, T. J. H. and Wilkinson, R., *Winchester and the Public Schools Elite*, Faber & Faber, London, 1967.

Blondel, J., *Voters, Parties and Leaders*, Penguin, London, 1963.

Bottomore, T. B., (a) 'The Administrative Elite' in Horowitz, I. L. (ed.), *The New Sociology*, Oxford University Press, New York, 1964.

—— (b) *Elites and Society*, Watts, London, 1964.

Brittan, S., 'The Irregulars' in Rose, R. (ed.), *Policy-Making in Britain*, Macmillan, London, 1969.

Budge, I., *Agreement and the Stability of Democracy*, Markham, Chicago, 1970.

Burnham, J., *The Managerial Revolution*, Day, New York, 1941.

Butler, D. E. and Stokes, D., *Political Change in Britain*, Macmillan, London, 1969.

Castle, B., 'Mandarin Power', *Sunday Times*, 10 June 1973.

Chapman, R. A., (a) 'Profile of a Profession: The Administrative Class of the Civil Service' in *The Civil Service: Surveys and Investigations* (Report of Lord Fulton's Committee, vol. 3(2)), HMSO, London, 1968.

—— (b) *The Higher Civil Service in Britain*, Constable, London, 1970.

Clements, R. V., (a) *Managers: A Study of their Careers in Industry*, George Allen & Unwin, London, 1958.

—— (b) *Local Notables and the City Council*, Macmillan, London, 1969.

Collisson, P. and Millen, J., 'University Chancellors, Vice Chancellors and College Principals: A Social Profile', *Sociology*, vol. 3, No. 1, January 1969, pp. 77–109.

Copeman, G., *Leaders of British Industry*, Gee, London, 1955.

Dahl, R., (a) 'The Concept of Power', in Polsby, N. *et al.* (eds.), *Politics and Social Life*, Houghton Mifflin, Boston, 1963.

—— (b) *Who Governs?*, Yale University Press, New Haven and London, 1963.

—— (c) *Modern Political Analysis*, Prentice Hall, Englewood Cliffs, NJ, 1963.

—— (d) *Polyarchy*, Yale University Press, New Haven and London, 1971.

Dale, H. E., *The Higher Civil Service*, Clarendon Press, Oxford, 1941.

Dennis, N., (a) *People and Planning*, Faber & Faber, London, 1970.

—— (b) *Public Participation and Planners Blight*, Faber & Faber, London, 1972.

Dodd, C. H., 'Recruitment to the Administrative Class 1960–64', *Public Administration*, vol. XLV, No. 1, Spring 1967, pp. 55–80.

Domhoff, G. W., (a) *Who Rules America?*, Prentice Hall, Englewood Cliffs, NJ, 1967.

—— (b) *The Higher Circles*, Random House, New York, 1971.

Edinger, L. J. and Searing, D. D., 'Social Background in Elite Analysis: A Methodological Enquiry', *American Political Science Review*, vol. 61, No. 2, June 1967, pp. 428–45.

Encounter, 'Suicide of a Nation?' (special issue), vol. 21, No. 1, July 1963.

Finer, S. E. (ed.), *Vilfredo Pareto: Sociological Writings*, Pall Mall, London, 1966.

Fox, J., 'The Brains behind the Throne', *Sunday Times*, 25 March 1973, pp. 46–57.

Frankenberg, F., *Communities in Britain*, Penguin, Harmondsworth, 1966.

Galbraith, J. K., *The New Industrial State*, Hamish Hamilton, London, 1967.

Gerth, H. and Mills, C. W. (eds.), *From Max Weber*, Routledge & Kegan Paul, London, 1948.

Giddens, A., 'Elites in the British Class Structure', *Sociological Review*, vol. 20, No. 3 (New Series), August 1972, pp. 345–72.

Goldstein-Jackson, K., 'The Judicial Elite', *New Society*, vol. 15, No. 398, 14 May 1970, p. 828.

Green, B., *Community Decision-Making in Georgian City*, unpublished Ph.D. thesis, Bath University of Technology, 1968.

Gunn, L. A., *Political Aspects of Administrative Change*, paper presented to the Conference of the Political Studies Association, Edinburgh, March 1972.

Guttsman, W. L., (a) *The British Political Elite*, MacGibbon & Kee, London, 1963.

—— (b) ed., *The English Ruling Class*, Weidenfeld & Nicolson, London, 1969.

Hacker, A., 'Political Behaviour and Political Behaviour', *Political Studies*, vol. 7, No. 1, February 1959, pp. 32–40.

Halsey, A. H. and Crewe, I. M., 'Social Survey of the Civil Service', being *The Civil Service: Surveys and Investigations* (Report of Lord Fulton's Committee, vol. 3(1)), HMSO, London, 1969.

Hampton, W., *Democracy and Community*, Oxford University Press, London, 1970.

Hart, D., 'Private Wealth for Public Good', *Daily Telegraph*, 7 April 1972, pp. 18–26.

Headey, B., (a) 'What Makes for a Strong Minister?', *New Society*, vol. 16, No. 419, 8 October 1970, pp. 624–7.

—— (b) *The Job of the Cabinet Minister*, George Allen & Unwin, London, 1974.

Herman, V., 'Patterns of Governmental and Ministerial Stability in Western Parliamentary Democracies', in Herman, V. and Alt, J. (eds.), *Cabinet Studies*, Macmillan, London, 1974.

Hewitt, C., 'National Policy-Making in Post-War Britain', *British Journal of Political Science*, Vol. 4, No. 1, January 1974.

Hirschman, A. O., *Exit, Voice and Loyalty*, Harvard University Press, Cambridge, Mass., 1970.

47

Hunter, F., *Community Power Structure*, University of North Carolina Press, Chapel Hill, NC, 1953.

Institute of Directors, (a) 'The Life and Times of a Director', *The Director*, October 1959.

—— (b) 'The Anatomy of a Board', *The Director*, January 1965.

—— (c) 'The Director Observed', *The Director*, April 1966.

Johnson, R. W., 'The British Political Elite, 1955–1970', *European Journal of Sociology*, vol. 14, No. 1, June 1973, pp. 35–77.

Johnson, T., 'Computers are not going to take over the world – but the Datacrats might', *The Sunday Times Business Supplement*, 14 December 1969.

Jones, G. W., *Borough Politics*, Macmillan, London, 1969.

Keller, S., *Beyond the Ruling Class*, Random House, New York, 1963.

Kelsall, R. K., (a) *Higher Civil Servants in Britain*, Routledge & Kegan Paul, London, 1955.

—— (b) *Graduates: The Sociology of an Elite*, Methuen, London, 1972.

King, A., 'Britain's Ministerial Turnover', *New Society*, vol. 8, No. 203, 18 August 1966, pp. 257–8.

Kornhauser, W., ' "Power Elite" or "Veto Groups" ', in Bendix, R. and Lipset, S. M. (eds.), *Class, Status and Power* (1st ed.), Free Press, New York, 1961.

Lasswell, H. D., (a) *The World Revolution of our Time*, Hoover Institute Studies, Series A, No. 1, Stanford University Press, Stanford, 1951.

—— (b) *The Comparative Study of Elites*, Hoover Institute Studies, Series B, No. 1, Stanford University Press, Stanford, 1952.

Lee, J. M., *Social Leaders and Public Persons*, Clarendon Press, Oxford, 1963.

Linz, J., Dogan, M. and Edinger, L. J., *Political Elite and Social Structure*, forthcoming.

Lipset, S. M. and Rokkan, S. (eds.), *Party Systems and Voter Alignments*, Free Press, New York, 1967.

Lockwood, D., 'The Distribution of Power in Industrial Society – A Comment', *Sociological Review Monographs*, No. 8, 1964, pp. 35–41.

Lutpon, T. and Wilson, C. S., 'The Social Background and Connections of "Top Decision Makers" ', *The Manchester School*, vol. 27, No. 1, January 1959, pp. 30–52.

McGinniss, J., *The Selling of the President*, Andre Deutsch, London, 1970.

McKenzie, R. T., *British Political Parties*, Heinemann, London, 1955 (revised edition 1964).

Marples, E., 'A Dog's Life in the Ministry', in Rose, R. (ed.), *Policy-Making in Britain*, Macmillan, London, 1969.

Meisel, J. M., *The Myth of the Ruling Class: Gaetana Mosca and the Elite*, University of Michigan Press, Ann Arbor, 1962.

Merelman, R., 'On the Neo-Elitist Critique of Community Power', *American Political Science Review*, vol. 62, No. 2, June 1968, pp. 451–60.

Michels, R., *Political Parties*, Free Press, Glencoe, Ill., 1959 (first published in New York, 1915).

Miliband, R., (a) *The State in Capitalist Society*, Weidenfeld & Nicolson, London, 1969.

—— (b) 'Professor Galbraith and American Capitalism', in Miliband, R. and Saville, J., *The Socialist Register 1968*, Merlin, London, 1968.

Miller, D. C., (a) 'Decision-making Cliques in Community Power Structures: A Comparative Study of an American and an English City', *American Journal of Sociology*, vol. 64, No. 3, November 1958, pp. 299–310.

—— (b) 'Industry and Community Power Structure: A Comparative Study of an English and an American City', *American Sociological Review*, vol. 23, No. 1, February 1958, pp. 9–15.

Mills, C. W., *The Power Elite*, Oxford University Press, New York, 1959.

Moore, B., *The Social Origins of Dictatorship and Democracy*, Penguin, London, 1967.

Morgan, D. H. J., 'The Social and Educational Background of Anglican Bishops: Continuities and Changes', *British Journal of Sociology*, vol. 20, No. 3, September 1969, pp. 295–310.

Morris, D. S. and Newton, K., (a) 'Profile of a Local Political Elite: Businessmen on Birmingham Council 1920–1966', *Discussion Paper*, *Series F*, No. 4, Faculty of Commerce and Social Science, University of Birmingham.

—— (b) 'The Social Composition of Birmingham Council 1930–1966', *Discussion Paper*, *Series F*, No. 2, Faculty of Commerce and Social Studies, University of Birmingham.

Morriss, P., 'Power in New Haven: A Reassessment of *Who Governs?*', *British Journal of Political Science*, vol. 2, No. 4, October 1972, pp. 457–65.

Mosca, G., *The Ruling Class*, McGraw Hill, New York, 1939.

Nettl, J. P., (a) 'Consensus or Elite Domination – the Case of Business', *Political Studies*, vol. 13, No. 1, February 1965, pp. 22–44.

—— (b) *Political Mobilisation*, Faber & Faber, London, 1967.

Newton, K., 'The Social Composition of Councils', *Discussion Paper, Series E*, No. 9, Faculty of Commerce and Social Science, University of Birmingham.

Nichols, T., *Ownership, Control and Ideology*, George Allen & Unwin, London, 1969.

Nicholson, E. M., *The System*, Hodder & Stoughton, London, 1967.

Olsen, M., *The Logic of Collective Action*, Schocken, New York, 1968.

Otley, C. B., (a) 'Public School and Army', *New Society*, vol. 8, No. 216, 17 November 1965, pp. 754–7.

—— (b) 'The Social Origins of British Army Officers', *Sociological Review*, vol. 18, No. 2, July 1970, pp. 213–39.

Pareto, V., *The Mind and Society: A Treatise on General Sociology*, Dover, New York, 1959.

Parry, G., (a) 'Elites and Polyarchies', *Journal of Commonwealth Political Studies*, vol. 4, No. 3, November 1966, pp. 163–79.

—— (b) *Political Elites*, George Allen & Unwin, London, 1969.

Paterson, P., *The Selectorate*, MacGibbon & Kee, London, 1967.

Poulantzas, N., 'The Problem of the Capitalist State', *New Left Review*, No. 58, November–December 1969, pp. 67–78.

Putnam, R. D., (a) 'Studying Elite Political Culture: The Case of "Ideology" ', *American Political Science Review*, vol. 65, No. 3, September 1971, pp. 651–81.

—— (b) 'The Political Attitudes of Senior Civil Servants in Western Europe', *British Journal of Political Science*, vol. 3, No. 3, July 1973, pp. 257–90.

Report of the Committee of Inquiry under the Chairmanship of Lord Fulton 1966–68, *The Civil Service*, vols. I–V, HMSO, London, 1968 and 1969.

Report of the Committee of Inquiry under the Chairmanship of Mr J. G. W. Davies, 1969, *The Method II System of Selection*, HMSO, London, 1969.

Rose, A. M., *The Power Structure*, Oxford University Press, New York, 1967.

Rose, R. (ed.), (a) *Studies in British Politics* (1st edition), Macmillan, London, 1966.

—— ed. (b) *Policy-Making in Britain*, Macmillan, London, 1969.

—— (c) 'The Making of Cabinet Ministers', *British Journal of Political Science*, vol. 1, No. 4, October 1971, pp. 393–414.

Roth, A. and Kerbey, J., (a) *The Business Background of M.P.s*, Parliamentary Profile Services, London, 1972 (earlier editions in 1963, 1965 and 1967).

—— (b) *Lord on the Board*, Parliamentary Profile Services, London, 1972.

Rule, J., *Private Lives and Public Surveillance*, Allen Lane, London, 1973.

Rush, M., *The Selection of Parliamentary Candidates*, Nelson, London, 1969.

Sampson, A., *Anatomy of Britain*, Hodder & Stoughton, London, 1962 (latest edition: *The New Anatomy of Britain*, Hodder & Stoughton, London, 1971).

Shils, E., *The Torment of Secrecy*, Heinemann, London, 1956.

Strang, Lord, 'Permanent Under-Secretary', in R. Rose (ed.), *Policy-Making in Britain*, Macmillan, London, 1969.

Subramaniam, V., 'Representative Bureaucracy: A Reassessment', *American Political Science Review*, vol. 61, No. 4, December 1967, pp. 1010–19.

Thoenies, P., *The Elite in the Welfare State*, Faber & Faber, London, 1966.

Thomas, H. (ed.), *The Establishment*, Blond, London, 1959.

Thompson, E. P., 'A Report on Lord Radcliffe', *New Society*, vol. 15, No. 396, 30 April 1970, pp. 737–8.

The Times, 'Whitehall's Needless Secrecy', 3 May 1973, p. 19.

Tunstall, J., *The Westminster Lobby Correspondents*, Routledge & Kegal Paul, London, 1970.

Urry, J. and Wakeford, J. (eds.), *Power in Britain*, Heinemann Educational, London, 1973.

Veblen, T., *The Engineers and the Price System*, Harcourt, Brace & World, New York, 1963 (first published in 1921).

Wakeford, J., *The Cloistered Elite*, Macmillan, London, 1969.

Weinberg, I., *The English Public Schools*, Atherton, New York, 1967.

Westergaard, J., 'The Withering Away of Class: A Contemporary Myth', in Anderson, P. and Blackburn, R. (eds.), *Towards Socialism*, Fontana, London, 1965.

Wilkinson, R., *The Prefects*, Oxford University Press, London, 1964.

Wolfinger, R., 'Non-Decisions and the Study of Local Politics', *American Political Science Review*, vol. 65, No. 4, December 1971, pp. 1063–80.

Worsley, P., 'The Distribution of Power in Industrial Society', *Sociological Review Monographs*, No. 8, 1964, pp. 16–34.

EMPIRICAL STUDIES

2. The Ideology of a Managerial Elite:
The National Board for Prices and Incomes 1965–1970

COLIN CROUCH

The re-emergence of industrial conflict into the British political arena has important implications for the structure of institutionalised capitalism which has been widely regarded as characteristic of this society.[1] The significance of these changes goes beyond the limited field of industrial relations itself to include the following major issues: the strategies which are employed by governments and economic elites to secure order, including the ideologies which support their position; that crucial question which stood at the centre of politics in an earlier industrial period, the political integration of a working class which has acquired certain rights of countervailing power; the basis of stratification within the society; and from the point of view of social and political theory, the concepts which are to be used in analysing its structure. In this paper only one small aspect of these recent developments can be examined in detail: the incomes policy of the Labour Government between 1964 and 1970, principally as exhibited in the reports on questions of incomes of the National Board for Prices and Incomes. This evidence will be used in two ways, first as a direct instance of the thinking of an elite, and second for what it reveals about the underlying structure. However, an attempt will be made to indicate some of the more general implications of the events described. In particular, there will be some exploration of the relationship between them and the concept of corporatism which several recent writers on contemporary industrial societies have found useful.[2]

An important feature of institutionalised capitalism has been its amelioration of the harshness of 'pure' or simple capitalist relations in the fixing of wages and the termination of disputes over them.[3] This is achieved through various forms of conciliation machinery, acceptance of formal rules and procedures, and so forth. In this way matters are resolved without the parties having recourse to their sheer

55

market strength. Those aspects of conciliation which are created by the state do not seek to impose the view of the government on the situation, but seek to find an accommodation acceptable to the parties. But it is important to recognise the historical context in which the outlines of the British system of institutionalised industrial relations took shape. It was a period when high unemployment imposed absolute restrictions on the market power of nearly all groups of manual workers; if the potential power of the working class was feared it was on account of its ability to create civil disorder. The position presented to organised labour by the structure of compromise was frequently more advantageous than that afforded by the market. It is perhaps this condition which made government and industry willing to extend a formal position to the unions; it is certainly this condition which has been radically changed since the commitment by governments to full employment during World War II.[4] In those situations where employees are able and willing fully to exercise their market strength, the traditional machinery of British industrial relations no longer serves simply to manage affairs in an orderly way. It may facilitate a real shift in the balance of market power such that labour is no longer so subordinate. Even more important, it may lead to situations where the power of labour is stronger outside the formal channels than within them.

It is important to clarify a major point on this development. By and large the effect of this change has not been to produce an overall change in the distribution of income between labour and capital, nor among different sorts of labour except over short ranges of the income structure. Pressure for increased income has been absorbed, partly by economic growth and partly by the process of inflation. This has been particularly important in changing the overall political implications of the growing power of organised labour from one concerning the class distribution of wealth to one of economic management and the general economic interest in a low rate of inflation.

Government attempts at dealing with this situation date from the earliest years of post-war full employment. The problem has been to shift back the balance of power within industry without dismantling the delicate system of compromise, and without sacrificing the politically important goal of full employment. Not surprisingly, given the difficulty of achieving this end, governments have frequently preferred to tolerate a modest rate of inflation.

The record of the earlier policies cannot concern us here, and it has been discussed elsewhere.[5] We shall here consider the most ambitious

56

of them all, the National Board for Prices and Incomes, the reports of which are extraordinarily clear in spelling out the aims of the policy of which it was the agent. They are therefore of considerable assistance in an attempt to characterise the nature of this innovation in the state's policy towards industrial relations.

THE IDEOLOGY OF THE NBPI

The National Board for Prices and Incomes[6] was established in an atmosphere of consensus; it had been preceded by a Declaration of Intent on prices and incomes policy signed by the Government, the Trade Union Congress and the employers' organisations. And in Parliament the Conservative Opposition, which had itself tried unsuccessfully to introduce an incomes policy, did not oppose but welcomed the establishment of the Board. The changes which took place in the attitudes of some of these groups during its lifetime will be considered later, but for the present the main task is to explore the ideology of the Board itself as revealed in its reports. We are here concerned, not with the Board's immediate proposals on industrial efficiency and so forth as such, but with their wider implications for matters related to social stratification: matters concerning the structure of inequality, the distribution of power and its legitimacy.

Legitimate forms of income inequality

A central question on which the NBPI was clear and explicit was that of the nature of an acceptable structure of income inequality. Consistently the Board argued that pay structure should be based on measurable differences of skill and responsibility.[7] The hierarchy of command should be reproduced in the hierarchy of income, from the level of the first-line supervision to that of higher management.[8] For example, in the Higher Civil Service, where differentials had become compressed at the very point where there was a significant increase in responsibility, the Board insisted that it was 'essential that this greater responsibility be acknowledged through an appropriate higher salary level'.[9] It also based its case for an increase in the salaries of top management in the nationalised industries on the fact that the small differentials between them and middle management made it difficult to raise the salaries of the latter to reward performance.[10] It was similarly insistent on the need to reward differences in skill level, criticising instances it encountered where semi-skilled workers were earning more than skilled workers.[11] Discussing its policy on differentials in general, the Board argued:

> Free collective bargaining, in so far as it consists of a competitive rivalry between unions to maintain their position relative to one another, leaves traditional differentials unchanged. One of the purposes of an incomes policy is to narrow differentials when they are too large, but also to enlarge them when they are too narrow. There is clearly a case, for example, for enlarging them when a projection of manpower needs indicates a future requirement for new skills. Perhaps too little attention has been given to this aspect in the various White Papers. It is, however, an aspect which the Board, in its own investigations, cannot entirely ignore. . . .[12]

In the next incomes policy White Paper[13] the Board's point was accepted and increases necessitated by a 'reform of the pay structure' were admitted among the criteria for preferential treatment.

Policy on low pay

Of course, the Board's policy of increasing certain differentials did not easily accord with one of the original criteria of the Government's policy: help for the low-paid. This caused the Board considerable difficulty. Politically, protection of the low-paid had been an important element in Ministers' defence of the incomes policy, particularly within the Labour movement. But in its first general report the NBPI had indicated the emphasis which it was likely to place on it:

> We conclude that the three objectives of help for the lowest paid, the better use of men, and the avoidance of inflationary increases in incomes are better secured through relating pay increases to the rate of national progress, with provisions for exceptions, than by relating them to the increases which it is thought that everybody else is getting.[14]

Later, the Board did attempt more direct means of assisting low-paid workers in individual references, and came to accept this task as part of its role.[15] However, given that it accepted a relative definition of low pay and its overall concern with differentials, the Board could evidently not be used as an instrument for the abolition of low pay.

It is significant that the Board could only really deal with low pay when it felt it possible to reconcile this criterion with its more dominant concern for securing differentials of skill and responsibility.[16] Thus, where differentials did not reflect differences of skill or responsibility, that is those which owed 'more to institutional than to economic or social factors'[17] the Board was happy to see their elimination and to criticise unions for not supporting this task; alternatively, the very existence of differentials could be used to help at least a few of the low-paid, through the recognition of levels of skill and responsibility within their ranks or by retraining workers so that they would become eligible for more skilled and hence better remunerated employment.[18]

Attitude to market forces

The Board's concern for the maintenance of certain differentials was partly, but only partly, related to labour market considerations. Its reports certainly made reference to market forces, sometimes accepting the need to resolve recruitment difficulties by granting pay increases.[19] Further, it was critical of monopolies on the grounds that they freed employers from price discipline making them less likely to resist pay claims.[20] And the Board identified market power, defined as 'the power to influence and indeed set prices and earnings at will' as a principal reason for maintaining a prices and incomes policy.[21] However, none of these points should be taken to mean that the Board advocated a market or neo-liberal solution to wage-setting, which would allow firms to outbid each other in the labour market until the less efficient were driven out or demand for the product reduced, creating unemployment. With the exceptions mentioned, the Board was extremely sceptical of attempts at responding to market fluctuations. It believed that pay increases would need to be very large before they had an effect on the labour market[22] and feared that competition for labour would be 'self-defeating'.[23] It would succeed only in 'bidding up' the price when labour was in short supply,[24] while when there was unemployment any increases would be unnecessary.[25] Where the Board acknowledged that an organisation had a recruitment problem, it preferred reforms which would improve the general attractiveness of the work[26] or increase the efficiency of the existing labour force.[27] It criticised firms which attempted to base their pay structures on 'the assumption that there exists a labour market, the prices in which have to be matched, though the assumption is often belied by the facts'.[28]

The NBPI's discomfort at market solutions was therefore partly a response to what it saw as the reality of the modern economy, but it may also be related to its concern for clear, stable pay structures, which it both preferred itself and saw as responding to the desires of many workers.[29] The market is always potentially unstable, and in a changing economy old skills lose their value while new occupations emerge which cannot readily be compared with existing ones in terms of skill and responsibility. Further, labour market shortages may emerge at certain points of a structure, to overcome which may involve disrupting a hierarchy of skill and responsibility. The Board sought to reconcile the need to respond to major market changes with its concern for the integrity and stability of existing structures,[30] but in so doing it had to give explicit recognition to the fact that skill and responsibility were not equivalent to market forces.[31] A similar difficulty emerged when the Board considered certain engineering firms which had been paying semi-skilled workers more highly than craftsmen. The Board recognised that this may have been a response to market factors, reflecting the unpleasant nature of the work, its boredom and so forth. But having noted this possibility, the Board immediately evaded the question[32] and all other references in the reports to an inverted differential between the skilled and the semi-skilled are unequivocally critical.

Manual-non-manual differences

The concern of the NBPI for clear structures based on skill and responsibility brought it into conflict with other deeply entrenched characteristics of the existing system of incomes distribution as well as with the operation of simple market forces. Particularly interesting among these is the general differential between manual and white-collar workers which the latter at least believed should be maintained. This barrier is an important one. Not only is it exceptionally difficult to make comparisons of skill and responsibility levels across this boundary, because of differences in the nature of the work; it has also traditionally been the boundary of different types of payment system, working conditions, concepts of the role and attitudes of different types of worker, and social status. In recent decades, however, the division has been made more complex, first by the growth of new technical occupations which fit readily into neither category; and second by the erosion of the usual expectation that the division will also represent a cut-off point in *size* of income.

The NBPI adopted as a long-term goal the abolition of all invidious distinctions between manual and non-manual labour, including the gradual extension of the salary system and its attendant security of income to manual workers:[33]

> A policy for productivity, prices and incomes is concerned with modifying attitudes making for resistance to increased productivity and to a closer relationship between movements in incomes and movements in productivity. It is concerned therefore with general reforms which may help to bring about changes of attitudes. We would suggest as one such reform the desirability of abolishing the division between the 'staff' and 'workmen'. The division is increasingly outdated – it is related to a past when greater co-operation was expected from the 'staff' than from the 'workers'; it is arbitrary and it can give rise to resentment.[34]

Consistent with this approach the Board was not prepared to accept the frequent assumption that the pay of non-manual workers should automatically be higher than that of manuals. It recognised as 'reasonable enough' the attempts of manual workers to catch up with the incomes of non-manuals,[35] and rejected severely claims made by white-collar workers for the maintenance or restoration of differentials over manual workers.[36] The Board's overall objective in this was to seek the replacement of the traditional practice in which manual and non-manual workers had different attitudes to work and to productivity. In place of the manual labourer responding merely to material incentives and being attached to his employer only by the cash nexus, it sought a worker who would co-operate, indeed participate, in the furtherance of the organisation's goals and the improvement of its productivity. And in place of the white-collar worker dependent on a paternalistic personal relationship with his employer, it sought an employee who, while certainly continuing the white-collar worker's tradition of co-operation, would do so as a member of a trade union and within a pay structure based on rational and objective principles.

Comparability

The manual/non-manual barrier is of particular interest because of its social significance, but it may also be seen as an instance of a more general phenomenon: the tendency for pay claims and pay expectations to be based on 'comparability'. This may be defined as the belief that one group of workers is entitled to an increase because a group which it takes as a reference group has received one. Comparability is extremely deeply rooted in British industrial relations, ranging from vague everyday comparisons made by groups of workers to the sophisticated exercises, based on job analogues and carried out by specialised staff, which are used to determine pay in certain areas of the public service. Comparisons have been important elements in the British consensus. They enable workers to articulate demands for relative justice within a narrow frame of reference, while not posing any threat to the overall structure of inequality. They frequently bear at least some relationship to differences of skill and responsibility and act as a useful guideline for employers when deciding on an increase. And, given their general acceptability, they provide useful benchmarks for negotiators and, most important, for third-party conciliators and arbitrators. Comparability is the principle on which such intervention is usually based.

Of course, when comparability truly reflected differences of skill or responsibility, the NBPI was content to follow it, but it frequently found that it did not do so. Further, it saw comparability as an important mechanism in the inflationary process of leap-frogging wage claims.[37] The incomes policy White Papers had encouraged the NBPI to place a decreased emphasis on comparisons, and it carried out this task enthusiastically,[38] criticising not only agreements made within industry,[39] but also the operation of official arbitration and pay review bodies which accepted comparability.[40]

The NBPI was thus a disruptive institution in that it attacked some of the fundamental assumptions on which pay determination and industrial relations had become based. In support of its preferred replacement (a hierarchy based on measured differences of skill and responsibility) the Board could argue that it would promote efficiency and help combat inflation. But it also sought to go beyond this and invoke moral criteria, freely using such concepts as 'equity', 'fairness' and 'justice' to describe its desired distribution. This becomes particularly interesting in that such concepts are unknown to market economics, and indeed one of the achievements of the capitalist system of income distribution is often considered to have been its liberation of such questions from casuistry and value judgement. Appeals for justice and equity do, however, figure prominently in the arguments of trade unionists and socialists, and hence it is also interesting to compare the content which the NBPI sought to give these terms with that of these other groups.

Ethics and income distribution

The NBPI would accept a desire for 'fairness' as a legitimate aspiration in a pay claim,[41] and the elimination of 'obvious inequity' was listed alongside the ending of 'confusion' and 'economic inefficiency' as an 'urgent need' in the reform of pay structures.[42] In the case of the engineering industry the Board went so far as to propose continuing outside intervention in pay determination in order to secure 'equity'.[43] By 'equity' the Board did not mean equality. This is most clearly expressed in its first report on the engineering industry:

> The actual structure of earnings within individual plants may give rise to differentials between different skills which may be so distorted or reversed as to cause as much concern on grounds of equity or justice as does the position of low-paid workers. For equity and justice require not only that the absolute level of pay be such as to provide an acceptable standard of living but also that skill and responsibility are fairly rewarded.[44]

An inequality would be unfair if it were the product of the disruptive use of market position:

> Without an incomes policy, groups in a powerful bargaining position or occupying strategic points in the economy are able to obtain pay increases not open to those in a weaker bargaining position or occupying strategically less important points; in other words, social injustice can arise from the undue use of market power. It is one of the purposes of an incomes policy to remedy this injustice. This purpose cannot be quickly achieved; it is all the more difficult to achieve when the balance of payments is adverse if groups of workers whose activities directly affect the balance of payments use the power which this gives them to obtain pay increases not open to others.[45]

Where a powerful bargaining position resulted from the possession of skill and responsibility, however, the Board referred to the ensuing differential in positive moral terms, even in contrast with the problems of the low-paid:

> ... if the labourer [earning £10 a week] works alongside a skilled
> man earning no more than £11, it might be economically unwise
> and socially unjust to give the labourer an increase of £1 and
> leave the skilled man's pay untouched.[46]

Behind the Board's notions of justice and fairness lay a major
second-order value: that of rationality. Its preference for a structure
of differentials based on differences of skill and responsibility rested
on the rationality of such a structure. By rationality is meant a
system whose features are overt and clear, calculable in precise terms
according to a body of internally consistent and logical principles.
This was a desideratum which the Board expressed explicitly. Discussing the introduction of properly structured salary systems for
white-collar staff, it said:

> ... there are certain principles which should be followed in any
> assessment of performances. First, the particular method adopted
> must be seen by the staff affected to be fair and equitable ...
> Secondly, it is important to assess only those factors which are
> directly related to performance. More general personality traits
> unrelated to performance are irrelevant to the process of per-
> formance appraisals. Thirdly, whatever system is adopted,
> quantifiable indicators of performance should be included
> wherever possible as they reduce the possibility of bias on the
> part of the assessor.[47]

Job evaluation and rationality

The absence of such criteria in pay structures provided the Board
with one of its most frequent sources of criticism,[48] and in nearly all
such cases its prescription was the introduction of job evaluation
schemes.[49] Job evaluation was described as 'the comparison of jobs
by the use of formal and systematic procedures ... in order, after
analysis, to determine the relative position of one job to another in a
wage or salary hierarchy'.[50] Obviously, such a process would enable
measurable values to be placed on different jobs, making possible
their comparison one with another in a rational and objective way.
However, despite the Board's great enthusiasm for job evaluation,
and its use of rationality and objectivity as crucial criteria for an
acceptable pay system, it was disarmingly willing to acknowledge the
essential subjectivity of job evaluation in practice: the impossibility

of eliminating bargaining and the intrinsic difficulty of making meaningful comparisons between different occupations.[51] Indeed, at times the Board would criticise a system for a misplaced sense of objectivity. The ambiguity of its attitude is clearly revealed in a passage from its report on salary structures:

> In the absence of clear-cut principles, the practical aim of managers has been to establish pay systems on a basis of acceptability to all concerned: that is to achieve a consensus about how salaries should be administered. Although job evaluation rests ultimately on a subjective foundation, as a technique it has proved most valuable in enabling pay structures to be rationalised and put on an acceptable basis.[52]

In one major reference, that on the pay of the armed forces, the NBPI was itself called upon to carry out a large exercise in job evaluation. It did so elaborately, making a series of sophisticated comparisons with civilian analogues for each service grade being evaluated. But despite this, the Board conceded the ultimate subjectivity of the whole exercise.[53] Further evidence of the Board's difficulty in practice of applying the criteria of rationality which in principle was its primary point of reference may be gleaned from those cases in which, in order to secure an 'acceptable' settlement, the Board sacrificed some of its concern for strictly justifiable agreements;[54] and also from its failure in specific instances to pronounce on what would comprise a fair distribution of the proceeds of a productivity agreement among workers, employers and consumers;[55] again a principle on which the Board was in theory insistent.[56]

Two important features of the Board's concern for rationality may be noted. First, the rationality being sought was not that of the free market. It was not advocating that salaries and wages be left to find their market rate; its concern was with the techniques which managements might employ in order to ensure that the internal relationships of their job hierarchies were based on consistent principles. Second, the Board's main concern in pursuing rationality was to seek structures which would be *accepted* as internally coherent rather than a precise substantive rationality according to its own criteria of skill and responsibility. This is not to argue that the Board was unconcerned with whether a salary structure 'really' corresponded to measurable differences in skill and responsibility. However, it has been shown that the Board was aware of the arbitrariness of several of its apparently objective methods, and its overriding concern in this matter was to produce structures which those directly concerned would accept as rational and hence (and in the Board's view *ipso facto*) as equitable. In this way alone is it possible to reconcile the Board's insistence on the need for rational structures with its acceptance of the practical impossibility of the task.

Attitudes to bargaining

The objective of the NBPI in proposing job evaluation, work measurement and so forth was at least in part an exercise in persuasion. It was seeking to encourage people in industry to accept a certain set of procedures for determining pay in preference to either custom and practice (as has been discussed above) or to another process which the Board treated ambivalently – bargaining.

The NBPI disliked bargaining. It constituted the 'bad' way of settling pay issues where job evaluation represented the 'good'.[57] It was contrasted with objectivity[58] and identified with unfairness,[59] and the Board sought evidence that many workers shared this view. In its early stages, it even tried to eliminate the use of the term 'productivity bargaining', preferring 'productivity agreement'.[60] But the Board was also a strong supporter of the formal process of collective bargaining, advocating its introduction in those industries where it was lacking. It sought to separate disputes over the grading and evaluation process from those concerning pay claims, and to have the former resolved by objective work-study while the latter should become a matter of exchanging improvements in productivity for pay increases. It was in this latter context that 'bargaining' of a kind became acceptable. What the Board was opposing when it criticised bargaining was the exercise of 'power' by work-groups or unions:

> We have read the Statement of Intent and the subsequent White Papers as meaning that trade unions and employers' associations have become powerful bodies, all the more powerful at a time of high employment . . . one group of employees may be better organised than another even in the same industry – manual workers may, for instance, be better organised than clerks; the more militant group may therefore operate to divert the distribution of income in its favour. The White Papers accordingly lay down rules to ensure that incomes and prices are not determined by the play of power and that the possible adverse consequences for others of actions by powerful bodies are better taken into

account. Arbitration or mediation called upon to terminate a dispute between two contestants is under a strong compulsion to pay primary regard to the interests of the contestants and therefore to ignore the implications of the settlement for others. It tends therefore to reflect and perpetuate the existing distribution of power and by its nature it is at variance with a policy which seeks to ensure that incomes are not determined by power alone.[61]

Bargaining, therefore, became illegitimate when it was a matter of workers exercising 'power'; and 'power' was used to refer to an attempt to shift the distribution of income in a direction other than that indicated by a quasi-rational process of job evaluation based on differences in skill and responsibility.

Productivity and acceptability

The appeal to rationality played an important part in the work of the NBPI, but the Board also made use of a more material inducement to consensus: the scope for improvements in productivity. Of course, the Board had several economic reasons for seeking increased productivity in addition to its need to make a prices and incomes policy acceptable, but it would be wrong to disregard this latter aspect. In nearly all its incomes reports the Board sought some means by which productivity could be improved in order to make possible (or justify) a pay increase.[62] Frequently it used the prospect of a productivity increase to sweeten the pill of a rejected claim, or it would hint, vaguely or in detail, at productivity improvements which might make possible the fulfilment of workers' income expectations. In general, where an increase in real wealth may be obtained, the possibility of a productivity agreement temporarily relaxes the major constraint of the relative scarcity of resources. The usefulness of productivity improvements as a means of escaping the problem of competition for scarce resources appeared most prominently with respect to low pay. As was discussed above, the problem of low pay gave the Board considerable difficulty; eventually it settled to the view that, like most other problems of incomes policy, it would be best resolved if it could be subsumed under the heading of productivity:

In so far as improving the position of the low paid is one of the purposes of a productivity, prices and incomes policy – which in our view it should be – the main remedy is to be found in the improvement of efficiency. Except in a minority of instances, therefore, we consider that the improvement of the position of the low-paid can be subsumed in the general problem of improving efficiency. [63]

And again:

In a period of economic stagnation gains in the living standards of the low-paid would have to be at the expense of other workers' living standards and this is bound to be resisted. When there are increases to be shared, it should be easier to give more to the low-paid. [64]

This principle is of course of greater potential application than the particular problems of the low-paid, and may be applied to the general question of income distribution; to that extent much of the Board's work in proposing productivity solutions to income disputes may be seen as a means of coping with the central political problem: the allocation of scarce material resources. [65]

The NBPI and managerial authority

Both rationality and productivity improvements were means by which the NBPI sought to secure the consent of workers to a particular system of incomes distribution. But income distribution is not primarily a matter of consent, whatever emphasis is placed on a 'voluntary' incomes policy by governments. Except in very exceptional circumstances workers do not decide the level of their own remuneration; resources being scarce, behind the process of bargaining and various degrees of consensus rest institutionalised sources of coercion which play the central role in determining incomes. Under simple capitalism this constraint is of course the market, and the labour market continues to be a major factor in the contemporary economy. As has been discussed above, the NBPI was wary of leaving pay determination solely to the play of the market. But obviously the Board itself could not fix incomes throughout the economy and in any case lacked the power to enforce its recommendations. The question therefore arises as to the source of the coercion which would secure the kinds of pay structure which the NBPI considered desirable. The Board's position on this was clear: it identified management as the function through which this task could be achieved, and sought to ensure that management possessed both the power to do so and the will to use that power.

The problem of leap-frogging wage claims between skilled and semi-skilled workers, whereby the latter could secure earnings beyond those merited by their skill, was one of the issues which most vexed the NBPI, and it diagnosed the problem as one of a loss of control. It saw such developments in the context of the broad political changes which had brought about full employment and thus reduced the uni-lateral power of management while moving power to the shop floor.[66] Many of the Board's proposals in specific references advocated the restoration of managerial control over a work force or payment system. As it summarised its own work in its final general report, the Board had 'tried to contribute to the improvement of industrial rela-tions by helping to develop situations in which management had a more effective control of the work situation based on the co-operation and consent of the workers concerned'.[67] It listed the restoration of managerial control among its reasons for supporting job evalua-tion;[68] when it advocated work measurement and work study it did so partly as means of securing managerial control over payment-by-results schemes;[69] it supported the proposals of the Donovan Com-mission[70] to the extent that they would help secure managerial control over inflationary earnings;[71] and finally, the Board maintained as one of its objectives in proposing pay-structure reforms the establishment of increased control for management.[72]

It was as a means for securing increased control that productivity bargaining again proved so useful to the Board.[73] Reporting on seven important productivity agreements, the Board identified as a common factor in them the realisation by management that they had lost con-trol of overtime and needed to recover it.[74] And following introduc-tion of the schemes managers had been able to secure 'nothing less than a revolution in managerial control over working hours and practices in many of the undertakings affected'.[75] In a later report it again cited examples in which the aims of productivity agreements included securing increased control and inculcating attitudes of 'total acceptance and adoption by workers of technical change, without specifying individual alterations in working practices'.[76]

But it is important to specify clearly the nature of this increased control which the NBPI advocated. It was not referring to the uni-lateral managerial prerogatives frequently sought by managerial groups; the Board was concerned with the overall integration of managers and workers in a collaborative exercise, as was indicated

69

above when considering the Board's concept of the modern worker in contrast with both the manual labourer and the white-collar employee of traditional practice:

> Our case studies showed that the end result of this broadening of the concept of co-operation and of the conclusion of a productivity agreement was usually a better controlled payment system and more effective use by management of the resources at its disposal. While this development might appear on the face of it to involve a derogation from the exclusive prerogative of management to manage, the consequences were beneficial to management as well as to employees. Indeed, increased managerial control was generally achieved through the consent and co-operation of workers and through greater participation by trade unions in decision-taking either through shop stewards or full-time officials. Productivity agreements have in short placed a premium on positive co-operation between management and workers in raising efficiency.[77]

The Board declared that participation by workers in reaching productivity agreements was 'the most practicable and fruitful approach to that elusive concept — industrial democracy'.[78] And as far as attitudes were concerned, 'productivity agreements would appear to have led to a greater "democratisation" on the shop floor, and this in turn has helped to create a more effective working relationship than existed before.'[79]

Superficially this emphasis on democracy and participation may seem at variance with the Board's severe criticisms of firms where workers had secured a strong *de facto* position in bargaining. The paradox is resolved by recognising the limitations on the degree and nature of the rights of unions and workers to share control, which the Board admitted. It saw the unity of management and unions in their pursuit of a wider interest: increased productivity and efficiency. It was the scope for this unity in modern conditions which made possible the shift from unilateral to shared management. Within that framework the Board fully recognised that workers and management had distinctive and possibly conflicting interests. It thus accepted that management and workers constituted two 'sides' of industry, but accepted this in such a way that management was undoubtedly the dominant partner, since it was the party which in the eyes of the Board was more completely identified with the common goal of

70

increased productive efficiency. Therefore the democracy and participation were based on the premise of overall acceptance of the prime role of management. This complex underlying framework of unity and pluralism, democracy and control is obviously not stated baldly in the Board's literature, but it may readily be inferred from it.

The role of trade unions

Consistent with this, the NBPI fully accepted trade unionism, and did not seek through its proposals for joint participation to undermine the position of unions. Discussing various proposed replacements for payment-by-results systems, the Board said explicitly:

Despite their emphasis on joint co-operation and workers' identification with the success of the firm, however, it is important that these plant-wide schemes do not appear designed to weaken the influence of unions.[80]

And in its third report the Board asserted the need for unions or their factory representatives to be involved in areas previously regarded as part of the managerial prerogative, such as the determination of work standards; the Board hoped this would lead to a decline in disputes on the shop floor, and to a start in increased participation in the affairs of an undertaking.[81] Again, the Board was able to reconcile these traditional areas of tension because of its confidence in the overall unity imparted by the search for increased productivity. It was not *any* kind of unionism which the Board approved, but what it regarded as 'responsible' unionism:

Not all union intervention can be turned into constructive channels by appropriate improvement and rationalisation of salary structure. Unhelpful union attitudes may be dictated by considerations quite outside a company's control, and may indeed be based simply on traditional thinking which is difficult to change. We would consider root and branch opposition to a system of pay linked to performance to come into this category. But in so far as rational responses govern union intervention we would expect their influence to be constructive in organisations having a planned salary structure combined with adequate techniques for its administration.[82]

Given that unions would make their task the discovery of ways in which pay increases could be matched by improvements in productivity, the NBPI was prepared both to maintain the importance for workers' interests of representation by strong trade unions and to call on employers in their own interest to help develop unions among their employees.[83]

This completes the review of the underlying premises of the NBPI on matters of the desired structure of inequality, the framework of authority, and the pattern of acceptable power relations. The distinctiveness of the Board's particular stance on these questions, and its relationship to theories of social stratification will be displayed to best advantage if two interesting questions are explored. First, how may the Board's position be contrasted with certain alternative ideal–typical forms of social and economic organisation? And second, assuming that it would be possible to construct a society based on the prescriptions of the NBPI, how would its system of social stratification best be described? An answer to the latter question will be reached through the discussion of the former.

THE SOCIAL STRUCTURE OF MANAGERIAL CORPORATISM

As has been indicated at several points above, the NBPI cannot be considered an expression of simple capitalism. It certainly considered that market mechanisms were important and that use should be made of them; but it is of the essence of capitalism that the market is allowed to be sovereign; it is not a device of which use may be made if it seems appropriate. The Board was prepared to assert over the dictates of the market the need for pay to reflect the hierarchy of skill and responsibility; and if anything was to be sovereign it was not the operation of market forces but the authority and discretion of management. Equally important, the very existence of the Board was evidence of at least a lack of confidence in market institutions, particularly during the periods when the Board was being employed as part of the apparatus of state control of incomes. A state-sponsored agency to advise on measures of industrial efficiency might be compatible with a capitalist economy, but an agency which was called upon to propose particular levels of remuneration or rates of pay increase in conformity with norms and criteria laid down by central government was certainly not; strictly speaking such a role would be irrelevant under capitalism since such matters would be resolved by the level of unemployment. Interestingly, it was as the Conservative

Opposition increasingly adopted a neo-liberal economic policy between 1966 and 1970 that it changed its attitude towards the NBPI. At first the majority of the Party's leadership had supported the establishment of the Board, and it was a dissident group of neo-Liberals who opposed it.[84] Most prominent among them was Mr Enoch Powell, MP, who while still a member of the Shadow Cabinet described incomes policy as a 'dangerous nonsense'. Within the House of Commons itself Mr John Biffen, MP, was the most outspoken advocate of Powell's ideas, particularly during the periods of statutory freeze and restraint when he employed the neo-Liberal argument to advocate free collective bargaining and a return to completely independent trade-union activity. However, as the incomes policy became part of a statutory freeze and lost general popularity, the Party's position shifted; first to advocating that the Board should act simply as a body investigating inefficiency and restrictive practices, and eventually to outright opposition to the Board.[85]

The Conservatives did not necessarily oppose the kind of criteria which the Board applied in its reports, but there is a significant difference in the language used. As has been seen above, the Board's emphasis was on 'skill and responsibility', or perhaps such terms as 'merit', 'special effort' and so forth: essentially the language which describes the work of employees in organisational structure. For Conservatives, on the other hand, it was 'enterprise', 'risk-taking' and 'initiative' which required rewards,[86] the language of entrepreneurship, even though often extended to refer to the work of employees. A further point of vocabulary, but significant nevertheless, has already been noted: the whole-hearted acceptance by the Board that ethical notions and ideas of fairness were legitimate criteria to apply to matters of incomes, again a perspective which has no place in thorough-going capitalism.

The work of the NBPI may also be distinguished from what has been called here institutionalised capitalism, or that set of compromises and acceptances of countervailing power which had gradually softened the rigours of simple capitalism in Britain over several decades. By its very nature this structure is less clearly defined than simple capitalism and it is hence not so easy to determine whether or not a particular practice is compatible with it. However, as was indicated at certain points in the above discussion, the role of the NBPI was clearly at variance with the most generous definition of institutionalised capitalism in some crucial areas. It attacked the process of comparability which was at the heart of orthodox conciliation;

criticised traditional habits of 'custom and practice' and sought to secure changes in them even where management and unions were content to continue in their habitual ways; and insisted on a 'rational' base for its recommendations. Of course, on occasions it found it advisable to make proposals designed to secure acceptance by the parties, but it certainly did not consider this to be its true role whereas it was precisely that of orthodox conciliatory bodies.

The NBPI had of course been established because the Government felt it necessary to move away from the practices of institutionalised capitalism under the pressure of inflation and balance of payments difficulties. The continuing commitment to full employment, and the use of a high level of state intervention suggest that this new policy of a Labour Government was not an attempt simply at stripping the compromises from capitalism, but an essay at an altogether novel strategy – of which the policies of the immediately preceding Conservative Government had been initial forays.

To consider briefly whether the new policy represented 'socialism' is particularly difficult to determine given the ambiguity of that term. But a debate over whether or not it did so was very important within the governing party. Ministers defended their policy as socialist on the grounds that (i) it asserted the public interest over the private interests of the parties involved in industrial relations; (ii) it sought to introduce order in place of the 'law of the jungle'; (iii) a party which advocated economic planning in all other sectors could not exclude wages from this process; (iv) it would encourage the modernisation of industry and help secure economic growth; and (v) it would assist the low-paid and those who lacked private strength.[87] Opponents of the policy, particularly during the tough statutory phases, argued that it was not socialist because (i) it sought to weaken the power of the unions, which were the representatives of the working class; (ii) it operated mainly as a means of wage restraint, while prices and profits escaped the net more easily; and (iii) the policy was operating in the context of an unequal society whose main contours were being left undisturbed.[88] This is not the place for an extended discussion of socialist philosophy, but the following observations may be made, based on the preceding analysis of the NBPI's work, which are relevant to some aspects of this debate. First, the Board's work was certainly concerned with the establishment of order, but the question must arise as to whether a system of order as such necessarily constitutes socialism; surely the nature of the order must be considered. In the case of the NBPI this order was that of industrial management;

74

the issue therefore becomes, to what extent is 'socialism' to be identified with the interests of industrial management? Second, the Board
certainly sought to introduce greater equity in income distribution,
but it did not mean by 'equity' the same as 'equality'; rather, it was
concerned to establish a structure of inequality based on differences
of skill and responsibility. As far as the division between capital and
labour was concerned, this was an issue with which the Board rarely
came to grips. Income from capital entered the Board's perspective
only with reference to prices and it did not therefore come under the
same kind of criteria which the Board applied to earned incomes.
The Board did request references specifically on dividends, but these
were not forthcoming from the Government. Also, in general reports
the Board would point out the need for restraint in earnings from
profit if wage-earners were to accept restraint, but this was not a
central plank in its strategy. As to the low-paid, the Board's difficulty
in tackling this criterion of the policy has been noted. The claims of
Ministers that the low-paid were a particular concern of the policy
may perhaps best be understood in a more general context: that if
overall restraint in incomes were forthcoming the rate of inflation
would be less and the low-paid would not fall behind. Supporters of
the Government's policy could, however, counter-argue that any
redistribution secured through free collective bargaining was not
necessarily redistributive from the rich to the poor. And although
union leaders speaking at conferences would advocate more social
equality as the necessary context for an agreed incomes policy, there
is little evidence that this demand was a relevant factor in the demands
of everyday shop-floor industrial relations. The range of comparisons
on which wage claims are based tends to be very narrow, while the
inflationary mechanism ensures that trade-union activity had little
overall effect on the respective shares of capital and labour.[89]

Important though the debate within the Labour Party over incomes
policy was, it is difficult to regard 'socialism' as a particularly useful
way of describing either the innovations of incomes policy or the
nature of union opposition to it. This concept, then, like that of
'simple capitalism' is of little assistance in an analysis of these developments, while the notion of 'institutionalised capitalism' represents
the very order which was under challenge.

In seeking alternative conceptualisations it is now appropriate to
ask: assuming that a society were constructed after the prescriptions
of the NBPI, what type of social structure would be produced? The
society would be a hierarchical one, based on differences of skill and

responsibility; but the hierarchy would comprise a series of fine gradations of different income and occupational positions rather than a small number of discrete classes clearly distinguished one from another, as is the case in most ideal–typical formulations of stratification systems. Neither, presumably, would the different positions impart traditional status-differences; the Board opposed claims for levels of income which were based on such considerations. Instead, the underlying legitimacy of the structure would clearly be rationalistic; and it would be the rationality of an administered bureaucracy, not that of the market economy. The dominant group within the society would be industrial management, since management was both the group at the pinnacle of the ladder of 'responsibility' which determines personal income, and that which held overall legitimate control within industry. Subordinate groups would have rights of organisation and opposition to the managerial interest, but this opposition would need to be limited in two important ways. First, it would need to accept the overall structure of inequality and the authority of management, the exercise of countervailing power being directed at the improvement of the position of labour within these confines. Second, the very need for opposition and dissent would be limited by the fact that an overall unity was imparted to the society by its scope for increasing efficiency and real wealth. In such circumstances all groups are able to advance their own interests in co-operation with, rather than in opposition to, those of others.

Obviously, a complete picture of a socio-political structure cannot be gleaned from the remarks of a body like the NBPI; the account must be limited to those aspects on which the Board had occasion to comment. However, sufficient material is available to enable us to relate this evidence to theories of stratification and political structure. The most relevant concepts for this purpose are managerialism and corporatism. The managerialism[90] of the NBPI is best seen in the contrasts between its policies and those of simple capitalism and socialism. Management plays the key role in controlling the pay structure despite the constraints of the market, in having an overall monopoly of legitimate authority within industry, and in receiving the highest incomes. Further, the whole emphasis of the reports' concern for ladders of skill and responsibility is oriented towards an economy of large-scale hierarchically organised corporations as opposed to structures of either entrepreneurship or egalitarianism. And the value-basis of organisation rationality may similarly be contrasted with the alternative rationalities of the market and the equality.

76

A more problematic concept than managerialism, that of corporatism, needs to be defined more closely.[91] It refers in general to a system in which the divisions of a heterogeneous society are enabled neither to express themselves in relations of conflict nor to dissolve themselves into small atomistic groups and individuals. Rather, an overall unity is proclaimed, and the different major interest groups so organised that their activities are subservient to the wider goal. Such a structure is frequently called 'organic'. Corporatism has its origins in Romantic Conservative thought, and received its development under fascism. In its practical manifestations, such as in Mussolini's Italy, corporatism has leaned heavily on the powers of the totalitarian state for successful operation, but in its ideological appeals it makes considerable use of nationalist symbol and myth as the basis of cohesion.

Now neither coercion nor patriotic appeals to the 'national interest' were absent from the incomes policy. However, it would clearly be an exaggeration to claim that the work of the NBPI was truly corporatist according to either of these characteristics. Symbols are of central importance to corporatism because they provide a source of unity to transcend the divisive heterogeneity of social interests contained within the society. But a modern industrial economy can provide a new basis for appeals to unity: the society has the capacity to produce constant increases in material wealth which may advance the interests of most members of the society without the need for the differences of interest which exist among them to be encountered. It is therefore possible for appeals to organic unity largely to dispense with what has hitherto been a crucial constituent of corporatism; in a sense, this may be regarded as a further development in the process of rationalisation:[92] the demystification of corporatism. Of the other major elements of organicism, however, the modern economy may well have need. The complexity of technology and the size of investment projects, the scale of corporate organisation and the deep involvement of the state render many of the characteristics of entrepreneurial capitalism irrelevant and involve a higher degree of organisation. Meanwhile, the position secured by labour in such societies, particularly when there is a commitment to full employment, means that new means have to be found to control labour's power if the existing economic and social structure is not to be disrupted.

To distinguish this singular form of corporatism it will here be called 'managerial corporatism', thereby linking the two concepts which have been useful in explaining those developments which have

77

formed the basis of this discussion. Thus redefined, the concept of corporatism is of value in describing certain characteristics of the work of the NBPI. The organisation of the two sides of industry was fully accepted, but an attempt was made to transmute their conflicts into technical disputes about the best means of securing the common general goal of increased productivity and efficiency. This latter goal provided the Board with a means of distinguishing between 'responsible' and 'irresponsible' behaviour. In several ways therefore the role of the NBPI implied a model of organic unity as in the theory of corporatism. It is, however, essential to link this with the idea of rationalistic managerialism for the NBPI was remote from the myth and romance of corporatism as that doctrine developed in Europe.

Corporatism and the state

Before the discussion of the character of managerial corporatism may be concluded, it is necessary to consider the problematic relationship between it and the state. As Lichtheim[93] has pointed out, the relationship between the state and class structure has been ambiguous since the emergence of the state as a public power in the later medieval period. Once the state ceases to be the private property of the dominant group in the society, the relationship between it and various elites will always be problematic. Such elites may influence or indeed dominate the state, but it will rarely serve their interests alone. Where early capitalism is concerned, of course, this question was particularly problematic because of the importance of the doctrine of the non-interventionist state. Modern economic conditions are likely to involve a more active state, but important limitations prevent the simple conclusion that even in a pure type of managerialism managers would dominate the state. First, management is not a 'class' in simple terms, being itself a very heterogeneous category. Second, the functions of industrial management, central though they are in a modern society, do not include several of the most important roles of the state. And third, once the state is at least formally an independent institution, it is always likely to follow the interests of other social groups or, indeed, the perspectives of its own political or administrative personnel.

A central difficulty for both management and all other modern social elites is that, while needing the power of the state to be allied with their own power, they cannot trust it. In consequence it is possible to formulate two distinct pure types of managerial corporatism.

The distinction between them is that which Nigel Harris[94] has defined as that between '*étatiste*' and 'pluralist' corporatism. In the former case the state takes a dominant role in co-ordinating the organic society. It intervenes continuously in co-operation with the organised interest groups, engaging in active planning, the state ownership of industry, interventionist incomes policies and so forth. In the pluralist case the state plays a more passive role, not unlike that of the night-watchman state of *laissez-faire* capitalism: it holds the ring, provides the framework of rules which affects the relative power of different interest groups, but it does not interfere in detail in their activities. But unlike the early capitalist situation, the parties around which the state holds the ring are not engaged in free, atomistic competition; they co-operate with one another through cartels, trusts, agreements and restrictive arrangements, offering their sense of social responsibility as the guarantee that they will not simply serve their private interests.

These two versions represent two alternative means of resolving the dilemma of elites in a modern state. In the former case the state is more actively engaged as a participant on management's behalf, but this may cause concern for individual managements since the state cannot be trusted; they would frequently prefer their own autonomy. Under pluralism, in contrast, there is considerable autonomy but the powers of the state are less readily available. A further difficulty of pluralism is the difficulty of defending it as such in the context of political democracy, since it amounts to a plea for autonomy and privilege unregulated by the external constraints of either government or market.[95]

Of course, empirical cases are not as clear-cut as pure types. The NBPI was not wholly an instance of either *étatisme* or pluralism, though it tended towards the former, particularly during the periods of statutory enforcement of the policy. It was the agency of a government which was following an interventionist economic policy; it interfered with the practices of particular firms and industries, freely criticising existing practices and proposing improvements; during the period of statutory enforcement the Government could postpone for several months the implementation of a pay increase which had been the subject of unfavourable report from the Board. It was as the result of this statutory intervention that managements and unions gradually became hostile towards the NBPI, and an incoming Conservative government committed to reducing state intervention abolished it. However, in its earliest phase, and again in the pre-election period of 1970, the Board was part of a firmly voluntary policy. It was not intended that the state should intervene statutorily, but that managements and unions would show restraint and pay attention to the reports of the Board and the White Papers on incomes policy. It was never envisaged that the state would be able to intervene in wage determination throughout the economy, so obviously there would need to be considerable dependence on voluntary restraint. And in any case a strong commitment to voluntarism was essential if the consent of the parties was to be secured. Thus alongside the tendencies towards *étatisme* within the incomes policy, there were opposing tendencies towards pluralism. This latter was best exhibited when the TUC and CBI offered to vet wage claims and price increases from their members as an alternative to legislative interference. This is perhaps as near to the pure type of pluralism as an empirical case can come, and demonstrates the distinctiveness of pluralistic corporatism from both *étatisme* and neo-liberalism.

SUMMARY

To place the work of the NBPI in the context of theories of managerialism and corporatism is useful, since it enables us to distinguish the operation of a policy of this kind from various alternative forms of social and economic organisation. There are however important limitations on the conclusions which one may draw from this concerning changes in the overall structure of the society. The impact of the Board was severely restricted in the following ways: (i) its activities were closely circumscribed by the Government, which prevented it from tackling some of the more controversial issues which arose;[96] (ii) the Board's success in changing established practices was very limited; (iii) the unions eventually adopted a position which insisted on the restoration of more traditional patterns of compromise; (iv) industrial management and the Conservative Party also moved into active opposition to the policy, and while they did not seek a return to simple institutionalised compromise, they did reject this particular exercise in *étatiste* corporatism.

It cannot therefore be concluded from a study of the NBPI that *étatiste* managerialism has become a deeply entrenched part of either British government or the underlying socio-economic structure. Further the class structure revealed by reports of the Board exhibited a confusion of characteristics: an important continuation of capitalist features; a similar persistence of traditional status barriers within the working population; and also a series of disruptive elements of shop-floor power which mark no class structure at all. Structures of reward which might more unambiguously be labelled 'managerialist' certainly exist, but they have to coexist with this tangled undergrowth. On the other hand, the NBPI was an important fact of political life; its genesis and the reasons for its existence mark the potential importance of *étatiste* managerialism in Britain; and its demise has not been marked by a return to the old ways of institutionalised compromise.

This study of the work of the NBPI has been able to trace important features of the peculiar stalemate which has been reached in Britain. Economic and organisational pressures continually lead to the weakening of institutionalised capitalism and its characteristic compromises. The inflationary processes with which it has become associated render its coexistence with full employment difficult for governments to tolerate. But at the same time it is deeply entrenched; it appears to represent a certain intricate balance in the triangular relationship of government, industry and organised labour. Attempts at transcending this outmoded compromise have tended towards corporatism, and in the period considered here they have been of a predominantly *étatiste* variety. But this has encountered opposition and resentment from most affected parties. Looking somewhat beyond the period under study, the Labour Government's interventionism ended in a return to traditional patterns; this was succeeded under the Conservatives by a different form of corporatism through legislative change (the Industrial Relations Act 1971), coupled with a return to neo-liberal policies of demand management. But even while this policy was being implemented renewed attempts were being made at restoring policies of conciliation among management and unions. And before the end of 1972 the Conservative Government had imposed a statutory prices and wages freeze and was planning the introduction of a voluntary incomes policy with statutory powers.

NOTES

1. For a survey of these characteristics see D. A. Martin and C. J. Crouch, 'England', in M. S. Archer and S. Giner, *Contemporary Europe*, Weidenfeld & Nicolson, London, 1971.

2. For example, J. A. Banks, *Marxist Sociology in Action*, Faber & Faber, London, 1970; and N. Harris, *Competition and the Corporate Society*, Methuen, London, 1972.

3. E. H. Phelps Brown, *The Growth of British Industrial Relations*, Macmillan, London, 1959.

4. B. C. Roberts, *National Wages Policy in War and Peace*, Allen & Unwin, London, 1958.

5. ibid., and also, V. L. Allen, *Trade Unions and the Government*, Longmans, London, 1960; H. A. Clegg and R. Adams, *The Employers' Challenge*, Blackwell, Oxford, 1957, Chs. 1, 3; H. A. Clegg, *The System of Industrial Relations in Great Britain*, Blackwell, 1970, Ch. 11.

6. The National Board of Prices and Incomes was appointed in 1965. Its task was to report to the Government on references made to it of prices and incomes questions. As guidelines the Government provided 'norms' of acceptable increases, and criteria under which exceptions could be made. At first the Board operated on an entirely voluntary basis, but its position was strengthened during the worsening economic situation of 1966. Under the Prices and Incomes Act 1966 the NBPI was placed on a statutory basis, and the Government took powers temporarily to delay implementation of pay and price increases during investigation by the Board. From August 1966 a statutory standstill was imposed on all proposed increases for six months, followed by a further six months of 'severe restraint'. After this period a strict policy continued to be adopted, the precise nature of the Government's delaying powers being varied under the Acts of 1967 and 1968. The Government's powers did not, however, extend beyond those of delay, and it certainly did not impose implementation of the NBPI's proposals. Towards the end of the Labour Government implementation of the policy became increasingly lax. The incoming Conservative administration in 1970 announced its intention to abolish the Board, and it finally disappeared in March 1971.

7. Reports of National Board for Prices and Incomes, HMSO, London: No. 18, *Pay of Industrial Civil Servants*, Cmnd. 3034, Ch. 4; No. 29, *The Pay and Conditions of Manual Workers in Local Authorities, the National Health Service, Gas and Water Supply*, Cmnd. 3230, paras. 89, 90; No. 105, *Pay of General Workers and Craftsmen in ICI Ltd.*, Cmnd. 3491, para. 28; No. 107, *Top Salaries in the Private Sector and Nationalised Industries*, Cmnd. 3970, para. 71.

8. NBPI Reports: No. 6, *Salaries of Midland Bank Staff*, Cmnd. 2839, paras. 39, 48; No. 8, *Pay and Conditions of Service of British Railways Staff*, Cmnd. 2873, para. 45; No. 49, *Pay and Conditions of*

Service of Workers in the Engineering Industry (*First Report*), Cmnd. 3495, para. 71; No. 146, *Pay and Conditions of Industrial Civil Servants*, Cmnd. 4351, para. 47.

9. NBPI Report No. 11, *Pay of the Higher Civil Service*, Cmnd. 2882, para. 11.

10. NBPI Report No. 107, (top salaries, op. cit.), paras. 70–81.

11. NBPI Reports: No. 24, *Wages and Conditions in the Electrical Contracting Industry*, Cmnd. 3172, para. 43; No. 91, *Pay and Conditions in the Civil Engineering Industry*, Cmnd. 3836, paras. 107–8; No. 126, *Smithfield Market*, Cmnd. 4171, para. 120.

12. NBPI Report No. 40, *Second General Report, July 1966 to August 1967*, Cmnd. 3394, para. 52.

13. *Productivity, Prices and Incomes Policy in 1968 and 1969*, White Paper Cmnd. 3590, HMSO, London, para. 26.

14. NBPI Report No. 19, *General Report, April 1965 to July 1966*, Cmnd. 3087, para. 67.

15. NBPI Reports: No. 48, *Charges, Costs and Wages in the Road Haulage Industry*, Cmnd. 3482, paras. 59 et seq.; No. 49 (engineering, op. cit.), para. 109; No. 110, *Pay and Conditions in the Clothing Manufacturing Industries*, Cmnd. 4002, para. 104; No. 146 (industrial civil service, op. cit.), para. 75.

16. The NBPI also sought to deal with problems of low pay through the solution of increased productivity, see page 67.

17. NBPI Report No. 169, *General Problems of Low Pay*, Cmnd. 4648, para. 124.

18. NBPI Reports: No. 29 (manual workers in local authorities, etc., op. cit.), paras. 31 et seq.; No. 101, *Pay of Workers in Agriculture in England and Wales*, Cmnd. 3911, para. 21; No. 152, *Pay and Productivity in the Water Supply Industry*, Cmnd. 4434, paras. 26, 29; No. 169 (low pay, op. cit.), para. 124.

19. NBPI Reports: No. 11 (higher civil service, op. cit.), para. 14; No. 32, *Fire Service Pay*, Cmnd. 3287, para. 38; No. 116, *Standing Reference on the Pay of the Armed Forces* (*Second Report*), Cmnd. 4079, Ch. 3.

20. NBPI Reports: No. 150, *Pay and other Terms and Conditions of Employment in the Fletton Brick Industry and the Prices Charged by the London Brick Company*, Cmnd. 4422, para. 58; No. 152 (water supply, op. cit.), para. 80; No. 164, *Standing Reference on the Remuneration of Solicitors* (*Second Report*), Cmnd. 4624, para. 64.

21. NBPI Report No. 122, *Fourth General Report, July 1968 to July 1969*, Cmnd. 4130, para. 25.

22. NBPI Report No. 16, *Pay and Conditions of Busmen*, Cmnd. 3012, para. 61 et seq.

23. NBPI Report No. 65, *Payment by Results Systems*, Cmnd. 3627, para. 42.

24. NBPI Report No. 44, *London Weighting in the Non-Industrial Civil Service*, Cmnd. 3436, para. 14.

25. NBPI Report No. 91 (civil engineering, op. cit.), para. 142.

26. NBPI Report No. 60, *Pay of Nurses and Midwives in the NHS*, Cmnd. 3585, paras. 28, 47.

27. NBPI Reports: No. 41, *Salaries of Staff employed by the General Accident Fire and Life Assurance Corporation Ltd*, Cmnd. 3398, para. 24; No. 63, *Pay of Municipal Busmen*, Cmnd. 3605, para. 36; No. 92, *Pay and Conditions in the Building Industry*, Cmnd. 3837, paras. 177 et seq.

28. NBPI Report No. 122 (general, 1968–9, op. cit.), para. 65.

29. NBPI Reports No. 17, *Wages in the Bakery Industry (Final Report)*, Cmnd. 3019, para. 41; No. 36, *Productivity Agreements*, Cmnd. 3311, paras. 9, 36; No. 65 (PBR systems, op. cit.), paras. 97, 194; No. 117, *Pay and Conditions of Workers in the Exhibition Contracting Industry*, Cmnd. 4088, para. 50; No. 120, *Pay and Conditions in the Electrical Contracting Industry*, Cmnd. 4097, para. 42.

30. NBPI Report No. 83, *Job Evaluation*, Cmnd. 3772, paras. 68 et seq.

31. NBPI Report No. 132, *Salary Structures*, Cmnd. 4187, para. 36.

32. NBPI Report No. 49 (engineering, op. cit.), para. 34. Attention is drawn to this passage as an example of the NBPI prejudging an issue in A. Fels, *The British Prices and Incomes Board*, Cambridge University Press, Cambridge, 1972, pp. 86–7.

33. NBPI Reports No. 51, *Pay and Productivity of Industrial Employees of the UKAEA*, Cmnd. 3499, para. 35; No. 146 (industrial civil service, op. cit.), para. 87.

34. NBPI Report No. 18 (industrial civil service, op. cit.), para. 51.

35. NBPI Report No. 132 (salaries, op. cit.), para. 40.

36. NBPI Reports No. 106, *Pay in the London Clearing Banks*, Cmnd. 3943, para. 46; No. 109, *Pay of Salaried Staff in ICI Ltd*, Cmnd. 3981, para. 49; No. 115, *Journalists' Pay*, Cmnd. 4077, para. 36; No. 152 (water supply, op. cit.), para. 64.

37. NBPI Reports: No. 65 (PBR systems, op. cit.), para. 42; No. 77, *Third General Report, August 1967 to July 1968*, Cmnd. 3715,

paras. 34, 37; No. 86, *Pay of Staff Workers in the Gas Industry*, Cmnd. 3795, para. 55; No. 98, *Standing Reference on the Pay of University Teachers in Great Britain (First Report)*, Cmnd. 3866, para. 37; No. 132 (salaries, op. cit.), para. 94.

38. Fels, op. cit., p. 104.

39. NBPI Reports: No. 50, *Productivity Agreements in the Bus Industry*, Cmnd. 3498, para. 70; No. 69, *Pay and Conditions of Busmen employed by the Corporations of Belfast, Glasgow and Liverpool*, Cmnd. 3646, *passim*.

40. NBPI Reports: No. 8 (railways, op. cit.); No. 10, *Armed Forces Pay*, Cmnd. 2881, para. 27; No. 18 (industrial civil service, op. cit.), Ch. 4.

41. NBPI Report No. 8 (railways, op. cit.), para. 18.

42. NBPI Report No. 83 (job evaluation, op. cit.), para. 121.

43. NBPI Report No. 49 (engineering, op. cit.), para. 132.

44. ibid., para. 33.

45. NBPI Report No. 122 (general report, 1968–9, op. cit.), para. 72.

46. NBPI Report No. 25, *Pay of Workers in Agriculture in England and Wales*, Cmnd. 3199, para. 11.

47. NBPI Report No. 132 (salaries, op. cit.), para. 69.

48. NBPI Reports: No. 29 (manual workers in local authorities, etc., op. cit.), para. 87; No. 49 (engineering, op. cit.), paras. 72, 119; No. 149, *Pay and other Conditions of Employment of Workers in the Pottery Industry*, Cmnd. 4411, para. 36.

49. NBPI Reports: No. 45, *Pay of Chief and Senior Officers in (1) Local Government Service and (2) the Greater London Council*, Cmnd. 3473, paras. 58, 59; No. 88, *Pay of Pilots employed by BOAC*, Cmnd. 3789, Ch. 5; No. 92 (building industry, op. cit.), Ch. 5.

50. NBPI Report No. 83 (job evaluation, op. cit.), para. 83.

51. ibid., paras. 8, 9.

52. NBPI Report No. 132 (salaries, op. cit.), para. 19.

53. NBPI Report No. 116 (armed forces (second report), op. cit.), paras. 70 et seq.

54. NBPI Reports: No. 5, *Remuneration of Administrative and Clerical Staff in the Electricity Supply Industry*, Cmnd. 2801, paras. 44, 45; No. 16 (busmen, op. cit.), Ch. 8; No. 42, *Pay of Electricity Supply Workers*, Cmnd. 3405, para. 71.

55. NBPI Reports: ibid, Ch. 3; No. 74, *Agreement relating to Terms and Conditions of Employment of Staff Employed by the Prudential and Pearl Assurance Companies*, Cmnd. 3674, para. 35;

No. 92 (building industry, op. cit.), para. 44; No. 101 (agriculture, op. cit.), para. 26; No. 109 (ICI salaried staff, op. cit.), paras. 196, 7; No. 123, *Productivity Agreements*, Cmnd. 4136, para. 101; No. 125, *Salaries of certain Staff employed by BICC Ltd*, Cmnd. 4168, para. 42; No. 131, *Pay of certain Employees in the Film Processing Industry*, Cmnd. 4185, para. 42.

56. NBPI Report No. 123 (productivity agreements, op. cit.), para. 131, guideline 5.

57. Compare Papers 6 and 8 in NBPI Report No. 65 (Supp.), *Payment by Results Systems (Supplement)*, Cmnd. 3627–I.

58. ibid., Paper 10, para. 13; and Paper 12, para. 18; also NBPI Report No. 79, *National Guidelines covering Productivity Payments in the Electricity Supply Industry*, Cmnd. 3726, para. 18.

59. NBPI Report No. 65 (Supp.) (op. cit.), Paper 8, para. 8.

60. NBPI Report No. 23, *Productivity and Pay during the Period of Severe Restraint*, Cmnd. 3167, para. 23.

61. NBPI Report No. 19 (general report, 1965–6, op. cit.), para. 86.

62. *Fels*, op. cit., p. 50.

63. NBPI Report No. 122 (general report, 1968–9, op. cit.), para. 59.

64. NBPI Report No. 169 (low pay, op. cit.), para. 122.

65. Fels (op. cit.) also stresses this point, and asserts that the Board 'did not regard the alteration of the existing distribution of income as one of the main purposes of incomes policy, unless greater efficiency or wage stability was likely to result' (p. 132). He also points out that the need for managerial efficiency provided a subject of consensus among the Board's members, which would not have existed had it been concerned with such questions as the justifiable return on industrial investment (p. 224).

66. NBPI Report No. 65 (PBR systems, op. cit.), paras. 59, 96.

67. NBPI Report No. 170, *Fifth and Final General Report, July 1969 to March 1971*, Cmnd. 4649, para. 60.

68. NBPI Report No. 83 (job evaluation, op. cit.), paras. 17 et seq.

69. NBPI Report No. 65 (PBR systems, op. cit.), Ch. 7.

70. The Royal Commission on Trade Unions and Employers Associations, established in 1965, which reported in 1968.

71. NBPI Report No. 77 (general report, 1967–8, op. cit.), para. 37.

72. NBPI Report No. 91 (civil engineering, op. cit.), para. 120; No. 132 (salaries, op. cit.), paras. 108 et seq.

73. This point is discussed at length and with perhaps excessive emphasis in T. Cliff, *The Employers' Offensive*, Pluto Press, London, 1970.

74. NBPI Report No. 36 (productivity agreements, op. cit.), para. 10.

75. ibid., para. 112.

76. NBPI Report No. 123 (productivity agreements, op. cit.), para. 27.

77. ibid., para. 92.

78. NBPI Report No. 40 (general report, 1966–7, op. cit.), para. 48.

79. NBPI Report No. 123 (productivity agreements, op. cit.), para. 96.

80. NBPI Report No. 65 (PBR systems, op. cit.), para. 153.

81. NBPI Report No. 77 (general report, 1967–8, op. cit.), para. 39.

82. NBPI Report No. 132 (salaries, op. cit.), para. 52.

83. NBPI Reports: No. 86 (gas industry staff, op. cit.), para. 53; No. 92 (building industry, op. cit.), paras. 161–3.

84. See, for example, the response of Conservative spokesmen: to the Declaration of Intent (*Hansard*, Vol. 704, cols. 382 et seq., December, 1964); to the establishment of the NBPI (ibid., Vol. 706, cols. 565 et seq., 11 February 1965); and during the debate on the Humble Address (ibid., Vol. 720, cols. 1155–278, 17 November 1965).

85. See, for example, the speech by Mr Edward Heath, MP, at Carshalton, 8 July 1967; and that by Mr Robert Carr, MP, *Hansard*, Vol. 750, cols. 1613 et seq., 17 July 1967.

86. Among the many speeches in which examples of this will be found are those of Mr Heath to the Conservative National Union, October 1965, and to the Scottish Conservative and Unionist Conference, 8 April 1967; and that of Mr Anthony Barber, MP, to the Conservative Conference, 9 October 1968.

87. The most outstanding instance was a speech by Mr R. H. S. Crossman, MP, Lord President of the Council, in Coventry on 9 September 1966, in which he described the proposals for statutory control over incomes as a major step towards socialism. A similar theme was taken up in speeches on 17 September by Mrs Barbara Castle, MP, Minister of Transport; Mr Ray Gunter, MP, Minister of Labour; and Mr Richard Marsh, MP, Minister of Power. See also the debates on prices and incomes at the Labour Party Conferences of 1966, 1967 and 1968.

88. Several examples will be found in the debates on the report stage and third reading of the Prices and Incomes Bill, 1966 (*Hansard*, Vol. 733, 9 and 10 August 1966); and also in debates on prices and incomes policy at the Labour Party Conferences 1966, 1967 and 1968.

89. Doubt has, however, been cast on this by A. Glyn and R. Sutcliffe, *British Capitalism, Workers and the Profits Squeeze*, Penguin, Harmondsworth, 1972. They argue that to some extent and at some periods firms have been prevented by international competition from raising prices, and that therefore pressure for increased wages does threaten profit levels.

90. Among useful recent discussions of the concept of managerialism are: J. Child, *The Business Enterprise in Modern Industrial Society*, Collier-Macmillan, London, 1969; F. Harbison and C. A. Myers, *Management in the Industrial World*, McGraw-Hill, New York, 1959; R. Marris, *The Economic Theory of 'Managerial Capitalism'*, Macmillan, London, 1964; T. Nicols, *Ownership, Control and Ideology*, Allen & Unwin, London, 1969.

91. This discussion leans heavily on N. Harris, op. cit., especially Ch. 4.

92. 'Rationalisation' is used here in the sense employed by Max Weber in his discussions of the growth of rationality in the West and the process of *Entzauberung*.

93. G. Lichtheim, *Marxism*, Routledge & Kegan Paul, London, 1961, Part VI, Ch. 3.

94. Harris, op. cit., *passim* but especially p. 18.

95. ibid., p. 226.

96. Fels, op. cit., p. 110 et seq.

3. Elite Recruitment and Political Leadership in Britain and Germany since 1950: A Comparative Study of MPs and Cabinets*

W. L. GUTTSMAN

The membership of legislatures and of the political executive in the post-World War II period has been regularly studied by those whose primary interest has been the functioning of parliamentary and governmental institutions as well as by the analyst of elections and the student of political parties. As a result a large amount of data is now available to permit the construction of longitudinal series of data as well as of inter-country comparisons such as is attempted here between Britain and Germany in the post-war period.[1] The data used here are thus inevitably based on existing sources even if originally not assembled in the form in which they are now presented.[2] It is hoped, however, that comparisons between countries of such widely differing political traditions as Britain and Germany will help to throw into relief certain general tendencies about elite recruitment and functioning. Furthermore in both countries two major parties arrayed on a left-right axis were in the post-war period competing for power and inter-party comparisons are thus of interest.

There are obvious ideological parallels between the British Labour Party and the German Social Democratic Party (SPD) yet there are also significant differences. The SPD lacks the close organisational and political ties with the trade union and co-operative movements which give the Labour Party mass support but which also cause frequent interest group conflict. The SPD, on the other hand, can claim a stronger and more centralised bureaucratic party organisation. The Conservative Party, politically more pragmatic but still largely hierarchical in its leadership pattern, also cannot be equated fully with the Christian Democratic (CDW/CSU) party complex which has more the character of a coalition of interests. Yet the two sets of parties are today not so dissimilarly placed within the

---

* This paper, related in some respects to earlier work of the author, is at the same time the by-product of a comparative study of social-democratic parties which has occupied him for some time.

national political system not to permit some analytical cross-referencing in respect of structure and social background of their leader cadres.

The German electoral system, though different in essentials from the British, knows today electoral districts and local candidate selection so that in one respect inter-party comparisons can be meaningful. On the other hand the existence of a system of proportional representation compared with our principle of election by simple majority has led to marked differences in the working of pressure groups within the political system which can be highlighted within the framework of a comparative study.

Britain and Germany: Social background and the strands of the political tradition

Great Britain and the German Federal Republic have today reached almost the same stage of their economic and social development. Indeed, Germany's industrial output has probably forged ahead of that of the United Kingdom while the national income per head of population has for some ten years exceeded that of Britain and the standard of living of its skilled working class is *probably* higher than that of its British counterpart. Following Western Germany's rapid population increase since the war the population of the *Bundesrepublik* (BRD) today equals that of Britain although urbanisation has not nearly reached the same proportions as here and German agriculture still occupies a more important part in the economy than in Britain. This and the religious bifurcation of the country (51 per cent Protestant against 45 per cent Catholic) constitute basic ingredients of the political tradition.[3] Thus the existence of a sizeable peasantry and the numerical strength of the Catholic minority — though not as large before 1933 as since 1949 — influenced for long the constitution of political forces in Germany. The political interests of the agricultural section of the population, their concern with protection, caused them for a long time to accept the leadership of the party of the large landowners. The political Catholicism uniting a variety of essentially conflicting economic interests in the Centre party (*Zentrum*) originally received its unifying impetus from the activities of the Catholic clergy who drew strength from the memories of the *Kulturkampf*. Both are important phenomena for the understanding of the German political system before 1933.

Not less important was the fact that under the impact of a deep-seated structural economic malaise, which the defeated country experienced after 1918, political opinion veered increasingly towards the political extremes and supported parties which appeared more interested in political collapse of the system than in the solution of the grave but fundamentally not insuperable problems which beset the infant republic.[4]

The inability of the infant of Weimar to defend itself against its enemies lay however not only in the adverse circumstances prevailing during its early years, nor was it just due to its internal enemies. It suffered from certain congenital defects which it had inherited from its antecedents in Imperial Germany. As researches penetrate into the transitional period between the Empire and the Republic it becomes clear how much was taken over from the political and administrative traditions of the former. Moreover, the underlying constitutional philosophy of the Weimar model did not succeed in reconciling parliamentary democracy with the State. The latter was still conceived as standing above the parties while the parties – though formally the organised basis of all power – 'Alle Gewalt geht vom Volke aus' ('all power derives from the people') as the Weimar Constitution put it were ideally expected not to act as pressure groups but to arrive at a common, national view. Hence the residual but eventually decisive powers given by the constitution to the *Reichspräsident*, hence the acceptance of civil servants and other allegedly 'unpolitical' men as ministers and even chancellors in the governments of the first German Republic, and the separation of the governmental from the party system. The Weimar Constitution, according to Stresemann, knew only the personal responsibility of *Reichsministers*, not the responsibility of the parliamentary parties (*Fraktionen*). Hence the response to the Nazi appeal to a 'politics above parties' and to their attacks on the '*Systempolitiker*', the men of the Weimar system, which found a sympathetic ear among the nationalistic but not radical middle class.[5]

The evolution of the political system of the BRD must be seen against this background and the earnest desire of the new political leadership which took over the reins after the twelve years of Nazi dictatorship, prodded not a little by Allied tutelage, was to create an institutional framework which would guarantee parliamentary supremacy, ensure stable government and prevent the potential disruption of constitutional government by political extremists. The 5 per cent minimum share of the popular vote needed to ensure representation in the *Bundestag* (the Federal Parliament), the outlawing of the West German Communist Party and of the neo-fascist SRP (*Sozialistische Reichspartei*) combined with a growing economic stability and prosperity, led to the decline of and disappearance of minor, mostly local parties and the emergence of what at present is a stable two-party system in which the CDU/CSU and the SPD share nearly 90 per cent of the votes and nearly 95 per cent[6] of the seats in the Bundestag. (See Table 1.)

TABLE 1: *West Germany and U.K.: Percentage share of votes going to the two major parties.*

West Germany*				U.K.	
	Votes	Seats		Votes	Seats
1949	60·2	67·1	1945	87·6	94·7
1953	74·0	81·1	1950	88·6	98·1
1957	82·0	88·3	1951	96·8	98·6
1961	81·5	86·6	1955	96·3	98·6
1965	86·9	90·1	1959	93·2	98·9
1969	88·8	94·0	1964	87·5	98·6
			1966	89·8	98·1
			1970	89·6	97·7

* CDU/CSU treated as one.

In as much as this development towards a two-party system did not take place without some constitutional midwifery its effects on the social character of the political leadership are difficult to assess. The disappearance of extreme left-wing parties as well as the virtual demise of the older type of Conservatives from the political scene has undoubtedly removed certain traditional groups from the political leadership. At the same time, the two-party system has inevitably widened the social basis of support for the two competing parties with resultant effects on the character of their leadership strata which now have to appeal to a somewhat wider social spectrum in the electorate.[7]

By way of contrast the British political system has remained virtually unchanged for more than half a century. In a country not defeated in two wars nor shaken by two revolutions, the basis of the present distribution of electoral and *formal* political power go back to the Parliament Act of 1911 and the Representation of the People Act of 1918. Subsequent changes in the electoral system or in the distribution of power between the two Houses of Parliament have only slightly altered the balance of political power. Three might-havebeens – proportional representation, devolution, and a substantial widening of power of individual MPs through the reform of parliamentary procedure, have so far only been repeatedly shelved. The non-adoption of the first, originally supported by the Labour Party, virtually destroyed the Liberal Party and prevented the rise of new parties.

The post-war political development was likewise accompanied by the re-establishment of a pure two-party system (at least in terms of parliamentary representation) which had been somewhat disturbed during the inter-war period when the Labour Party took over the Liberals' position as the counter-establishment party, while in Germany such a system was *de facto* established after the first Bundestag election.

It seems therefore appropriate to concentrate our analysis on the respective two major parties in the two countries.

Electoral System, Party Structure and the Selection of Candidates

Recently attention has again been focused on the effects of the electoral system on the structure of political competitions and the functioning of intra and inter-party democracy. Clearly not only electoral qualifications and the system of voting are important but the system of representation and the formal basis of allocating votes to parties is of equal significance for the selection process of candidates and, through that, on the type and character of the candidates put forward by the parties.

The British system has *ab initio* been based on the territorial unit of the constituency. Since 1884 these have been sufficiently large and similar in size not to affect the selection process of the type of candidate who came forward, although the social character of the constituency, its degree of 'urbanness' or rural isolation has continued to be significant. The University constituencies, abolished only in 1948, were the sole exception to the principle of territorial constituencies and they brought a certain amount of flexibility into the system.

Local patronage, and later local constituency parties, have generally determined the person of the candidate, but even the centralised and powerful party organisations have not been able to exercise much influence on the selection of candidates for Parliament in the post-war period, except in a negative way of vetting the list of candidates. In a similar way the principle of election by simple majority has been the most powerful influence towards the evolution of a two-party system – modified only in a limited way by the chances which a declining number of multi-member constituencies finally abolished only in 1948 gave first to the Radicals and later to the Labour Party.[8]

The establishment of a mixed system of representation in Germany after the war was by way of an attempt to overcome the tendency towards a multi-party system which was endemic in the Weimar system of election based on pure proportionality.[9] As modified in 1953 the West German electoral system provides for the election of 247 (248 in 1965) deputies in individual constituencies while an equal number are selected on the basis of *Länder* lists. Election for the so-called *Direkt-Mandate* is by simple majority but the total number of seats gained by a party is determined by the share of the popular vote received by the party on the basis of the second, i.e. 'list', votes cast by each voter. On the basis of the distribution of what may thus be termed the popular vote, and using the d'Hondt system the fixed number of parliamentary seats are shared out between the parties and then between the *Länder* parties or combinations of them. From the total number of seats allocated to the party in a *Land* the candidates who were victorious in the constituency elections are deducted. The rest of the seats are allocated to each party on the basis of the list of candidates which each party puts up in each of the *Länder*.

For the selection of candidates the dual system has two formal consequences. As far as the selection of local constituency candidates is concerned it places decisive power over selection and in about 60 per cent of the cases also effectively election, in the hands of the local party activists, in a similar way as in Britain. The system of proportional representation too guarantees the parties a significant proportion of seats on the basis of the expected continuation of support for the party by its traditional adherents. One recent estimate put the figure of 'safe' *Land mandats* as high as 203 of the 248 MPs returned on the basis of lists in the individual *Länder*.[10]

In theory the composition of the *Land* lists could be quite independent of the local candidates and the selection more influenced by the party leaderships. In the early Bundestag election this was to some extent still the case but recently the two groups of candidates which must by definition contain a large number who will not be elected have become increasingly similar. In 1965, only fifty candidates were not contesting constituencies, and the major problem which the selectors of the *Landesliste* have to face is to determine the place of the candidates on the list as it is this rank-order which determines the chances of success or failure.[11]

The task of selection is left to the party *Land* delegates' conference numbering usually only between one and two hundred. Such a body may decide the political character and personnel of a significant proportion of their party's parliamentary strength. This is especially so in the case of the SPD which gains the majority of its seats from the *Länder* lists. Thus in 1957 the candidates list for the *Land* of North Rhine–Westfalia furnished forty-one of the 169 seats gained by the party throughout the Federal Republic apart from Berlin.

Given the two methods of candidate selection with their different rationales one would like to be able to answer the question whether this is reflected in the type of candidate chosen. No clear answer can be given, if only because on the formal plane the two slates of candidates are today largely identical. Any significant comparison would therefore have to be between candidates with high-ranking list places and poor prospect of local success and those in 'safe seats' who, in consequence, are often given a low place on the list. The most we can say is that those who are favourably placed on the lists appear to represent more often party and interest group leaders and officers than those who are essentially constituency candidates. Yet the safe constituencies are also subject to wirepulling manoeuvres by central party organisations or by those with strong local influence, including sometimes a retiring member, in favour of a popular politician or a personal protégé.

If social differences emerge in consequence they will be on the occupational, not on the class plane. Employees of organisations, public officials and occasionally academics who tend to be prominent among the group of leaders and experts whom the parties would like to have in Parliament, figure in the land list selections while independent professional men and entrepreneurs would more easily find a place in the group of candidates favoured by constituencies.

Unlike Germany, where the role and personality of the parties is enshrined in the constitution (Basic Law §22) and where the operation of the Party system, including the nomination of candidates is regulated by the law about political parties passed eighteen years later,[12] political parties have no locus standing in English constitutional law, and there is no legal obstacle to those who would seek entry into Parliament beyond the minimal requirement about proposers and deposit. In practice competition is restricted to three parties and effective control, as already stated, is shared between two. In Germany, on the other hand, although the Burkean principle of the MP as a servant and not a slave of his constituents is enshrined in

95

the constitution, the power of the party over the deputy seems in effect greater.[13] The law relating to political parties provides for the election by secret ballot of all delegates to conferences (including Selection Conferences). It prescribes that the lowest unit of party organisations should be small enough to provide for a meaningful democratic decision and lays down that there must not be any mandating of the delegates. If any of the provisions about party organisation and selection procedure is not complied with recourse can be had to the courts. The ratio of party members to supporters is at least as high in Germany as in Britain but the number of activists, the *Parteibürger* is smaller. In Britain some 100,000 people are probably involved in the selection of parliamentary candidates. In Germany the figures are considerably lower, yet the power of the local selectorate is probably greater, especially in the *Wahlkreise* – the 248 electoral districts referred to earlier. Since the introduction of the electoral law in 1956 which laid down criteria to ensure the democratic participation in candidate selection even a prominent politician may have to go 'cap in hand' from one constituency to another to find a safe seat.[14]

German parties are generally less loyal to their parliamentary representatives than their counterpart in Britain where the number of retirements of sitting MPs at each general election between 1950 and 1966 accounted for only 7·6 per cent of all seats held by the party and where resignations at general elections for other causes (e.g. appointments to offices incompatible with membership of Parliament or succession to the Peerage) was even rarer – less than 1 per cent of the total.[15] While each of these cases may hide instances of incompatibility between a member and his constituency, cases of overt conflict between members and their constituencies resulting in threatened or effective non-readoption are rare.[16] In Germany, on the other hand, turnover due to non-selection rather than non-election is greater. In the election to the third Bundestag in 1957 Kitzinger found that 'a sixth of the members of the second Bundestag were deprived of their seats against their wishes, not by the electorate but by their party selection committee' and another unspecified but not insignificant proportion seem to have secured readoption only after a contest.[17] Twelve years later the number of constituency members who stood for re-election in the CDU/CSU was 162 (of 206 retiring members) and in the SPD 151 (of 207). But of the CDU/CSU candidates 13 per cent had to face opposition at readoption and of the SPD 22 per cent shared this fate.[18]

The greater volatility of the German selectorate contributed to the considerably shorter parliamentary service of the average deputy compared with the British MP, which emerges from the figures given in Table 2.

TABLE 2: *Seniority of Members of the Bundestag (1969) and House of Commons (1970)*

Year elected	1969 Bundestag		1970 House of Commons	
	N	%	N	%
Before 1945	–	–	16	2·0
1945–1959			270	43·0
1949–1953	41	8·0		
1953–1957	49	9·5		
1957–1961	67	13·0		
1960–1970			194	31·0
1961–1965	85	16·5		
1965–1969	120	23·0		
1969	156	30·0		
1970			150	24·0
	518	100·0	630	100·0

Sources: Kaack, op. cit. 1971, p. 658;
D. Butler & M. Pinto-Duschinsky, *The British General Election of 1970*, Macmillan, London, 1971, p. 300.

This can be explained in terms of electoral geography and party organisation. The average constituency in the United Kingdom comprises just under 60,000 electors while the average German *Wahlkreis* has an electorate of about 150,000. The body which selects the candidate in Germany – the *Wahlkreis-delegierten-Konferenz* corresponds to our constituency selection meeting but often comprises a number of local parties. It is therefore frequently, though not always, constituted as an *ad hoc* body brought together for this particular purpose. The delegates who choose the candidates are thus subject to a variety of local pressures and these bring about the contests which some sitting members have to face and casts others entirely into limbo. At the same time it lacks the cohesion which the Management Committee of, say a Constituency Labour Party, which meets regularly on a variety of business, experiences.

In Britain neither party organisation nor the selection process for parliamentary candidates has been subject to any legal regulation or public control beyond that provided by the parties themselves, though quasi-primaries have been tried in a number of instances mainly by Conservative MPs seeking to defeat moves to oust them made by local party executives. The general evolution of political parties from loosely organised committees of notables to the mass-membership parties of the second half of the twentieth century has ensured the emergence of a system of candidate selection through local party selection meetings on which the membership is directly or indirectly represented.[19]

The formal regulation of selection procedures, however, whether by law as in Germany or by customary procedure or party-constitutional provision as in Britain, cannot legislate against such personal influence which party officers or socially influential members may have in the pre-selection procedure or even in the course of the formal selection meeting itself.[20]

This applies even more strongly to the system of short-listing procedures undertaken by Officers or by the local Party Executive Committee which may *ab initio* rule out the consideration of certain candidates. As Schattschneider has put it, 'he who can make nomination is the owner of the party' and we shall only gain a full understanding of the process of elite recruitment, including the causes for the changing social composition of the political leadership, if we can gain further insight into that part of it which goes on behind closed doors.[21]

This applies *a fortiori* where the choice of candidates becomes in fact an act of acclamation. In Britain, where selection conference will generally have a number of candidates before them, this is a rare occurrence, but in Germany single choice candidature in the case of constituency members is much more common. In 1969 a total of one hundred candidates contesting an election for the first time were selected without opposition as against seventy-three who faced a contest – though rarely a multiple one – at their selection conference.[22]

In the case of the German *Länder* lists a selection procedure based on the formal solicitation of support by prospective candidates are *de facto* excluded. Here the Land Party Executive is the formal nominating agency. The party constitutions lay down that the selection should be done by the delegates' conference, but this body cannot in practice select twenty to thirty and occasionally even more candidates whom the party can expect to see returned, let alone decide

98

on the whole slate of candidates. The Conference may discuss the first few names on the list which also provides the party's *tête de combat* but will inevitably vote on, say, number nine to thirty-nine *en bloc*. It will generally be able to do so only because it has secured beforehand the approval of its constituent bodies for the composition of the list. In the case of the SPD the distribution of places on that list will be based on a key which takes account of the electoral strength of the districts, with possible allowance for representation from such bodies as the Young Socialists (*Jungsozialisten*) or the women's organisation in the party.[23]

In the case of the CDU the *Proporz*, i.e. the system of distributing seats according to some general principle of proportionality, laid down by the party will generally be based on the desire to achieve representation of the various functional groups inside the party which represent the interests of e.g. the industrial or the trade union element in the party.[24] In this way Interest Groups can exercise a direct influence on party policy and the party can utilise the specific linkage of interest group candidates to their sponsors and adherents for an appeal among these groups for general support for the list of candidates. Thus in Schleswig-Holstein, a land containing a potentially wide range of electoral support for the CDU, ranging from Farmers and Expellees to artisans and sections of the industrial working class, the desire for a wide popular appeal was in conflict with the strongly entrenched position of the farmers in the membership and in the decision-making groups of the party activists. Taking elections singly and over a period farmers have indeed had the lion's share of representation but in selecting Bundestag candidates for the *Landeslistes* in 1958 a bitter and prolonged struggle went on right through to the seventh and hopeless place so that in the end it could be claimed with some conviction that the list, as constructed, gave a 'mirror image of the social breadth of the CDU'.[25]

It is thus the combination of a loosely structured party organisation with considerable *ex officio* power of local and regional party executives and the system of slates of candidates which gives the CDU its alleged character as a representation of interest groups.[26]

Such traditional ties as existed between the British Conservative Party and economic interest groups, e.g. the National Farmers Union, the County Landowners Association or the Rochdale Cotton Spinners Federation have virtually all disappeared and in the case of the limited sponsorship exercised by organisations like the NUT, a link with the Conservative Party – or for that matter with any party

— is fortuitous, depending on a teacher candidate being selected by a Conservative Constituency Organisation.[27]

The British system of candidate selection does not preclude the utilisation of the political *career* ladder by economic and social interest groups, but the influence of the lobby in Britain is exercised directly on the Executive and indirectly on members of Parliament, and not through the Party organisations. Trade unions apart, interest groups infiltrate into Parliament not via the selection process but through the appointment of MPs to honorary positions on their committees and occasionally through the payment of retainers to MPs in addition to the usual promotional activities.

As a result, full-time officers of interest groups have rarely entered the House of Commons[28] and Mr John Davies, who entered Parliament in 1970 following on his General Secretaryship of the CBI provided with Ernest Bevin and Frank Cousins one of the few examples of a transition from a powerful pressure group position to a strategic post in the government.

The Bundestag, on the other hand, has customarily and continuously seen officials of economic organisations pass through its ranks so that one can speak of a *Verbandsfärbung* — a colouration — of the parliamentary cadres of the political parties, especially the CDU. The Second Bundestag, elected in 1953, contained thirty members who held leading positions, paid or unpaid, in economic interest groups and a further thirty-eight who were officers or officials of Employers Associations, including twenty-three active in the Farmers' Union (*Bauernverband*).[29] An analysis of the membership of the Third Bundestag suggests that the percentage of interest-group representation exceeds substantially the 14 per cent who had indicated this in the official biographies.[30]

The Social Background of Political Leadership Cadres in Britain and Germany

We must inevitably accept the limitations of a formal analysis of the leadership cadres of political parties, here exemplified by the party representations in the House of Commons and the Bundestag, the Cabinet and the Federal Government respectively. Cross-national comparisons are bound to involve some simplification in the categories used, if only to overcome the discrepancies in the individual national analyses, whether these are due to differences in names or the result of genuine differences in the social structure and occupational–status hierarchy of Britain and Germany.

100

Yet without stretching our analyses on a Procrustean bed of compatible but meaningless categories we can observe one major trend in the development of the political elite of both countries, in spite of their inherent differences. That is a narrowing of the social gulf which used to separate leadership groups of the two parties (or, in the case of Weimar Germany, groups of parties) of the left and the right. This process has been the result of a contraction of the bases of recruitment, relatively, if not absolutely, within each party. In other words both parties have become more 'middle-class' in character, shedding in the course of this development a certain portion of recruits from the two ends of the social spectrum. This process has been most marked in the case of the two parties of the Left, and, above all, the Labour Party, although a similar tendency can be observed in the case of the two parties of the Right, especially the British Conservative Party, which has lost over the years a certain number of its leaders of aristocratic and/or upper class origin. If during the past two decades this process has not been as marked on the Right as the corresponding one in the parties of the Left, it is because the inverted *embourgeoisement* of conservative parties has proceeded apace gradually over a period of a century or more, whereas the parallel movement on the Left has been more recent and more rapid. As far as Germany is concerned, the long juxtaposition between a popularly elected but powerless Parliament and a sovereign bureaucracy not accountable to it, has meant that the traditional ruling class subsumed under the short-hand term of Junkers and Officer-corps, was not as strongly represented in the Reichstag as the landowning class was in the House of Commons.

In the assessment of the social background of British MPs the education received is a surer guide than occupation, if only because the cost of public school education makes it a clear prerogative of the well-to-do. If we analyse the composition of the Conservative Party representation in the House of Commons since 1950 we find an underlying basic differentiation between a large and largely upper middle-class contingent which shows itself most clearly in the 70–80 per cent of Conservative MPs whose educational background is that of public school education followed in most cases by attendance at university, mostly Oxford or Cambridge, and a much smaller element mainly of middle-class or lower middle-class background whose members received their secondary education in grammar schools and of whom a significantly smaller percentage proceeded to university.[31]

Within this overall trend slight troughs and peaks can be observed

TABLE 3: *Aristocrats and Landowners in the Reichstag and in the House of Commons, ca. 1880–1930*

in %

Reichstag[a]		House of Commons	
Aristocrats	Landowners	Aristocrats	Landowners
1880	33	26	1880	ca. 25	16–19[b]
1912	14	17	1909	16[c]	13–14[d]
1930	4	4	1928	15[c]	

(a) K. Demeter: 'Die soziale Schichtung des deutschen Parlaments seit 1848', *Vierteljahresschrift fur Sozial- und Wirtschaftsgeschichte*, 1952.
(b) W. L. Guttsman, op. cit., 1963.
(c) H. R. G. Greaves, 'Personal Origins and Interrelation of the House of Commons', *Economica*, 1929, pp. 173–84.
(d) J. A. Thomas, *The House of Commons, 1832–1901*, 1939, and *The House of Commons, 1906–1911*, 1958.

according to the size of the party's parliamentary representation. Thus in 1955 and 1970, two peak years of Conservative success, the percentage of MPs with a public school background was slightly lower than in 1966, the year of the lowest Conservative representation since 1945 when the percentage of public school educated rose to an all time high of 80 per cent.

Looking at Conservative parliamentary candidates as a whole we can observe a correlation between type of constituency in electoral terms, and type of candidate. We find a gradation in the saliency of selected social characteristics, notably education in public schools and selected institutions within that group, in respect of the likely electoral success of the constituency.

As Rush states in his analysis of the selection process of Conservative candidates for Parliament, 'there does appear to be some substance in the view that the more traditional types of constituency prefer the more traditional type of Conservative candidate'.[32]

The early history of Labour's parliamentary representation shows a similar tendency. Those who represented 'safe' constituency seats were during the period 1918–35 more proletarian in origin than the men who filled up the Labour benches in the electoral landslides of 1923 and 1929. Not only was the share of trade-union sponsored MPs the greater the smaller the party's parliamentary representation

TABLE 4: *Education of British MPs 1951–70*[*]

	1951 Cons %	1951 Lab %	1955 Cons %	1955 Lab %	1959 Cons %	1959 Lab %	1964 Cons %	1964 Lab %	1966 Cons %	1966 Lab %	1970 Cons %	1970 Lab %
School												
Elementary only	1·2	26·4	2·3	33·9	1·6	35·7	1·0	31·2	0·8	22·0	0·6	20·6
Secondary (Grammar)	24·0	53·5	22·1	43·7	26·4	46·1	23·7	51·1	18·6	59·8	24·6	58·5
Public school	74·8	20·1	75·6	22·4	72·0	18·2	75·3	17·7	80·6	18·2	74·8	20·9
TOTAL	100·0	100·0	100·0	100·0	100·0	100·0	100·0	100·0	100·0	100·0	100·0	100·0
University												
Oxford	31·8	13·2	30·5	10·5	28·5	13·2	30·3	13·4	32·5	14·9	30·0	17·1
Cambridge	20·6	6·1	22·4	6·1	21·6	4·6	22·0	6·2	24·1	7·9	21·5	8·0
Redbrick/Other	13·1	22·0	10·5	23·1	9·5	21·3	10·9	24·2	10·3	28·4	11·5	28·6
TOTAL	65·5	41·3	63·4	39·7	59·6	39·1	63·2	43·8	66·9	51·2	63·0	53·7

[*] Derived from the respective Nuffield Election Studies by David Butler and various collaborators.

TABLE 5: *Occupations of Conservative MPs**

	1951 N	%	1955 N	%	1959 N	%	1964 N	%	1966 N	%	1970 N	%
Professions												
Barrister	61		66		72		65		55		60	
Solicitor	11		11		14		14		15		14	
Doctor, Dental Surgeon	4		2		5		3		2		6	
Architect, Surveyor, Civil Engineer	8		6		20		5		3		4	
Chartered Secretary, Accountant	2		11		9		6		6		6	
Armed Services	32		47		37		28		19		24	
Civil Servant, Local Government	9		12		14		18		13		12	
Teachers:												
School	1		2		–		2		3		6	
Adult Education	2		–		3		1		–		2	
University	2		2		3		2		1		1	
Ministers of Religion	–		–		–		–		–		–	
Consultants, Scientists	–		–		–		–		–		14	
	132	41·2	159	46·1	177	45·7	144	47·4	117	46·2	149	45·2
Commerce and Industry												
'Business'/Small Business	4		–		3		1		2		3	
Company Director	76		62		68		45		40		80	
Company Manager	18		16		20		13		12		14	
Commerce/Insurance/ Management/Clerical	19		23		22		21		21		4	
	117	36·5	101	29·4	113	31·0	80	26·3	75	29·6	101	30·6
Workers												
(Railway) Clerks	–		–		–		–		–		–	
Miners	–		–		–		–		–		–	
Skilled Workers	1		1		1		2		2		2	
Semi-skilled/Unskilled	–		–		–		–		–		–	
White Collar	4		4		4		5		7		1	
	5	1·5	5	1·5	5	1·4	7	2·3	9	3·6	3	0·9
Miscellaneous												
Private means	27		11		4		4		5		4	
Politicians/Political Organisers	12		17		11		11		2		10	
Journalists, Publicists	13		19		26		20		17		30	
Farmer	15		31		38		35		27		31	
Housewife	–		1		1		–		1		1	
Student	–		–		–		–		–		–	
Local Administrator	–		–		–		–		–		1	
	67	20·8	79	23·0	80	21·9	70	23·0	52	20·6	77	23·3
Not known							3	1·0				
TOTAL	321	100	344	100	375	100	304	100	253	100	330	100

* Derived from the Nuffield Election Studies.

TABLE 6: *Occupations of Labour MPs**

	1951 N	1951 %	1955 N	1955 %	1959 N	1959 %	1964 N	1964 %	1966 N	1966 %	1970 N	1970 %
Professions												
Barrister	28		27		27		31		36		34	
Solicitor	12		9		10		15		18		13	
Doctor, Dental Surgeon	9		8		7		9		9		7	
Architect, Surveyor, Civil Engineer	1		–		2		6		4		4	
Chartered Secretary, Accountant	–		2		3		5		5		6	
Armed Services	2		3		3		2		3		–	
Civil Servant, Local Government	9		9		8		7		9		3	
Teachers:												
School	18		25		22		32		33		33	
Adult Education	9		4		4		9		15		10	
University	15		10		10		10		24		13	
Ministers of Religion	–		3		2		2		–		–	
Consultants, Scientists	–		–		–		–		–		14	
	103	31·5	100	36·6	98	38·0	128	40·4	156	42·9	137	47·8
Commerce and Industry												
'Business'	4		–		–		–		–		–	
Company Director	4		2		1		2		3		4	
Company Executive/ Manager	7		4		5		4		11		10	
Commerce/Insurance/ Management	2		6		3		11		13		5	
Clerical	11		14		5		10		3		7	
Small Business	–		9		12		7		2		2	
	38	12·9	35	12·6	26	10·1	34	10·7	32	8·9	28	9·6
Workers												
(Railway) Clerks	12		10		8		10		9		4	
Miners	35		33		34		31		32		22	
Skilled Workers	23		29		22		41		47		33	
Semi-skilled/Unskilled	38		25		26		21		21		17	
White Collar	12		5		6		11		22		3	
	120	40·7	102	36·7	96	37·2	114	36·0	131	36·1	79	27·6
Miscellaneous												
Private means	–		–		–		–		–		–	
Politicians/Political Organisers	6		7		7		7		9		11	
Journalists, Publicists	33		27		25		27		29		27	
Farmer	2		5		3		2		2		1	
Housewife	3		2		3		5		4		1	
Local Administrator	–		–		–		–		–		3	
	44	14·9	41	14·7	38	14·7	41	12·9	44	12·1	43	15·0
TOTAL	305	100	278	100	258	100	317	100	363	100	287	100

* Derived from Nuffield Election Studies.

but even among the constituency-party sponsored candidates the percentage of men of working-class origin was inversely related to the magnitude of the party's victory at the polls.[33]

Since the war this trend has been reversed. The percentage of trade-union sponsored MPs has ranged from 35 per cent to 39 per cent in the six General Elections since 1950 and the fluctuations are not clearly correlated with the size of the Parliamentary Labour Party. Moreover, of those sponsored by trade unions, a not insignificant minority are today recruited not from the industrial field but consist of trade union members without industrial connection with the sponsoring union.[34]

More important still, the percentage of Labour MPs who according to their occupation and increasingly also according to their social background must be counted as middle-class has advanced inexorably and nothing seems likely to stop this trend. This trend emerges already from the analysis of educational experience presented in Table 4 which shows the decline in the number of those who received only elementary schooling from one-fourth in 1951 to one-fifth in 1970 and a rise in the percentage of university-educated from 41·3 per cent to 53·5 per cent during the same period.[35] It is even more apparent from the occupational breakdown given in Table 5. In 1951 four MPs in ten has started their occupational career as manual workers or clerks, but by 1970 their share was down to 28 per cent.

If we compare the candidatures for safe seats with those for others we receive ample confirmation of the fact that we are concerned with underlying trends which have deeply affected political selection procedures in traditional working-class communities. As R. W. Johnson in his ingenious analysis of this phenomenon states, 'the penetration by middle-class candidates of Labour's safest seats has also certainly rung the death knell of effective working-class representation. If the trends of the 1964–70 period continue we could expect to see a Parliamentary Labour Party, entirely bereft of manual working-class MPs by the end of the century.'[36]

We shall be able to judge the validity of this assertion better once we have looked at the comparable development in Germany during the same period.

Even in the earlier leadership cadres of the German Social Democratic Party men who did not belong either to the artisan strata or the industrial working-class milieu figured more prominently than in the Parliamentary Labour Party which for the first twenty years of its existence was composed entirely of men of working-class origin. And

106

TABLE 7: *Education of Members of the Bundestag*

	1953([a])		1961([b])		1965([c])		1969([d])	
	CDU %	SPD %	CDU %	SPD %	CDU %	SPD %	CDU %	SPD %
School								
Grundschule (to 14)	30·0	56·2	18·4	38·0	10·0	23·0	2·0	5·9
Mittelschule* (to 16)	1·6	4·3	2·4	8·0	12·3	28·6	19·6	35·5
'Hoehere' Schule† (to 18)	67·2	39·5	74·5	44·0	74·5	43·6	77·6	57·0
Not known	1·2	–	4·7	10·0	3·2	5·1	0·8	1·7
TOTAL	100·0	100·0	100·0	100·0	100·0	100·0	100·0	100·0
University	43·6	20·2	60·3	33·4	61·4	30·9	64·0	40·5
Number of MPs	255	162	251	203	251	217	250	237

Notes:
(a) Bethusy-Huc, op. cit., 1958.
(b) Trossmann, *Der Deutsche Bundestag*, 1963.
(c) Kaack, op. cit., 1971.
(d) Ibid.
* For 1961 and 1965 these include *Fachschulen* (i.e. further education or vocational training, more universal in Germany than in Britain).
† Not all those who attended a Grammar School stayed the course to the final examination (*Abitur*). According to Bethusy-Huc, who gives a detailed breakdown, the figures for 1953 include a percentage – 8·6% – for the CDU and SPD who did not do so. This percentage may have been high on account of the War.

although the Social Democratic *Fraktion* in the Reichstag was before 1914 also predominantly composed of men who had started life as skilled workers or craftsmen and had then generally proceeded to careers as party and trade union leaders, it contained from the beginning a fair proportion of professional men, small shopkeepers, publicans, master-craftsmen and even a few men of substance.[37] As in the Labour Party the percentage of middle-class recruits to the leadership rose during the course of the century from an estimated 16 per cent in 1903 to an estimated 35 per cent in 1930.[38]

This process of *embourgeoisement* proceeded apace in the post-war period. As a development it is the more remarkable because for all practical purposes the SPD was after 1945 the only left-wing party – the Communist Party, whose leadership in the inter-war years was much more proletarian in character than that of the SPD, had never regained its former strength and was prohibited in 1956.

As Tables 7 and 8 show, the Bundestag *Fraktion* of the resurrected SPD contained from the beginning a sizeable middle-class element. Given the rigidity of the German educational system, which, because of the absence of maintenance grants etc. was until recently heavily

TABLE 8: *Occupational Background of the SPD*

	1953([a])	1961([b])	1969([c])
Workers, Artisans (white collar)	24	16	1
Employees (Angestellte)	15	5	7
Teachers	–	–	27
Lawyers	–	12	7
Public Servants	21	48	57
(Other) Professions	26	16	7
Commerce and Industry	2	17	10
Journalists	–	24	7
T.U. Officials	⎫	31	41
Party Officials	⎬ 63	25	53
Officers of Associations	⎭		
(*Verbandsfunktionäre*)	–	–	12
Housewives	7	6	3
Other	–	–	–
None, not known	1	–	4
Farmers	3	3	1
	162	203	237

(a) Bethusy-Huc, op. cit.
(b) Triesch, 'Struktur der Landtage', *Politische Meinung*, 1962, Heft 74.
(c) Kaack, op. cit.

weighted against the advancement of children of working-class background, the number of the university-educated provided basic evidence for this trend and this alone shows a doubling of the percentage of *Akademiker* from 20 per cent (1953) to 40 per cent (1969).

The occupational breakdown suffers from the inevitable confusion and overlap of categories used but if we amalgamate the rubric of workers, artisans etc., and combine them with officials of working-class organisations, we observe a decline in the share of these two groups from 53·5 per cent (1953) to 40 per cent (1969) and a corresponding rise in the percentage of public officials, teachers and members of the professions from 29 per cent to 43 per cent in the same period.

The German Christian Democratic Party, as we saw, is politically and socially much more a coalition than the Conservative Party in Britain and the various strands which have entered into its composition, from Farmers and expellees to the 'Christian' part of the trade union movement and industry and commerce tend to be represented directly and indirectly in the party's *Fraktion* in the Bundestag (see Table 9). The latter thus includes a few full-time trade union officials, though unlike the SPD, none who occupy prominent positions in individual unions or in the DGB, the German Federation of Trade Unions, and leaders of the Farmers Unions as well as industrialists and officers of trade associations.

TABLE 9: *Occupational Background of the CDU/CSU*

	1953([a])	1961([b])	1969([c])
Workers, Artisans (white collar)	40	10	—
Employees (*Angestellte*)	17	9	3
Teachers	—	9	27
Lawyers	—	19	9
Public Servants	39	60	47
(Other) Professions	45	15	—
Commerce and Industry	19	52	38
Journalists	—	9	8
Trade Union Officials			
Party Officials	} 47		
Officers of Associations			
(*Verbandsfunktionäre*)			36
Farmers	32	47	23
Housewives	9	6	3
Other	—	—	—
None, not known	7	—	1
	255	236	195

(a) Bethusy-Huc, op. cit.
(b) Triesch, op. cit.
(c) Kaack, op. cit.

Numerically these groups are overshadowed in the CDU and even more so in the CSU, by what even today can still best be described as *Honoratioren* [i.e. notables], men who are sometimes disparagingly referred to as parish pump politicians (*Dorfpolitiker*) and perennial backbenchers who constitute, it is alleged, the silent lobby fodder of the party.[39]

Given the regional diversification of Germany and the absence of a capital city like London which acts as a social and cultural centre in addition to its political role, it is not surprising that the majority of constituency MPs have roots in their constituency or its region. According to Kitzinger, about 80 per cent of all *Wahlkreiskandidaten* resided in the electoral district which returned them to Parliament.

But the type of *Honoratiorenpolitiker* is of course subject to those general changes which have affected the character of party organisations and the democratisation of the latter has reduced the chances of the mere notables. As Kaack has pointed out, local 'eminence' in Germany is today in this respect intimately mixed up with office-holding in party organisations and with membership of interest groups. Analysing the starting positions of German MPs newly elected in 1969 he found that of seventy-three Christian Democratic representatives forty had held party office (twenty-eight at local level) and thirty — largely overlapping, one imagines — were elected local government representatives. In the SPD the percentage of those holding local elected and party office is even higher. Only little more than one-third did not hold party office and 62 per cent were elected representatives in local government compared with 41 per cent among the newly elected members of the CDU/CSU.[40]

In Britain the importance of local connections and the extent of local government experience has sometimes been overlooked. Especially in the Labour Party the local man has frequently been subsumed under the label of the trade-union sponsored candidate and a more refined analysis would seem to be indicated although the data for this, involving a step-by-step study of the pre-parliamentary *cursus honorum* of candidates, are not easily available.[41] The overall percentage of 'local' candidates is not insignificant, especially in the Conservative Party — 62·8 per cent among the candidates contesting incumbent seats between 1950 and 1966.[42]

While *Honoratiorenstatus* or positions in the ranks of the territorial grandees have by now virtually ceased to influence leadership selection in the British Conservative Party — the career of Sir Alec (Lord) Douglas Home is clearly an anachronism — other institutional factors influence the *cursus honorum* and, consequently, the social composition of the governmental personnel in the two countries as much as the electoral system and party organisation influence the selection of candidates and the character of Parliament. In Britain the Cabinet is of course only the apex of the governmental hierarchy, the size of which is now in the region of one hundred. There is thus a real and measurable career ladder for the parliamentary representative and entry into this ultimate resting place of parliamentary ambition is delayed and attenuated. Indeed, after the upheaval of war and post-war period which provided opportunities for meteoric careers and extra-parliamentary roads to political office, the road to the Cabinet has again become more traditional in character and membership is attained on the average only fourteen and a half years after entry into Parliament.[43]

The *Bundeskabinet* — numbering between sixteen and twenty-two

110

— was until recently, when a junior ministerial rank was instituted in the form of the *Parlarmentarische Staatssekretär*, the sole governing group in Germany.[44] Unlike its predecessors before 1933 the Federal Government has been composed almost entirely of members of the Bundestag without the marked admixture of permanent civil servants who figured so largely in the Cabinets of the Empire and the Weimar Republic.[45] And due largely to the political stability of the Bonn system of government and the balance of electoral power for twenty of the twenty-three years since 1949 the turnover of ministerial office-holding has been one of the lowest ever in the recent history of democratic political systems. Between 1949 and 1969 only sixty-nine individuals held Cabinet Office and if we concentrate on the Ministers belonging to the major party in the coalitions, the CDU/CSU, the turnover is even smaller. Even so it is smaller than in Britain where the Conservative Cabinet under Eden, Macmillan and Home (1955–64) turned over approximately two and a half times while members of the Labour Cabinet of 1964–70 saw on average about thirty-two months in office.

Socially the composition of Conservative Cabinets in Britain shows the same stability which has characterised its parliamentary representation. We find however that in terms of class origin and, at least for the period before 1964 but not so obviously in respect of its educational background, Conservative Cabinets continue to be more exclusively recruited than the wider group of Conservative MPs from which it is primarily recruited.[46] It is most marked in respect of the admittedly small aristocratic element. This amounted to ten out of fifty-three, or 19 per cent for the period 1955–64 and it still accounts for one-fifth of Mr Heath's Cabinet in its first year of office. At this level it is greater than on the Conservative benches of the House of Commons and it suggests that the process of a gradual decline in the number of aristocrats in the Conservative Cabinet has now ceased, 'producing a situation of complete stasis'.[47]

If minor trends in the social evolution of the Conservative Parliamentary Party are thus not necessarily reflected in the Cabinet after the inevitable delay due to the parliamentary seniority of Cabinet Ministers, the membership of Labour Cabinets has accentuated such trends rather than followed them. Labour Cabinets have from the beginning of the party's governmental career been more middle-class, more 'professional' and 'university-educated' in their background than the Parliamentary Labour Party as a whole. This trend has proceeded apace in the Labour governments of the 1960s. As originally

111

TABLE 10: *Socio-Economic Background of the British Conservative Cabinets, 1955–64, and of the CDU/Coalition Cabinets, 1949–64**

	Conservative Cabinets		CDU/Coalition Cabinets	
	N	%	N	%
Class				
Aristocrats	10	19	3	6
Middle-Class	37	79	39	72
Working-Class	1	2	6	11
Unknown	—	—	6	11
TOTAL	48	100	54	100
Education				
Elementary School only	—	—	4	8
Secondary (Grammar)/ Public School only	10	21	7	13
Secondary (Grammar)/ Public School and University	38	79	43	79
TOTAL	48	100	54	100

Schools: Eton, 20; Harrow, 4; other major public schools, 15; Grammar school, 9.
Universities: Oxford, 26; Cambridge, 10; other universities, 2.

* For figures on Conservative Aristocrats, see Johnson, loc. cit. Analysis of the German Cabinet was derived from Zapf, op. cit., 1965.

constituted, Mr Wilson's Cabinet of twenty-three still contained ten men with a working-class background. But these men gradually 'lost out' and when they left office they tended to be replaced by what has sometimes been called with slight acidity 'Labour Intellectuals'. Thus Mr Wilson's last Cabinet contained only three men who had followed a working-class occupation and one of them was at that stage a recent recruit to the leadership.[48]

The social background of German Cabinet Ministers stands in a similar relationship to the social composition of the parliamentary parties from which they are recruited to that which we find in Britain.

However only the group of Cabinet Ministers who sat in the CDU-led governments of the period 1949–69 is large enough to enable us to place some reliance on the results of a sociological analysis. Up to 1963–4 fifty-four men held Cabinet office and of those only six are known to have come from a working-class background and only one is known to have followed a manual occupation. Only three, or 6 per cent, belonged to the aristocracy compared with 12 per cent under Weimar or 65 per cent in the governments of civil servants which characterised the Empire.

Educationally the members of the CDU Cabinets were equally a group of higher achievement than the bulk of the parliamentary membership of the party and its minor coalition partners in the Bundestag. Of the fifty-four all but eleven were *Akademiker* and twenty-six of the forty-three had obtained a doctorate, though, one assumes, mostly in law which did not demand such a prolonged course of study as that leading to a Ph.D degree in the Humanities.[49]

What is remarkable about the as yet correspondingly small group of SPD Ministers is that overall one-half of SPD Ministers came from a family background in the older middle-class occupations in the professions and in administration which for so long provided the traditional background of German politicians and holders of elite positions in public life,[50] while the career of the other half has been largely determined by a more traditional background of Labour leaders: office holding in party organisations and trade union activity and office. Among the twelve SPD Ministers in the coalition of 1969 two had been prominent trade union leaders, viz. Chairmen of the Miners' Union and of the Mineral Industries' Trade Union respectively. Among the twelve SPD Parliamentary Secretaries of State, perhaps more typical of the younger generation, seven had had a university education while the rest came mainly from the organisations of the Labour or trade union movement.

We can better assess the social positions of Cabinet Ministers – the apex of the political elite – if we look at their whole career, including that part which follows on their government service. Such data for British post-war Cabinets are given in Table 11 and they illustrate the important trends which also distinguish the British political elite from its German counterpart. In the first instance the figures show that Cabinet office is, by and large, political office, and that its holders are men who are committed to a political career which they will leave only in case of age or for highly prestigious public office or a major position in industry. Among the forty-eight Conservative Cabinet Ministers who held office between 1955 and 1964 only 25 per cent took the latter course; a similar proportion stayed in politics, mostly in the House of Commons in the hope – eventually justified – of continuing in high political office. Another seven did so, in the same spirit, one imagines, only to be disappointed. None, incidentally, were defeated at the polls as were some former Labour Ministers in 1970.

TABLE 11: *Subsequent careers of selected British Cabinet cohorts since 1951*

Career Position, if any	Labour 1951 at c. 1961	Conservative 1955–64 post-1964	Labour 1964 at 1970
Cabinet, 1964–	2	n.a.	—
Cabinet, 1970–	n.a.	13	n.a.
MP (not in government if applicable)	3	7	14
Retired from politics, no significant occupation, deceased	8	16	6
Major Party Office	—	1	—
Major Public Office, Diplomat, etc.	—	4	1
Business, Private and Public Corporation (major office)	2	5	1
High Office in Education, etc.	—	2	—
TOTAL	15	48	22
Total ennobled after leaving Cabinet	4	17	3

No less significant is the fact that nearly all those who did not continue in parliamentary politics received a peerage, if they did not have one already, and generally a hereditary one. It suggests that Conservative Cabinet Ministers – with the exception of Harold Macmillan – are not destined to die as ordinary mortals while the majority of former Labour Ministers seem to share the latter fate.

The former members of German Cabinets, on the other hand, are by comparison a less exclusive group who, if they leave the government while still in their fifties and sixties, will often return to the more ordinary careers which they had followed before entering politics. Thus of fifty-four men who sat in the Christian-Democratic coalitions

114

between 1949 and 1964 only fifteen were still in the Bundestag after 1969. Sixteen had died before 1969, eight may be thought to have retired as they had all nearly reached or passed their seventieth year but thirteen had left politics mostly for minor industrial office and only two, Luebke and Heinemann, advanced from ministerial positions into high office, in their cases the Federal Presidency.

CONCLUSIONS

The comparative study of political elites, defined here as groups holding legislative and ministerial office, must deal with three interrelated areas.

1. The formal career patterns and turnover of office holding.
2. The social background of candidates and the institutional factors which determine success or failure of political aspirations.
3. The relationship between the political leader cadres and the directing group of economic and social organisations which bring pressure to bear on the political arena.

As indicated earlier, these factors must be seen against the background of the political traditions of the countries concerned and the extent of social cleavage and overt conflict. Here the role of the parties of the Left, representing traditionally the 'underclass' society, is both crucial and illustrative of the changing relationship between the social character of the political leadership and the masses of the followers.[51]

Under the powerless Parliament of the German Empire the SPD was, in the words of Max Weber, a 'social Ghetto-Party' and this social isolation, coupled with a strong ideological commitment, caused the party to concentrate on the perfection of its organisational efficiency and on the building up of a 'counter-state' rather than present itself as an alternative government, especially when confronted with the attempt by the Right to influence public opinion through its integral connection with or sponsorship of powerful interest groups.[52]

By way of contrast the British Labour Party felt from the beginning more integrated in the political process, willing to act as a pressure group and, broadly speaking, accept the basic social structure of British society and the traditional means for effecting changes within the established rules of the game.

As a consequence of these different developments, the widening of the social basis of the SPD political elite in Germany proceeded until

1933 largely through the social differentiation within the elaborate party organisation which provided a veritable 'state within the state', while the corresponding *embourgeoisement* of the Labour Party leadership reflected to a greater extent the support received by the party from a section of the middle and lower middle-class as voters and party activists. While such support was, in the inter-war years, also sought, and partly gained, by the SPD, the system of proportional representation encouraged the articulation of sectional middle-class interests.

In the post-1945 political system in Germany these interests increasingly identified with the CDU. But given the trend towards a two-party system, the Christian Democratic Party, unlike the sectional interests which formed it, has been compelled to attempt to turn itself from an interests and *Honoratioren* party to a voters' party while the SPD, traditionally a 'members' party, has sought to shed its past identification with ideological commitment and offer itself as a popular party of national appeal.[53]

In Britain both parties are now regarding themselves as national parties, but this has not produced a perceptible widening of the social catchment area of the political leadership. On the contrary, the political elite has over the years become more middle-class in character and the marginal widening in the basis of recruitment of the Conservative political leadership has been more than offset by the decline in the traditional working-class politicians on the Left, both in Britain and in the Federal Republic. The 1970 House of Commons actually contained a majority of MPs who were educated at public school and/or Oxbridge, forty-three more than twenty years earlier when the corresponding figure was 306.[54] It seems unlikely that this phenomenon is directly correlated either with the distribution of intellectual ability throughout the nation or with the possession of political flair among a random chosen sample of the university-educated or the secondary school leavers.

Election by simple majority, however, guarantees at least that the candidate has passed through a certain popularity contest and for safe seats near London the list of applicants may run into three figures.[55] In Germany we noticed a much smaller degree of personal competition for parliamentary candidatures and larger constituencies with smaller selection bodies apart from the fact that half the candidates, even though mostly formally adopted by a constituency, owe their election to the position on the list rather than to their being chosen at the local level.

116

While in Britain the boundaries of constituency and party organisation are conterminous, the basis for the selection of candidates in Germany is in the case of constituency MPs mostly and in the case of the *Land* list, always, federative in character. Hence the apparently greater influence of the local party leadership in the selection and the emergence of an elaborate system of rules and conventions – *Proporz* etc. – to make up for the lack of scope for the direct democratic selection of candidates and the absence of a national panel from which electorally well-placed constituencies can choose an attractive candidate. And it is by such mechanisms that we obtain the close correlation between local elected office and/or party office and parliamentary candidature in Germany.[56]

It is thus at the electoral level and via the selection of candidates that the influence of interest groups is being brought into play. This is especially important in the case of the CDU. As a study of the German election of 1961 formulated it with deliberate simplification, the CDU operates during elections especially in rural districts as the political expression of a variety of existing institutions which normally have another purpose.[57]

Today the British party system knows little direct pressure group influence at the selection or constituency election level. Interest groups operate either at the pre-election stage on a national level[58] or by way of pressure on the Executive or on MPs over specific issues, as well as by the general alignment of members of pressure groups, especially influential ones, with one or the other of the two parties. In practical parliamentary politics such influence becomes operative through the policy-making of the dominant party by what S. E. Finer has called the 'Esau phenomenon' by which the party is often speaking for its lobby. 'The voice is Jacob's voice: but the hands are the hands of Esau.'[59]

Interest-group pressure in Germany not only launches certain men into politics; it may also cause their withdrawal from the political arena back into the world of the organisation or of business. In the case of the CDU it causes a certain widening of the occupational spread of those who enter parliamentary politics and in both parties the greater power of the party organisation – at least at the local and *Land* level – can bring about the non-readoption of MPs, so that the average length of service in Parliament is shorter than in Britain where defeat, death and resignation are the primary causes which end a political career.

If men leave politics while still in the working stage of life they will, of course, generally return to their previous occupation, but in Germany the multiple levels of political representation including the elected positions in local government enable the ex-MP to enter – or re-enter as the case may be – a secondary career in politics.

There is thus a wider penumbra of political office – including public service, party officialdom and service in interest groups or economic and professional associations – the German *Interessen* and *Spitzen-Verbände* – which through direct personal connection or by way of their semi-official function can be included in this group, which Dahrendorf, drawing the circle even more widely, has termed the 'Service Class'.[60] Politicians move within this group and this interconnectedness of elected and appointed public office seems to be on the increase. Among the younger group of members of the third Bundestag (1957–61) prior office holding in elected office had occurred in 58 per cent of all cases (220) and 51 per cent had held non-elected posts in the public sphere – 31 per cent as party and/or interest group employees and nearly 20 per cent as government officials or other public employees.[61]

And unlike Britain, where the party hierarchy usually runs parallel to the elected political leadership and the group of ministerial office-holders, we observe in Germany a positive correlation between levels of status and power in the parliamentary parties and in the party organisations, either past or present. The more powerful politicians in the Bundestag are at the same time more 'professional' politicians, more likely to hold high party office either in the Executive Committees of the parties or in specialist Sub-Committees or at *Land* or District level.[62] Party organisation acts thus paradoxically as a super-interest group.

Links such as the above are not absent in Britain but the political elite still exercises leadership function partly by operating directly on the mass of its followers and the nation – as Adenauer, and now Brandt, have sought to exercise on a personal plane.

If the political leadership cadres of the two parties in the two countries are thus today possibly more remote from the bulk of the followers this is in Britain largely due to the continuing existence of a wide social gulf between the elected and the majority of the electors, while in Germany, where the political elite occupies a somewhat wider spectrum, a complex electoral system and bureaucratic selection procedures are interposed between voter and representative and we observe a communication gap between the electorate and its representative.

In Britain, candidate selection which effectively happens mostly at time of resignation is potentially subject to democratic pressures operating at the level where the eventual choice at the polls is exercised. Here the character of politicians can gradually be adjusted to changing political attitudes.

In Germany we saw that the turnover of candidates is greater but effective choice smaller. Thus the corresponding influences operate even more indirectly and institutional forces, including interest groups, are influential at that level. At the same time the greater correspondence of parliamentary politics with party politics makes for greater dependence of the political leadership on the organisation, so that changes of personnel are more difficult to effect but potentially more rapid.

These two mechanisms might ensure that candidate selection is responsive to the changing wishes and view of the electorate. The problem of how to guarantee a close and continuous identification of supporters, or even party activists, with their leaders remains for both countries. The Labour Party has moved a long way from the days when a closed and solidaristic working-class community sent men with strong local or industrial ties with the constituency into Parliament. The post-war SPD, now for the third time in the Federal Government, is today anything but a social pariah party in which leaders and followers were united by a fervent belief in a radically new society. In their attitude to politics, though not in their ideological stances now so curiously reversed, these two parties have moved closer together. At the same time the character of their leadership has come closer in character to that of the two parties of the Right, while these, in turn, are moving hesitantly towards a more democratic system of organisation.

NOTES

1. Cross-national elite comparisons are still comparatively rare. The ambitious study of 'world revolutionary elites' undertaken by D. H. Lasswell and associates did not get beyond a general conspectus. See D. H. Lasswell *et al.*, *The Comparative Study of Elites*, Hoover Institute Studies, Stanford University Press, Stanford, 1952, and D. H. Lasswell, *The World Revolution of our Time*, MIT Press, Cambridge, Mass., 1951, and some suggestive case studies, including

M. Knight, *The German Executive, 1890–1933*, Stanford University Press, Paolo Alto, 1955.

For a useful compilation of data on political elites up to 1950 see Donald R. Mathews, *The Social Background of Political Decision Makers*, Random House, New York, 1954.

2. Reference to sources will be given throughout the text. In general see for Britain: W. L. Guttsman, *The British Political Elite*, MacGibbon & Kee, London, 1963; Peter G. J. Pulzer, *Political Representation and Elections in Britain*, Allen & Unwin, London, 1967; J. F. S. Ross, *Parliamentary Representation*, Eyre & Spottiswoode, London, 1943; R. W. Johnson, 'The British Political Elite, 1955–1970', *European Journal of Sociology* Vol. XV, no. 1, June 1973, pp. 35–77; and for Germany see: K. von Beyme, *Die politische Elite in der Bundesrepublik Deutschland*, Piper, Munich, 1971 and V. Bethusy-Huc, 'Die soziale Struktur deutscher Parliamente' (Dissertation, Bonn, 1958).

3. Any comparison of the BRD with pre-war Germany must bear in mind that the division of the country resulted in a state with a considerably larger Catholic population than under Weimar where Catholics accounted only for one-third of the population.

4. The literature on the collapse of the Weimar Republic is legion, but see in particular: D. Bracher *et al.*, *Die Auflösung der Weimarer Republik*, Ring, Villinger, 1960; F. Neumann, *Behemoth*, Oxford University Press, New York, 1942; E. Mathias and R. Morsey (eds.), *Das Ende der Parteien*, Droste, Düsseldorf; and Th. Eschenberg (ed.), *Der Weg in die Diktatur*, 1962.

5. For a discussion of some of the basic aspects of the constitutional system of Weimar see: M. Weber, 'Parliament and Regierung im neugeordnete Deutschland' in his *Gesammelte Politische Schriften*, Drei Masken, Munich, 1921; E. Fraenkel, *Deutschland und die westlichen Demokratien*, Kohlhammer, Stuttgart, 1964; and G. Leibholz, *Strukturwandel der modernen Demokratie*, Müller, Karlsruhe, 1952.

6. A decline in the number of parties can also be observed at the *Land* Parliament level although no specific constitutional device operated here. At the first elections in 1945 there were seventy-three named parties seeking election; of these only fifteen were still represented in 1949–52 and the number fell further to ten in 1962. Of 1,350 seats in *Land* Parliaments in 1962, 1,169 were held by either the CDU/CSU or the SPD. The hurdle erected to prevent the formation of splinter-group parties at the national level became progressively

120

more severe. At first the 5 per cent quota applied only to a single *Land* but in 1966 it was made to apply to the whole of the BRD and the number of constituencies which a party had to gain as an alternative qualification was raised from one to three.

7. See S. M. Lipset and S. Rokkan, 'Cleavage Structures, Party Systems and Voter Alignments', in their *Party Systems and Voter Alignments*, Free Press, Chicago, 1967, and other essays in this volume; R. Wildenmann *et al.*, 'Auswirkungen von Wahlsystemen auf das Parteien- und Regierungssystem der Bundesrepublik', in E. K. Scheuch and R. Wildenmann (eds.), *Zur Soziologie der Wahl*, Westdeutscher Verlag, Cologne, 1965.

8. For an account of how this system was used by the Labour Party in its beginning, see F. Bealey and H. Pelling, *Labour and Politics 1900–1906*, Macmillan, London, 1958.

9. Weimar Germany was divided into thirty-five 'constituencies' each with lists of candidates in a rank-order fixed by the party and not changeable by the voter. The quota was established by dividing the total number of votes cast by the number of seats in the Reichstag, allocating mandates accordingly in each constituency and even permitting a transfer of residual votes to a national list.

10. Cf. H. Kaack, *Wer Kommt in den Bundestag*, Leske, Opladen, 1969.

11. Given this large overlap between the two lists, the first places on the *Land* list will frequently be occupied by candidates who are already assured of election in a safe constituency, while the places immediately below them will be given to those politicians who did not secure a promising *Wahlkreiskandidatur* but whom the party would like to see in Parliament. Paradoxically, the chances for this decline the greater its electoral success. It may thus lead to the entry of men put up to draw second votes who may not be good constituency MPs. The effects of this dual system are curious and it seems to me wrong to suggest that because the total number of seats gained by a party is determined by the party's share in the popular vote, the system of *Direktmandate* has functioned like a system of proportional representation as Conradt suggests in 'Electoral Law and Politics in Western Germany', *Political Studies*, Vol. XVII, no. 3, September 1970, pp. 341–56, although the number of constituencies where the direct candidate receives significantly more votes than the list-candidate is small.

12. The relevant passage of the German Basic Law states that 'the parties participate in the formation of the political will of the people'

and in doing so it makes a previous paragraph (para. 20) that 'all political power is derived from the people', already contained in the Weimar constitution, more specific.

13. Para. 38 of the Basic Law states that 'deputies are the representatives of the entire nation, not bound by mandates or directives and subject solely to (the dictates of) their conscience.'

14. Cf. Unkelbach *et al.*, *Wahler, Parteien, Parliament*, 1965, p. 82.

15. M. Rush, *The Selection of Parliamentary Candidates*, Nelson, London, 1969; see also the various Nuffield election surveys, for example, D. Butler and M. Pinto-Dushinsky, *The British General Election of 1970*, Macmillan, London, 1971, pp. 295–6.

16. Cf. N. Nicolson, *People and Parliament*, Weidenfeld & Nicolson, London, 1958; L. D. Epstein, 'British MPs and their local parties: the case of Suez', *American Political Science Review*, Vol. LIV, no. 2, June 1960, pp. 374–91.

17. Cf. U. Kitzinger, *German Electoral Politics*, Oxford University Press, London, 1960, p. 78; and Th. Ellwein, *Das Regierungssystem der Bundesrepublik*, Westdeutschen Verlag, Cologne, 1965, p. 163, who suggests that 'one-third of all MPs who sat in the previous Parliament were either not readopted or withdrew voluntarily'.

18. Only five and four respectively were defeated.

19. Cf. A. Ranney, *Pathways to Parliament*, Macmillan, London, 1965; Rush, op. cit.

20. In the case of the Labour Party, the Standing Orders for the conduct of selection meetings preclude any discussion of the merits of respective candidates. In the case of the Conservative Party the actual procedure seems more flexible and 'guidance' therefore more possible.

21. E. E. Schattschneider, *Party Government*, Farrar, New York, 1942, p. 64, quoted by Ranney, op. cit., p. 269.

22. Cf. H. Kaack, *Wer Kommt in den Bundestag (1971)*, Westdeutscher Verlag, Cologne, 1971, p. 616. (The proportion is similar for the two parties.)

23. Cf. Kaufmann *et al.*, *Kandidaten zum Bundestag*, Kiephenheuer & Witschal, Cologne, 1961, pp. 100–127.

24. Cf. ibid., pp. 59–91.

25. H. J. Varain, *Parteien und Verbände*, Westdeutscher Verlag, Cologne, 1966.

26. Cf. Unkelbach *et al.*, op. cit.; G. Schulz, 'Die CDU' in *Die Parteien in der Bundesrepublik*, 1955.

27. For a theoretical discussion of the role of interest groups in the

British political system, see H. Eckstein, *Pressure Group Politics*, Allen & Unwin, London, 1960, especially Chapters 1 and 5; also S. E. Finer, *Anonymous Empire*, Pall Mall, London, 1958.

28. Cf. J. D. Stewart, *British Pressure Groups*, Oxford University Press, London, 1958. Stewart lists only three officials of interest-group organisations in addition to trade union officials, and Rush (op. cit.) found that of 230 new candidates for Conservative-held constituencies between 1950 and 1966 only thirty-two were officers or officials of national Conservative organisations.

29. R. Breitling, *Die Verbände in der Bundesrepublik*, Hain, Meisenheim, 1955.

30. Cf. G. Loewenberg, *Parliament in the German Political System*, Cornell University Press, Ithaca, 1967, p. 113. In total Loewenberg found 40 per cent interest-group representation in the CDU and 20 per cent in the SDP (ibid., p. 126).

31. Taking the average of the six elections analysed we find that of the public-school educated MPs 66 per cent went on to university, compared with 48 per cent of the grammar-school educated.

32. Rush, op. cit., p. 90.

33. For an analysis of this, see Guttsman, op. cit., pp. 237–9.

34. Rush, op. cit., p. 182.

35. To a small extent these changes must have followed the expansion of the educational system and the greater opportunity for secondary and university education in the immediate post-war period compared with the 1920s and early 1930s.

36. Johnson, loc. cit.

37. Of 166 Social Democratic MPs who sat in the Reichstag between 1893 and 1912, party and trade union officials accounted for 59 per cent, journalists and publicists 10 per cent, professional men 4 per cent, public officials 2 per cent. (Cf. Molt, *Der Reichstag vor der improvisierten Revolution*, Westdeutscher Verlag, Cologne, 1963.)

38. R. Hunt, *German Social Democracy, 1918–1933*, Yale University Press, New Haven, 1964, p. 92.

39. Similar criticism has been levelled at Conservative MPs by Lord Kilmuir, who as Sir David Maxwell-Fyfe was the architect of the 'new look' of the Conservative Party, who thought that of the men newly elected in 1955 an unduly large proportion were 'obscure local citizens with obscure local interests'. Cited Rush, op. cit., p. 78.

40. Cf. Kaack, op. cit., 1971, pp. 617–19.

41. Cf. the brief but illuminating analysis of local government background of MPs elected in 1951 in W. J. M. Mackenzie's 'Local

Government experience in Parliament', *Public Administration*, Vol. XXIX, no. 4, Winter 1951, pp. 345–56.

42. Rush, op. cit., p. 60. Local connections as defined by Rush include ties in the constituency, by virtue of residence and/or occupation, as well as wider regional connections.

43. Cf. F. M. G. Willson, 'Entry into Cabinets, 1959–1968', *Political Studies*, Vol. XVIII, no. 2, 1970.

44. It must be remembered, of course, that the appointment to the most senior rank of the bureaucracy, that of *Staatssekretär*, is also often made on political grounds and that it is not uncommon for the holders of these posts to be changed with a change of government.

45. Civil servants accounted for approximately 50 per cent of the membership of cabinets in the Empire and for about 25 per cent of that of the Republic. See W. Zapf (ed.), *Beiträge zur Analyse der deutschen Oberschicht*, Piper, Munich, 1965, p. 63.

46. In respect of university education, each of the post-war Conservative Cabinets has contained a higher percentage of Oxbridge educated than the group of Conservative MPs as a whole.

47. See Johnson, loc. cit.

48. i.e. Mason and Mellish. For the figures quoted see Johnson, loc. cit.

49. These figures are derived from H. Gerstein and H. Schellhoss, 'Die Bonner Exekutive' in Zapf, op. cit., pp. 55–76. The analysis presented there gives also an interesting breakdown of the occupational background of office holders in respect of all Ministries, showing the predominance of lawyers in all departments and the absence of any marked relationship between the area of administrative responsibility and professional expertise, except in the case of the Ministry of Food (*Ernaehrung*) which has generally been held by agricultural interest-group representatives and hence shows three agriculturalists as office-holders.

50. Cf. Von Beyme, op. cit., p. 43.

51. Cf. F. Parkin, *Class Inequalities and Political Order*, Mac-Gibbon & Kee, London, 1971, pp. 121–36.

52. Cf. E. Fraenkel, op. cit., 1964.

53. Cf. U. Lohmar, *Innerparteiliche Demokratie*, Eube, Stuttgart, 1963, p. 12. The change of appeal was exemplified in the changed style of party leadership from Ollenhauer to Brandt. See also: Unkelbach *et al.*, op. cit., p. 126 et seq.

54. If we take graduates only the difference between the parties is today only marginal – Conservatives 63 per cent, Labour 54 per cent.

55. Cf. Rush, op. cit., p. 77.

56. Joint service in *Land* and Federal Parliament, common during the early days of the BRD, has since been proscribed by the parties.

57. Cf. E. K. Scheuch and R. Wildenmann, op. cit. Especially noticeable in this respect are the activities of the Farmers' Union, cf. Kitzinger, op. cit., p. 248.

58. The direct intervention of pressure groups in elections is, of course, severely circumscribed by the strictly applied provision of the law relating to election expenditure. On pressure-group campaigns, see R. Rose, *Influencing Voters*, Faber, London, 1967.

59. S. E. Finer, op. cit., p. 52.

60. Cf. R. Dahrendorf, *Society and Democracy in Germany*, Weidenfeld & Nicolson, London, 1968, pp. 90–4.

61. Cf. G. Loewenberg, op. cit., p. 93.

62. Cf. Kaack, op. cit., 1971, pp. 663–73; Loewenberg, op. cit., pp. 128–30, and Tables 22, 24, 26.

4. A Changing Labour Elite:
The National Executive Committee of the Labour Party 1900–72

VICTOR J. HANBY

THE NEC OF THE LABOUR PARTY

Of all the executive organs of the Labour Party, we know least about the NEC. Traditionally it is envisaged as performing a Cinderella role between delusions of grandeur on the part of the party's rank and file and expedient democratic protestations on the part of the parliamentary leadership.[1] Whatever the nexus between truth and imagination over this problem, there is little doubt that the NEC is an important locus of power when the party is in opposition and has considerable influence when it is in power.[2] Yet in reality, we know very little about the men and women who have filled positions on this committee. Customary though it is in some contemporary academic circles to equate the changing social structure of political leadership with changing policy preferences,[3] the NEC has been largely ignored in this and other respects. This deficiency is even more startling when we consider firstly, the primacy of the NEC (then the Labour Representation Committee) in the formative years of the Labour Party, and secondly, the fact that the NEC has often in the past been the scene of traditional skirmishes between Labour 'left' and Labour 'right'.

One would be reticent at this juncture to endorse wholeheartedly Guttsman's claim 'that even within the Labour movement social background and career lines are correlated with political attitudes';[4] nevertheless, an appraisal of the social and career antecedents of the incumbents of the NEC should reveal significant avenues of interest along related lines. Has the NEC followed the path of *embourgeoisement* that the parliamentary leadership, according to Guttsman,[5] has already travelled and along which constituency organisations, according to Hindess,[6] are now meandering? If the Annual Conference is the 'Parliament of the movement',[7] as Attlee suggested, is the NEC representative of the movement at large, or indeed, has it ever been?[8]

Fred Rogers and A. Wedgwood Benn were the party chairmen in 1900 and 1972 respectively, and stand as polar opposites in our period of study. One the son of a labourer, the other the son of a knighted former Labour Cabinet Minister; one consecutively errand boy, labourer, bookbinder; the other journalist and man of the media. Rogers was a committed life-long trade unionist, Benn has no active union background. The one, openly sceptical of the working-class vote,[9] was in later years a Conservative councillor; the other is a Fabian socialist. Yet do such differences really mark basic underlying ideological similarities? Benn is and Rogers was an active Labour journalist; Rogers was as fiercely unequivocal about Labour representation in his day as Benn is now. Or conversely, do such paradoxical differences tell us more about society and the Labour Party role within it, than they do about the characters under discussion?[10] A definitive solution to this consideration is beyond the scope of this study but analysing changes in the social composition of the NEC may illustrate trends which are of a partial explanatory nature. First of all, however, we need to know whether such changes occurred and whether such trends are in fact discernible.

Social Composition 1900–72

Two hundred and thirty-two[11] people have filled places on the NEC with an average length of service of just under seven years. Of these 232, forty-eight persons sat for just one year, 143 (i.e. 61 per cent of the total) served for five years or less and the remainder, eighty-nine, were incumbent for more than five years. Of the final eighty-nine, sixty-two or 27 per cent of those who have held office, served for periods of ten years or more. Eight individuals (Susan Laurence, Barbara Ayrton-Gould, James Griffiths, Clement Attlee, Sam Watson, Barbara Castle, Tom Driberg, Ian Mikardo) served from twenty to twenty-four years while six others (Arthur Henderson, John Clynes, Ramsay MacDonald, Herbert Morrison, Hugh Dalton, Alice Bacon), served twenty-five years or over. One would agree with McKenzie that 'these figures do not necessarily suggest that there has ever existed a tight-knit oligarchical control of the Executive'.[12] Nevertheless, comparison between his findings and the above would seem to suggest that over the last twenty years, a higher proportion of positions than hitherto has been taken up by incumbents who have been sitting for ten years or more. While the period 1953–72[13] only shows a 3 per cent increase in the total of those who sat for less than five years, there is a 6 per cent increase in the number of positions occupied by individuals who have been on the Executive for more than ten years. These figures are, however, too tenuous for one to do more than merely speculate on them. But they would seem to indicate, that while on average there has been a fairly steady turnover of personnel – two to three changes in executive positions per annum – nevertheless, at any given time since the war, one could find a nucleus of long servers who, if not constituting a tight-knit oligarchy, could together have provided a pressure group on policy which might have proved difficult to resist in certain circumstances. The essentially though not exclusively parliamentary nature of this group is one of its most salient features.

It could be crucially significant that there has been this consolidation of positions on the NEC in the last twenty years. Guttsman argues that 'from a loose federation of trade unions and socialist societies composed almost entirely of working-class men and women, it (the Labour Party) grew into a nation-wide organisation, . . . with a significant portion of its members belonging to the middle-class'.[14] If it is the case that the NEC manifests similar features, then it would seem that in the last twenty years, the NEC has been witnessing a consolidation of power by the middle-class.[15]

An examination of the occupational background of the fathers of the NEC members indicates that the bulk of the NEC was overwhelmingly of working-class[16] background (Table 1). One hundred and seventy-one or 74 per cent of the sample came from parental backgrounds which could be described as working-class, with miners and labourers in most evidence. Forty-two or 18 per cent of the total have middle-class fathers, with owners of small businesses being the most prominent group. Parental occupation on its own, however, is not necessarily a sufficiently good indicator of social class. Social mobility and educational background are two features which commonly complicate any assessment of social class.

Analysing incumbents' own occupational background (for details see Table 1) we see that the overall picture has changed to a significant extent. The proportion of individuals of working-class background has decreased to 58 per cent while those of middle-class occupations has risen to 34 per cent. Within the former category miners are joined by railwaymen as the preeminent occupational grouping, while in the latter, journalists, teachers, lecturers and union officials[17] comprise the major elements. This transition from the overwhelmingly working-class character of their parental background would seem to indicate that the *embourgeoisement* of the parliamentary party perceived by Guttsman, had a parallel in the NEC. The social mobility rate[18] within the context of incumbents of

128

TABLE 1: *Father's and Incumbent Occupation**

FATHER		INCUMBENTS	
Not known	18	Not known	18
Labourers	34	Labourers	7
Miners	25	Miners	22
Railwaymen	10	Railwaymen	22
Agricultural workers	6	Railway clerks	7
Textile operatives	4	Textile operatives	7
Blacksmiths	3	Dockers	7
Compositors	3	Compositors	3
Military Forces (ranks)	3	Steelworkers	6
Seamen	3	Shipyard	3
		Seamen	3
Miscellaneous manual	9	Engineering workers	12
Unspecified manual	72	Carpenters	2
Self-employed businessmen	12	Electricians	2
Shop-keepers	2	GPO	2
Legal profession	5	Miscellaneous manual	9
Teachers	2	Unspecified manual	25
Members of Parliament	5	Self-employed businessmen	7
Professors	2	Journalists	12
Civil Servants	3	Teachers	14
Churchmen	2	Lecturers	7
Miscellaneous non-manual	5	Trade Union Officials	13
Unspecified non-manual	4	Professional	7
		Civil Service	6
		Social Work	3
		Miscellaneous non-manual	6

* These are the occupations in which they spent the bulk of their adult lives.

Sources: Who Was Who; Who's Who; Who's Who in the Labour Party 1924, 1927; The Herald Book of Labour Members; The Times Guides to the House of Commons 1950–1970; Dictionary of National Biography; individual Biographies; Labour Party newspaper files, Transport House.

the NEC has been a strikingly high 22 per cent. The NEC would seem to be moving away from its working-class origins. This movement is not complete, but the trend is apparent.

From an examination of the levels of educational background, one would be tempted on the basis of mere comparative proportions to consider the NEC in its early years as being composed of individuals with only minimal educational standards. Any scurrilous implications can of course be safely disregarded. But it is a fact that in the period 1900–31 about 63 per cent of persons on the NEC had an elementary education only. This percentage decreases to 50 per cent when one looks at the whole period. In many cases even this elementary education was interrupted by the rigours of working as a half-timer. Of these 50 per cent, 8 per cent supplemented their elementary education by attendance at either night classes or Labour colleges of one form or another. Thirty-six per cent of the total had a secondary education and in addition 57 per cent of this latter group also went to university or public school or both.

Within the NEC there seems to be a certain polarisation on educational grounds with one sector attending elementary schools only and the bulk of the other having both secondary *and* higher education. The lines of educational demarcation would seem to be as firm as this suggests with very little confluence between the two groups. It is also significant that as one draws nearer to the present day, the percentage of NEC members with university education increases.

If one considers longevity of incumbency and social origin together, a similar, rather more striking picture than before, appears (see Table 2). With incumbency divided into four cohorts and examining the class composition of each cohort, two predominant trends emerge.

The longer the period of incumbency, the greater the proportion of members with middle-class origins. Secondly, over all the cohorts the closer one draws to the present day, the higher the proportion of middle-class individuals. In the last forty years the NEC has moved from a situation in the 1930s of potential domination by the middle-class, to one of fact in the period 1940–72. This feature is further substantiated by the fact that of the total man-years in the period 1900–72, 47 per cent is accounted for by middle-class incumbencies, while in the period 1940–72, 68 per cent of the total man-years is attributable to middle-class incumbents.

It might be argued that age is a significant factor in these findings. However, this does not prove to be the case. Over the life of the NEC the mean age of incumbents on election to the committee is forty-four years. The mean age of all middle-class members is forty-five years. Only a very small minority of middle-class individuals show a signi-

130

TABLE 2: *Class Composition and Length of Tenure*

PERIOD AND CLASS COMPOSITION (in %)

TENURE IN YEARS	1900–18		1918–31		1931–45		1945–51		1951–64		1964–72	
	W/C	M/C	W/C	M/C	W/C	M/C	W/C	M/C	W/C	M/C	W/C	M/C
Under 5	93	7	81	19	78	22	77	23	77	23	76	24
6–10	100	—	93	7	86	14	83	17	72	28	69	31
11–20	83	17	67	33	59	41	56	44	50	50	—	—
Over 20	67	33	43	57	42	58	33	67	—	—	—	—

W/C = Working-class
M/C = Middle-class

ficant deviation from this mean and they are too small in number to indicate a viable trend. Whatever the rationale or explanation of long incumbencies, it does not lie with age. One needs to look further, at the broader scenario of the party at large, for example, and certain individuals' roles within it.

Such general formulations as have been argued here do little more than indicate relative changes that have taken place within the social antecedents of the members of the NEC during its lifetime. Crucial though these changes are, they themselves can do little more than indicate that certain trends exist and the primary concern now is therefore to locate temporally the emergence of such patterns and relate them to the socio-political context of their era.

Accordingly the life of the NEC has been divided into six periods, in order to assess what the actual trends have been. These divisions are not as arbitrary as one might imagine, and they should be immediately significant to anyone conversant with labour history.

1900–18

Within this period the NEC was overwhelmingly working-class. Comparing parental and incumbent background, one finds that the proportion of working-class occupations was 89 per cent[19] and 91 per cent respectively. This result ought not to be surprising. The uneasy alliance that constituted the Labour Party was gaining growing electoral support.

Fostered by a trade union movement whose leading members were in the main staunchly working-class both in origin and political orientation, the Labour Representation Committee in the first years of its existence had looked to the working-class to provide its leaders and its support[20] and in this it was singularly successful. Since 1906 when the Labour Representation Committee had received the 'imprimatur' of being called the Labour Party, labour representation in Parliament had increased dramatically. Though still dependent in many circumstances on tacit Liberal support for its candidacies, its appeal to the working-class had had a positive result. It saw the working-class of the country as its constituency and appealed directly to them for support. 'In its beginnings the strength of the Party had lain in its lack of a clearly defined policy: in its deliberately empirical approach to the problem of the day. It had been created to advance the cause of the working-classes.'[21]

Eighty-seven per cent of the individuals in this period had received only a basic elementary education. A clear majority had experience

132

of being half-timers. The party in Parliament and the NEC in particular was dominated by the politics of individuals whose names and careers are almost synonymous with that of the Labour Party, and whose own backgrounds effectively predetermined the policy and electoral imperatives of the party they were trying to create. Fundamentally limited in its aims at its inception, the Labour Party made no attempt in the first years of its life to move to any broader electoral appeal. Indeed any such move would have been contrary to the original intentions of the party and completely anathema to the majority of its founders. On the NEC therefore miners, labourers, railwaymen and weavers comprise the bulk of incumbent occupations. Middle-class representation was a mere 7 per cent, being composed for the most part of Fabians[22] (Pease) and sons of self-employed professional men (W. Barefoot and R. J. Wilson). If ever the Labour Party was primarily a working-class party, and if ever the NEC mirrored such representation, it was in the period 1900–18.

1918–31

The new constitution[23] of 1918 precipitated widespread and significant changes in party organisation and consequently in the social composition of the NEC. Three features of this reorganisation are particularly pertinent. First, individuals could join the party as individuals and not just as members of a corporate body. Persons who were ineligible to join trade unions or trades councils and whose antipathy to socialist societies had prevented them from participating, were therefore free to join the party at large and could thus be considered for election to the NEC if they were well enough known. Secondly, the formation of a Women's Section on the NEC meant, as it turned out, the subsequent introduction and consolidation of a large middle-class element. Thirdly, after 1918 the party had, almost as a by-product of the new constitution, its first substantial, formal policy statement, *Labour and the New Social Order*. This document, mainly drafted by the Fabian, Sidney Webb, was an explicit commitment to socialism. But the socialism was of a moderate, evolutionary, gradualist kind and 'no suggestion was made that a Labour Government on coming to power would promptly introduce more than a very small instalment of socialism'.[24]

Two additional extraneous features are crucial for understanding internal party changes during this period. The collapse of Liberalism effectively released on to the open market a politically homeless section of the electorate, and more important, of the political elite. Parts

133

of these groups containing both moderate and radical elements from all classes were to find sanctuary in the Labour fold. Secondly, Ramsay MacDonald's obsession with respectability, his undisguised disdain for his own working-class colleagues, and his antipathy to closely defined socialist policies ensured that the party as a whole followed a moderate, middle course throughout the 1920s. The net result of all the above features was that the party, from constituency to the NEC levels, expanded its catchment area.

Amongst newcomers to the NEC, therefore, working-class representation decreases in this period. Sixty-six per cent had parents who were working-class, while on their own occupations only 63 per cent were working-class. Twenty-seven per cent of the newcomers had fathers whose occupations were middle-class while 32 per cent had occupations themselves which could be classified as middle-class. Given that there was some difficulty in determining the occupations of a small group of fathers amongst both sectors, one can only isolate a minimum social mobility rate amongst newcomers in this period of about 5 per cent, with the possibility remaining that it could be higher.

The number with only elementary education had fallen to 50 per cent, while 24 per cent had received university education. This 24 per cent is in fact exclusively middle-class and represents 80 per cent of that group. This point is even more telling when one considers that at the time the bulk of these individuals were at university, the national percentage of those aged eighteen to twenty-four attending university was 1·15 per cent.[25] In addition, 3 per cent of the NEC middle-class newcomers in this period went to public school but not to university.

All of the above details refer to individuals who *became* incumbent on the NEC during the period 1918–31. One really needs to consider in addition *all* incumbents in the period, newcomers plus persons who were already members from the earlier period. Such analysis reveals a similar picture though the class divisions are slightly more firmly drawn. Of all incumbents during the period, 64 per cent were working-class, while 34 per cent were middle-class. By 1931 therefore, slightly in excess of one-third of the NEC came from middle-class backgrounds. This really is a most significant and striking advance from the 7 per cent of the earlier period who were middle-class.

The working-class is still well represented by labourers, miners and railwaymen, but one notes the ever-increasing proportion of teachers, lecturers, and solicitors among individuals' occupational backgrounds. Sons and daughters of businessmen have been joined by sons and daughters of baronets, professors, doctors and engineers.

134

The bulk of the middle-class component in this period is explained primarily by individuals of middle-class occupations who had fathers with similar class background, rather than by patterns of upward mobility between generations, even though there was a certain element of this.

The emergence of these specific occupations as significant during this period is explained solely by the same factors which account for the radical changes in the social composition of the committee. The political middle course steered by Ramsay MacDonald moved the party away from its original working-class orientation to a wider and more indeterminate political position. 'In each of his major theoretical works and in his day-to-day political dealing MacDonald's socialism emerged as a promised land, not an attainable one, portrayed only in attractive-sounding generalisations.'[26] Ramsay MacDonald's socialism, and hence his party,[27] could be (and often was) all things to all men. The Liberal débâcle of the 1920s pushed many prominent ex-radical Liberals into the Parliamentary Labour Party and hence some emerged on the NEC. Without exception, those on the NEC were of middle-class backgrounds (Charles Trevelyan, Josiah Wedgwood). For all those reasons that make middle-class women more prominent and active in politics than their working-class equivalents, the formation of a Women's Section saw the consolidation of a significant middle-class group on the Committee. In addition, certain opportunistic individuals, some with what could be considered traditional, middle-class political pedigrees but with a more radical disposition than was likely to lead to success within the old Conservative Party, saw the Labour Party in the 1920s as the alternative government and as a means to political advancement,[28] and felt no hesitation in aligning themselves with a party which had James Ramsay MacDonald, not James Keir Hardie, as leader.

The original working-class links with the miners and railwaymen still exist in this period, because of traditional union links on the NEC but the above features document the emergence of teachers, lecturers, and professional men as the most significant changing characteristic of the NEC in the period 1918–31. The professional middle-classes — administrators not agitators[29] — have appeared for the first time as an important group on the Committee, and theirs was to be a pre-eminent role henceforth.

1931–45

In simple electoral terms one would characterise this period as one of collapse, consolidation and then growth. Within the NEC, except for the obvious exceptions, there was no drastic change. A normal rate of turnover is apparent, but so is the continuation of the trend established over the two initial periods. Amongst newcomers to the Committee, on both parental and incumbent background, the proportion of working-class is depressed to 58 per cent and 55 per cent respectively. Although the proportion with middle-class fathers had only risen marginally from the period 1918–31, there was nevertheless a 4 per cent increase to 36 per cent in the number of middle-class when based on the individuals' own backgrounds. Again one can only isolate a minimum social mobility rate of 5 per cent, though the possibility remains that it could be higher given the fact that there is again a small group for whom father's occupation is not available. These individuals are not, of course, included in these calculations. It is difficult during this period to draw any serious inference from the educational background of the committee because earlier changes in the educational structure in 1902 and 1907 were calculated to redress the balance, if only partially, in educational opportunity at secondary school level. Of the new incumbents, however, 20 per cent went to university, of whom all had social backgrounds which could only be described as middle-class, in terms of both their own and their fathers' occupation.

If one looks at *all* incumbents rather than simply newcomers the same trend is revealed, though again rather more strikingly. Forty-nine per cent of the incumbents during this period were from the working-class while 41 per cent were middle-class in origin. The period 1931–45 again shows a gradual consolidation of power by the middle-class in the NEC: a more gradual movement than before but still significant. Two features emerge as salient during this period. One, the increasing gap in terms of social composition between the middle- and working-class segments on the NEC. Not only were there differences of occupational background but such differences were buttressed by an increasing differentiation in educational levels. This characteristic in turn exacerbates the second important phenomenon of this era. This period witnesses the emergence into prominence on the NEC of individuals who are destined later to play larger, more important roles on the parliamentary stage. Attlee is the most prominent from the middle-class. At the other end of the class spectrum Bevan appears for the first time. Attlee had public school and university credentials (Haileybury and Oxford), while Bevan's education encompassed Sirhowy Elementary School and the Labour

College in Earls Court. The policy schisms of the late 1940s and 1950s are at least in part a paraphrase of such differences. The growing problem of the hiatus between the two classes on the NEC and within the party at large, remains unrecognised and largely unresolved even today.

1945–51

Amongst the new incumbents this period witnesses the most dramatic upsurge of middle-class representation of any of the periods under discussion. The characteristics of parental background again reveal a decrease in the proportion of working-class to 53 per cent and an upsurge of 6 per cent in the middle-class element to 33 per cent. Comparing the occupational background of the individuals themselves, however, a strikingly different picture emerges. Of the newcomers to the NEC, 53 per cent illustrate middle-class characteristics with journalists the most prominent group, with a mere 33 per cent coming from the working-class. Thirty-three per cent of the total or 63 per cent of the middle-class had been to university while only one of the working-class group exemplified this feature. This exception is interesting, being the daughter of a miner, who qualified as a teacher and remained in this occupation until becoming an MP and subsequently being elected to the NEC. The most salient feature of this period is undoubtedly the social mobility patterns experienced amongst newcomers to the Committee. Of those whose parents were working-class, no less than 30 per cent were socially mobile during the earlier part of their lives preceding their election to the NEC. In addition the overall class balance of the Committee swung firmly in favour of the middle-class. Indeed, of all incumbents during the period, and not solely newcomers, 40 per cent were of working-class background, while 54 per cent were middle-class.

There are essentially two problems with this period, in terms of an assessment of the above results. Firstly, the sample is rather smaller in this period than in others, due not to turnover, which is average, but rather to the fact that the period is comparatively short. Secondly, the results are rather atypical in view of their rather dramatic nature. Nevertheless one may conjecture as to the reasons for this sudden dramatic reversal of class proportions. Presumably with Labour in power the pre-eminence of MPs within the party would be assured, so that it was only natural that a high proportion of MPs should be elected to the NEC during this period of Labour ascendancy. Indeed, MPs filled the bulk of new positions on the Committee, flooding the

Women's, Constituency and Societies' Sections and constituting a clear majority of the Committee. Moreover the majority of these MPs were of ostensibly middle-class background. The predominantly middle-class composition of the NEC between 1945 and 1951 would seem to be at least in part a function of the inordinately high number of MPs who were elected to that body during the period. This obviously is the continuation of earlier trends but it is certainly more pronounced than previously. The movement of the main arena of Labour politics from the NEC to the PLP and therefore the rise in potential importance of the MP within the party at large, ensured the favourable acceptance of parliamentarians within all spheres of party activity, as well as giving to such individuals' chances of election to the NEC the added bonus of social position and political prominence. The period 1945–51 seems to have been the decisive watershed in the 'Parliamentary Labour Party's successful fight to gain control of such extra-Parliamentary institutions within the Labour Party as the Executive, the annual delegates' conference and the party machine.'[30]

The growth of importance of the MP, however, is really only half the explanation of the changes to the NEC in the period under discussion. There is another related and equally important factor to be considered. Changes in the party organisation and personnel which came to fruition in this period were really the culmination of trends initiated by MacDonald and which snowballed throughout the late 1930s and 1940s under the guidance of Attlee; namely the recruitment and formalisation of a relatively efficient party organisation which projected the credibility of its capacity to govern and made the necessary electoral appeal to ensure such capacity. One tangible result was that teachers replaced miners as the strongest occupational group on the Labour benches; another was the emergence into prominence on the NEC of certain types of individuals with certain types of occupational backgrounds.[31]

The successful reorganisation of the party in the 1930s and 1940s necessitated the recruitment of individuals who, unlike the majority of their pre-1930 predecessors, thought politically with their brains and not with their hearts, of individuals with professional and administrative skills, or who in Bauman's words were administrators not agitators. The reciprocity of their relationship was an exacting one. The party needed their political skills, they on the other hand needed a vehicle for such skills. As the party moved to the middle ground in the mid-1930s and 1940s the opportunity for their alliance was formed. Such persons served their political apprenticeships prior

138

to our period under discussion and hence emerge into national prominence in the era 1945–51. On the NEC therefore former civil servants, teachers and journalists emerge as the prominent groups, all
fitting the above pattern, all invariably middle-class.

The need for and consequent rise of these professional classes
within the party, coupled with the correlative growth of importance
of the MP within the party, effectively ensured that the majority of
individuals gaining election to the NEC in the period 1945–51 were
professional, middle-class or members of Parliament, and in the
majority of cases, usually all three.

1951–64

In electoral terms, one could characterise this as one of the periods of
perennial Labour reassessment. Both in policy and ideological terms,
this would adequately categorise the many schisms and disputes
which arose within the party. On the NEC, it might be characterised
as a period of grass-roots and trade union reassertion of their position within the Labour movement.[32] However, this would only really
present half the picture of the dynamics of NEC positions as the ideological cleavages of the 1950s and 1960s must be seen against the
background of actual changes in the social composition of the
committee itself. Such changes were themselves the culmination of
emergent trends from past periods.

Three important features emerge from this period. The proportions
of middle-class representatives are again high, with journalists, lecturers and teachers being the most predominant. This time 49 per
cent of new incumbents are of middle-class background with 53 per
cent of this group having attended university. This is in striking contrast to the working-class group where only *1 per cent* had attended
university. In addition, of all incumbents 49 per cent were from
middle-class backgrounds with 41 per cent being working-class.
Though the middle-class proportion for both new and existing incumbents reveals a slight slippage from the figures of the earlier period,
the figure is nevertheless approximately what one has come to expect
from the analysis of earlier periods. From period to period there has
been a significant growth in middle-class representation on the NEC,
throughout the life-span of the Labour Party. The second crucial
feature of this period is the social mobility rates of the new incumbents. Thirty-two per cent of those who had working-class fathers,
were socially mobile and occupationally joined the middle-class. The
closer one draws to the contemporary era, the higher the social

139

mobility levels exhibited by members of the Committee. In terms of domination of the Committee, occupationally the NEC has moved far from traditional Labour Party working-class links. This should not be too surprising as the trend has been firmly in evidence since the 1920s.

The third crucial feature of this period is again the role of the MP. While MPs on the Constituency and Women's Sections explain a significant proportion of this 49 per cent, a further proportion is accounted for by MPs who are on the trade union section of the NEC. The period 1951–64 sees not only a further consolidation of the role of the middle-class but also of the MP, with the latter again constituting a majority of the NEC. It comes as no surprise then, during the debates of the Gaitskell era, to find middle-class, intellectual MPs appearing on both sides of the dispute. It is perhaps a singular tribute to Harold Wilson that in only three years he was able not only to develop broad enough electoral support to win a general election, but in so doing, was able to convince the average Labour rank-and-filer that there was a significant role for him to play in a party organisation increasingly dominated by MPs both in and out of Parliament.[33] Whether the rank-and-filer remained convinced is a moot point.

The perpetuation of the strong professional and middle-class influence in the Committee is explained by the same factors which accounted for the emergence into prominence of such groups in the period 1945–51, and therefore needs little recapitulation here. If anything, a party in opposition with a revitalised organisation to build is more dependent than ever on the administrative and political skills at the disposal of its personnel. And in a complementary fashion, the party which in the early sixties saw itself as introducing a new efficiency to Whitehall and a new technology to the nation, obviously needed to attract to its fold individuals with such necessary skills. The infusion into the NEC of the professions in large numbers is simply a function of all these factors, mentioned here and earlier.

In part, this also explains the continued growing importance of the MP, as most of the middle-class members were MPs. It does not explain, however, the continued presence of middle-class MPs in the *trade union* sector. The political fortunes of these individuals will all have been forged in vastly different circumstances to those persons who rise to prominence in the Constituency or Women's Section. Indeed there is some evidence to suggest that parliamentary experience is seen by some union leaders as detrimental to a person's chance of election to the NEC. An anonymous union official quoted in M.

Harrison, *Trade Unions and the Labour Party Since 1945*, when asked about his union's possible vote, stated in reply, 'we've got enough MPs already . . . Padley's a politician . . . He's really nothing in the industrial side of the movement.'[34] But given the numbers of MPs who are returned to the trade union sector, this probably suggests that such comments are not typical or at least are typical only of certain union leaders, or of certain unions. This is more obviously true when we consider that any candidate who is particularly unacceptable to more than one large union has only a limited chance of election. The explanation of the middle-class trade union MP therefore would seem to lie in the fact that the unions of which they are members regularly nominate MPs for election, replacing one incumbent MP by another. Invariably, these are white-collar unions whose political nominees are often middle-class, as are many of their members. In addition certain other unions have established traditions of nominating MPs to the union sections of the NEC, the two most prominent being USDAW and NUGMW. Both types of unions are, of course, likely to have vastly differing standards of political acceptability, the one traditionally linked with the poorer paid sections of the working-class, the other middle-class and more inclined towards professionalism and the professional classes. Such differences, allied to these unions' predilections for nominating MPs, account for the increasing numbers of middle-class and working-class MPs on the union section. Within such numbers, however, the middle-class element is by far the stronger.

1964–72

This era is too fresh in the minds of most people to necessitate any detailed commentary. The middle-class comprised 42 per cent of the total number of new individuals within this period, with teachers and journalists again responsible for the bulk of individual careers. Seventy-one per cent of the middle-class group had attended university while not one of the working-class group, which made up 47 per cent of the representatives, had any university experience. In terms of educational opportunities and standards, this period manifests similar characteristics to those discussed earlier. An increasing number of NEC members received more than just an elementary education but this increase in numbers coincided with the increase in middle-class representation. One feature is therefore simply a function of the other and does not represent a more widespread application of educational opportunity. Like its predecessors this period too illustrates high

141

social mobility levels among the new incumbents. Of those whose fathers were working-class, 36 per cent were socially mobile and moved into the middle-class in the earlier part of their career preceding their election to the NEC. One of the most significant features to emerge from the study so far would seem to be the fact that over the last forty years, an average of about one-third of the new incumbents of the NEC had changed their social situation and moved up the class ladder. Relatively low levels of social mobility were experienced during the first years of the committee but this feature is totally eclipsed by the fact that social mobility levels increased in each successive era as one approached the contemporary period. Overall, therefore, 37 per cent of all incumbents during the period 1964–72 were working-class, while 56 per cent were middle-class. Once again the class balance of the NEC has swung firmly towards the middle-class who have regained the majority they originally had in 1945–51. Since 1930 at least 40 per cent of the members of the NEC have been middle-class; on two occasions greatly in excess of 50 per cent have come from this stratum. If this trend continues as it has been doing in the past, one wonders what its continuation will mean to the Labour Party. Having compared different background cohorts, we reach the end of our period with the general conclusion that the essentially working-class homogeneity of the early period has been gradually replaced by a simple dichotomy of working-class and middle-class and by an occupational heterogeneity which reflects this basic cleavage. More importantly, the middle-class composition of newcomers in this period is reflected in the fact that all of the 42 per cent are MPs. Again, this effectively means that in the period MPs were in an even clearer majority position than hitherto. By 1972 two groups dominate the NEC, the middle-class and MPs and in the majority of cases the two groups are synonymous.

I have argued that MPs play an increasingly important role on the NEC as well as noting the growing middle-class representation which largely parallels this growth of MPs' influence. To what extent, therefore, is there a growing gap, not just between the working- and middle-classes but between the MP and other segments of the Labour movement, as reflected in such class disparities?

Trade Unions

Of those individuals who sat in the trade union section of the NEC, 76 per cent came from working-class backgrounds, while a mere 12 per cent[35] were discernible as being middle-class. The trade union

142

section in 1972, in class terms, manifests similar characteristics to its predecessor in 1900. The overwhelming class homogeneity of this section is probably the most predictable and expected feature of the social composition of the NEC. In addition, only 13 per cent of trade union members had been MPs at the time of their elections, with the bulk, about 60 per cent, of this 13 per cent manifesting working-class occupational characteristics. This middle-class residue, however, could be important, even though universally it is rather small. The trade union section would seem to be essentially of the political and social background that is considered the traditional home of Labour politics. However, the proportion of MPs on the trade union section is not constant and recent developments indicate significant changes. Since 1951, 31 per cent of newcomers to the trade union section were MPs at the time of their election. The role of the MP is therefore increasing amongst the trade unionists on the NEC, so that the traditional working-class mores, in terms of occupational background, which these individuals exhibit, may be ameliorated by other less traditional considerations. 'With few exceptions, Labour MPs submit like others to the traditions of the place and succumb to the *genus loci*. Parliamentary life itself becomes an educative and moderating influence. The mores of the House lessen antagonism . . . New loyalties are created.'[36] The parliamentary man, with original working-class antecedents, may be vastly different from his class peers who have not experienced parliamentary influences acting on their traditional values. In addition to the expanding role of the MP on this section there is another changing feature which merits documentation. This concerns the actual length of the period of manual occupation that the unionists worked before becoming full-time union officials. In the period 1900–18, the average number of years in manual occupations of the working-class members of this section was twenty-four years. This figure had diminished to about sixteen by 1931, to about twelve by 1940 and in the period 1945–72 averages at about eight years.[37] Though the majority of members in this section have been working-class, yet this evidence would seem to indicate that even within this 'working-class' criterion significant qualitative changes may have been taking place, which would be ignored by too casual a use of the terms working- or middle-class.

Constituency Section

The increasing bi-polarity along class and institutional lines is probably nowhere better reflected than in the Constituencies Section of

143

the NEC. Sixty-seven per cent were middle-class, while 33 per cent were of working-class background. The traditional working-class representative has been pushed aside, it seems, by individuals whose backgrounds we presume indicate initial loyalties different to those expected of working-class representatives. In addition, since 1931, the beginning of a long period of reconstruction and consolidation, 83 per cent of the Constituency Section came from middle-class segments of the population. This change is further reinforced by the fact that, again since 1931, 87 per cent of the individuals elected to the constituencies section were MPs at the time of their election. In addition, 8 per cent subsequently became MPs during the course of their tenure. Individuals who were elected in the last forty years on to that section of the NEC which is reserved for constituency representatives, have been overwhelmingly of a parliamentary and middle-class background. The working-class, non-parliamentary representative from the constituency is extremely difficult to find on the NEC, and one might almost say, is in danger of extinction altogether. One does not have to look far to explain this phenomenon. 'In the constituency and women's divisions of the Labour executive . . . one is elected because one is known.'[38] Being an MP would obviously provide the basic platform from which to be known. The rise of the middle-class and of the MP at all levels within the party and the fact that the clear majority of MPs in the Constituency Section were from this social stratum leaves little room for any working-class, non-parliamentary representatives. Under present circumstances, the difficulty is for any single individual without a ready-made parliamentary position to make himself known sufficiently widely within the party to ensure election. For all the reasons that sociologists know so well, it is consequently more difficult for the working-class than for the middle-class individual to make his presence felt under such limitations. Probably the simplest answer 'is that, in the Labour Party, constituency workers choose to be represented by Members of Parliament',[39] and of those individuals who stand for election the vast majority of the successful ones are MPs and middle-class, with a residual category of persons who are MPs *and* working-class or *just* middle-class with no parliamentary background, though the latter too have almost dwindled to extinction.

Women's Section

Though the increasing domination of the NEC by the middle-class and MPs is best exemplified on the Constituency Section, similar characteristics are found in the Women's Section. Persons here were overwhelmingly from the middle-class stratum of society (89 per cent), with a minimal working-class representation of 11 per cent of the members. Again the bulk of this group has parliamentary experience, with 48 per cent having been MPs at the time of their election and an additional 22 per cent becoming MPs during the course of their incumbency. These results should not on *a priori* grounds be too surprising, though the high proportion of MPs should possibly generate some debate.

Finally, if one turns to the *Societies*[40] Section, similar class findings to those of the trade union section are exhibited. Sixty-four per cent were of working-class background, while 36 per cent were middle-class. But the parliamentary influence is again similar to most of the other segments of the NEC, with 46 per cent of incumbents being MPs before they were elected and an additional 27 per cent subsequently being elected to Parliament during their tenure.

Political Careers

This section does not intend to document whether or not individuals became Cabinet Ministers or MPs but merely to provide the broad political framework under which the bulk of members received their early political training prior to their incumbencies on the NEC. Even within what one might imagine to be broad communalities of experience there exist vast discrepancies of background which add another dimension to the patterns of existing social differentiation. Taking overall considerations first, 152 or 66 per cent of the total incumbents had trade union experience[41] of one form or another, either full- or part-time. In addition to this group, thirty-six or 16 per cent had experience in socialist, co-operative societies, or miscellaneous organisations. The remainder, forty-four, or 18 per cent of the total, spent most of their early political apprenticeships working for the party at either local or national level. There is therefore considerable differentiation amongst primary political activity. These categories are in a sense slightly misleading, however, as although they refer to the primary political sphere of experience of the incumbent's life, many members had multiple interests and were not simply restricted to one field of activity. Examining the secondary political experiences of the different sections should reveal aspects of these multiple interests as well as hopefully providing sources of contact between them.

Within the trade union section of the NEC slightly under half the members had also been associated with local party organisations. Of those individuals who sat on sections other than the trade union section, 40 per cent had some trade union experience, 25 per cent had Fabian or Co-operative Society experience, 16 per cent had been active in the party organisation and the remainder are scattered through various fields, trade councils, SDF, political journalism and the ILP. It is apparent therefore that there are considerable areas of overlap amongst the primary and secondary political activities of the NEC incumbents. Only two fields of experience remain relatively unrelated. Only a small minority of Fabians and Co-operators had trade union experience, and only a small group of trade unionists had Fabian or Co-operative backgrounds. It would appear that the traditional mutual distrust between the Fabians and the unions tended to ensure that their respective devotees for the most part remained quite faithful to their original affiliations. 'The leaders of the Labour movement also behaved towards the Fabians in the same sort of way as the Fabians did to them. They did everything possible to restrict the participation of the Fabians in the running of the new-born Labour Party and they regarded with suspicion the projects for legislation submitted by the Fabians to its parliamentary wing.'[42] Some Fabians do have trade union experience, but they are very much in the minority. On the other hand, the fact that many trade unionists had also been active in local party affairs, together with the quite wide experience of trade union and other activity amongst the Constituency and Women's Sections, is testament to the basic politeracy of these groups. The original party-trade union links were therefore maintained by sections of the organisation which one might have thought had already disregarded such links. In addition, the original eclectic foundation of the Labour movement is well demonstrated by the proliferation of secondary organisations which have emerged from this analysis.

Since 1945, however, a strikingly different picture emerges. The trade union experience of these other NEC sections has diminished to 16 per cent, Fabian and Co-operative activities account for 29 per cent of the incumbents, while local party roles total 38 per cent of the secondary activity. An additional 17 per cent is accounted for by political journalism. Amongst those individuals on the NEC, therefore, whose primary careers were not in the unions, the last thirty years has seen a significant change in secondary political activity. Fewer and fewer individuals spend their time on union activities, while an increasing number participate in Fabian, local party or journalistic activities. This would again seem to indicate a growing

146

TABLE 3: *Background Characteristics of NEC Members*

	1900–31	1931–72
(a) Class Background*		
Aristocracy	2	—
Middle-Class	25	55
Working-Class	85	50
Not known	—	15
(b) Occupation		
Professionals	17	42
Commerce and Industry	8	2
Trade Union Officials	2	11
Manual	84	52
Not known	—	13
(c) Education – School		
Elementary	69	45
Grammar	14	31
Public	4	12
Private tuition	5	—
Secondary/Technical College	6	17
Not known	13	15
(d) Education – University		
None	81	74
Oxford	1	16
Cambridge	4	1
Others	12	14
Not known	13	14
	n = 112	n = 120

Sources: Who Was Who; Who's Who; Who's Who in the Labour Party 1924, 1927; The Herald Book of Labour Members; The Times Guides to the House of Commons 1950–1970; Dictionary of National Biography; individual biographies; Labour Party newspaper files, Transport House.

* The class scheme adopted was that laid out in footnotes 16 and 17.

rift between union and non-union members of the NEC, particularly as primary differences are already quite distinct; with the Fabians and the political journalists being drawn mainly from the middle-classes and according to Hindess and Bauman,[43] with the local parties becoming increasingly dominated by the middle-class, this would seem to be an extra dimension to the social differentiation which has already been seen to be increasing amongst the incumbents of the NEC.

Conclusion: A Labour Elite or not: Lessons for Tomorrow

Tables 3 and 4 present in a digest form the main class findings of the research. In addition to noting the increasing *embourgeoisement* of the NEC over time, a second striking feature has been the growth of the role of the MP. MPs now constitute the bulk of members of the Constituency, Women's and Societies Sections as well as contributing in a significant manner to the incumbents on the trade union section.[44] The NEC in the seventy years of its life therefore witnessed two major structural changes. Firstly, the middle-classes now com-

TABLE 4: *Career Patterns of NEC Members, 1900-72*

	1918	1931	1931–1945	1945–1951	1951–1964	1964–1972
Aristocratic or upper middle-class background with professional or entrepreneurial career	1	4	3	1	1	–
Middle or lower middle-class background with professional or entrepreneurial career	2	12	8	4	7	5
Middle-class background with career as trade union official (or similar organisation)	–	2	1	–	2	1
Working-class background with a professional or business career leading to middle-class status	2	4	3	4	4	4
Working-class background with career as an official of a trade union (or similar organisation)	–	1	3	–	5	3
Working-class background with a career occupationally defined as working-class	44	40	22	4	16	4
Not known	–	–	5	3	3	4
TOTAL	49	63	45	16	38	21

Note: The categories in this table are adapted from W. L. Guttsman, *The British Political Elite*, p. 242.

prise about 56 per cent of its membership. Parallel with such middle-class growth has been the emergence of MPs as a potential voting bloc on the committee. Since 1945 about 55 per cent of the NEC have been MPs at any one time. Though one feature is a partial function of the other, nevertheless, one cannot, except in the period 1964–72, completely equate middle-class growth with growth of MPs' membership. Often MPs on the Trade Union Section have working-class antecedents, while occasionally members on the women's section are middle-class but without a parliamentary career. The significance of the MP on the committee is probably reinforced by a point made earlier concerning the longevity of certain incumbencies. A corpus of individuals who have served for ten years or more emerges since 1945, and it is a salient feature of this group that the majority are MPs. Indeed, the usual custom is one of higher turnover on the trade union section with the constituency and women's sections remaining static for long periods of time.[45] What considerations therefore could one give to notions of a 'Labour elite' emerging on the NEC?

Technically, we could argue that the NEC is already an elite. If we adopt Parry's definition of elites as 'small minorities who appear to play an exceptionally influential part in political and social affairs'[46] then within the Labour movement in this country it would be relatively simple, though essentially trite, to show that the NEC constitutes one kind of Labour elite. As a small core of individuals elected from within the Labour movement at large, the NEC by definition would seem to comprise an elite. More importantly however, can one perceive of another group of individuals within the NEC who themselves constitute so to speak an elite within an elite?

It is again a relatively simple task to indicate since 1945, firstly the overwhelmingly strong MP representation on the NEC and secondly the comparatively long tenure of the bulk of these individuals. MPs who were newcomers to the NEC in the period 1945–72, sat on average for eleven years. This figure is considerably depressed due to the inclusion of present-day incumbent MPs who have only been sitting for a couple of years or so. There is considerable overlap in terms of service amongst this parliamentary group. One could therefore identify a parliamentary corpus within the NEC, with certain individuals common for long periods and new parliamentary blood being injected from time to time, who themselves then remain for considerable periods of tenure. It is therefore an easily recognisable parliamentary nucleus of individuals but it is not, in any sense, a tight-knit oligarchy. Two additional features would need to be considered also, before one could decide whether this was an elite in Parry's terms. Firstly, all the individuals need to resubmit themselves for annual election, so that any long-term policy plans envisaged by a minority could only be tentative. This point could be mitigated by the fact that prospects of consistent re-election could be known to be high. The uncertainty still remains from year to year, however, and the NEC does have the habit of producing quite unexpected changes of personnel, even within sections noted for their relative quiescence.[47] Secondly, it is one thing to impute collusion to any group of individuals but it is another to prove it. It is therefore exceedingly difficult to substantiate any arguments that this parliamentary group 'play an exceptionally influential part' in the formulation of policies emanating from the NEC. Mackenzie's inference that this is indeed the case suffers rather badly from a lack of conclusive evidence.

The significance of increased representation of MPs is, however, best exemplified in conjunction with the growing *embourgeoisement* of the NEC as a whole.

As this and more specifically other research has shown, the Labour Party has never been a completely working-class organisation but it would be surely equally dubious to claim that it has changed from a working-class to a middle-class party. Certainly its growth as a formal organisation entailed the inevitable enrolment of individuals with the necessary political and administrative skills to maximise the party's electoral advantages.[48] Such skills, it seems, are more likely to be located within the middle-class strata of society. Electoral success therefore had the additional consequence of attracting an increasing middle-class element into the party organisation at all levels. Labour electoral support amongst the middle-class has not grown at anything like the same rate.[49] There is consequently a considerable class imbalance from the national to the constituency level. Hindess is partly correct when he says, 'What has happened rather, is that certain types of interests have been squeezed out of the general coalition represented by the Labour Party.'[50] More specifically middle-class and parliamentary interest now dominate the major policy structures.

This argument is not the dubious one of correlating social background with political attitudes but is merely stipulating that the alliance which built the Labour Party, could now, in a rather insidious fashion, be its undoing. As emphases and interest within this alliance diverge from traditional and expected ones, so expectations of policy and performance must adapt to meet such changes. Because the realization of changing emphases has not been quickly assimilated by

150

the bulk of the party, traditional expectations of performance remain. And it is such traditional concerns, as a result of the transformed social structure of the party, which are the most difficult to satisfy.

A priori, one could have assumed that the NEC, through its trade union element at least, was now the last repository of traditional Labour support and values. This patently is not the case. The parliamentary ethos is disproportionately represented and like the Cabinet, Parliament, and the constituency organisations, the NEC has likewise witnessed the continuing growth of the influence of the middle-class. The growing gap between Labour leaders and Labour led, is nowhere better exemplified than by the changing structural characteristics of the NEC. With a Party and constituency leadership growing increasingly isolated from its traditional support,[51] the rank-and-filer who looks to the NEC as the last bastion of traditional Labour politics against the growing parliamentary and middle-class influence, is being sadly deluded.

Labour's traditional response to charges of 'leadership unrepresentativeness' has been in keeping with its essentially ambivalent attitude to any problems that confront it. On one hand, it makes pleas for more working-class representatives and for closer ties with its traditional support (most recently Wedgwood Benn, Chairman of the 1972 NEC, felt constrained to deliver this appeal). On the other hand it concerns itself with party-convulsing debates on how to broaden its national appeal, consolidate its electoral support, and win the next election.

Like the other sections of the party organisation, the NEC has moved far from its original working-class beginnings. Such a trend was the natural concomitant of the party's growth from a sectional movement to a fully-fledged national party. Just as experiences in government introduced strains into the Labour movement, so these changes in the social composition of the NEC present additional strains. Beatrice Webb saw 'the firm anchorage of the Labour Party in the working-class organisation' as 'a guarantee that Labour administrations will continue to represent adequately four-fifths of the population'.[52] If present trends within the party and on the NEC continue, it remains a possibility that the only working-class anchorage will be a statutory one which will pose interesting problems for such notions of representation. The *embourgeoisement* of the NEC casts into sharp perspective the essentially antipathetic and mutually destructive nature of those forces which came together to form the

151

Labour Party. The uneasy balance between egalitarianism and electoral ambition that has characterised all spheres of party life throughout its history has produced a contemporary situation, within the party and on the NEC in particular, where problems of diminishing social equality and increasing social differentiation between leaders and led, call into question the founding ideological precepts of the organisation. This is not the place to solve this problem or even to offer suggestions, but there is little doubt that the growing social gap between political elite and rank-and-file is one of the more pressing institutional problems in the Labour Party today. If the *embourgeoisement* of the NEC continues unabated, then one wonders how long it will be, before 'the myth of the worker who becomes an NEC member has taken over from that of the shoe black who made himself a millionaire'.[53]

NOTES

1. See particularly R. McKenzie, *British Political Parties*, Mercury, London, 1964, 2nd edition, pp. 516–26; J. Blondel, *Voters, Parties and Leaders*, Penguin, London, 1963, pp. 113–27; R. Rose, *Politics in England*, Faber, London, 1965, pp. 144–5; A. Sampson, *Anatomy of Britain Today*, Harper & Row, New York, 1965, pp. 121–3; M. Harrison, *Trade Unions and the Labour Party Since 1945*, Allen & Unwin, London, 1960.

2. See Stephen Haseler, *The Gaitskellites*, Macmillan, London, 1969, pp. 10–14 and pp. 152–4; A. Sampson, *The New Anatomy of Britain*, Hodder & Stoughton, London, 1971, pp. 46–9. The debate of course continues unabated today.

3. Both Guttsman and Hindess are culpable of this dubious academic exercise. Of the two, Hindess at least makes an attempt to relate changing policy imperatives to the changing social structure but is only partially successful. See W. Guttsman, *The British Political Elite*, MacGibbon & Kee, London, 1963; B. Hindess, *The Decline of Working-Class Politics*, MacGibbon & Kee, London, 1971. See also Z. Bauman, *Between Class and Elite*, Manchester University Press, Manchester, 1972, p. 285.

4. W. Guttsman, p. 226.

5. 'Labour politicians have, in the course of their rise in the governing hierarchy, tended to become absorbed in the wider political ruling class.' (W. Guttsman, p. 373.)

6. 'Changes in the Labour Party . . . have led to the differentiation

of the political demands, concerns and orientations of party members and supporters . . . In this differentiation the orientation of the middle class areas have been compatible both with the interests of the party leadership and with the response of the party organisation to its own changing institutional environment.' (B. Hindess, p. 164.)

7. C. Attlee, *The Labour Party in Perspective*, Victor Gollancz, London, 1937, p. 93.

8. See J. Blondel, pp. 121–7 for a discussion of some aspects of the representativeness of the NEC.

9. See the entry on Frederick Rogers in Joyce M. Bellamy and John Saville (eds.), *Dictionary of Labour Biography*, Macmillan, London, 1972, p. 290.

10. On the relationship between changes in party organisational structure and its role in society see Z. Bauman, *Between Class and Elite*. Bauman's essentially structuralist analysis at times tends to over-read the available evidence and his oftentimes highly personalised response to historical events tends on occasions to weaken his arguments, though the scope of the study is impressive.

11. This total excludes H. Brill (Coalporters) of 1900–1, who only sat for two months, but includes C. Lacey of the League of Youth.

12. R. McKenzie, p. 520.

13. This period is chosen so as to make these figures relevant to McKenzie. His research on the NEC stops at 1952.

14. W. Guttsman, p. 226.

15. This is consistent with J. Blondel, p. 121. However his research is only based on the period 1952–62 and has no comparative aspect with any other period.

16. The usage of the terms working- and middle-class is primarily based on the usual distinction between manual and non-manual workers. The 'lower' class alternative was chosen wherever cases were borderline or where my information was ambiguous. See S. Hall and D. Caradog Jones, 'The Social Grading of Occupations', *British Journal of Sociology*, Vol. I, January 1950; also J. H. Goldthorpe *et al.*, *The Affluent Worker in the Class Structure*, Cambridge University Press, Cambridge, 1969, especially Appendix A, pp. 196–7. Theirs is a comparatively cogent description of the problems in this area but their usage of an 'intermediate' scale rather leaves the issue unresolved. Also D. Butler and D. Stokes, *Political Change in Britain*, Pelican, London, 1971, pp. 90–103, present a particularly intelligent but nevertheless not definitive class classification. Their findings in particular indicate the essential contentiousness of the problem.

17. Salaried employees of 'white-collar' unions are obviously middle-class, but there is still a singular difficulty in classifying other union officials. Union bureaucrats were therefore for the most part classified in the main occupation that they had followed before entering the union and usually this was a manual one. If however, all of their working lives had been spent within the union with no other outside occupation, they were classified as middle-class. This procedure posed no problems of classification.

18. Establishing the acceptability of a general measure of social mobility remains a perennial problem for social science. For this study social mobility was calculated by totalling all those individuals who were perceived as having changed their class situation when based on parental and then on personal occupation, and then computing this as a proportion of their original class. On the difficulties inherent in constructing social mobility rates see Kenneth Macdonald and John Ridge, 'Social Mobility', in A. H. Halsey, *Trends in British Society Since 1900*, Macmillan, London, 1972, pp. 129–48.

19. These figures do not represent any form of reverse mobility, merely that for the fathers' occupations, there was a slightly larger group about whom information was unobtainable. In some instances in subsequent sections the percentages do not total to 100. This is explained by the small percentage of unknowns in each sector. This cannot materially affect the findings as the middle-class proportions can only rise, should information concerning these individuals come to light.

20. See Z. Bauman, *Between Class and Elite*, p. 193.

21. F. Williams, *Fifty Years March, The Rise of the Labour Party*, Odhams, London, 1950, p. 197.

22. In this early period it would appear that the Fabians were present on the Committee only through the sufferance of the unions. 'Their origins and the class ties which they retained separated the Fabians from the groups of working-class socialists, who were distrustful of these rich, sophisticated highbrows from the ruling class.' Z. Bauman, *Between Class and Elite*, p. 180. See also A. McBriar, *Fabian Socialism and English Politics*, Cambridge University Press, Cambridge, 1962.

23. The organisation established in 1900 consisted of a twelve-member committee with an unpaid secretary, with seven representatives of the trade unions, one of the Fabians and two each from the ILP & SDF, and with each section electing its own representatives. In 1905 it was agreed that the socialist societies should be jointly repre-

sented, i.e. they would have a total of three representatives rather than one for the Fabians and two for the ILP. (The SDF had withdrawn from the Committee in 1901.) In 1918 the NEC was reconstituted to consist of twenty-three members — thirteen representatives of affiliated organisations (trade unions, Co-operative and Socialist societies), five representatives of local Labour parties, four women and the Treasurer. Except for the Treasurer who could be nominated by any section, each section nominated its own candidates, but in all cases the nominations would be voted upon by the entire conference. Since 1929, the Leader has sat *ex officio* in the Committee. The only basic modification to this occurred in 1937. Constituency representation was increased from five to seven, and it was decided that the trade union and socialist societies' representatives should be elected separately by their own sections. The constituency nominations were also to be elected by the vote of the constituency delegates alone. Nominations for the women and Treasurer are still elected by vote of the whole conference. By 1937 the Committee therefore consisted of twelve trade union members, seven constituency party members, one socialist and co-operative societies representative, five women members, the Treasurer of the party, and the Leader of the party (*ex-officio*). In 1935 a League of Youth section was added but was subsequently removed before the year was out. In 1953 the Deputy Leader of the party also joined *ex-officio*, and except for this there have been no additional changes to the Committee since 1937. But in 1972 the Annual Conference voted to amend the Constitution and allow a Young Socialist representative on the Committee.

24. G. D. H. Cole, *British Working-Class Politics 1832–1914*, Routledge, London, 1941, p. 245.

25. Figures adapted from tables presented in A. H. Halsey, 'Higher Education', in A. H. Halsey (ed.), *Trends in British Society Since 1900*, Macmillan, London, 1972.

26. Z. Bauman, *Between Class and Elite*, p. 224.

27. There was a very real sense in which the party could have been considered to be 'his' creature. A specific MacDonald cult developed in the 1920s. See Z. Bauman, *Between Class and Elite*, pp. 225–6; Lord Elton, *The Life of Ramsay MacDonald*; E. Shinwell, *The Labour Story*, Macdonald, London, 1963, pp. 77–89.

28. Bauman sees this as one of the major causes for the formation and consequent success of the Labour party, its creation providing an alternative avenue to political and social position and acceptability. Z. Bauman, *Between Class and Elite*, pp. 170–220.

29. The distinction is a Lasswellian one. See H. Lasswell, *Psychopathology and Politics*, Free Press, New York, 1951; also Z. Bauman, *Between Class and Elite*, for an extensive application to the Labour Party.

30. Z. Bauman, *Between Class and Elite*, p. 293.

31. See W. Guttsman, *The British Political Elite*, p. 243, pp. 275–7; and Z. Bauman, *Between Class and Elite*, pp. 302–23, for an analysis of the relationship between electoral efficiency and organisational professionalisation.

32. See particularly S. Haseler, *The Gaitskellites*, for the most comprehensive analysis of NEC schisms and disputes during the period. The analysis ought to be considered against the background of changes in the social composition of the NEC. Also M. Harrison, *Trade Unions and the Labour Party Since 1945*, pp. 307–23.

33. Hindess, for example, finds that significant differences already exist between leaders and the led on matters such as economic policy, and sees this as a growing, not diminishing, trend. B. Hindess, *The Decline of Working-Class Politics*, p. 78.

34. M. Harrison, *Trade Unions and the Labour Party Since 1945*, p. 313.

35. It was not possible to obtain sufficient information about the outstanding 12 per cent of individuals who sat in the Trade Union section.

36. W. Guttsman, *The British Political Elite*, p. 247.

37. See also Z. Bauman, *Between Class and Elite*, p. 319, for similar findings amongst his union elite.

38. J. Blondel, *Voters, Parties and Leaders*, p. 126.

39. ibid., p. 125.

40. This includes all individuals who in the early period sat on the Trade Council section, plus Lacey of the League of Youth.

41. Obviously part of this total is made up of individuals from the non-union sections. In addition, this aspect of the paper is based on the following distinction between primary and secondary political career routes. Primary routes are the major sources of political activity in the years preceding election to the NEC, but it does not include MPs as a separate category. An individual who has spent most of his political life as an MP will have been classified within the party category. An MP who has spent most of his life working for a trade union will be classified amongst the union section, etc. Secondary activity therefore concentrates on examining those political activities in which members participated, in conjunction with their primary

careers, but which are considered less significant in terms of total years of involvement for any individual.

42. Z. Bauman, *Between Class and Elite*, p. 182.

43. Hindess, *The Decline of Working-Class Politics*, pp. 136–63; Z. Bauman, *Between Class and Elite*, p. 283. See also J. Blondel, *Voters, Parties and Leaders*, pp. 101–3.

44. For a complementary analysis of the role of the MP in the committee, see R. McKenzie, *British Political Parties*, p. 421; J. Blondel, *Voters, Parties and Leaders*, p. 125; B. Hennessy, 'Trade Unions and the British Labour Party', *American Political Science Review*, December 1955, p. 1060. Z. Bauman, *Between Class and Elite*, p. 294, is in fact wrong when he says, 'in the early days of the Labour Party's existence there was a statutory limitation on the number of MPs who could be members of the party executive'. The 1908 Party Conference carried two resolutions to this effect but both were defeated and no subsequent efforts were made to circumscribe the number of the PLP on the Committee. There has always been considerable unease about their strength however.

45. The higher turnover of trade unionists is explicable firstly, in terms of their official positions within their trade unions, causing them to relinquish the seat rather than their being defeated in the elections and secondly, partly due to the practice of allowing smaller or medium-sized unions a certain number of seats. As a matter of interest, while it is generally correct to assume that the bulk of unionists on the NEC are not General Secretaries, nevertheless, it seems that a seat on the NEC could be considered a necessary milestone in a trade union career. Seventy-four per cent of the union incumbents on the committee rose to be either Assistant General Secretary, or General Secretary (or the equivalent in some unions) during the course of their union careers. Sixty-two per cent of the group rose to be General Secretary of their union. As most General Secretaries prefer to sit in the General Council of the TUC, unionists on the NEC are usually second, third or lower rankers in their union hierarchy but incumbency on the NEC would seem to be a relatively good predictor of who will later rise ultimately to the top of the union hierarchy. For that reason most union incumbents cannot therefore be simply dismissed because they are second or even third rankers. In opposition to Guttsman's notions, their importance and influence is a potential one and ought to be considered for that reason alone. On this issue see particularly W. Guttsman, *The British Political Elite*, p. 225n; J. Blondel, *Voters, Parties and Leaders*, p. 120; R.

McKenzie, *British Political Parties*, p. 519; M. Harrison, *Trade Unions and the Labour Party Since 1945*, pp. 311–13.

46. G. Parry, *Political Elites*, Allen & Unwin, London, 1969, p. 13.

47. Witness Lady Eirene White's unexpected departure in 1972. See also M. Harrison, *Trade Unions and the Labour Party Since 1945*, pp. 310, 314–15.

48. On this and related concepts see E. Spencer Wellhofer, 'Dimensions of Party Development', *Journal of Politics*, Vol. 34, February 1972, pp. 153–83, and T. Hennessey and E. Spencer Wellhofer, this volume. Also Bauman, *Between Class and Elite*, Ch. 4.

49. P. Pulzer, *Political Representation and Elections in Britain*, pp. 102–9. It is of course, both interesting and paradoxical that when the NEC was *most* working-class it had least working-class electoral support; when it was least working-class, it had *most* working-class votes.

50. B. Hindess, *The Decline of Working-Class Politics*, p. 146.

51. At least this is so if we accept Guttsman, Hindess and Bauman.

52. Beatrice Webb, 'The Disappearance of the Governing Class', *Political Quarterly*, 1930, pp. 104–9.

53. With apologies to Z. Bauman, *Between Class and Elite*, p. 299.

METHODOLOGICAL STUDIES

5. Some Comments on the Use of Directories in Research on Elites, with Particular Reference to the Twentieth-Century Supplements of the Dictionary of National Biography

COLIN BELL

> Not of the great only you deign to tell
> The stars by which we steer
> But lights out the night that flashed and fell
> Tonight again are here
>
> SIR HENRY NEWBOLT

Introduction

In the literature on the composition of elites we frequently notice remarks to the effect that there are problems about defining precisely who the elite are. Yet despite the real theoretical problem of the boundary between the elite and the non-elite in practice we find that the elite is all too easily bounded. The familiar theoretical tautology of many elite studies – variations on the theme that those who have power are the elite and the elite are those who have power, is frequently confounded for all practical purposes with a procedural tautology, the theme of which is that the elite have entries in directories and that the entries in directories are the elite. The purpose of this brief paper is to remind its readers that entries in a directory are the end product of a social process of nomination that can be studied in its own right. This must be understood as a substantive as well as a methodological point for these nomination processes are good data and may be as significant in studying the elite as is describing the entries in directories. The systematic biases of directory entries are clues to the social imagery of directory editors – the biases to be discovered in directories are the result of the editors' view of the social system.

Directory-Based Research on Elites

Directories will certainly go on being used in research on elites. *Who's Whos, Who Was Whos, Peerages, Dictionaries of National Biography*

(DNB), and the like are peculiarly seductive sources of data. They appear to yield easily data on what Lasswell over twenty years ago said was needed – 'from whom to whom and systematic trend analysis'.[1] This is no doubt why directories have provided the basic data for notable studies by amongst others: C. Wright Mills, Baltzell, Warner and Abegglen, Bendix and Geiger.[2] In addition directories, unlike the subjects in them, are easily available, do not refuse to be interviewed and so on. The data contained in each entry are frequently full (for example the data in each entry in the British DNB are fuller than that used by Blau and Duncan in their now classic *American Occupational Structure*), always well ordered alphabetically and cross-referenced and apparently certified correct. Upon closer investigation however many analysts have noticed biases in these directories – usually in a somewhat perfunctory early paragraph. These biases are rarely investigated systematically or treated as data in themselves. An exception to this are Digby Baltzell's remarks on *Who's Who in America*, which he pointed out was too heavily weighted towards educators and churchmen relative to the organising elites of business, government and labour; that it is none too helpful about power in America as many who exercise it are not respectable and so do not merit an entry; and that some people are included more because of their prestige or prominence than because of any real achievement in a functional sense.[3] These biases are significant when one remembers that assertions as to whether or not the American social structure is becoming more rigid are made on the basis of what is essentially a description of the contents of directories.[4] Baltzell's comments isolate three problems in the study of elites, firstly that of the *composition* of the elite in general and its *nomination* in particular; secondly of the *power* of the elite; and lastly the *resource* base of particular parts of the elite. In this paper we shall be concerned mainly with the first and last problem. The last problem – that of the changing resource base – can be seen as the underlying central sociological hypothesis of elite studies that have resorted to directories for their data.

'*From Ascription to Achievement*'

This Parsonian neologism sums up the hypothesis that many wish to test on data from directories. Suzanne Keller puts it like this, 'recruitment mechanisms, however varied in practice, reflect only two fundamental principles: recruitment on the basis of biological (and implicitly, social) inheritance and recruitment on the basis of personal talents and achievements'.[5] Once you regard elite composition as a sequence of change in the biographical characteristics of those who are members of the elite, that is in the comparative frequency of selected characteristics in the life histories of elite members at different times, as Lasswell and his collaborators do, then not only are directories the most obvious source of data but the 'ascription to achievement' is the most likely analytical framework. From this follows two opposed positions that may be called the 'change' and the 'continuity' positions respectively.

Daniel Lerner's remarks in a volume he wrote with Lasswell are representative of the former position:

> The most obvious transformation of the European elite by true revolutionary movements was in terms of social origins. Under the imperial dynasties that ruled most of Europe during long centuries, people were defined as elite *by birth*. Status was inherited by the test of blood. The democratic transformation certified by the American and French Revolutions at the end of the eighteenth century changed all this. Under the new democratic dispensation, status was earned by the test of merit. Birth was replaced by skill as the central criterion of elite membership[6] [his emphasis].

In contrast to this view of the composition of elites in the 'democratic' countries (which means all the advanced industrial powers except Russia, Italy and Germany), Max Beloff claims that Britain had the

> . . . additional advantage that derives from the continuity of institutions and of personnel. There has been no radical break of the kind that gives an air of unreality to so much discussions of Russian foreign policy, where one has to take into account the almost total replacement of one *governing elite* and its institutions by another. No doubt the *British elite* has evolved over this period, but there has been no abrupt transformation. The permanent hierarchies, civil and military, have a continuous history, and in political life one parliament succeeds another with a carry-over of membership sufficient to make the process of change a continuous one.[7]

Directories such as the DNB are frequently resorted to in an attempt

163

to resolve the conflict between the 'change' and the 'continuity' position on elite composition.

The DNB as a Source of Data

The editors of the DNB have disapproved of the use to which their Dictionary, along with other directories, has been put by social scientists interested in the composition of the elite. Sir Sydney Lee, the DNB's second editor, wrote in his *Principles of Biography* that the

> true biography is no handmaid of ethical instruction. Its purpose is not that of history. It does not exist to serve biological or anthropological science. Any assistance that biography renders these three great interests — ethical, historical, and scientific — should be accidental; such aid is neither essential nor obligatory.[8]

What is both essential and obligatory is that the social scientist who wishes to use the DNB as a source of data for studying say, social mobility or the changing composition of the elite, should investigate the DNB carefully. How are the biographies collected, how is it decided who should be included? The answers to these questions involve an understanding of the social construction of this, and other directories. Without this understanding the DNB is indeed the 'hideous package' to which its founding editor, Sir Leslie Stephen was wont to refer.[9] In attempting to test the 'from ascription to achievement' hypothesis there are particular difficulties in using the DNB. In a *Peerage* all the entries are high on ascriptive rank — though of course this high position is itself finely divided. In the DNB *all* are high on achieved rank — though some may also have high ascribed rank. *Who's Who* combines both those high on ascribed and achieved rank and unlike the DNB and the *Peerages* some people refuse to go in. The entries in the DNB are 'obituaries' — the assessments of the achievements may be tempered by affection but nobody refuses permission for an entry to the DNB. Nobody 'opts out'. Neither *Who's Who* nor the DNB admit to coercion or persuasion — entries are conferred not bought.[10] There is a sense in which conferment of an entry in the DNB is nomination or confirmation of membership of the elite. Given that authority, achievements and rewards are unequally distributed in any society, those who finish enshrined in the DNB score very highly on at least one of these dimensions. There are though considerable differences in the deference given to high scores on these dimensions such that not all of the high scorers will be considered worthy of the DNB.

164

Some of the Worthies (as the entries to the DNB are collectively known) are included regardless of the achievements, e.g. King George V at one extreme whereas others are there only for their achievements. However, this now familiar ascription/achievement dimension is a distinction that is difficult to maintain. One Duke may be a great scientist while another may achieve nothing of note yet both Dukes may get an entry in the DNB. In her Encyclopaedia article Keller sums up this point:

> Conspicuous achievements are still often facilitated if not determined by high social and economic position, since wealth and high social standing open many doors to aspiring candidates and instil in them great expectations for worldly success.[11]

The nexus between achievement and ascription is not easily unravelled.

We are told somewhat cryptically in the first twentieth-century supplement to the DNB, the 1901–11 volume, that 'the principles of selection and treatment are already familiar'. As this was written in the first twentieth-century supplement it can only refer to the main DNB. Lord Annan, in his masterful biography of Leslie Stephen, tells us that 'By printing twice a year in the *Athenaeum* the names which were considered worthy of inclusion and by asking readers to suggest additions, Stephen escaped the charge of editorial partiality. . . .'[12] For the twentieth-century supplements, whilst Stephen and his successors can escape one kind of charge of editorial partiality they are open to others – for example, that of viewing the world from the position of upper middle-class literary intellectuals. Whilst the occasional trade unionist, especially if he becomes an MP, thrusts himself into view, many industrialists do not. They seem surest where rank and hierarchy can be clearly established and where their taste as literary academics can be called into play – bishops, generals and novelists are their *forte*. But what is the industrial equivalent of being the Bishop of Bath and Wells? The editors of the first volume classified the Worthies in that volume (who include Queen Victoria and Edward VII) in a way that easily shows the way their minds worked. They wrote '. . . the memoirs embrace comprehensively all branches of the nations and the empire's activity' (this should be treated as a hypothesis). They went on pointing to a difficulty that has also to be faced by any one who attempts to use the DNB as a data source. 'In any endeavour to classify the vocations of the persons commemorated,

165

allowance must be made for the circumstance that in a certain proportion of cases the same person has gained distinction in more fields than one.' However they claim that

> If the chief single claim to notice be alone admitted in each instance the callings of those whose careers are described in (the 1901–11) volume may be broadly catalogued under general headings[13] thus:

	N	%
1. Administration of government at home, in India and the colonies	194	11·9
2. Army and Navy	120	7·3
3. Art (including architecture, music and the stage)	225	13·8
4. Commerce and Agriculture	50	3·1
5. Law	74	4·5
6. Literature (including journalism, philology, philosophy, printing and lexicography)	372	22·7
7. Religion	173	10·6
8. Science (including engineering, medicine, surgery and exploration)	291	17·8
9. Social reform (including philanthropy and education)	97	5·9
10. Sport	39	2·4
TOTAL	1635	100·0

The classification is of course a sociological hodge-podge, confounding further the confusion between occupation and industry. Academics for example turn up under Art, Law, Literature, Religion, Science and Social Reform. It is predominantly a male elite – in the 1901–11 volume, 71 (4·3 per cent) of the entries were women, included 'on account of services rendered in art, literature, science and social or educational reform'.

If systematic comparisons are made between the DNB and other sources then the kind of bias in any study of elite composition based only on the DNB can be revealed. Erikson's study of British industrialists[14] is based on the biographies of 525 steel manufacturers operating between 1850 and 1950, and 475 Nottingham hosiers. The two groups included only active managing partners; chairmen of limited companies; vice-chairmen or deputy chairmen; managing directors; general managers of large partnerships or sole ownership firms.

In the study of the steel industry only manufacturers using the Bessemer or open hearth process qualified for inclusion in order to limit the scope of the inquiry to the heavy steel industry and then to the larger type of public company in contrast to the relatively small, less heavily capitalised, manufacturing units of the hosiery industry.

While differing from the point of view of company size these two industries were similar in that they both experienced their main period of innovation and of change to 'modern' factory production methods during the second half of the nineteenth century.

It was not possible to separate out from this sample a complete group of industrialists who would qualify for entry to the post-1901 DNB as their dates of death are seldom given. Out of the total of 525 steel men, twenty-three appear in the DNB of which twelve are in the post-1901 volumes. None of the hosiers are in the post-1901 DNB and only two are in the pre-twentieth-century volumes.

The list of men and women compiled from John Gross' study[15] of men of letters is more haphazard and not necessarily complete – some of the people mentioned in the book are not in the index; but as he gives dates it was possible to eliminate fairly accurately those who would not have been eligible for inclusion in the 1901–50 DNB volumes. All the people picked out would fit into the DNB category of the institutional realm of literature. At least nine could possibly have died too late to have been eligible for the last DNB volume, but are not traceable in any other directory. From a possible total of 145 eligibles 107 are included in the DNB.

The steel men famous as innovators and inventors are mainly in the pre-1901 DNB. Only one of the twelve in the twentieth-century volumes is remembered chiefly as an inventor and FRS. All of the twelve are either owners or company chairmen. Apart from H. L. Hichens who was chairman of Cammell Laird from 1911 until 1941 and is remembered for the part he played in the reconstruction of the firm and for his modern attitude to labour relations, they all held some position of distinction in addition to that of company head. One was part founder and one-time president of the Institute of Iron and Steel and received a baronetcy for services to the industry. The rest held recognised positions outside the steel industry; seven, of whom six received hereditary titles, were MPs. Two were the sons of peers. One of these was knighted for his public services as a member of a government commission. The other inherited the title of Duke of Devonshire and was also noted as a promoter of science and engineering teaching at Cambridge University by the provision of several generous endowments.

It would seem that if a Worthy achieves in a non-traditional sphere, prior recognition of an individual's elite status by other members of the elite is a necessary precondition for inclusion in the DNB. The only two Nottingham hosiers included in the DNB were nationally known as radical MPs. One of these is Samuel Morley. His son is not in, despite the fact that he was created 1st Baron Hollenden and became head of the family firm which was one of the oldest established and largest hosiery manufacturers in England and had by this time expanded its operations outside the Nottingham area.

The problems in the case of the men and women of letters is to decide in certain cases why they have been excluded from the dictionary. Popular or critical success during a writer's lifetime, or membership of the literary circles represented in the old established or widely recognised literary reviews and journals, seems a fairly good guarantee for inclusion but there are exceptions to this rule that seem pretty arbitary. Writers neither successful nor respectable as far as contemporary literary tastes were concerned probably tend to be excluded. Rupert Brooke is in, Wilfred Owen not. (Gerald Manley Hopkins who died in 1889 is another example of a now well-known poet not in the DNB.) All the critics picked out for special mention by John Gross are in the DNB, except for Christopher Caudwell, a Marxist writer killed in 1937 while still in his twenties. The best guarantee for non-inclusion is obviously to be 'unrespectable' *and* short-lived.

The Social Process of Nomination

Inclusion in the DNB is the end product of a rather inarticulate sifting of obituaries and utilisation of the network of social relationships of people who 'know'. That the whole process is thought to be obvious should put the sociologist on his guard. We were told that 'in any volume the people who obviously go in amount to about 80 per cent and the remainder just have to put up a fight for it . . . have to convince us of their claim in one way or another'.[16] As for more precise criteria:

> sometimes a man will have done just one thing of significance –
> like inventing the vacuum cleaner; or he is someone *whom we*

168

think people will still want to know about in fifty years time.[17]
[italics added]

Despite our earlier comments about rank, those at the DNB say that, 'in the professions the very top rank is tantamount to automatic inclusion, for if they don't who does, but we think of them in terms of individuals getting in and not in terms of rank.' Steadfast adherence to achievement criteria characterises the DNB editorial policy. The actual process was described like this:

> Basically we start from the obituaries, mainly those in *The Times*. I put these into professions and number them up (a), (b), (c), which being interpreted means Possible, Marginal, Reject. The lists are made up along these lines and, in the case of people like soldiers, lawyers, doctors, they are sent to two or three personal contacts in those professions who are asked to number them up according to their own way of thinking. We then sort out the results and the answer is usually pretty clear.
>
> There is a committee to deal with more general lists such as authors, public men, and so on. It has no fixed membership or time for meeting: from time to time a few knowledgeable people are invited to meet and give their views on who should go in and suggestions for contributors of the notices.

What 'knowledgeable' means here covers a multitude of taken-for-granted assumptions about the British social structure – the elite nominates its successors. They share a similar social imagery. Those included in the DNB are a rather peculiar elite biased towards the established professions and *literatures*. There is of course nothing wrong with studying such an elite but at least we should be aware that that is what is being studied and probably most social scientists would find the nomination process more interesting than the end result.

NOTES

1. Harold D. Lasswell, *et al.*, *The Comparative Study of Elites*, Hoover Institute Studies, Stanford, 1952, p. 22.
2. C. Wright Mills, 'The American Business Elite: a Collective Portrait', *J. Econ. Hist.*, No. 5, 1945; E. Digby Baltzwell, *Philadelphia Gentleman: The Making of a National Upper Class*, Free Press of

Glencoe, New York, 1958; W. Lloyd Warner and J. C. Abegglen, *Occupational Mobility in American Business and Industry 1928–1952*, University of Minnesota Press, Minneapolis, 1955; R. Bendix and F. W. Howton, 'Social Mobility and the American Business Elite', *British Journal of Sociology*, Vol. 8, 1957; T. Geiger, 'Intelligentia', *Acta Sociologica*, Vol. 1, 1955.

3. E. Digby Baltzwell, 'Who's Who in America' and 'The Social Register: Elite and Upper Class Indexes in Metropolitan America', in R. Bendix and S. M. Lipset, *Class, Status and Power*, 2nd edition, Routledge & Kegan Paul, London, 1967, p. 271.

4. See for example Bendix and Howton, op. cit.

5. Suzanne Keller, 'Elites', *Int. Encl. of the Social Sciences*, Macmillan Free Press, New York, Vol. 5, p. 28.

6. Daniel Lerner (with Harold D. Lasswell), *World Revolutionary Elites: Studies in Coercive Ideological Movements*, MIT Press, Cambridge, Mass., 1965, p. 258.

7. Max Beloff, *Imperial Sunset, Vol. I: Britains Literal Empire 1897–1921*, Methuen, London, 1969, p. 8.

8. Sydney Lee, *Elizabethan and Other Essays*, Oxford University Press, Oxford, 1928, p. 39.

9. Quoted in Noel Annan, *Leslie Stephen, his Thought and Character in Relation to his Time*, Harvard University Press, Cambridge, Mass., 1952, p. 79.

10. The differences between types of directories can be summarised like this:

High Status by:

	Ascription	Achievement	Can opt out
Peerages	**	–	x
Who's Who	*	*	√
DNB	*	**	x

** necessary and sufficient condition of entry
* sufficient condition of entry
– irrelevant
√ happens
x does not happen.

11. Keller, op. cit., p. 28.

12. Annan, op. cit., p. 77.

13. The 1922–30 volume of the DNB uses a different classification: Royalty, Politicians, Dominion Statesmen, Colonial Administrator,

Services, Letters and Scholarship, Science and Engineering, Great Adventurers. The 1941–50 volume's preface reflects that on the Worthies included in the following manner,

Some met violent deaths, by accident or by enemy action; a few died by their own hand. Most, however, their labours done, died in their own beds. These labours varied exceedingly [note the assumption that they had all done something]. Yet in one way or another, all the men and women to be met here revealed in their several labours qualities which marked them out from among their fellows.

14. Charlotte Erikson, *British Industrialists: Steel and Hosiery, 1850–1950*, Cambridge University Press, Cambridge, 1959.

15. John Gross, *The Rise and Fall of the Man of Letters*, Weidenfeld & Nicolson, London, 1969.

16. All quotations in this section are from private communications from the editorial office of the DNB.

17. An additional difficulty is that the size of the volume changes from decade to decade – the first being about twice the size of any since. The chances of 'making the grade' (their term) is effected by the size of the volume.

'And the marginal people will have a better chance of getting in in some decades when there have been fewer swells than they will in others.'

6. Some Social and Educational Characteristics of Selected Elite Groups in Contemporary Britain: A Research Note based on a 'K means' Cluster Analysis

JOHN AND FRANCES WAKEFORD AND
DOUGLAS BENSON

The vagueness and variety of conceptual definition of the notion of elite evident in classical elite theory persists in contemporary terminological wrangles. Perhaps it is partly a reflection of his confidence that he has found the 'missing link' which 'points the way to gathering the right facts' that led to Kadushin's statement that 'all the parts for building good elite studies are, in fact, lying about'.[1] His optimism does not yet seem warranted, for certainly few British sociologists can claim to have provided or attempted to provide empirical data to substantiate a particular identification of a dominant group or groups in Britain. In fact few would probably claim to have added significantly to Bottomore's discussion of elite theories published nearly a decade ago.[2] W. L. Guttsman's study, *The British Political Elite*, and Lupton and Wilson's insights gleaned from the disclosures of the Bank Rate Tribunal remain as two of the more notable but rather solitary published empirical investigations of elite groups in Britain until the Cambridge research programme yields results.[3]

The limited quantity and sometimes ambiguous quality of such studies as do exist has not discouraged assertions and counter-assertions. For example Blondel writes·

> The 30 per cent or so of old Etonians whom one finds in the Cabinet, in the banks, in the insurance companies, have greater influence than their numbers warrant, because, being old Etonians, they have more contacts. They supply information about other old Etonians who are influential in other walks of life; they are go-betweens, they are the instruments of compromises in the sectors of British political, social, and economic life in which they are numerous.[4]

Anthony Sampson feels in a position to assert, however, that significant changes have taken place and suggests that during the 1960s 'clever grammar school boys', 'the new meritocrats', have been displacing 'the old boy nets of ruling families and public schools'.[5] John Rex, on the other hand, explicitly puts forward a ruling class thesis and suggests that 'a model of a ruling class effectively exercising economic and political power, while also organising legitimation and consent to its rule' is still appropriate for Britain.[6]

In the literature various 'new class' theses vie with more general assertions about 'classlessness' and, despite certain research findings to the contrary, about *embourgeoisment* in terms of cultural values and political outlook, Burnham referred to a 'managerial class', Galbraith more recently has referred to the educational and scientific 'estate', and Dahrendorf to a 'service class' working with the ruling groups and elites.[7] Giddens has specifically focused on assertions about the supposed 'decomposition' of class relationships 'at the top':

> The view that the ruling class has ceded place to a more amorphous and differentiated set of 'leadership groups'.[8] There is no longer, it is argued, a distinctive 'upper class', still less a 'ruling class', in contemporary Britain. Elites are no longer drawn from a background of minority privilege, and they are no longer cohered by the common social and moral ties which were once created by the gentlemanly ethos of the 'Clarendon' schools (i.e. the top nine, public schools) and the ancient universities.[9]

Discussion of such evidence as is available asserts that members of certain delineated elite groups share links through kinship, common schooling at a small number of prestigious schools, common membership of a few colleges at the two ancient English Universities and of a small number of exclusive London clubs and a range of other channels of everyday association. Often it is further suggested that such groups are relatively 'closed', with a common culture contributing to a certain *rapprochement* over the particular issues of the day. Westergaard for instance favours a 'non-pluralist' perspective and delimits a dominant grouping thus:

> The dominant grouping is that of a small, homogeneous *elite* of wealth and private corporate property — politically entrenched in the leadership of the Conservative Party; strongly represented in, or linked with, a variety of public and private bodies; assured of

173

the general support of the press, if not at the overt political level of the publicly controlled mass media; its members sharing for a large part a common, exclusive educational background, and united by fairly close ties of kinship and everyday association . . . It is an *elite* which, while its economic base is that of financial and industrial capital, yet has its own uniquely British features, in part inherited from the agrarian-mercantile nobility and gentry of the pre-industrial era. It is neither a tightly closed group – indeed much of its viability may derive from its absorbtive capacity – nor a monolithically united one. But internal divisions remain generally confined to particular issues, and do not develop into major fissures of a durable kind.[10]

Studies in this field have generally been limited to the analysis of a single link at a time – for instance the proportions of various elite groups who have attended the same school, attended the same university or were members of the same club. Thus it has been difficult to distinguish the contribution made by each link – a crucial issue when such factors are interactive.[11] The development of a new technique for seeking out clusters among a large number of individuals and using a number of attributes simultaneously provided the opportunity to examine which individuals among the 'elite' share various selected educational and social characteristics to the greatest degree.

Method

As Giddens has emphasised, until some working definitions have been measured against sociological 'realities' in systematic research, the decision to include or exclude positions is rather arbitrary. We have basically used Bottomore's definition of the term 'elite(s)' as now generally applied 'to functional, mainly occupational, groups which have high status (for whatever reason) in a society'.[12] But we have also included the top wealth-holders, the upper stratum of the aristocracy and life peers, and like Giddens we have cast the net wide, and although there are differences, we have included a similar range of groups with a cut-off at a similar level to that which he proposes.[13]

Twenty-one categories of people considered representative of those prominent in public life were selected for this study, people who, it might generally be agreed, were in a position to be exercising some of the greatest political and economic power in Britain. Using available published sources their membership was listed and details recorded of date of birth, social background, kinship links, education, club

174

membership and interests.[14] At this stage three categories originally
intended for inclusion had to be omitted through lack of information
– the directors of the four largest finance houses, property companies
and investment trusts – but data on the secondary schooling, higher
education and club membership and other associations of the people
holding 934 of the 1,141 positions in the other eighteen categories
(82 per cent) was obtained to provide the basis for further analysis.

TABLE 1: *Membership of eighteen selected elite groups, 1971*

	Number in group	Number included in study
The Cabinet	40	40
Senior Civil Servants (Permanent Secretaries and Permanent Under Secretaries with salary at least £9,000 per annum)	19	17
The Wealthiest Businessmen (from The Times 15.12.67. 'The £400m League')	41	29
The Chairman of the fifty largest industrial companies (from The Times 1000 1970–71)[1]	50	32
Board Members of the major nationalised industries (BEA, BOAC, National Coal Board, Electricity and Gas Councils, Railways Board, Steel Corporation and the Post Office)	70	59
Senior Officers in the Armed Forces		
(i) Army – (Field Marshals, Lieutenant Generals and Major Generals)	124	106
(ii) Navy – (Admirals of the Fleet, Vice and Rear Admirals)	80	46
(iii) Air Force – (Marshals, Air Chief Marshals and Air Marshals)	31	28
Directors of the Bank of England	19	19
Directors of the 'Big Four' clearing banks (Barclays, Lloyds, Midland and National Westminster)	113	90
Directors of the four major British insurance companies (Prudential Assurance, Royal Insurance, Legal and General, Commercial Union)	67	40

175

The Monopolies Commission	18	15
Bishops of the Church of England	37	35
University Vice Chancellors and Principals[2]	120	103
Controllers of the media (Governors of the BBC, Members of the Independent Television Authority and the Proprietors of the seven major national daily newpapers)	33	26
High Court Judges	91	81
Top Aristocracy (Dukes and Royal Dukes)	21	18
Life Peers	167	150
TOTAL	1,141	934

Notes:

1. *The Times 1000: Leading Companies in Britain and Overseas,* Times Newspapers, London, 1971.

2. For definition see P. Collins and J. Millan, 'University Chancellors, Vice Chancellors and College Principals', *Sociology,* Vol. 3, no. 1, 1969. See also A. H. Halsey and M. A. Trow, *The British Academics,* Faber, London, 1971, pp. 160ff.

There has been a rapid increase in the techniques available for numerical classification over the last decade, and the most important consideration for sociological analysis is the ability of a number of these more recent strategies to handle classificatory data, a facility which is not available with Inverse Factor Analysis (Q-analysis). One of these strategies – the K-means clustering procedure – was employed in the present study. After splitting the population of 934 randomly into two halves A and B the data was classified into disjoint clusters using the RELOC option available within the CLUSTAN 1A computer package.[15]

Each split half was initially randomly classified into thirteen clusters ($k = 13$). The similarity between each object and the k centroids were then computed. Each object, considered in turn, was then moved between clusters if this results in a reduction in the error sum of squared distance between the objects and the centroid of their cluster. The centroid of the two relevant clusters are recalculated at each iteration. The initial starting points for each cluster are thus successively modified during each iteration of the relocation cycle. Stability is reached when no further re-allocation takes place. There is a danger that within certain data sets convergence to stability may not obtain. To prevent the occurrence of oscillation a maximum value can be placed on the number of relocation cycles to be gone through. In this study the maximum value assigned was ten, sufficient for most analyses.

The next stage involves the reduction of the k clusters to k–1. This is obtained by fusing the two 'nearest' clusters. The programme then returns to the relocation phase until stability is reached for the k–1 clusters. At the end of each relocation phase the results for that value of k are then printed out. All of the members of each sample were classified into one of the clusters. That is the 'residue' option was not used. The result of this is that 'unclassifiable' objects have been classified, reducing the homogeneity of the resultant clusters.

TABLE 2: *Secondary Schooling of those holding elite positions, 1971*

	N	%
Eton	117	13
Winchester, Harrow, Rugby, Charterhouse or Marlborough (the 'Clarendon' group of schools)	128	14
One of the other seventy-six major English Public Boarding Schools[1]	191	20
Other Public or Private School (including Scottish private schools and all direct grant schools)	212	23
Grammar School	207	22
Other State Secondary School	29	3
Secondary education abroad	32	3
No secondary education	15	2
Privately educated	6	1

Note:

1. All independent boarding schools in England and Wales with the headmaster a member of the Headmasters' Conference and which have at least a third, and at least 200 boarders. (Full the full list see John Wakeford, *The Cloistered Elite*, Macmillan, London, 1969, pp. 213–14.)

From an examination of the dendograms produced by the programme it was decided to consider the results at the eight cluster level
in one half (A) and the ten cluster level in the other (B).

Results

The figures for the whole group of 934 elite positions are summarised
in Tables 2, 3 and 4.[16]

Ninety-seven per cent of the elite positions are held by men, mostly
aged between fifty and seventy and married in the 1930s or 1940s.
Thirteen per cent had attended a single school (Eton) between the two
world wars, 14 per cent the other five major elite 'Clarendon' group of
public schools, 20 per cent one of the other major public boarding
schools and 23 per cent some other private or direct grant school.
Only 3 per cent had attended an 'ordinary' secondary school of the
type attended by over three-quarters of the population. Half of the
total had been to one of the two ancient universities while one-fifth
had had no higher education at all. Seventy-five per cent were members of at least one of a small number of exclusive London and
provincial clubs.

TABLE 3: *Higher Education of those holding elite positions*[1]

	N	%
Cambridge University	243	26
Oxford University	228	24
London University	67	7
Other English University	47	5
Other University in Great Britain (including		
Trinity College, Dublin)	69	7
University abroad	28	3
Military academy (Sandhurst or Woolwich)	68	7
Dartmouth College	23	3
Cranwell	9	1
No Higher Education	186	20
Technical College	29	3

Note:

1. Some attended more than one institution. Figures indicate
attendance and do not necessarily indicate that a degree or other
qualification was obtained.

178

TABLE 4: *Reported Club Membership of those holding elite positions*

	N
Athenaeum	117
Army and Navy, or Naval and Military	66
Carlton	55
Brooks's	52
MCC (Lord's)	51
Royal Automobile or Royal Scottish Automobile	42
Pratt's	38
United Service	37
Reform	34
White's	34
Oxford and Cambridge University	32
Royal Yatch Squadron	32
Cavalry	26
United University	24
Turf	23
Garrick	23
Boodle's	20
Beefsteak	16
The Bath	15
Caledonian	15
Hurlingham	15
Travellers'	15
Buck's	14
Savile	14
Leander	13
Royal Thames Yacht	11
Royal Ocean Racing	10
University Women's	10
Junior Carlton	8
Alpine	7
Savage	5
TOTAL	874

Eight other London clubs with one or two members from the elite	10
National political associations	8
Other sporting clubs	92

179

Other forces clubs	55
Clubs abroad	35
Other, mainly provincial, clubs	145

| No club membership indicated | 238 |

The clustering procedure produced an indication of seven distinct clusters which included 75 per cent of the population in the study. Although there were weaker indications of other groupings, in no case did they appear in both split halves. The first three, referred to in turn as *The Vice Chancellors, The Military* and *The Judiciary* emerge clearly. They, together with a rather different cluster centred on the Life Peers, clearly contrast with the three other clusters, discussed later, which were largely based on educational background.

The *Vice Chancellors* are outstanding for the high proportion with grammar school education. Few had attended major public schools. Although most had been at either Oxford or Cambridge, the group also contained a higher proportion of members who had been at Scottish, Welsh and Irish universities than the rest of the elite. Apart from a high proportion with membership of the Atheneum (and for women the University Women's Club) the other affiliations demonstrated are few.

TABLE 5: *Cluster 1: The Vice Chancellors*[1]

	A N=45	B N=45
Present Affiliation		
Vice Chancellors	43	45
Life Peer	1	—
Senior Civil Servant	1	—
School		
Eton	—	1
'Clarendon' Group of schools	2	3
Public Boarding School	3	5
Other Public or Direct Grant School	13	8
Grammar School	24	26
Other State Secondary School	4	—
Private Education	—	1
Abroad	1	1

Higher Education
Oxford	18	17
Cambridge	10	9
London University	6	5
Other English University	2	9
Other University in Great Britain	15	9
Abroad	3	2

Other Affiliations (past and present)
Controllers of the media	1	—
Life Peers	1	1
Business and Banking	2	—
Law (other than High Court Judges)	1	—

Club Membership[2]
Athenaeum	23	21
Oxford and Cambridge Universities	3	1
Savile	4	—
United University	4	1
University Women's	4	4
Other clubs (mainly provincial)	6	6
Other sporting clubs	3	—
Total club membership	56	43
No club membership	7	14

Binary Frequencies Ratio > 2 in both halves[3]
Grammar School	2·5	2·5
Other University in Great Britain	4·5	2·7
Female	2·6	4·0
Atheneum	4·4	3·5
University Women's Club	6·9	10·4

Notes:

1. The title of each cluster refers to the largest common factor(s) and does not indicate that all members share this attribute.

2. All clubs with more than one member in the cluster.

3. The 'Binary Frequencies Ratio' is the percentage occurrence in the cluster divided by the percentage occurrence overall. (A value of 1 would indicate a frequency in the cluster *equal* to that in the whole population, a value of 2 a frequency in the cluster *double* that in the whole population etc.)

The second cluster, *The Military*, is made up almost entirely of senior army officers, with a common education at one of the two military academies (amalgamated in 1946). Nearly all were members of at least one London club, particularly popular being the Army and Navy, Cavalry, Naval and Military, and United Service. They also show a tendency to have attended a small number of the major public schools. Of all the clusters this shows the greatest similarity of age, nearly all members being aged between fifty and sixty in 1971. Thus the sharing, in many cases as contemporaries, of school and military college membership, backed by common club membership suggests a second significant grouping among the elite.

TABLE 6: *Cluster 2: The Military*

	A N=33	B N=37
Present Affiliation		
Senior Army Officers	33	34
Cabinet	—	1
Judiciary	—	1
Life Peer	—	1
School		
Eton	1	2
'Clarendon' Group of schools	10	7
Public Boarding School	19	16
Other Public or Direct Grant School	2	2
Grammar School	1	10
Higher Education		
Oxford	2	2
Cambridge	4	1
London University	—	2
Other English University	1	2
Other University in Great Britain	—	1
Sandhurst or Woolwich	27	25
No Higher Education	2	4
Other Affiliations		
Business and Banking	1	2
Law	—	1
Aristocracy	—	1

182

Club Membership

Army and Navy (or Naval and Military)	19	24
Cavalry	2	7
MCC (Lords)	2	1
Royal Yacht Squadron	3	—
United Service	5	3
Clubs abroad	3	1
Other clubs (mainly provincial)	3	1
Other sporting clubs	6	7
Other forces clubs	3	2
Total club membership	50	54
No club membership	1	1

Binary Frequencies Ratio > 2 in both halves

Public Boarding School	2·7	2·2
Sandhurst/Woolwich	11·6	9·0
Army and Navy/Naval and Military Clubs	9·6	8·0
Cavalry Club	2·2	6·8
United Service Club	3·7	2·1

Most of *The Judiciary* had attended a public boarding school, a high proportion at one of the five 'Clarendon' group of schools. The majority (nearly all of one of the split halves) had been at a single university, Oxford. Though less evidently than 'The Military', many were members of a small group of clubs.

TABLE 7: *Cluster 3: The Judiciary*

	A N=28	B N=57
Present Affiliation		
High Court Judges	28	22
Life Peers	—	12
Directors of the 'Big Four' banks	—	5
Church of England Bishops	—	4
Senior Civil Servants	—	3
Monopolies Commission	—	3
Senior Army Officers	—	3
Directors of the Bank of England	—	2
Cabinet	—	1
Senior Air Force Officer	—	1
Chairman of one of the largest fifty companies	—	1

School		
Eton	1	1
'Clarendon' Group of schools	9	20
Public Boarding School	14	13
Other Public or Direct Grant Schools	2	18
Grammar School	2	3
Other State Secondary Schools	—	1
Abroad	—	2

Higher Education		
Oxford	16	55
Cambridge	12	1
London University	1	2
Other English University	—	2
Other University in Great Britain	1	2
Abroad	—	5

Other Affiliations		
Director of one of the 'Big Four' banks	—	1
Vice Chancellors	—	2
Life Peers	5	1
Law (other than High Court Judges)	—	4
Aristocracy	1	—
Political organisations: Conservative	2	1
Liberal	—	1
Labour	1	1

Club Membership		
Atheneum	3	7
Garrick	6	6
Leander	—	2
MCC (Lords)	3	5
Oxford and Cambridge Universities	2	6
Pratt's	1	3
Reform	—	3
Royal Yacht Squadron	—	2
Travellers'	—	2
United University	2	3
Other clubs (mainly provincial)	4	8
Other forces clubs	—	3
Total club memberships	36	71
No club memberships	7	15

184

Binary Frequencies Ratio > 2 in both halves

'Clarendon' Group of schools	2·3	2·6
Oxford University	2·4	3·8
Garrick	9·1	4·1
Junior Carlton	3·3	2·7
Oxford and Cambridge Universities (club)	2·4	2·7
United University	2·6	2·2

The fourth cluster, based on Life Peers, shows a different pattern of associations. Apart from the different basis for membership, it has characteristics which contrast strikingly with the three previous clusters. It is more heterogeneous, having members from a considerable range of the eighteen categories; it has a considerable proportion (though still less than half) of members with grammar and other state schooling; it contains some with experience of a technical college and several with neither higher education nor secondary education. It has a greater proportion of women than the rest of the elite, also of the elderly (seventy-year-olds) and participation in Labour Party activities. Only one London club appears, the Reform.

TABLE 8: *Cluster 4: Life Peers*

	A N=44	B N=55
Present Affiliation		
Life Peers	29	29
Wealthiest Businessmen	1	5
Senior Army Officers	—	5
Directors of the 'Big Four' banks	2	3
Aristocracy	1	3
Senior Naval Officers	2	2
Directors of the four major insurance companies	1	2
Senior Air Force Officers	1	2
Boards of nationalised industries	—	3
Monopolies Commission	2	—
Directors of the Bank of England	2	—
Cabinet	1	—
Senior Civil Servant	1	—
Controller of media	1	—
Chairman of one of the fifty largest companies	—	1

185

School		
Eton	1	6
'Clarendon' Group of schools	1	2
Public Boarding School	2	3
Other Public or Direct Grant Schools	8	17
Grammar School	12	13
Other State Secondary Schools	8	1
Private	1	2
Abroad	5	2
Elementary School only	7	5

Higher Education

Oxford	2	2
Cambridge	3	8
London University	3	4
Other English University	1	5
Other University in Great Britain	1	3
Abroad	4	2
Sandhurst/Woolwich	—	4
Cranwell	—	4
Dartmouth	—	4
No Higher Education	28	21
Further Education at Technical College	3	5

Other Affiliations

Wealthiest Businessmen	2	—
Director of the Bank of England	1	—
Aristocracy (Dukes)	—	5
Monopolies Commission	—	1
Senior Army Officers	—	3
Senior Air Force Officers	—	4
Senior Naval Officers	—	3
Boards of nationalised industries	2	—
Life Peers (non-life Peers only)	3	—
Chairman of one of the largest industrial companies	1	—
Business and Banking	5	7
Law	2	1
Aristocracy (other than Dukes)	—	10
Political Organisation: Conservative	1	—
Liberal	1	—
Labour	12	14

Club Membership
Reform	2	—
Total club membership	2	—
No club membership	42	55

Binary Frequencies Ratio > 2 in both halves
Born 1890–1899	2·6	2·6
Married 1910–1919	3·6	4·2
Female	4·0	4·6
Elementary School only	8·3	7·1
State Secondary School (other than Grammar School)	4·6	5·1
Privately educated	3·6	2·8
Further educated at Technical College	2·7	2·5
No Higher Education	2·7	2·3
Associated with political activity (Labour Party)	7·5	7·4
No club membership	3·7	4·0

While the first four clusters are associated most closely with a single current affiliation, the most prominent attribute of members of the other three clusters is their common educational background, a characteristic used to provide our headings — *Eton and Oxford, Public Boarding School and Cambridge* and *Grammar School.*

Both halves of the first of these clusters were almost entirely composed of Old Etonians who had attended Oxford, or to a much lesser extent Cambridge. This was the only cluster to contain any significant number of thirty to forty-year-olds. The great majority of them were members of one or two London clubs, in particular the Beefsteak, Brooks's, Pratt's or White's. While members of the aristocracy, the Cabinet and the boards of directors of the 'Big Four' clearing banks are particularly numerous among them, members of the cluster were to be found as members of fourteen of the eighteen groups that make up the elite population in the study, a position further strengthened by their other affiliations in the business and political spheres.

TABLE 9: *Cluster 5: Eton and Oxford* (*University*)

	A N=46	B N=43
School		
Eton	46	36
'Clarendon' Group of schools	—	4
Grammar School	—	3

Higher Education

Oxford	23	37
Cambridge	16	1
Abroad	—	1
Sandhurst/Woolwich	3	5
No Higher Education	5	1

Present Affiliation

Wealthiest Businessmen	1	1
Cabinet	4	9
Directors of the 'Big Four' banks	13	10
Directors of the four major insurance companies	3	7
Church of England Bishops	—	1
High Court Judges	3	1
Controllers of media	3	—
Aristocracy	4	2
Senior Army Officers	3	2
Senior Air Force Officers	—	1
Boards of nationalised industries	2	—
University Vice Chancellors	1	2
Life Peers	7	6
Chairman of one of the fifty largest companies	2	2

Other Affiliations

Wealthiest Businessmen	—	1
Cabinet	1	1
Directors of the 'Big Four' banks	2	2
Directors of the four major insurance companies	2	2
High Court Judges	—	2
Controllers of the media	2	—
Senior Army Officers	1	—
Senior Air Force Officers	1	—
University Vice Chancellors	2	—
Life Peers	1	4
Business and Banking	15	18
Law	2	8
Aristocracy	9	9
Political Organisation – Conservative	5	6

Club Membership

Army and Navy/Naval and Military	—	—
Beefsteak	5	3
Boodle's	2	1
Brooks's	10	8
Buck's	—	4
Carlton	6	11
Cavalry	4	2
MCC (Lords)	4	5
Pratt's	8	8
RAC/RSAC	—	2
Royal Yacht Squadron	3	—
Turf	6	—
White's	8	6
Clubs abroad	1	2
Other clubs	10	12
Other sporting clubs	3	1
Other forces clubs	7	2
Total club membership	87	83
No club membership	5	5

Binary Frequencies Ratio > 2 in both halves

Born 1930–1939	3·4	2·2
Eton	9·4	5·8
Oxford	2·1	3·4

Present Affiliation:

Cabinet	2·1	4·6
Directors of 'Big Four' banks	3·1	2·3
Aristocracy	4·5	2·4

Other Affiliations:

Cabinet	10·2	10·8
Directors of the 'Big Four' banks	2·5	2·2
Directors of the four major insurance companies	2·0	3·6
Aristocracy	5·1	3·1
Political Organisation – Conservative	3·6	3·6

Club Membership:

Alpine	3·4	2·7
Beefsteak	4·2	8·1
Brooks's	4·2	3·1

Carlton	2·4	4·1
Pratt's	5·4	3·8
White's	5·4	3·4

The second of these clusters was based (to different degrees in the two halves of the sample) on the major public schools and Cambridge. Its members shared no other outstanding attribute beyond containing among them a rather high proportion of bishops of the Church of England, but they are the largest cluster in both split halves of the analysis and provide members for every one of the eighteen categories used in the study.

TABLE 10: *Public Boarding School and Cambridge* (*University*)

	A N=60	B N=95
School		
Eton	—	21
'Clarendon' Group of schools	—	19
Public Boarding School	60	30
Other Public or Direct Grant School	—	19
Grammar School	1	—
Abroad	—	5
Higher Education		
Oxford	5	—
Cambridge	28	95
London University	2	2
Abroad	2	1
Cranwell	1	—
No Higher Education	23	—
Technical College	1	—
Present Affiliation		
Wealthiest Businessmen	4	3
Cabinet	6	7
Senior Civil Servants	2	2
Directors of Bank of England	2	5
Directors of the 'Big Four' banks	9	18
Directors of the four major insurance companies	4	5
Church of England Bishops	6	8

190

High Court Judges	—	15
Controllers of the media	1	3
Aristocracy	—	2
Monopolies Commission	1	—
Senior Army Officers	5	7
Senior Air Force Officers	3	1
Senior Naval Officers	4	—
Boards of nationalised industries	5	3
University Vice Chancellors	1	4
Life Peers	4	9
Chairman of one of the fifty largest companies	3	3

Other Affiliations

Directors of Bank of England	—	1
Directors of the 'Big Four' banks	—	2
Directors of the four major insurance companies	2	4
Boards of nationalised industries	—	1
Life Peers	1	7
Business and Banking	19	27
Law	3	7
Aristocracy	1	10
Political Organisation: Conservative	—	6
Liberal	—	1
Labour	1	1

Club Membership

Army and Navy/Naval and Military	1	2
Athenaeum	5	14
The Bath	2	3
Boodle's	2	5
Brooks's	4	16
Buck's	—	3
Carlton	3	8
Cavalry	4	1
MCC (Lord's)	7	5
Oxford and Cambridge Universities	1	8
Pratt's	1	6
Reform	4	2
RAC/RSAC	3	2
Royal Yacht Squadron	2	7

Royal Thames Yacht Club	—	2
Turf	1	4
United Service	1	2
United University	2	7
White's	3	8
Hurlingham	2	3
Other clubs	11	19
Leander	1	3
Other sporting clubs	5	11
Other forces clubs	3	3
Total club memberships	75	150
No club memberships	18	12

Binary Frequencies Ratio > 2 in both halves

| Church of England Bishops | 2·6 | 2·3 |

The final cluster share almost without exception an education at a maintained grammar or other state secondary school. None had attended public school. The majority had been to one of a wide range of universities, but about one in three had no higher education. Unlike the two previous clusters, a small proportion of them had further education at a technical college. Most were members of London clubs, without favouring any one club except the Reform, and they contributed to fourteen of the eighteen categories, being particularly evident among Senior Civil Servants and the Boards of Nationalised Industries (though still being a small minority of both). They had no members among the Vice Chancellors, the Monopolies Commission, the Directors of the Bank of England or the Aristocracy.

TABLE 11: *Cluster 7: Grammar School*

	A N=56	B N=53
School		
Grammar School	48	53
Other State Secondary Schools	5	—
Abroad	3	—
Higher Education		
Oxford	6	4
Cambridge	6	11

192

London University	10	6
Other English University	5	5
Other University in Great Britain	8	11
University abroad	2	—
Cranwell	1	—
Dartmouth	—	1
No Higher Education	18	15
Technical College	4	5

Present Affiliation

Wealthiest Businessmen	5	—
Cabinet	2	—
Senior Civil Servants	4	2
Director of 'Big Four' banks	1	4
Director of the four major insurance companies	3	3
Church of England Bishops	1	4
High Court Judges	2	3
Controllers of the media	3	8
Senior Army Officers	6	—
Senior Air Force Officers	4	1
Senior Naval Officers	2	6
Boards of nationalised industries	14	16
Life Peers	6	—
Chairman of one of the fifty largest companies	3	2

Other Affiliations

Wealthiest Businessmen	2	—
Director of 'Big Four' banks	—	1
Controllers of the media	—	1
Boards of nationalised industries	2	—
University Vice Chancellor	1	—
Life Peers	1	2

Club Membership

Army and Navy/Naval and Military	2	—
Athenaeum	5	6
The Bath	—	2
Caledonian	1	3
Carlton	2	1
Garrick	1	2

Hurlingham	2	—
MCC (Lord's)	2	—
Reform	8	6
RAC (RSAC)	9	4
Savile	2	—
Travellers'	3	1
United Service	4	3
Clubs abroad	3	—
Other clubs (mainly provincial)	3	5
Other sporting clubs	7	3
Other forces clubs	4	1
Political clubs	—	4
Total club memberships	65	44
No club memberships	8	16

Binary Frequencies Ratio > 2 in both halves

Grammar School	4·1	4·3
Further Education at Technical College	2·8	2·6

Present Affiliation:

Boards of nationalised industries	3·9	4·9
Senior Civil Servants	3·7	2·2
Reform Club	3·3	3·8

An examination of the contribution each of the three clusters based on educational background makes to the eighteen categories which are taken to constitute the elite suggests that the Cabinet contains a particularly high proportion of both Eton and Oxford and Public School and Cambridge clusters. It also indicates the high contribution to the Directors of the 'Big Four' Banks, the four major Insurance Companies and the Aristocracy made by these two clusters.

Cluster 6 contributes nearly one-third of the Church of England Bishops and high proportions of the Wealthiest Businessmen, Senior Civil Servants, the Directors of the Bank of England and High Court Judges. On the other hand members of cluster 7, based on grammar school education provide a significant proportion of the Board Members of the Nationalised Industries, the Controllers of the Media and Senior Civil Servants.

Quite apart from ambiguities in their conceptual assumptions it is clear that empirical studies of this kind raise a considerable number of methodological problems. The data readily available in published form is variable in quality and incomplete. The social ties apparently

TABLE 12: *The Contribution of Clusters 5, 6 and 7 to the eighteen elite categories*

	Cluster 5 Eton and Oxford	Cluster 6 PBS & Cambridge	Cluster 7 Grammar School	Total in study
Wealthiest Businessmen	2	7	5	29
Cabinet	13	13	2	40
Senior Civil Servants	—	4	6	17
Directors Bank of England	—	7	—	19
Directors of 'Big Four' banks	23	27	5	90
Directors of four largest insurance companies	10	9	6	40
Church of England Bishops	1	14	5	35
High Court Judges	4	15	5	81
Controllers of media	3	4	11	26
Aristocracy	6	2	—	18
Monopolies Commission	—	1	—	15
Senior Army Officers	5	12	6	106
Senior Air Force Officers	1	4	5	28
Senior Naval Officers	—	4	8	46
Board Members of nationalised industries	2	8	30	59
University Vice Chancellors	3	5	—	103
Life Peers	13	13	6	150
Chairmen of fifty largest industrial companies	3	6	5	32

most significant for such a study may neither be sought by the compilers of the directories nor willingly exhibited by their contributors.[17] Nevertheless, the consistency shown in the two randomly selected halves of the elite population examined in our analysis lends support to the suggestion that within the upper levels of British public life there are sets of individuals who, it could be maintained in terms of educational experience and current social and occupational links, appear to display at least a potential for a degree of similarity of outlook. This does not of course in any way specify what would be the crucial decisions on which any degree of accord is likely among elite groups, or the manner in which such accord might be reached.

1. C. Kadushin, 'Power, Influence and Social Circles: A New Methodology for Studying Opinion Makers', *American Sociological Review*, Vol. 33, no. 5, October 1968, p. 685. Kadushin maintains in his article that this missing link is the concept of 'social circle' and discusses methods of studying social circles of 'producers of opinions which influence others'. Certainly Diane Crane has used this concept in an interesting way in her study of scientists who work on similar research problems: Diana Crane, 'Social Structure in a Group of Scientists: A Test of the "Invisible College" Hypothesis', *American Sociological Review*, Vol. 34, no. 3, June 1969.

2. T. B. Bottomore, *Elites and Society*, Penguin Books, Harmondsworth, 1966 (first published 1964).

3. W. L. Guttsman, *The British Political Elite*, MacGibbon & Kee, London, 1963, pp. 359ff.; Tom Lupton and C. S. Wilson, 'The Social Background and Connections of "Top Decision Makers" ', *The Manchester School*, Vol. 28, no. 1, January 1959. See also T. J. H. Bishop and R. Wilkinson, *Winchester and the Public School Elite*, Faber, London, 1967; R. K. Kelsall, *Higher Civil Servants in Britain*, Routledge & Kegan Paul, London, 1955; for a more recent example see R. W. Johnson, 'The British Political Elite, 1955–72', *European Journal of Sociology*, Vol. 14, no. 1, June 1973. The conceptual and methodological assumptions of the Cambridge study are contained in Anthony Giddens, 'Elites in the British Class Structure', *Sociological Review*, Vol. 20, no. 3, August 1972; Anthony Giddens, 'Elites', *New Society*, Vol. 22, no. 528, 16 November 1972.

4. J. Blondel, *Voters, Parties and Leaders*, Penguin Books, Harmondsworth, 1963, p. 243.

5. Anthony Sampson, *The New Anatomy of Britain*, Hodder & Stoughton, London, 1972, pp. 659ff.

6. John Rex, 'Power', *New Society*, Vol. 22, no. 522, 25 October 1972, p. 26.

7. See J. Burnham, *The Managerial Revolution*, 1941; J. K. Galbraith, *The New Industrial State*, Penguin, Harmondsworth, 1967; R. Dahrendorf, 'Recent Changes in the Class Structure of European Societies', *Daedalus*, Vol. 93, no. 1, 1964. See also T. B. Bottomore's contribution to *Contemporary Europe: Class, Status and Power*, edited by M. Scotford Archer and S. Giner, Weidenfeld & Nicolson, London, 1971, pp. 388–407.

8. Anthony Giddens, 'Elites in the British Class Structure', op. cit., p. 346.

9. Anthony Giddens, 'Elites', op. cit., p. 392.

10. J. H. Westergaard, 'Sociology: the Myth of Classlessness', in Robin Blackburn (ed.), *Ideology in Social Science*, Fontana, London, 1972, pp. 140–1.

11. See. J. N. Morgan and J .A. Sonquist, 'Problems in the Analysis of Survey Data, and a Proposal', *American Statistical Association Journal*, June 1963.

12. T. B. Bottomore, *Elites in Society*, op. cit., p. 14.

13. Anthony Giddens, 'Elites in the British Class Structure', op. cit., p. 361. The range is also similar to those used by Guttsman (op. cit., 1963, pp. 359ff.) and Lupton and Wilson (op. cit.), although one or two rather differently defined categories are also included in the present study — 'the wealthiest businessmen', 'the aristocracy' and life peers.

14. The main references were *Who's Who 1971*, Adam and Charles Black, London, 1971, and *Whittaker's Almanack 1971*. Other works of reference were used as necessary. We are grateful for the assistance of Sarah Laughton with this part of the research.

15. The prime reason for selecting the k-means method is the avoidance of the necessity of calculating the $1/2n(n-1)$ similarity coefficients required by the more rigorous hierarchical techniques. Thus where computing time is at a premium this method can be used on larger data sets. Also within this particular option there are a number of choices available to the user at each stage of the procedure, giving a high degree of flexibility in possible clustering strategies. The sample was split to produce a better estimate of the reliability of the types found, with an added advantage that it again reduced the amount of computing time needed to handle the data.

The concept of distance as a measure of similarity is not new, Sokal mentions the work of Heincke in 1898. However, its use in taxonomic methods is more recent having to await the arrival of computers to take the massive load of computation involved. With regard to continuous variables the basic idea is simple. If there are two objects measured on n variables, then the n variables are taken to define an n-dimensional space within which the two objects are situated according to their scores on the n variables. The similarity of the two objects is then the euclidian distance between the two objects in the space so defined.

With binary (classificatory) data the principle is the same when the appropriate transformations have been made. Using the common 2×2 table, the 'distance' between two points is given by

$$d = (b+c)/N, \text{ where } N = a+b+c+d.$$

It can be seen from this that the centroid of a cluster is that point which is equidistant from all points within that cluster and that a cluster's homogeneity can be considered as a function of the sum of squares of the distance between each point in the cluster and its centroid.

For a discussion of this and other transformations see R. R. Sokal and P. Sneath, *Principles of Numerical Taxonomy*, Freeman, San Francisco, 1963. See also R. R. Sokal, 'Distance as a Measure of Taxonomic Similarity', *Systematic Zoology*, Vol. 10, pp. 70–9.

16. The analysis throughout is of *holders of the positions* on the eighteen groups and therefore those who occur as members of more than one category appear more than once in the total group. The 934 positions were in fact held by 793 individuals.

17. For a discussion of the use of inclusion in a directory as an elite index see Baltzell, *Who's Who in America* and ' "The Social Register": Elite and Upper Class Indexes in Metroplitan America', in R. Bendix and S. M. Lipset, *Class, Status and Power*, New York, Collier Macmillan, 1966, and the contribution by Colin Bell in the present volume.

7. Elite Background and Issue Preferences: A Comparison of British and Foreign Data using a New Technique

DENNIS FARLIE AND IAN BUDGE*

ABSTRACT

Recent research has cast doubt on the ability of standard demographic characteristics to predict elite attitudes. This finding is important because it implies that (a) these characteristics are not linked with invariant socialisation experiences which might serve as general explanations for the presence and direction of certain attitudes; (b) more broadly, the assumption implicit in most studies of elite social background — that we know what background data mean attitudinally — is wrong. This paper undertakes a further study of attitudinal-background relationships using a new focus, some new data along with old, and a new technique. The focus is on one set of particularly important attitudes (issue-preferences). The data consist of background characteristics and issue preferences of local and national legislators in the United Kingdom, United States, Venezuela and Israel. The technique produces a multi-variate classification of preferences more sensitive to background influences than any used hitherto. Results from the investigation generally uphold the conclusions of earlier studies. Although background characteristics in combination successfully predict issue-preferences (with one exception) they do not have the same relationship with preferences in different areas. Background characteristics thus do not serve as invariant indicators of preferences at cross-national or indeed cross-regional level. Generalisations based on the assumption that they do are suspect, and this conclusion has implications for theories of the Power Elite.

* This is the second of a series of collaborative papers in which the order of the names is alternated to indicate the studies are in every case a joint endeavour. We wish to thank while absolving Don Searing for his support and theoretical and practical help with this paper. We are grateful to Roger Barlow for his careful and competent analysis of all the data reported in this paper.

I *Relevance and Importance of the Relationship between Characteristics and Attitudes.*

Most fundamental assertions about politics in liberal-capitalist democracies depend upon an implicit equivalence between background characteristics and political attitudes. The fact that decision-making positions are predominantly held by individuals from an exclusive 'Establishment' – defined in terms of social and educational background – is often taken as *prima facie* evidence for the content of actual decisions. It is assumed, quite plausibly, that individuals of this social type will not be disposed to challenge the fundamentals of the existing order – the capitalist free-market economy itself.[1] What might seem independent evidence on the part played in actual decision-making by business, research councils, foundations and other interest groups becomes germane to the Power Elite thesis only on the assumption that these bodies, through the social characteristics of their members, are agents of the Establishment.

The sophisticated recent advocates of this thesis admit the possibility of disagreement among the members of the Power Elite constituted by the Establishment. Such differences are however tactical rather than fundamental. They concern the best ways to preserve the existing structure of society – by outright resistance to change or by intelligent adaptation. All elite members are nevertheless "agreed over the existing economic and social system of private ownership and private appropriation".[2] This raises an operational problem which elite theorists consistently evade: how to distinguish fundamental issues on which Western decision-makers are agreed from less fundamental issues on which they may disagree?[3] Until this distinction is clearly specified it will be impossible to make a proper empirical test of the central hypothesis about the Power Elite – that their common interests and background shape central decisions in the Western democracies. For unless they can be shown to agree on the 'fundamental' issues the whole argument falls to the ground.

It is however clear that the fundamental issues on which the Power Elite are hypothesised to agree are unlikely to be of the specific type we consider below. Domhoff remarks: 'The world . . . is pluralistic . . . So is the American power structure – if we take a very short time span, deal with a myriad of specific issues of varying importance on a moment-by-moment basis. . . .'[4] The same point could be made in regard to Britain. Thus – even although our study is concerned with legislative elites in capitalist democracies – its concentration on background influences over the very types of issue instanced in Domhoff's quotation renders it incapable of providing direct evidence for or against the existence of a Power Elite. Nevertheless important indirect inferences are still possible. Some specific issues such as nationalisation and planning touch more closely on private ownership than others: are the elites consequently more agreed in these areas, or are different background factors consistently related to radical and conservative views in that area? Does a consistent relationship between social characteristics and issue-preferences extend across all the issues considered, thus providing support for the pluralist assertion that distinctive leadership groups compete for mass support on issues which although specific have profound effects for everyone (e.g. British entry to the Common Market)? Does the same pattern of relationship extend across nations, and between central and local levels, so that there is scope for generalisation of some sort to all Western liberal-capitalist democracies? Or on the contrary do cultural and social differences produce idiosyncratic political patterns which seem to confound demographically-based generalisations of either the Marxist or pluralist variety?

Not simply pluralism or elitism but wider assumptions about the effects of elite background are affected by answers to these questions. Most studies of the social background of elites, whatever their other presuppositions or ideological bias, have assumed that there is an obvious one-to-one relationship between particular attitudes and particular characteristics. Elite characteristics are also studied in order to determine the structure of political and material opportunities in the society and the effects on politics of long-term changes in social values.[5] But analysts have generally agreed with Donald Matthews, in his classic review of the literature, that 'the study of the social backgrounds of political decision-makers . . . contributes to a deeper understanding of the actions and decisions of those in positions of authority.'[6]

It is of course tautological that political attitudes are developed 'within a frame of reference determined by . . . total previous experience'.[7] Matthews and other students of elite background are however arguing for a narrower and potentially falsifiable hypothesis: that the standard known characteristics of elites available from biographical data — their family, education, religion, career characteristics, etc. — are consistently related to their political attitudes. This hypothesis carries the powerful implication that characteristics of this type usually produce the same attitude — higher education for example is usually associated with greater conservatism or liberalism as the case may be. For otherwise – if higher education sometimes produced conservatism and sometimes liberalism within the same attitudinal area – it would not function as a useful indicator nor contribute to deeper understanding of elite decisions. Encapsulated within this argument is the further assumption that characteristics like education produce the same attitudinal effects across different countries and cultures. For if different effects are produced in different cultures, interactive cultural influences, as well as pure social background, need to be considered.

It would be a grave injustice to Matthews' thoughtful discussion to imply that he ignores the provisional nature of his assumptions. On the contrary he tries where possible to produce relevent data. At the time of writing however the only available information was American: correlations between legislators' votes and certain demographic characteristics which Matthews noted could be spurious.[8] Most other analysts of elite background have taken the relationship for granted and devoted their main efforts to the compilation of standard demographic data which are assumed to say something about influences on decisions.[9] A cross-national analysis of the relation between demographic characteristics and attitudes thus carries enormous implications for one of the most closely researched areas of elite analysis.

II *Research Background*

The verity of the relationship has in fact been recently thrown into doubt as a result of the pioneering investigations undertaken by Edinger and Searing.[10] Their inability to find attitudinal-background connections which were cross-nationally generalisable led to the following conclusions:

1. Some background characteristics have more relevance than others for elite attitudes within political systems.

2. Some attitudes are more strongly related than others to background characteristics within political systems.

3. The relative importance of relationships between background and attitude varies from one system to another.

It is in short simply not obvious from their investigations what attitudes the standard background characteristics indicate, especially in cross-national comparisons. While Edinger and Searing did get some relationships between background and attitude these were often not connections which could have been reasonably predicted in advance. *A priori* use of background characteristics as attitudinal indicators was further inhibited by reversals of relationships for different elite groups in different countries.

Such confusion in the relationship between background and attitudes may be partly due to the grossness and crudity implicit in the categorisation of standard demographic characteristics. But in his review of the research Searing raises the more fundamental question of why background characteristics should be expected to classify similar socialisation experiences anyway.[11] Elite members with similar levels of education may differ fundamentally according to the type of school attended, the effort expended to achieve education and so on through a lot of other characteristics which the educational measure, no matter how finely scaled, is inadequate to tap. Even if it were adequate for this purpose within a single society and institutional setting, individuals in varying cultural and institutional locations would probably react differently to the same stimuli. On this argument there is no reason to think that standard social characteristics classify similar attitudes and thus that they can be used as known and invariant attitudinal indicators.

The implications for theories of the Power Elite are far-reaching here. For if this conclusion is accepted, gross similarities between the social background of top decision-makers cannot be used as proof of attitudinal agreement. Pluralist competition between elite groups even on fundamental issues would still be possible in spite of a shared, exclusive social background, because such backgrounds could be associated with different types of attitude.[12]

For the technical literature on the social background of elites the implications of Searing's findings are also significant. Most elite studies simply present background data under the assumption that everyone knows what these data mean attitudinally. But this evidence casts doubt on the *a priori* forecasting ability of the standard background items. These might still be compiled in order to indicate the opportunity structure for political recruitment or to trace long term change in the relationship of social factors and politics. But they could not be presented on the assumption that they told us something about political attitudes.

A third implication from Searing's discussion is that background characteristics cannot be used to predict or explain political attitudes — at least, not in their standard form or without full understanding of the complex, interactive socialisation processes which intervene. It is this conclusion which underlies the implications already drawn for the Power Elite and social background literature. Its bearing on research strategy is central and startling: for a time at least the quest for generalised demographic determinants of elite attitudes and behaviour should be abandoned in favour of massive depth studies of particular elites, and of the way their backgrounds and institutional socialisation react to produce controlling norms and preferences. Given the findings we have just discussed this direction would certainly be the best to take. But just because it involves such a radical reorientation, the existing evidence deserves further examination of the kind presented here, before a new direction is taken.

One independent German investigation has already produced further evidence for the absence of consistent relationships between background and attitudes.[13] Findings from a related area – that of legislative recruitment – do however suggest that some of these negative conclusions might be open to reinterpretation. In selecting characteristics which distinguished five sets of British local councillors and legislators from corresponding populations it was obvious that the most discriminating characteristics were strongly of the standard demographic type discussed above.[14] From bivariate comparisons with census data on the populations, which are available for large numbers of countries in the literature already cited on social background, it does seem true that legislative elites generally come from highly exclusive backgrounds. The implication of this for our recruitment analysis was that among our British legislative elites none of the standard demographic variables except age and political status (for obvious reasons) was successful at predicting who would stay in political life and who would drop out. In discriminating among elite members, in other words, the standard demographic characteristics did not function well because the elite groups were almost completely homogeneous in terms of their relatively exclusive background.[15]

This finding may extend beyond attempts to predict change and continuity in political careers to any prediction of legislators' attitudes and behaviour from background characteristics. Thus the absence of consistent relationships between background attitudes within elites could paradoxically indicate the importance of background influences. Only these might appear in differences between the attitudes of elites and population, rather than within the socio-economically controlled elite environment itself. Should we discover a broad measure of political agreement among legislators, in conjunction with their known exclusive background, the Power Elite hypothesis in the form advanced by Domhoff and Miliband would receive

204

considerable support, particularly if elite attitudes were found to diverge from those of the corresponding population. This is a question to which we shall return in our conclusions.

III *Research Focus*

Any attempt to probe deeper into the questions raised by Edinger and Searing should concentrate upon more specific types of attitudes than the comprehensive range appropriate to the original analysis.[16] For its purposes different attitudes elicited by independent investigations in different countries, e.g. basic values in Venezuela, specific issues and perceptions in Israel and the USA – were viewed as equivalent. Some findings indicate however that the influence of background factors may vary between different types of attitude.[17] We should in any case be better able to discover cross-national regularities by focusing upon a particular type of attitude. We have chosen to concentrate upon preferences on specific issues. It is true that this focus omits the question of who defines the issues – the problems of agenda-setting and of effectiveness in bringing items into political debate. This is unfortunate because the question of what issues are not debated (e.g. the question of socialism vs. the free-market economy) is central to the Power Elite hypothesis. On the other hand the whole topic of how to measure such norms is obscure: the investigations which produced much of the secondary data available to us for analysis had no intention of focusing on such norms and produced very ambiguous questions on them, whereas the questions on specific issues are reasonably clear and interpretable. Moreover in regard to one of the central problems of this area of investigation – how far attitudes relate to subsequent behaviour, another crucial assumption of the social background literature – it is obscure how these very general norms would be reflected in legislative behaviour. In regard to issue-preferences on the other hand there is clear if limited evidence that in a relatively free voting situation issue-preferences are carried over to behaviour.[18] Because we should like our investigation to carry some policy-related implication, we wish to generalise our attitudinal findings to actual behaviour and so confine our attention to the specific issue preferences which have been shown to correlate with behaviour.

IV *Data*

Such issue-preferences have been elicited from different legislative groups at divergent times and places, with substantially different purposes in mind. This wide spread presents opportunities as well as

205

problems. On the positive side, findings derived from the British data can be extensively checked against a variety of cross-national evidence. On the negative side, questions about comparability obtrude, both in regard to the conditions under which interviews were held and of exact questions asked. By focusing on specific issue-preferences we avoid most difficulties connected with the formulation of survey questions, but not problems associated with the different conditions and times at which interviews were conducted. These are summarised for each data-set below, along with other relevant information:

1. GLASGOW   Eighty-two out of 113 (elective) city councillors were interviewed from February to July 1966 concurrently with a city-wide systematic sample of electors.[19]

2. BELFAST   Forty-five out of sixty (elective) city councillors were interviewed from June to September 1966 concurrently with a city-wide systematic sample of residents.[20] Both the Belfast and Glasgow surveys, and the interviews with councillors and residents, covered identical topics concerned in part with representation and communication of preferences on five issues current in the locality.

3. LONDON   Fifty-nine out of an original random sample of eighty candidates and backbench MPs from Greater London seats were interviewed from February to June 1962, concurrently with a systematic sample of residents from a Parliamentary constituency selected as reasonably representative of all Greater London constituencies.[21] The purpose of the survey was to compare agreement on nine current issues of national import, as well as on other points.

4. UNITED STATES   Five hundred and four State legislators in both legislative Houses of New Jersey, Ohio, California and Tennessee, constituting over 90 per cent of the legislators, were interviewed from January to June 1957. Interviews focused on role conceptions for the self and others, but questions on specific issues and personal background were included.[22]

5. VENEZUELA   Twelve hundred and forty-eight members of the 'Venezuelan elite', identified by a panel of experts using positional criteria (e.g. offices held) from among 5,500 respondents, were interviewed in 1963 about important political issues, social stratification; regime orientations; modernisation priorities and conceptions of social justice. Information on demographic characteristics was also elicited.[23]

6. ISRAEL   Ninety-three members of the Israeli Knesset, out of a total of 120 were interviewed in 1962 on their preferences on current issues; general political attitudes; perceptions of the legislative pro-

cess, recruitment and of major foreign powers; demographic characteristics were also ascertained.[24]

It will be noted that not all members of the elites interviewed were actual legislators: in London there were in addition Parliamentary candidates, in Venezuela army officers, officials, trade unionists and businessmen. Nevertheless all the elite groups contain legislators as a central element, and four out of six consist exclusively of legislators. Preferences on specific, current issues were included in all cases as a central element in the study design.

Local legislators (British councillors, American State legislators) form three out of the six groups examined. In terms of the complexity and size of the governmental unit, local areas like Glasgow or New Jersey compare with small states like Israel (as of 1964). In terms of the importance of issues the politico-religious problems of Belfast in 1966 are fraught with consequences as momentous as any of the issues confronted by a national parliament. Thus the local-national distinction does not constitute an insuperable obstacle to analysing responses comparatively, although the difference between governmental levels should be borne in mind. Enough similarities between the data-sets do appear to make comparative analysis feasible, even if the justification for using these particular data-sets remains that they are the only ones presently available.

The American, Venezuelan and Israeli data were used in Searing's original investigations, so that our analysis has the potential of validating his findings through another approach.[25] The British data-sets are analysed for the first time in this connection. Besides their inheren interest for what they tell us about British politics they have two other advantages: (a) they extend the range of cross-national comparisons, (b) similar questions were asked of members of corresponding populations at the same time. Thus there is an opportunity to enquire below whether background factors operate to distinguish the preferences of elite from mass in these areas, whether or not they discriminate between the preferences of elite members themselves.

v *Research Purposes*

Edinger's and Searing's findings are of course the product of their particular data-sets, but also of a particular technique. This is based on a Robot Data Screening Programme which produces three statistics: (a) a 'predictability measure . . . which indicates the percentage of correct respondent classifications on a dependent attitudinal variable made by an independent background variable': (b) a 'scope index

207

(which) represents the total number of all elite attitudes in a study predicted by a background variable at the ·05 level': (c) a 'strength measure . . . the mean predictability for this set of attitudinal predictions'.[26]

A main impulse to further examination of attitudinal-background linkages derives from the suspicion that the simple placement of individuals inside or outside an attitudinal category may not be a sufficiently sensitive measure of background effects. Our own technique, as will become apparent, allows background factors to influence the likelihood that an individual may belong in one category rather than another. This increases the potential effect that a background factor can exert and reduces the possibility that measurement uncertainty is responsible for any negative findings. Another contrast between the techniques lies in the encouragement given by our procedure to multivariate analysis of background effects. As explained below, its whole rationale is to use numbers of background factors in combination to derive likelihood scores for issue-preferences. This methodological stance seems fully justified in the present context: socialisation experiences and reference groups are more likely to be shared by e.g. male Catholic Labour working-class trade unionists than by individuals grouped in any one of these categories in isolation.

The negative findings of Edinger and Searing may derive in part from the concentration of their main attention upon bivariate relationships, each background factor in turn being related to each attitude. At one point Searing certainly extended comparisons to two-, three- and four-variable combinations of background characteristics, with rather disappointing results.[27] The whole philosophy of our approach is however to discard the hope that we could ever explain the variety and complexity of elite preferences with one background characteristic. Rather we start with a prediction derived from all the background characteristics available and weed out those which make no contribution.

The danger of this procedure is that we may end up with characteristics which predict preferences well but which are grouped in complex combinations so specific to time and place that they are neither generalisable nor easily interpretable. Since the two latter goals rather than pure predictive ability are our main objectives, this danger must be borne in mind when interpreting results.

The optimum finding from our point of view would thus be a set of characteristics which were sufficiently subtle and discriminating to isolate common socialisation experiences producing similar issue-preferences, while not so extended as to be uneconomic and non-generalisable. In combination, such a set might function as a reliable indicator of preferences across political systems – at least within a given issue-area. Inside the set the work done by any one characteristic might fluctuate, for all evidence stresses that no single characteristic will prove a reliable indicator of all preferences under all circumstances. But the decline in its contribution could well be consistently offset by an increased contribution from others within the set. Thus the predictive capacity of the set as a whole would remain constant. The search for such a set has a practical justification in that its discovery would isolate some characteristics as predictively powerful out of the jungle of potential indicators that confront us. It has theoretical justification in our knowledge that different issues stimulate different responses – draw on different socialisation experiences, relate to different symbols and different groups – but that the range of issues is not limitless and may be fairly indicated for most issues by a limited set of background characteristics. Such a set or sets of characteristics our technique is well adapted to uncover.

VI *Technique*

The procedure devised for use in this and related investigations aims essentially at using specified characteristics to estimate the likelihood of a given individual's location in categories of a dependent variable. The procedure takes its start from a matrix such as the one presented in Table 1. The issue forming the Column variable is agreement or disagreement with a proposal to abolish fee-paying in all Corporation schools in Glasgow. Each category of every background characteristic used in subsequent analysis of Glasgow councillors (to whom entries relate) is located at the side of the full matrix, which cannot be shown here. Dots indicate the missing categories. Matrix entries are the proportions of councillors (out of all those who agree or disagree with the proposal, respectively) who fall into the categories of each background variable. Proportions thus run to 1·00 for each background variable down each column. Looking across the columns these proportions give the likelihood that a person in a given category (e.g. Labour, Catholic, Woman) will agree or disagree. Each person has an array of social characteristics and each characteristic has a given likelihood of agreement and disagreement. In combination each person's total set of characteristics produces a vector of likelihoods that he agrees or disagrees. For example a vector (·40, ·60) shows that an individual councillor is most likely to disagree but not much more

Probability Matrix for Glasgow Councillors on the Issue of Abolishing Fees in all Corporation Schools

		Abolish Fees:	
		AGREE	DISAGREE
PARTY	Progressive	·15	·69
	Labour	·85	·28
	:	:	:
DENOMINATION	Presbyterian	·44	·72
	Episcopalian	·00	·02
	Other Prot	·09	·02
	Nonbeliever	·26	·09
	Catholic	·15	·11
	:	:	:
SEX	Male	·89	·83
	Female	·11	·17

likely than to agree. This likelihood vector can be compared to the assignment vector obtained from the previously known characterisation of the individual as agreeing or disagreeing – e.g. (0·00, 1·00). A mathematical presentation of the procedure is made in the appendix to the paper on 'Background Characteristics and Political Recruitment' cited in footnote 14. It is obtainable on application to the authors.

The likelihood scores derived from the matrix sum to 1·00. An individual can be placed at some point between 'agree' and 'disagree' in terms of his likelihood score. Given two categories the total distribution of individuals in term of their likelihood scores can be graphically presented through their location on a line between two points. Given three categories (e.g. 'Agree', 'Disagree', 'Neutral') the distribution is over a triangle, with four over a pyramid, and so on. Table 2 presents a distribution of Glasgow councillors – produced by this process – in terms of their propensity to agree or disagree with the proposal to abolish fee-paying. Since there are only two points involved, a greater likelihood of agreeing entails a corresponding reduction of the likelihood of disagreeing, so the likelihood scores are in this case mirror images of each other; e.g. an individual with a ·8 likelihood of agreeing has a ·2 likelihood of disagreeing.

Of course the likelihood scores, being predicted from background characteristics, are not infallible. Table 2 presents distributions separately for those councillors who actually agree with the proposal and those who actually disagree. Although the bulk of each group has scores in the appropriate direction, five of the councillors who are

TABLE 2: *Distribution of Glasgow Councillors in terms of their likelihood of Agreeing or Disagreeing with Abolition of Fee-paying in Corporation Schools*

Likelihood of agreement with proposal in terms of background characteristics	Councillors actually agreeing with proposal	Councillors actually disagreeing with proposal	Likelihood of disagreement with proposal in terms of background characteristics
$1\cdot00 > S \geqslant \cdot9$	28	5	$0 < S \leqslant \cdot1$
$\cdot9 > S \geqslant \cdot8$	1	1	$\cdot1 < S \leqslant \cdot2$
$\cdot8 > S \geqslant \cdot7$	0	0	$\cdot2 < S \leqslant \cdot3$
$\cdot7 > S \geqslant \cdot6$	0	1	$\cdot3 < S \leqslant \cdot4$
$\cdot6 > S \geqslant \cdot5$	0	1	$\cdot4 < S \leqslant \cdot5$
$\cdot5 > S \geqslant \cdot4$	0	0	$\cdot5 < S \leqslant \cdot6$
$\cdot4 > S \geqslant \cdot3$	0	3	$\cdot6 < S \leqslant \cdot7$
$\cdot3 > S \geqslant \cdot2$	1	1	$\cdot7 < S \leqslant \cdot8$
$\cdot2 > S \geqslant \cdot1$	0	0	$\cdot8 < S \leqslant \cdot9$
$\cdot1 > S \geqslant 0$	4	34	$\cdot9 < S \leqslant 1\cdot00$
TOTAL	34	46	

Lambda = ·647. Goodman and Kruskall Tau$_a$ = ·485.

N = 80 (two councillors were neutral on the proposal and so are not located above).

S represents standardised likelihood score.

shown as likely to disagree in terms of their background characteristics had actually expressed themselves as agreeing with the proposal. Seven of those who had actually disagreed are shown as more likely to agree (scoring ·5+ towards agreement).

In estimating the predictive success of the background factors used in relation to this issue we shall in this paper regard such placements as error.[28] With the two neutral councillors this makes fourteen councillors out of eighty-two misplaced on this issue, or 17 per cent. This percentage is not in itself an adequate indicator of the predictive success of the background factors, for a greater number might have been accurately placed had we used some simple guessing rule such as placing individuals in the largest category. By comparing our classification (dichotomised at ·5) with the distribution in terms of councillors' actual opinions, we can assess the gain from using our procedure

211

through such well-known statistics as Lambda and the Goodman and Kruskall Tau$_a$.[29] The high values of these statistics in Table 2 demonstrate the predictive power of the background variables over preferences on this issue.

Since a large set of background factors is employed to make this classification we also need to know what they are and which are contributing usefully to the likelihood scores, and which not. The contribution of each factor can be estimated from associated information values presented in Table 3 below.

TABLE 3: *Information Values and Rankings of Background Characteristics used to predict Glasgow Councillors' preferences on the Proposal to Abolish Fee-paying in Corporation Schools*

Background characteristics	Information value	Rank
Father's occupation	1·096	1
Own Party affiliation	1·069	2
Father's Party affiliation	0·789	3
Self-assigned class	0·647	4
Description of persons in own class	0·449	5
Age	0·437	6
Second class mentioned by R in discussion of class structure	0·397	7
Denomination	0·355	8
Length of education	0·384	9
Number of class mentioned above own class in discussion of class structure	0·352	10
People in second class mentioned by R in discussion of class structure	0·248	11
R's class awareness	0·243	12
Membership of trade union or professional organisation	0·197	13
R's occupation	0·194	14
Church attendance	0·175	15
The number of classes R sees in discussion of class structure	0·147	16
Length of time R has lived in Glasgow	0·104	17
Sex	0·073	18
Whether R is retired or not	0·033	19
Whether R would be happy to leave Glasgow or not	0·018	20

212

Information values are the difference between the average movement in the correct direction and the average movement in the wrong direction associated with each background characteristic. It is always positive. Absolute values are not comparable between one issue and another — what can be compared are the rankings made on the basis of absolute information values. Table 3 presents both the absolute values and rankings of background characteristics based on their success in placing councillors on the Fees issue. The first point that emerges is the diversity of background characteristics used to predict preferences. Had we a free choice of background predictors to use in the study we would certainly have made a rather different selection from that forced on us by the necessity of secondary analysis. However the characteristics used in Glasgow and Belfast do include the standard characteristics used in elite studies, such as occupation, sex, party, denomination, education and father's background. Both the diversity of characteristics and the inclusion of most standard characteristics are true of the other data-sets employed below.

Looking specifically at relationships with the Fees issue, there is obviously a distinct break between the two or four most predictive characteristics and the rest. This does not appear for every issue — for some, indeed, most of the higher-ranking characteristics are close in terms of information-values. These differences point to the utility of reporting information-values as well as rankings in subsequent analyses. It is obvious however that characteristics after rank 10 contribute little in the way of further predictive power. This is generally true of all issues examined, for all data-sets: hence only the ten highest ranking characteristics will be listed in subsequent tables.

VII *Placement of Elite Members on Issue-Preferences*

Before reporting information values we must however confirm generally that elite members' issue preferences are being correctly predicted in terms of their background characteristics, on a better than chance basis. We can do this by summarising, for each issue in every data-set, similar information to that already presented for the Glasgow fees issue in Table 2. For each issue we shall report values of Lambda and Tau_a. Instead of giving the full distribution of respondents over all likelihood scores we shall however simply report the total percentage correctly placed — correctly in the sense of having a $\cdot 5 +$ likelihood of agreeing or disagreeing when they actually do agree or disagree. In terms of the fees issue this percentage is 83 per cent, and is reported as such in Table 4.

213

TABLE 4: *Glasgow and Belfast Councillors' Summary Statistics showing Distribution of Issue-Preferences and Degree of Correct Prediction of Preferences by Background Characteristics*

GLASGOW

Issue Proposal Preference:	For %	DK/ Neutral %	Against %	Per cent councillors correctly placed %	Goodman and Kruskall	
					Tau$_a$	Lambda
Abolishing school fees	43	*	57	83	·485	·647
Placing pubs in housing estates	86	*	14	89	·111	·100
Extending parking meters	76	*	24	87	·405	·474
Mixing Catholic and Protestant school-children	85	*	15	92	·460	·500
Changes in city government	86	*	14	88	·160	·182
Raising local rates	45	12	43	84	·532	·711

BELFAST

	For	DK/ Neutral	Against	Per cent correctly placed	Tau$_a$	Lambda
Opening park swings on Sundays	74	*	26	80	·202	·272
Extending State aid to (Catholic) Mater Hospital	69	13	18	84	·464	·533
Naming Lagan Bridge after (Protestant) Carson	67	17	17	74	·256	·313
Mixing Catholic and Protestant tenants in public housing	73	*	27	78	·162	·231
Changes in city government	87	*	13	87	·000	·000
Raising local rates	59	*	40	74	·393	·563

Asterisks * mark cases where a response was endorsed by so few respondents that they were omitted in the generation of likelihood scores.

Tables 4, 5, 6, 7 and 8 also give the distribution of respondents in terms of their original endorsement of alternatives on the issue — in the case of the Fees issue for example 43 per cent of Glasgow councillors originally agreed with the proposal for abolition, while 57 per cent dissented. The original percentages for agreement and disagreement are important for two reasons. In the first place they show whether elites are highly agreed in conserving the status quo, which is at least a first step towards checking Power Elite as opposed to pluralist hypotheses. Secondly a predictive failure of background characteristics may in some cases be due to the fact that so many elite members agree or disagree with a proposal that it is impossible to do better than the simple guessing rule of putting them all in the largest category. This is not really a predictive failure, however, for it reflects the inability of background characteristics to distinguish between opposed preferences in a situation where preferences are not opposed, and in fact where the shared background of the elite may be prompting strong agreement, either in contrast to or in sympathy with the population.

Fairly extensive agreement exists in fact on four out of six issues among Glasgow councillors. On the fees issue, which approaches most closely to a class confrontation (fee-paying being the distinctive mark of a middle-class education) councillors are strongly divided, as also on the question of higher local taxation (raising rates). Where agreement reaches its highest level, on change in city government and allowing the sale of drink in public housing, prediction from background characteristics is inhibited simply because the percentage of persons correctly scored cannot be vastly higher than the percentage in the largest category. Predictive success is not confined to issues where there is disagreement however because it is also fairly high on the extension of parking meters and the integration of school-children.

Surprisingly, in view of later developments, there was more general agreement among Belfast than Glasgow councillors over the range of issues confronting them.[30] The swings, hospital, bridge and housing questions were all related to the politico-religious division between Protestants and Catholics, which in terms of violence and involvement appears as more fundamental to Northern Irish politics than class or economic issues. Over all these issues as well as the raising of rates, background characteristics yield a fair degree of predictive success. Only in regard to changes in city government, where agreement is high, does this slump drastically to zero.

The immediate conclusions to be drawn from Table 4 are twofold. First in terms of general bearings on the Power Elite hypothesis, the more class-related issues are the most divisive. Also, as we will see in Section X below, high general levels of agreement among councillors reflect similar views among the populace. Secondly, the background characteristics available do on the whole successfully 'place' councillors in terms of their preferences. Where their predictive success is not much greater than that of a simple guessing rule, this is because of councillors' high agreement which could itself be attributed to their background homogeneity.

This is a problem which does not arise with the preferences of London MPs and candidates. The original responses of this group on what to do about the problems listed at the side of Table 5 were coded into an extended set of 10–12 categories. For purposes of our analysis the most popular response or group of responses have been contrasted with all other replies. Disagreement has thus in a sense been maximised for purposes of this analysis: had respondents been confronted with simple 'agree-disagree' choices, like most of the other

TABLE 5: *Greater London MPs and Parliamentary Candidates: Summary Statistics showing distribution of Issue-Preferences and Degree of Correct Prediction of Preferences by Background Characteristics*

Issue Proposal Preference:	For	Other	Per cent MPs/ Candidates correctly placed	Goodman and Kruskall	
	%	%	%	Tau$_a$	Lambda
More vigorous action within existing policy framework on monopolies	33	67	82	·357	·474
More aid to help achieve racial integration on immigration	32	68	85	·544	·473
Flexible attitude to negotiations with Russians on Berlin	51	49	79	·320	·551
Technical improvements in building methods on housing	66	34	76	·190	·300
Increase expenditure on education	53	47	83	·439	·900
Take Britain into the Common Market under certain conditions	69	31	88	·526	·611
Government policy of general restraint on wages	29	71	87	·554	·647
Technical proposals to improve efficiency of public transport	41	59	78	·440	·428

groups we discuss, agreement might well have appear higher. Nevertheless it is abundantly clear from the original study[31] that these responses reveal considerable elite disagreement on class-related socioeconomic issues as well as the rest. In interpreting the summary statistics given in the table it is important to remember that the 'Other' heading groups numerous diverse preferences: thus the fact that 71 per cent opposed Government policy on wages does not mean that they were in complete agreement over the alternatives to Government policy.

The other statistics in Table 5 show that over three-quarters of the MPs and candidates were correctly placed in terms of their background characteristics on every issue, and the values of Tau_a and Lambda show that such placements represented in every case a fair and sometimes considerable enhancement of predictive ability.

Table 6 shows that this conclusion generally applies to State legislators in the United States, whether as a combined group or within

TABLE 6: *US State Legislators: Summary Statistics showing Distribution of Issue-Preferences and Degree of Correct Prediction of Preferences by Background Characteristics*

Issue Proposal Preference:	Agree	DK/ Neutral	Disagree	Per cent correctly placed	Goodman and Kruskall Tau$_a$	Lambda
	%	%	%	%		
USA (four States combined)						
Government is responsible for welfare	50	7	43	72	·330	·446
Businesses should be free from regulations	59	11	30	70	·244	·194
There should be more State taxes	33	5	62	76	·285	·271
Suspected Communists should not be allowed to teach	59	19	22	69	·096	·248
School needs are by nature:	Financial	DK	Administrative			
	%	%	%			
	49	18	33	69	·257	·400
NEW JERSEY						
Government is responsible for welfare	57	3	40	84	·447	·618
Businesses should be free from regulations	61	9	30	73	·241	·323
There should be more State taxes	53	4	43	78	·342	·541
Suspected Communists should not be allowed to teach	70	19	11	82	·356	·417
School needs are by nature:	Financial	DK	Administrative			
	%	%	%			
	49	15	36	82	·551	·684

TABLE 6 (*continued*)

Issue Proposal Preference:	Agree %	DK/ Neutral %	Disagree %	Per cent correctly placed %	Goodman and Kruskall Tau$_a$	Lambda
			OHIO			
Government is responsible for welfare	44	3	53	79	·335	·541
Businesses should be free from regulations	64	9	27	79	·341	·444
There should be more State taxes	35	0	65	77	·228	·351
Suspected Communists should not be allowed to teach	51	24	25	65	·501	·586

School needs are by nature:	Financial %	DK %	Administrative %			
	43	7	50	77	·329	·541

			TENNESSEE			
Government is responsible for welfare	53	0	47	83	·425	·630
Businesses should be free from regulations	58	14	27	82	·469	·564
There should be more State taxes	29	2	69	81	·287	·389
Suspected Communists should not be allowed to teach	46	24	30	73	·338	·493

School needs are by nature:	Financial %	DK %	Administrative %			
	53	15	32	82	·478	·607

			CALIFORNIA			
Government is responsible for welfare	64	0	36	82	·377	·513
Businesses should be free from regulations	49	12	39	79	·412	·581
There should be more State taxes	33	0	66	84	·395	·514
Suspected Communists should not be allowed to teach	68	12	20	78	·255	·368

School needs are by nature:	Financial %	DK %	Administrative %			
	56	32	12	78	·367	·308

218

their separate States. A significant feature of this table is however the generally greater predictive success attained within each State compared to the combined group of legislators. This may indicate that characteristics are differently associated with preferences within each State, thus lowering the predictive power they exert when used in combination. Such a possibility can be checked through the information values associated with each characteristic in the separate States (Section VIII below).

TABLE 7: *Israeli National Legislators: Summary Statistics showing Distribution of Issue-Preferences and Degree of Correct Prediction of Preferences by Background Characteristics*

Issue Proposal Preference:	Agree %	DK/ Neutral %	Disagree %	Per cent correctly placed %	Goodman and Kruskall Tau$_a$	L ambda
Civil (non religious) marriages should be allowed	45	*	55	90	·638	·775
Medical care should be taken over by the State	43	*	57	85	·496	·649
The publicly owned fertiliser plant should be sold	60	14	26	79	·369	·472
Priority should be given to agriculture over industry	24	12	62	82	·410	·515
The best sources of capital are:	Public %	DK/ Neutral %	Private %			
	48	12	40	70	·357	·413
Priority should be given to education for:	Professions %	Liberal/ Arts %	Agriculture %			
	66	6	28	65	·000	·000
Income should be allocated on basis of:	Family size %	Skill %				
	25	75		79	·282	·364
The standard of living should be:	Unchanged %	Lowered for rich %	Lowered for all %	Raised for poor %		
	31	24	10	35	55	·248	·397

219

Associated with the generally high predictive success shown in Table 6 is fairly extensive disagreement on most issues: this is most widespread on the question of Government responsibility for welfare, but is also apparent — less consistently — on the regulation of business and on taxation. Agreement is highest in support of the illiberal suggestion that suspected Communists should not be allowed to teach. The nature of school needs is a technical question, but undoubtedly questions of Government intervention in society and economy appear as ones on which these legislative elites are least agreed.

TABLE 8: *Venezuelan Natural Elite: Summary Statistics showing Distribution of Issue-Preferences and Degree of Correct Prediction of Preferences by Background Characteristics*

Issue Proposal Preference:	Agree %	DK/ Neutral %	Disagree %	Per cent correctly placed %	Goodman and Kruskall Tau$_a$	Lambda
Oil firms should be nationalised	25	4	71	64	·074	·000
State should take over all industry	12	2	86	85	·115	·000
All industry should be in private ownership	38	4	58	63	·186	·124
Wages should be regulated	29	2	69	63	·036	·000
Workers should be taxed more	21	*	79	62	·025	·000
State should control land prices	65	3	32	63	·070	·000
Eliminate party influence in trade unions	75	7	15	74	·058	·000

Military influence in politics should be:	Zero %	Limited %	Unlimited %			
	62	35	3	56	·008	·005

Church in politics should have:	No influence %	Guiding influence %	Unlimited influence %			
	53	45	2	55	·068	·114

In economic development priority should be given to:	Poor %	Capital %				
	39	61		61	·037	·006

Israel contrasts sharply with the United States and less sharply with Britain in being a country where Government intervention in all spheres of life is well established. All the issues covered in Table 7 with the exception of marriage law and types of education concern the degree of Government intervention: questions of income allocation and sources of capital are central to the development of the economy on public or private lines. Disagreement is extensive about the sources of capital, standard of living and medical care, but is not absent for the issues of income allocation, the sale of the public fertiliser plant or the relative position of agriculture and industry. Although marriage law is a non-economic question it is central to societal values and here disagreement is extensive.

Partly because of the prevalence of disagreement, background characteristics serve to type Knesset members successfully on all issues but the technical one of educational priorities.

The issues available for Venezuela also include several proposals related to a fundamental restructuring of the economy. Most members stand out against very radical measures, such as State control of all industry, nationalisation of the foreign oil firms from which the bulk of Government revenue derives, or priority for the economic interests of the poor against those of capital. But almost 40 per cent support this last proposal, and a quarter support nationalisation of oil. Most elite members are on the other hand against the extension of private ownership of economic discrimination against workers, and two-thirds feel the State should take the fairly far-reaching step of controlling land prices.

The other group of issues—natural in a situation where competitive politics had been but recently restored—relate to the influence of parties and two powerful interest groups—Army and Church. The majority opinion is in all cases against vested interests having any influence, though in the case of Army and Church there is disagreement over the extent of influence which could be permitted.

Generally there is a fair dispersion of opinion over the issue-preferences—which underlines the real failure of the background characteristics to locate elite members very successfully on any issue, and in most cases in fact to locate members less successfully than could be done through pure guesswork. This negative result is not due to the peculiarities of the background characteristics available for Venezuela, since these include all the standard characteristics which have been used successfully in the other data-sets. A more likely explanation lies in the mixed composition of the group selected

221

as the Venezuelan elite, which differs from the other groups of legislators and aspirant legislators in also including army officers, business men, trade unionists and civil servants. (Legislators cannot be identified as a separate group.) This factor may combine with the radically different nature of a developing society to reduce the predictive power of the background characteristics. All our other data-sets come from elites in developed Northern countries. Israel may seem an exception here but in fact the elite groups are largely Ashkenazi and Northern European in origin.

What seems to be revealed in Venezuela, perhaps as a result of the *coup d'état* of the late fifties and the incipient revolutionary movement of the early sixties, is a situation where immediate reactions to current issues are less constrained by long-term background influences than in the more stable developed countries. This is understandable, given fluidity and rapid regroupings in politics under semi-crisis conditions.[32] But it means that background characteristics cannot yield much information about likely stances on issues under such circumstances. This means that our further analysis must be confined to the developed Western countries, and that any generalisations we derive from that analysis must be limited to such countries.

Although the outcome of the Venezuelan analysis is negative it is of considerable substantive interest to find that the country which came nearest to a revolutionary, Marxist-oriented restructuring of economic and social relationships shows least connection at elite level between background characteristics and issue-preferences.

VIII *Contribution of Different Characteristics to the Placement of Elite Members on Issue-Preferences*

The successful placement of Western legislators in terms of their characteristics does not imply that the assumptions of the social background literature are all upheld even within this limited culture area. For these assumptions do not relate to all the characteristics we have perforce employed in our predictions, but only to those which are characteristically employed to type legislators: family background, occupation, education, party, sex, age, region of origin, religion, etc. We are searching for a set of such variables which will exert a reasonably constant effect across various issues in different areas and countries. A first step in determining whether such a constant effect is exerted, is to examine the information values associated with the top ten characteristics (all those which exert much predictive effect) for each of the placements of British, American and Israeli legislators reported in Tables 4–7 above.

The first point to note about Tables 9–13, which present our findings on the consistency of effects, is that ranks are intercomparable –

TABLE 9: *Information Values of Ten Most Informative Background Characteristics Giving Rise to Successful Placements of Glasgow Councillors Reported in Table 4*

ISSUES:

RANK	FEES	PARKING METERS	RATES	MIXING SCHOOL CHILDREN
1	Father's occupation 1·096	Second class mentioned by R ·681	Party 5·096	Denomination 1·024
2	Party 1·069	Length education ·429	Father's party 2·833	Father's party ·999
3	Father's party ·789	Organisation membership ·426	Father's occupation 2·732	Description of persons in second class mentioned 1·024
4	Self-assigned class ·646	Party ·425	Self-assigned class 2·392	Organisation membership ·810
5	Description of persons in own class ·449	Length of time in city ·367	Denomination 1·957	Number of classes mentioned above own ·786
6	Age ·436	Father's occupation ·353	Occupation 1·794	Feelings about leaving Glasgow ·786
7	Second class mentioned ·397	Description of persons in second class mentioned ·346	Description of persons in second class mentioned 1·485	Party ·738
8	Denomination ·385	Denomination ·343	Second class mentioned 1·468	Self-assigned class ·693
9	Length education ·383	Description of persons in own class ·317	Length education 1·411	Church attendance ·687
10	Number of classes mentioned above own ·352	Occupation ·297	Class awareness 1·392	Second class mentioned by R ·633

between issues and between data-sets – while the raw information-values on which they are based can be used only to assess the relative effect of characteristics within each issue. Information-values themselves, it will be remembered, represent the difference between the average movement in the correct direction and the average

223

movement in the wrong direction, associated with each background characteristic. Thus the absolute values depend on the average movement of individuals on the issue, which may be affected by the number of options open on the issue, among other things.[33] The relative importance of characteristics on each issue, expressed by the rankings at the side of the tables, is comparable, and it is on the relative stability of particular characteristics at particular ranks that we base our assessment of the generalisability of characteristics across issues and across different areas.

TABLE 10: *Information Values of Ten Most Informative Background Characteristics Giving Rise to Successful Placements of Belfast Councillors Reported in Table 4*

ISSUES:

RANK	SWINGS	HOSPITAL	BRIDGE	RATES	MIXING TENANTS
1	Denomination	Denomination	Length of time in city	Father's occupation	Denomination
	·622	1·809	1·918	·725	·517
2	Feelings about leaving Belfast	Length education	Denomination	Self-assigned class	Description of persons in own class
	·487	1·755	1·550	·564	·482
3	Party	Organisation membership	Father's occupation	Father's party	Father's party
	·433	1·488	1·243	·526	·436
4	Father's party	Age	Retirement status	Denomination	Party
	·414	1·442	1·240	·508	·434
5	Father's occupation	Self-assigned class	Father's party	Length education	Second class mentioned
	·388	1·440	1·099	·431	·307
6	Class awareness	Feelings about leaving Belfast	Number of classes mentioned	Description of persons in own class	Self-assigned class
	·369	1·319	1·004	·359	·291
7	Self-assigned class	Sex	Length education	Number of classes mentioned	Age
	·357	1·248	·974	·225	·285
8	Length of education	Party	Feelings about leaving Belfast	Party	Number of classes mentioned
	·354	1·193	·958	·212	·249
9	Length of time spent in city	Church attendance	Occupation	Number of classes mentioned above own	Organisation membership
	·314	1·160	·938	·202	·238
10	Number of classes mentioned	Second class mentioned	Self-assigned class	Occupation	Occupation
	·300	1·122	·873	·186	·215

224

In the case of Glasgow party varies between ranks 1 and 7 over the four issues on which background prediction was successful, while denomination rises from rank 8 to rank 1 on the question of integration of schools, where religious feeling is primarily involved. These are the only two purely demographic characteristics which appear among the leading ten over all four issues, but others such as length of education and father's education appear on three out of four issues. Otherwise perceptions and feelings about the class structure loom large – not surprisingly, since Glasgow politics tend to emphasise class cleavages over against other types of division.

In Belfast, not surprisingly, denomination takes a leading place on the four politico-religious issues considered, and helps affect feelings about rates. No other demographic characteristic ranks among the top ten on all issues, but several do for four out of five: party, fathers' party, length of education. Feelings about class are somewhat less prominent than in Glasgow but still evident (self-assigned class appears on all five issues).

Generally there is enough similarity between the demographic characteristics linked to preferences between issues, and between Glasgow and Belfast, to encourage further investigation of the consistency of effects between the two cities (Section IX below). There is also a question however of the extent to which similar characteristics shape preferences elsewhere.

The London data offer some support to the idea that they may. Given the greater number of issues, denomination, party, length and type of education, father's occupation appear frequently among the leading ten characteristics, as they did in Glasgow and Belfast. The most stable characteristic is one on which there was no data for Glasgow and Belfast – parents' income. The presence of this characteristic along with others linked to family background suggests that early socialisation experiences may have as much relevance to the formation of British policy preferences as current affiliations and characteristics, in direct contrast to Searing's findings about foreign elites.[34]

The absence of feelings about class from the characteristics mainly affecting Parliamentarians' preferences is an unfortunate artefact of the available data: no detailed information about class feelings was collected in London. This is true also of the American and Israeli sets. It would have been interesting to see whether – as often asserted – class had a peculiarly strong effect on British attitudes as compared

TABLE 11: *Information-Values of Ten Most Informative Background Characteristics Giving Rise to Successful Placements of London MPs and Candidates Reported in Table 5*

ISSUES:

RANK	MONOPOLIES	IMMIGRATION	BERLIN	HOUSING	EDUCATION	COMMON MARKET	WAGES	TRANSPORT
1	Parent's income ·600	Parent's income ·959	Region of origin ·319	Father's occupation ·549	Party ·501	Party ·710	Length of father's education ·992	Type of house Ownership ·611
2	Type education ·343	Family income ·676	Parent's income ·243	Length father's education ·429	Age ·471	Father's occupation ·700	Parent's income ·855	Party ·427
3	Number organisation memberships ·323	Father's occupation ·618	Age ·223	Church attendance ·391	Parent's income ·417	Type of education ·535	Father's education ·690	Type of education ·410
4	Length father's education ·263	Party ·487	Family income ·202	Parent's income ·379	Family income ·342	Church attendance ·525	Type of house ownership ·559	Father's occupation ·313
5	Age ·251	Length father's education ·484	Party ·176	Length education ·215	Father's occupation ·268	Length father's education ·410	Party ·491	Region of origin ·213
6	Denomination ·234	Type of education ·440	Length of education ·158	Region of origin ·205	Trade union member ·249	Parent's income ·393	Family income ·437	Age ·209
7	Type house ownership ·228	Region of origin ·254	Denomination ·140	Age ·186	Denomination ·219	Denomination ·315	Type of education ·256	Parent's income ·142
8	Length education ·193	Type house ownership ·245	Length father's education ·137	Party ·163	Church attendance ·200	Sex ·305	Age ·252	Family income ·137
9	Family income ·192	Church attendance ·233	Church attendance ·110	Trade union member ·157	Type of education ·189	Family income ·227	Length education ·215	Number organisation memberships ·121
10	Region of origin ·179	Age ·184	Type of house ownership ·062	Type house ownership ·153	Type of house ownership ·177	Trade union membership ·160	Region of origin ·212	Church attendance ·096

to those in other countries, but this remains unanswered by the available data.

Table 12 summarises information values and ranks for the combined group of American State legislators and for each of the separate

TABLE 12: *Information-Values and Ranks attained in separate States for Ten Most Informative Background Characteristics Giving Rise to Successful Placements of Combined American State Legislators Reported in Table 6*

ISSUES:

RANK	WELFARE	BUSINESS REGULATION	TAXES	COMMUNISTS TEACHING	SCHOOL NEEDS
1	Govt./Party function before legislature	Urban/Rural upbringing	Govt./Party functions before legislature	Urban/Rural upbringing	Urban/Rural upbringing
	4·277	4·983	3·450	2·876	2·933
	(2,2,7,7)	(2,3,4,2)	(5,2,1,14)	(8,1,4,2)	(15,8,2,2)
2	Length of education	Relatives in political office	Status of previous offices	Parent's occupation	Parent's occupation
	3·060	4·550	3·197	2·510	2·787
	(1,18,12,14)	(26,4,3,2)	(6,19,5,21)	(9,8,2,2)	(3,1,6,1)
3	Party offices	Length of education	Number relatives in political office	Length of education	Income
	3·004	4·270	3·172	2·462	2·594
	(26,13,25,26)	(10,5,1,24)	(7,13,13,9)	(6,2,1,15)	(4,2,3,3)
4	Party	Income	Legislative experience	Number of relatives in political office	Number of relatives in political office
	2·845	4·020	3·169	2·449	2·451
	(10,1,5,8)	(16,6,2,4)	(15,8,15,7)	(26,3,3,5)	(8,3,2,6)
5	Membership of House or Senate	Parent's occupation	Previous official positions held	Income	Length of education
	2·798	3·597	3·111	2·415	2·175
	(9,15,2,4)	(13,7,5,7)	(26,21,20,22)	(2,6,5,4)	(5,4,4,12)
6	Status of present official position	Marital status	Length of education	Marital status	Party offices
	2·778	3·488	3·092	1·952	1·895
	(17,6,6,1)	(26,8,6,9)	(4,10,12,13)	(5,5,6,14)	(23,9,25,17)
7	Present official positions	Denomination	Status of present official position	Denomination	Marital status
	2·778	2·114	3·044	1·388	1·802
	(14,3,4,3)	(7,2,9,5)	(12,3,11,2)	(20,4,24,6)	(7,7,5,8)
8	Denomination	Party offices	Membership of House or Senate	Party offices	Region of birth
	2·766	2·066	3·015	1·170	1·283
	(5,7,1,5)	(25,9,12,11)	(9,7,7,3)	(25,14,21,18)	(6,5,22,25)

227

Table 12 (*continued*)

ISSUES:

RANK	WELFARE	BUSINESS REGULATION	TAXES	COMMUNISTS TEACHING	SCHOOL NEEDS
9	Legislative experience	Region of birth	Branch Govt. in which present positions are held	Protestant denomination	Denomination
	2·755	2·014	3·011	1·169	1·136
	(12,4,9,6)	(11,1,24,20)	(14,2,8,1)	(13,13,12,6)	(13,6,7,7)
10	Branch of Govt. in which present positions are held	Present official positions	Primary occupation	Age	Party
	2·714	1·422	2·979	1·089	0·747
	(16,4,3,2)	(14,10,8,6)	(8,15,9,11)	(1,9,10,16)	(14,23,19,11)

Ranks for States are given in the order New Jersey, Ohio, Tennessee, California.

States. However the data for the separate States have necessarily been summarised. Entries in the body of the table represent the leading ten characteristics and their information-values for the combined group of State legislators: following this are the ranks attained by the characteristic on the issue in each of the States, in the order: New Jersey, Ohio, Tennessee, California.

Again new characteristics, not available for Britain, appear among the leading ten. Such are legislative experience, party offices and other characteristics related to the political careers. However some of the demographic characteristics already encountered are more stable than these — e.g. length of education appears for all five issues: denomination appears for four although in the lower ranks: income appears on three. Party does not appear often, seeming less constant and important than the number of relatives in political office. Urban-rural upbringing emerges as the principal factor associated with preferences on three issues. Generally there seems a fair mix of characteristics associated both with past socialisation and present career experiences in this American data.

The range of individual State ranks attached to each characteristic for each issue gives some idea of its consistency of effect between areas. Although there are cases in which the variation in ranks is limited, on the whole there is a fairly wide range between States. The possibility of producing a set of indicators for preferences which would be relatively invariant between regions seems correspondingly more limited for the United States than it does for Britain.

228

The background characteristics available for Israel are more restricted than is the case for the other areas reviewed. One point emerges quickly however – the pre-eminent role of party in typing preferences over all issues. The maintenance of living standards is the only question on which it does not rank first. This presents a considerable contrast with all the previous data-sets, where party influence was limited. Length of education exerts respectable effects over five out of six issues, as does the type of (Jewish) education. Organisational factors are more important here than with previous data-sets, and occupation also assumes more prominence. The type of socialisation into Israeli society naturally affects preferences in a way which finds no parallel elsewhere.

TABLE 13: *Information-Values of Ten Most Informative Background Characteristics Giving Rise to Successful Placements of Israeli Members Reported in Table 7*

ISSUES:

RANK	MARRIAGE	STATE MEDICINE	FERTILISER PLANT	PRIORITY AGRICULTURE	SOURCES OF CAPITAL	INCOME ALLOCATION	STANDARD OF LIVING
1	Party	Party	Party	Party	Party	Party	Date arrived Israel
	1·232	1·065	2·793	2·409	1·957	3·849	3·249
2	Type of Jewish education	Occupational sector	Type of Jewish education	Occupational sector	Date arrived Israel	Age	Length education
	·764	·528	1·707	2·006	1·346	3·811	2·772
3	Length education	Arrived with family or party	Length of education	First occupational sector	Legislative experience	Membership professional organisation	Type of Jewish education
	·748	·463	1·461	1·531	1·329	3·730	2·343
4	Legislative experience	Importance in organisations	Occupational sector	Length of education	First occupational sector	Length of stay in present home	Party
	·244	·326	1·289	1·403	1·912	3·703	2·042
5	Age	Type of Jewish education	Date arrived Israel	Age	Age	Type of Jewish education	Membership professional organisation
	·222	·292	1·246	1·397	1·127	3·377	1·909
6	Date arrived Israel	Date arrived Israel	Stay in present home	Arrived with family or party	Length of education	Length of education	Age
	·163	·231	1·112	1·263	·935	3·306	1·848

229

Table 13 (*continued*)

ISSUES:

RANK	MARRIAGE	STATE MEDICINE	FERTILISER PLANT	PRIORITY AGRICULTURE	SOURCES OF CAPITAL	INCOME ALLOCATION	STANDARD OF LIVING
7	First occupational sector	Legislative experience	Arrived with family or party	Membership Jewish organisation	Occupational sector	Organisation memberships before Israel	Legislative experience
	·150	·205	·985	1·183	·855	3·225	1·757
8	Membership professional organisation	Stay in present home	First occupational sector	Date arrived in Israel	Membership Jewish organisation	Importance in organisations	Arrived with family or party
	·138	·140	·906	1·151	·872	3·101	1·734
9	Arrived with family or party	First occupational sector	Membership Jewish organisations	Membership professional organisations	Arrived with family or party	Arrived with family or party	Organisation memberships before Israel
	·094	·102	·699	·952	·808	2·913	1·640
10	Importance in organisations	Membership professional organisations	Importance in organisations	Type Jewish education	Membership professional organisations	First occupational sector	Stay in present home
	·086	·082	·647	·910	·711	2·817	1·444

Table 14 summarises the implications of this section in presenting for each area the mean rank attained by each of the standard demographic characteristics[35] available, over all issues. The ranks in this table are not those reported previously but relate to the position attained by the information-value of each standard characteristic in comparison with information values for all the other standard characteristics reported in Table 14.

This adjustment is made necessary by the fact that the number of characteristics associated with each data-set varies enormously — from fifteen in Israel to forty-three in the United States. Obviously standard characteristics would as a result of the accidental availability of information for the United States be more likely to attain low rankings there than in Israel, if we did not standardise on the basis of the characteristics reported for each set in Table 14. Many characteristics available elsewhere are missing for Israel and so we must discount some of the very high ranks attained there: comparisons are made in terms of five characteristics compared to ten or more elsewhere.

230

TABLE 14: *Ranks of Information-Value for Standard Background Characteristics over all Issues for Each Data-Set*

Characteristic	GLASGOW Mean rank	GLASGOW SD ranks	BELFAST Mean rank	BELFAST SD ranks	LONDON Mean rank	LONDON SD ranks	ALL USA Mean rank	ALL USA SD ranks	NJ Mean rank	NJ SD ranks	OHIO Mean rank	OHIO SD ranks	TENN Mean rank	TENN SD ranks	CALIF Mean rank	CALIF SD ranks	ISRAEL Mean rank	ISRAEL SD ranks
Occupation	6	1·5	6	1·3	7	3·0	7	1·3	3	2·2	8	0·7	6	2·1	8	1·4		
Father's occupation	4	2·1	4	2·0	5	3·6	5	3·0	7	2·7	6	3·0	5	2·1	5	3·7		
Income					3	1·9	5	1·7	5	2·1	4	1·5	5	3·0	3	0·6		
Parent's income	5	2·1	1	0·5	8	3·4												
Denomination							4	1·5	7	3·0	4	1·5	5	3·6	2	1·9		
Region of birth							6	0·8	7	1·7	3	1·4	8	2·0	7	2·8		
Urban/rural upbringing	4	1·9	4	2·0	7	2·9	2	1·3	7	3·3	4	1·9	3	1·7	4	3·1	4*	1·2
Length of education							2	1·2	3	1·4	4	1·5	3	1·6	7	1·5	3	0·8
Type of education					6	3·2	6	0·8	6	2·1	7	1·9	7	1·3	7	1·3	3	1·2
Organisation membership					9	2·6												
Trade union membership	4	2·4	5	1·8	9	1·9												
Age	4	2·1	4	2·0	5	1·9	9	1·5	6	3·5	8	1·4	6	2·3	7	3·3	3	1·3
Sex	2	1·9	6	1·7	11	1·0	7	2·9	6	2·8	7	5·3	7	3·2	5	1·4		
Party	3	1·7	4	2·1	3	1·6	6	2·9	5	2·8	6	5·3	6	3·2	4	1·4		

* Rural/Urban employment on arrival in Israel.

Note: Blank cells indicate unavailability of information on the characteristics for a given area. Ranks are assigned for each area only for the set of characteristics shown in the table as available for each area.

The size of the standard deviation of ranks indicates the degree to which different characteristics are important for different issues within the same area.

Some characteristics in Table 14 show surprising consistency in their importance between areas – father's occupation, for example, varies only between 4 and 7. Region of birth is 6th, 7th or 8th except in Ohio. The spread is rather greater with characteristics like sex. Other factors however show greater variation: age varies widely between Glasgow and the United States, as does denomination between Belfast and New Jersey. More disquietingly for the prospects of generalisation, those characteristics such as denomination or party which assume leading ranks in one area sink to middling or low positions in others.

The situation is similar between issues within areas, as revealed by the standard deviations presented in the table. In some cases such as denomination in Belfast and party in Israel, the standard deviation is small, indicating the considerable importance that these characteristics attain across all issues (Tables 10, 13). Generally however the standard deviations are moderate to large for most of the characteristics in most areas, indicating at best a limited potentiality for generalising on a demographic basis across different issue-areas.

This conclusion can be applied to the totality of findings examined in this section. They do not absolutely preclude the possibility of predicting preferences from a limited set of background characteristics for all areas and issues. But they certainly do not encourage optimism about the success of such a generalisation. So many of the standard characteristics vary across issues and areas or give only a slight boost to successful prediction that they counterbalance the stronger effects and greater stability of such characteristics as father's occupation.

IX *Generalisation of Background Predictions between Different Areas*

'It may be possible but likely not' is an unsatisfactory conclusion on which to leave discussion. Fortunately our technique permits further analysis. Provided that the characteristics and issues involved are the same and have identical codings we are able to use the weights generated from the relationship between preferences and characteristics in one area to type elite members in another area. To simplify somewhat: if being a male member of the more conservative party, in a non-manual occupation with fifteen years of education, forty-five years old, a non-trade unionist of rather upper class background who has spent a lifetime in the city, types Glasgow councillors as

232

disagreeing with a likelihood of ·9 + with the proposal to raise rates, how far will we improve on guesswork by typing Belfast councillors in exactly the same way? The transfer of scores based on background characteristics between areas, in this way, directly answers the question of how useful background characteristics are as attitudinal indicators, by seeing how invariant the relationship is when applied elsewhere.[36]

Glasgow and Belfast offer a minimal test of generalisability because they are geographically close, share a variety of socioeconomic and cultural characteristics and have already shown some similarity in the background influences at work (Tables 9, 10). The range of issues in each city is rather different however: of issues successfully predicted the rates proposal is identical in both cities and the questions of religious integration in schools and housing seem sufficiently similar to support an attempt at the transfer of scores.

Very little predictive success is attained when Glasgow scores are used to type Belfast councillors in terms of agreement or disagreement with issues. Lambda and Tau_a are zero for the transfer of scores on the integration issue (as also when Belfast scores are used to type Glasgow councillors on the issue). Slightly more success is attained with rates: Glasgow scores applied to Belfast raise the summary statistics to just under ·20, and this is increased somewhat when Belfast scores are applied to Glasgow. Given extensive similarities between the cities this is hardly an encouraging result.[37]

The other areas where the identity of coding and issues allows transference of scores are the American States. Since differences in the relative influence of background characteristics are greater here (Table 12) it is hardly surprising that the transference of scores produces uniformly worse results than in the case of the British cities. Although we lack the ability to transfer scores at national level, due to the noncomparability of our data, the failure to make successful predictions between cities and regions inside one country argues that national transfers would be even less successful.

The attempt to transfer scores thus leads to the definite conclusion that no set of background characteristics can be isolated which acts as an invariant — or even relatively invariant — predictor of issue-preferences. Such a conclusion is of course subject to the severe limitations of the data at our disposal. But it is entirely consonant with the results of previous research on the relationship, using somewhat different data and different techniques.

Theoretical implications from our generally negative findings will be drawn in the Conclusions (Section XI). There is however one unsettled point which deserves further consideration. We pointed out earlier that background characteristics might affect issue-preferences not only by distinguishing one section of an elite from another section, but also by differentiating elite preferences as a whole from those of the corresponding population. The relatively exclusive background which distinguishes all elite groups makes such a differentiation plausible and its presence would constitute a general effect of background characteristics upon preferences even although the relationship between specific characteristics and preferences takes a different form among different elites.

In order to check the correspondence we need identical data on elites and population from the same area. We have this in the case of the British groups but not in the case of other elites.

Carrying through identical analyses to those performed on elites in Sections VII and VIII above, we found that knowledge of background characteristics enabled us to type electors' preferences less well than we could type those of elite members but still rather better than we could by pure guesswork. Predictive success varied over different issues, as with elites, but the values of Tau_a and Lambda averaged ·20 over all issues.[38] The characteristics affecting preferences proved to be generally the same amongst the population as amongst the elite: thus in Belfast for example denomination ranked first on the issues of Swings, Integration and Bridge, and second on the Hospital, much as it did among councillors. Thus the same characteristics seemed to produce similar divisions among population and elite, and to this extent British elite groups seem to reflect general opinion.

Perhaps more direct evidence of preferential correspondence between elites and populace is afforded by product-moment correlations between percentages endorsing different policies among elite and population. These ranged from ·44 to ·61, indicating a fairly substantial agreement between politicians and electors over the issues confronting them.[39]

These correspondences do not say anything about the direction in which influence flows, and are just as compatible with elite manipulation of popular preferences as with elite responsiveness to popular feeling. But the evidence does in general suggest that some correspondence exists, at least in Britain, and that elites' exclusive background does not generate exclusive elite preferences.

Technical implications are perhaps easier to derive from our investigation than broader theory. Searing's earlier finding that it is simply not obvious what attitudes the standard background characteristics indicate when used cross-nationally, is confirmed by our analysis. It is misleading to compile standard social background data on different elite groups in order to infer their political preferences and attitudes, for social background seems to be differently related to preferences in different Western polities. Outside such polities our predictive failure to type Venezuelans' preferences suggests that under the semi-crisis conditions endemic in developing countries social background may not be a good indicator of preferences at all.

The import of our findings is not wholly negative however, for inside each of the Western areas examined we have been able to type preferences fairly accurately on the basis of background characteristics. The precise form and direction of the relationship is peculiar to each elite group but it is there: within the area, preferences are consistently related to certain characteristics. This must lend a certain predictability to the political positions taken up by the elite, which may be necessary for rational bargaining and coalition-formation and in turn for political stability. The unexpected contrast between Venezuelan and Western elites on this point could be the most important conclusion of the whole analysis.

Another interesting and illuminating finding is the extent to which pre-adult socialisation experiences relate to the preferences of British elite groups. This contrasted with the mixed characteristics (both current and past) which appeared as important among American and Israeli legislators: and contrasted so strongly with Searing's general findings about his five foreign elite groups. Perhaps we have here a statistical reflection of the traditionalism often noted as a characteristic of British political culture: past experiences seem to retain their influence on present attitudes longer than they do in other countries.

In terms of future research strategy our conclusions point strongly to more intensive work on the socialisation of individual elites, with a view to uncovering the processes which render certain factors more influential than others and which relate them differently to issues in different systems and to diverse issues. Such research may have the incidental effect of generating better indicators of background effects than the ones we have been operating upon.

Throughout the paper we have been concerned with its bearings upon those Power Elite hypotheses which emphasise the effects of

235

elites' exclusive background upon the content of decisions. We accept that the specific time-bound issues we have examined cannot conclusively test these hypotheses. Nevertheless we have not found a peculiarly pronounced elite consensus on issues related to a fundamental restructuring of the economy, nor on issues which might be regarded as fundamental by other criteria (such as politico-religious issues in Belfast). The attitudinal effects of social background vary so much even between British cities that general inferences can hardly be drawn from the exclusive characteristics shared by all elites. Moreover similar preferential divisions seem to exist among British elites as among the corresponding populations, similar characteristics show broadly similar relationships to issue-preferences and these preferences themselves generally correspond. Certainly popular preferences are strongly affected by the institutional alternatives available, and our findings may reflect some manipulation of populace by elites and a certain false consciousness among the population. But the import of our findings is generally against the thesis of concurrent elite action in defence of the *status quo*, even in its fundamental aspects. The onus of proof is now on elite theorists to identify fundamental issues and to show that they are affected differently by social background than those we have examined.

NOTES

1. Following from a number of earlier studies, this view is put most plausibly on a solidly researched basis by G. W. Domhoff, *The Higher Circles*, Vintage, New York, 1971, for the US, and by Ralph Miliband, *The State in Capitalist Society*, Weidenfield & Nicolson, London, 1969, for the UK, with side glances at France. The link between demographic characteristics and political attitudes is also accepted by many non-Marxist scholars without the same implication of a ruling elite: e.g. Jean Blondel, *Voters, Parties and Leaders*, Penguin, Harmondsworth, 1963, pp. 139–48; W. L. Guttsman, *The British Political Elite*, MacGibbon & Kee, London, 1963, Chs. 6 and 7.

2. Miliband, p. 69; Domhoff, p. 107.

3. Miliband makes the distinction less clear by following the quotation in the text with the remark: 'it must be stressed again that this basic consensus between bourgeois politicians does not preclude

important and genuine differences between them, not only on issues other than the actual management of the economic system, but on that issue as well' (p. 71). A distinction might be abstracted from p. 72: (Western) 'politics . . . (is) . . . about different conceptions of how to run the *same* economic and social system and not about radically different social systems'. However it is difficult to know what is, operationally, a radically different system. Presumably nationalisation, worker participation in management, etc., do not count. Perhaps ultimately the 'agreement' of the Power Elite is for Miliband negative: their common non-consideration of radical socialist measures. Domhoff offers no guidance to the distinction between fundamental and other issues.

4. Domhoff, pp. 354–5.

5. D. Matthews, *The Social Background of Political Decision-Makers*, Random House, New York, 1955, p. 5.

6. ibid., p. 4; see also pp. 3, 5, 38, 40–1, 60.

7. ibid., p. 4.

8. ibid., pp. 39–41.

9. See the series of studies in the Hoover Elite Series: also Guttsman, op. cit.: J. Meynaud, *Decisions and Decision-Makers in the Modern State*, UNESCO, Paris, 1967.

10. L. J. Edinger and D. D. Searing, 'Social Background in Elite Analysis: A Methodological Inquiry', *American Political Science Review* (hereafter cited as *APSR*), Vol. 61, 1967, pp. 428–45; D. D. Searing, 'The Comparative Study of Elite Socialisation', *Comparative Politics*, Vol. 1, pp. 471–500.

11. 'Comparative Study', p. 474; 'Social Background', p. 445.

12. Of course elite theorists like Domhoff could refuse to accept this evidence on the ground that relationships to highly specific attitudes within a short time span do not tell us anything about relationships to fundamental issues. But the onus is then on the elite theorists to investigate relationships with fundamental issues.

13. A replication of Searing's studies, which produced substantially similar conclusions, has been undertaken by Uwe Schleth: 'Once again: Does it pay to study Social Background in Elite Analysis', pp. 99–118 of *Sozial Wissenschaftliches Jahrbuch für Politik*, Rudolf Wildenmann (ed.), Munich and Vienna, 1970.

14. Ian Budge and Dennis Farlie, 'Background Characteristics and Political Recruitment', unpublished MS.

15. ibid. Indicators which were more subjective in character, which were not particularly successful in distinguishing legislators from

corresponding populations, proved good discriminators between drop-outs and stayers within an elite group.

16. 'Comparative Study' footnotes 8 and 11 describe the general nature of opinions elicited: they included foreign and domestic issues, procedural orientations, perceptions and evaluations of home and foreign politics and of the socioeconomic structure of the country concerned.

17. Edinger and Searing note the better performance of their background factors in relation to 'salient political issues' over their French and German data ('Social Background', p. 445, footnote 39). This finding was apparently not upheld on the wider comparisons with American, Israeli and Venezuelan material ('Comparative Study', p. 493).

18. The link between attitudes and behaviour is largely unprobed, as Searing notes ('Comparative Study', pp. 494–5). The inconsistencies commonly noted are examples of mass behaviour (cf. David Marsh, 'Political Socialisation: The Implicit Assumptions Questioned', *British Journal of Political Science*, Vol. 1, 1971, pp. 453–66). As Dahl notes, inconsistencies are less likely to appear in the case of elites: R. A. Dahl (ed.), *Political Opposition in Western Democracies*, Yale, New Haven and London, 1966, pp. 370–1. The main empirical evidence for the close relationship between legislators' issue-preferences and vote comes from American representation studies, cf. W. E. Miller and D. E. Stokes, 'Constituency Representation in Congress', pp. 287–306 of C. Cnudde and D. E. Neubauer, *Empirical Democratic Theory*, Markham, Chicago, 1969.

19. Detailed information about the Glasgow surveys is given in Appendix A of Ian Budge, J. A. Brand, M. Margolis, A. L. M. Smith, *Political Stratification and Democracy*, Macmillan, London, 1972.

20. Full details about the Belfast surveys are reported in Appendix A of Ian Budge and C. O'Leary, *Belfast: Approach to Crisis*, Macmillan, London, 1973, Appendix A.

21. For details see Ian Budge, *Agreement and the Stability of Democracy*, Markham, Chicago, 1970, Appendix D.

22. A full report of design and results of the survey is made in John Wahlke, H. Eulau, W. Buchanan, L. C. Ferguson, *The Legislative System*, Wiley, New York, 1962, Ch. 2 and Appendices. We wish to thank these authors for the generous provision of their data for secondary analysis.

23. The Venezuelan study is briefly described in Searing, 'Comparative Study', footnote 8. The design is discussed in detail in F.

238

Bonilla, and J. A. Silva Michilena, *A Strategy for Research on Social Policy*, MIT Press, Cambridge, Mass., 1967, pp. xiv–xviii. We wish to thank these authors and their collaborators for making data available for secondary analysis.

24. 'Comparative Study', footnote 8. The main report of the interviews is in L. Seligman, *Leadership in a New Nation*, Atherton, New York, 1964. Problems of transference reduced the effective numbers for our analysis from 93 to 89. We wish to thank Professor Seligman for making his data available for secondary analysis.

25. The German and the French data used in Searing's and Edinger's original investigation were unfortunately not available for our use at the time of writing.

26. All quotations are from 'Comparative Study', p. 474.

27. ibid., pp. 488–9.

28. Such placements may not in fact be error. Viewed in a longer time perspective they may identify those most likely to switch preferences on the issue.

29. Lambda, and Goodman and Kruskall's Tau_a, are based on the calculation:

$$\frac{\text{No. of errors made using} \atop \text{naive guessing rule} \; - \; \text{No. of errors made using} \atop \text{likelihood scores}}{\text{No. of errors made using naive} \atop \text{guessing rule.}}$$

For Lambda the naive guessing rule is simply to place everyone in the largest category: for Tau_a it is to assign individuals so as to reproduce the marginal distribution of preferences. In order to calculate these statistics we have however to dichotomise likelihood scores at .5.

30. For discussions of this finding and its relationship to the subsequent crisis, see Budge and O'Leary, *Belfast*, Chs. 11 and 13; also Ian Budge and C. O'Leary, 'Cross-cutting Cleavages, Agreement and Compromise', Vol. XV, 1971, pp. 1–30; and 'Relationships between Attitudinal and Background Cross-cutting', Vol. XVII, 1973, of *Midwest Journal of Political Science*. The aggregate agreement of councillors masks a split in the ruling Unionist Party which can be regarded as ultimately responsible for the breakdown of order.

31. Budge, *Agreement*, Ch. 7.

32. It does not apparently apply to more basic attitudes: Searing found no less a relationship between background factors and attitudes in general in Venezuela than in the other countries included in his study. 'Comparative Study', pp. 474–7.

33. Movement along a straight line (two preferences) is necessarily more limited than movement in a triangle (three preferences).

34. In contrast, Searing concluded that in relation to general political attitudes (including issue-preferences) current affiliations and behaviour were substantially more important than early socialisation for the elites he examined ('Comparative Study', pp. 477–8).

35. According to a review of over 200 inventories of elite characteristics the most frequently used background characteristics are: occupation, education, age, region of birth and religion. F. W. Frey, 'Social Background of Political Elites' cited in Searing, 'Comparative Study', p. 484. All are included in Table 14 though some are not available for all data sets.

36. While in principle a similar operation could be carried out between different issues within the same area, or between different issues in different areas, dissimilarities between data-sets and issues limit analysis in this direction at the present time. However a negative result to the minimal test proposed in the text makes it unlikely that more ambitious transfers of values would be successful.

37. The negative results are certainly not an artefact of the technique, since similar transferences of scores for the activist-elector distinction were successful for five British cities. Budge and Farlie, 'Background Characteristics', op. cit.

38. Thus rather going against the idea that background characteristics are more consistently related to popular than to elite preferences, as suggested for example by Dahl, *Political Oppositions*, pp. 370–1.

39. For the method of comparison and results see Budge *et al.*, *Political Stratification*, p. 94; Budge and O'Leary, *Belfast*, p. 294.

STUDIES IN ELITE THEORY

8. Property, Class and the Corporate Elite*

PHILIP H. STANWORTH

Introduction

An influential strand of social thought has incorporated the notion that the advance of industrialisation has been matched by a decline in the importance of property. Those writers inclined to this opinion have emphasised the idea that technocratic and meritocratic principles have become, or are in the process of becoming, the dominant elements in the stratification of industrial societies. Moreover, the change from 'class structure' to 'stratification' has been seen as part of a more general development toward the gradual erosion of ideological and institutional differences between industrial societies with contrasting political and economic systems which will eventually culminate in societal 'convergence'. Accordingly it has been argued that the class structure of capitalism, and in particular the upper class asserted to be characteristic of bourgeois society, has dissolved as the essentially classless character of industrial society has become manifest. Perhaps greatest stress has been put on the irresistible progress of the managers of corporate enterprises, characterised at one extreme as bureaucratic zombies, but also more sympathetically as benign administrators. The rise of a corporate elite of propertyless administrators and business leaders has frequently been cited as evidence of the decline, or even disappearance of the upper class, and the enervation of property.

The consequent concern with those who control company assets is in part a reflection of a tendency to concentrate on a more general, theoretical level, and with the decision-making aspects of power, though it may be noted that remarkably few studies of British elites have in fact combined the analysis of social backgrounds, career paths and the like with the intensive investigation of the series of important decisions. Be that as it may, there has been an inclination to assume

* I would like to thank Anthony Giddens and Dr Robert Blackburn of the Faculty of Economics and Politics, University of Cambridge, for their comments and advice in the preparation of this paper.

that the real structure of power is very close to the formal structure of decision-making. This has obscured other features of power relationships which cannot be considered by reference to decision-making alone. Similarly the influence of the classical elite theory has been toward an almost exclusive concentration on political power and decision-making. Hence attention has been directed away from property, and the significance granted to it as a source of power and inequality has diminished. Mosca and Pareto, of course, conceived their somewhat similar theories as a thorough-going critique of socialist theories and ideals, and the concepts of 'political class' and 'governing elite' were formulated with a pungent emphasis on the primacy of political power in an explicit rejection of Marxist theories of class structure.[1]

Although Marx failed to provide a single systematic statement of his views on class it is at least clear that he regarded property relationships as a fundamental component of class structure. In this Marx was continuing to employ a well-established usage, a fact he openly acknowledged.[2] Therefore, in dismissing the historical materialism and class analysis that were the bedrock of Marxist thinking, Pareto and Mosca were also repudiating that conception of property which placed it at the centre of prior and existing systems of social inequality. They put emphasis on political power as the primary component in the structure of domination, and in so doing, moved control of the means of administration to the centre of the stage at the expense of the ownership of the means of production. Thus studies of elites which have addressed the problem of power have generally concentrated on decision-making and only rarely given systematic consideration to the context of class structure as a significant phenomenon of power.[3] It often seems to be assumed that to the extent that elites can be shown to 'exist' and to have 'autonomy' then class structure is relatedly less significant. Therefore to a large number of social theorists the elite concept is both a critique of, and alternative to, class analysis. Some Marxist writers see a similar contradiction in that class analysis is seen to negate the assumptions that lie at the base of classical elite theory. Poulantzas,[4] for example, reasons in his review of Miliband's *State in Capitalist Society*[5] that the elite concept is incompatible with the correct conception of the Marxist 'problematic'.

This point of view would be valid if the use of the term 'elite' by necessity carried the assumptions of superiority, solidarity and power associated with Pareto's theories. While some writers continue to 'build-in' these characteristics there is no necessary theoretical or

244

empirical reason why this must be the case and compelling arguments why certain issues should be left open for enquiry. As Aron, Bottomore and Giddens[6] have emphasised the problems of the recruitment, structure, and power of elites are all points for empirical investigation. If the term elite is used simply to denote those who occupy senior positions of formal authority in various institutions then the characteristics of elites can be examined and their relationship to class structure analysed. The systematic examination of the relationship of class structure to elite formation in Britain remains a pressing task for social scientists, in view of the general importance of the British case to discussions of the so-called 'decomposition' of capitalism, and the surprising neglect by sociologists of the British upper class.

The Decline of Property

Social and political theorists have given frequent consideration to the institution of property and its relationship to social inequality although there have been wide differences in the manner in which the association has been construed. Two broad approaches can be discerned, although it must be emphasised that neither necessarily constitutes in any sense a tradition of school. First, there are those writers who have emphasised the centrality of private property to the structure of inequality within society. Authors such as Rousseau and Millar argued that private property emerged at the point when the natural equality of men was destroyed: 'The first man who, having enclosed a piece of ground, bethought himself of saying "this is mine", and found people simple enough to believe him was the real founder of civil society.'[7] Not only was property at the source of inequality, it was for these writers the continuing basis of the unequal distribution of power in society. Perhaps the most sophisticated, and certainly the most influential writer in this vein was Marx. Marx maintained that private property was the consequence of alienated labour[8] and that those who owned the means of production stood in contradiction to those who had only their labour to sell. All relationships of power in capitalist society, as in other types of class society, were linked to basic property relationships. Marx's stress on property relations and class structure has remained a fundamental component of Marxist theory though some avowedly socialist authors have categorically rejected its continued validity.[9]

Another approach which takes a position contrary to that just outlined is gathered around the theme that private property, once an important component and source of inequality in classic capitalism,

245

has now declined in its general social significance. More particularly, those who support this view state that private ownership is no longer an important basis of power in society, and has, furthermore, been supplanted in the very context in which property might be expected to retain its importance most tenaciously, that of the industrial enterprise. Increasingly modern writers of this persuasion are wont to refer to 'post industrial', 'post capitalist'[10] or simply 'the industrial society'[11] in order to express their conviction that 'capitalism' is now an obsolete term. Moreover, some hint that the concept 'socialism' is about to suffer a similar fate as a consequence of the inexorable progress of industrialisation which has the effect of eradicating the distinction between the major economic and political systems.

The idea that the decline of property would be an inevitable result of industrialisation is not a new idea. Since the early days of the nineteenth century, when embryonic industry was growing rapidly, certain writers have projected this image of the future, just as more contemporary observers have sought to confirm and extend the trend. Saint Simon's work is particularly prescient in this respect, not because his predictions on the future of industrial society were particularly accurate, but because the thoughts he expressed have found frequent echo in the writings of others.[12] It was his conviction that future industrial societies would be arranged around what he termed 'production' rather than property. Saint Simon believed that the key to power in industrial society would be knowledge, and that scientists, engineers, creative artists, financial and industrial experts would constitute the political leadership of the future. This he contrasted with the situation of his own time in which men of property were paramount. By this unambiguous declaration that the pivotal role of property was but a temporary phase, soon to be replaced by a more technocratic principle, Saint Simon succeeded in estranging his bourgeois supporters for whom such a vision resembled a spectre rather than the millennium. They must have felt happier with Saint Simon's erstwhile secretary Auguste Comte who took a more conservative, though in some respects similar, position in regard to the industrial future. While he conceded that the role of men of property, pure and simple, would be severely curtailed in the future, Comte recoiled from the thought that property would or should be unimportant. It was Comte's opinion that rulers should always be substantial property owners, but property should go only to those of great merit. Merit, of course, accrued to those who demonstrated a proper understanding of Positivist knowledge.[13] While Comte's conception of the future was much more rooted in the past than that of Saint Simon the fundamental theme was also that of the accentuation of the role of knowledge and the emergence of a technocracy.

Although Durkheim wrote little specifically about property in industrial society it is clear that he was sympathetic to Saint Simon's views on the diminishing significance of property in industrial society.[14] He argued that the continuing development of the division of labour would erode the position of property as the primary component of social hierarchy, for an increasingly complex differentiation would place a premium on the personal 'internal' qualities and intellectual abilities of individuals.[15] In particular, the inheritance of property, by which general social advantage and considerable power were bestowed on the receiver would disappear; 'A day will come when it will no longer be permitted a man, even by way of testament, to leave his fortune to his descendants, just as he has not been allowed (since the Revolution) to leave them his social function or his high offices.'[16] However, Durkheim was unwilling to await the elimination of inheritance in the fulness of time for he advocated its virtual abolition during his own lifetime.

Saint Simon, Comte and Durkheim were in the main writing about the future in the sections of their work to which reference has been made. However, a number of more recent contributions to the discussion have maintained either that the emasculation of property is already well advanced, or that it is an accomplished fact. Perhaps the most renowned aspect of this point of view has been the prominence given to the so-called 'managerial revolution' and that most publicised of all divorces, of ownership from control. The arguments have been widely repeated and variously summarised and criticised.[17] However, the main points can be restated in so far as they impinge on the role of property in present-day industrial societies. One note of caution must, unfortunately, be intoned. As Beed has emphasised, 'the real as opposed to the formal relations between ownership and control in companies has yet to be empirically investigated'.[18] As with many debates in the social sciences this condition of fundamental ignorance has been overlooked in the heat of discussion. What should be a hypothesis is stated with the conviction of a confirmed proposition.

The Rise of the Managers

In its strongest version the 'managerialist' argument has encompassed

247

the claim that the capitalist ruling class has been replaced by a new class of managers. Burnham,[19] for instance, stated that a new managerial class was displacing, and would eventually succeed, the bourgeoisie. The growing predominance of the managers, in his opinion, was an expression of their indispensability in an age of technological and organisational complexity. It was this factor which delivered control of the business enterprise and ultimately society into their hands. Burnham did not dismiss property 'ownership', however, for he thought that the common distinction made between ownership and control was fundamentally misleading. Thus he referred to the managers as a ruling class because they 'own' by virtue of the control they exert: 'ownership means if there is no control, then there is no ownership . . . if ownership and control are in reality separated, then ownership has changed hands to "control", and then the separated ownership is a meaningless fiction . . . the sources of wealth are the basic instruments of production . . . [and] are to be directed by the managers; and the managers are then, to be the ruling class.'[20] Burnham claimed, therefore, that the alleged divorce between ownership and control was a fiction. All that had changed was the social location of ownership. But this complete identification of ownership with control ignores other aspects of ownership and property relations which will be examined, briefly, below.

The idea that the power of the managers springs from their functional indispensability, and that the ownership of property is in comparison of little significance, has been stated with particular vigour by Drucker, although he did not follow Burnham's example by using the term class.

> A new ruling group has emerged in our society – management . . . it derives its authority and responsibilities squarely from function . . . and not from anything it possesses such as property [etc.] . . . nor does it derive its position from the authority of superior knowledge . . . Its position, its power, its responsibilities rest on indispensable functions.[21]

These remarks were directly primarily toward the USA but it is clear that Drucker regarded this development as one which would be manifested in all advanced industrial societies. It is curious to note that although he regarded property ownership as of minor importance, he bestowed considerable significance on a process he claimed to discern,

248

by which the rights associated with occupational position were increasingly similar to those normally associated with ownership. However, the general implication that power is associated with functional indispensability, and not property, is unmistakable.

Burnham and Drucker promulgated 'strong' versions of the managerialist thesis for they argued that the decline of the capitalist ruling class had been matched by the emergence of a new ruling corporate elite or class. However, there is another version of managerialism which places the development of a non-owning managerial group within the general context of a movement away from a ruling class situation, to one in which a plurality of institutional elites and groups representing diverse interests contend to have their particular, and often opposed, policies realised by means of government action. The corporate elite wields power within fairly well-defined institutional limitations, and has no position of particular advantage in competing with other interests over issues of general concern. As the centre of this competitive activity, the political system, which is also the institutional focus of decision-making, is given a position of particular significance. Politics, for these writers, is essentially concerned with compromise and the reconciliation of oppositions within the framework of a consensus which reflects the common interests of all. Property, shorn of its political privileges, and excluded by the realities of shareholding from control of the corporate economy, becomes one interest among many, albeit for more sophisticated pluralists such as Dahl and Polsby, an interest with a position of relative advantage. Business leaders, divested of any substantial stake in property, and isolated from the political arena, more than ever before have to take careful note of public opinion and orient their policies appropriately.

In common with 'moderate' managerialists Parsons emphasises the professional and technical competence of managers in contrast to the ascriptive rights of the owners under 'classic' capitalism. He also implies that the property-based industrial economy is an archaic form, since it is in the nature of industrial society that a well-defined elite of professional career executives should emerge. Parsons is quite unequivocal that this is already the case in the USA: 'I must stress that the business elite is no longer primarily an elite of property owners'.[22] Property is thus replaced by professional competence as the basis of authority in the highly complex industrial and financial organisations in which the vagaries of inheritance and mere wealth have no place. The new corporate elite operates within clearly defined

249

institutional limits such that its political influence compares most unfavourably with the power of property in the days before the political emasculation of the ruling class.

Given the removal of property as a potent force in the political arena, and the democratic representation of diverse interest groups, political programmes based on the articulation of class interests, or purely ideological considerations, lose any broadly based appeal they might have had and become obsolete. Literally there is an 'end to ideology'[23] in this sense, and class politics disappear as a result of the technical logic of industrialisation.

The imperatives of technology are pin-pointed by Galbraith as the chief factor in the emergence of a new locus of power within the economy which he terms the technostructure.[24] The technostructure, an admittedly vague formulation, consists of all those who contribute specialised knowledge to the process of group decision-making, of which the managerial sector is but a small element. In capitalist societies, Galbraith argues, the entrepreneur has more or less disappeared, while the corporation has escaped control of its legal owners and become largely self-reliant in terms of finance. The authority of the market has evaporated and is gradually being replaced by the guiding hand of the state, which becomes the general orchestrator of the economy although industry 'calls the tune'. However, Galbraith thinks the technostructure is ill-equipped for effective direct political action, unlike the entrepreneurial class of the past. Increasingly business has become indifferent to the particular party in office and adopts a chameleon attitude to ideological considerations, for government policies demonstrate a growing similarity regardless of the political rhetoric of whichever party is in office. In return for this spirit of co-operation and since government needs access to their specialised knowledge the business corporations have gained influence on decisions central to their own interests, particularly those which affect the general level of demand. Accordingly the technostructure has become a primary influence on the formulation of policy although it has no *formal* part in actual publicly declared political decisions. The pattern is one in which the technostructure has established its needs in regard to the economy and these have been passed on by the producers to the consumer. Galbraith therefore sees the 'needs' of the technostructure as the paramount organisational principle at work in industrial societies, so much so, that ideological considerations become irrelevant. Thus, communist and capitalist societies can be expected to converge[25] under the exigencies of technology and the desire to maintain a predictable level of production and demand combined with a stable social order.

The alienation of control from the owning class has been seen to have crucial consequences for the experience of owning in that the owners and controllers of large-scale business have lost their desire to support the rights of property. In the process of economic aggrandisement, the entrepreneur has been bureaucratised out of existence. Whereas ownership of an enterprise once involved the direct experience of control this has now been transformed into the passive and impersonal possession of shares. Consequently the motivation to defend both business and the interests of private property has declined:

> The capitalist process, by substituting a mere parcel of shares for the walls of, and machines in, a factory, takes the life out of the idea of property. It loosens the grip that once was so strong . . . Eventually there will be nobody left who cares to stand for it.[26]

Schumpeter and Geiger[27] lay particular emphasis on this supposed change in motivation between owner and managers and between the capitalist proprietors and the inert rentier. Thus legal owners have little commitment to the preservation of private property, and the managers who control giant corporations have a minimal, and waning, adhesion to property themselves. It is reasoning of this kind that lies behind the conviction that the controllers of privately owned corporations are more liable to be susceptible to the interests of the public, as opposed to those of property, by virtue of their institutional differentiation from the *de jure* owners. Hence the 'soulful' corporation.

The crux of these arguments excepting Galbraith's emphasis on the diffuse nature of the techno-structure, is that although the ownership of a public company lies with its shareholders, be they thousands or millions, the actual administration of the enterprise, from broad policy decisions to more mundane matters, is carried out at the behest of a few professional directors recruited mainly for their managerial skills. The power of this group and a few large shareholders, it is said, goes far beyond any ownership stake they might collectively have in the corporation. Most large corporations, especially those that constitute the 'top 100'[28] which dominate the economy, more or less conform to this model, and consequently control of the greater part of the economy has been wrested from the owners by a process of organisational development to be condensed and concentrated into the hands of a tiny managerial elite.

This situation is compared with the days of classic family capitalism when enterprises were owned and operated by the same people and who themselves constituted a 'ruling class'. The ensuing bifurcation of ownership and control therefore has involved, it is claimed, the emasculation of the capitalist class and its eventual replacement by an economic elite whose power stems from their professional skills and their position at the head of the bureaucratic structures of large corporations. Opinions differ as to the power of the corporate elite when compared with other social groups, but with the exceptions of Burnham, the general conclusion among managerialists seems to be that it is much more limited than that of the now defunct capitalist class. Private property is no longer the fundamental basis of power within the economy or society at large.

There are a number of problems raised by the ownership and control argument which are important to the discussion of the distribution of power in industrial societies. Firstly the debate is primarily about the control of the property.[29] It is stated that property ownership in and of itself generates no power within a particular enterprise except in the case of very substantial shareholdings. Now there appears to be much validity for this point of view from the perspective of the majority of shareholders who rarely, if ever, play an active role in company affairs. Only in the case of infrequent exceptions such as takeover bids, when small shareholders may reject the advice of their board over the question of who shall in future control the company assets and vote or sell accordingly, are there decisive shifts of control away from the directors and the large shareholders. However, despite the loss of control associated with certain forms of property other aspects of the power associated with property ownership are still firmly linked to the private owners.

The concept of ownership has two important dimensions, sociological and legal. From the legal point of view the principle concern is with the rights associated with possession, while the sociologist may be more interested in the analysis of the actual content and consequences of property relationships. The legal content of ownership is of course subject to variation over time and between different systems of law. In Britain, property owners are guaranteed certain rights which vary in respect to the property object.[30] However, certain general observations may be made. First, property owners receive income generated by various forms in which property is held, be it rent, profit, dividends, or capital gains. Like any other form of income property income yields purchasing power, that is the ability

252

to command certain resources on the market subject to their availability. In the case of owners of substantial property, the income from this source is probably crucial in ensuring access to those goods and services which lie beyond most earned incomes and are, at the same time, associated with an upper class style of life. In particular the children of the wealthy are liable to have access to those educational processes which are known to be vital in maximising their life chances. Only a small proportion of parents can afford the fees needed to complete an education at a reputable public school[31] and it is reasonable to suppose that most of the sons of the upper class attend this type of school. The dominance of ex-public school pupils in elite positions has been well-documented and the extent to which the upper class is over-represented may be taken as an indication of one aspect of the power of property.[32] Furthermore entry into elite positions often entails long periods of university and professional training which constitutes a formidable obstacle to those of slender means. In this sense property is significantly linked to whatever power may be linked to elite positions. Ownership yields income that can be transformed into educational privilege which, in turn, bestows considerable advantage in gaining access to elites.[33]

Of course, those with substantial property share access to the goods and services which have an important bearing on life chances with the salary rich, but property ownership has an important attribute which is not characteristic of most occupational positions — wealth can be conveyed to those of one's choice. In Britain there are few restrictions on the manner in which property is transmitted at, or before, death, other than death duties. It would appear that the possession of property, combined with the ability to pass it on to descendants, substantially intact, has been a vital factor in the enduring capacity of many upper-class families to place their sons over several generations in positions of key importance in British society. Indeed, research on the respective roles of inheritance and accumulation as the bases of large fortunes[34] has confirmed the impression that the upper-class 'extended' family, like that of the working- and middle-classes, continues to act as an important medium for the transmission of physical, financial and ideological assets.[35] Long ago Hobhouse[36] commented that inheritance was the most powerful factor shaping the social conditions of his time, and in 1926 Stamp[37] outlined a detailed programme for the analysis of the processes by which wealth was transmitted from one generation to the next. This suggestion has been largely unheeded although the excellent work of Wedgewood,

Harbury and Atkinson has confirmed the view that the inheritance of substantial wealth remained the foundation of most large fortunes. Death duties once promoted as a means of redistributing wealth throughout society have in fact proved to be 'voluntary taxes' and their only effect has been to substantially increase 'inter-vivos' giving. All the available evidence supports the impression that the general concentration of wealth remains substantially what it was sixty years ago, except that wealth is now held by more than one member of wealthy families being 'spread' through several generations in order to minimise the tax burden on property income and to avoid death duties.[38] This is impressive evidence of the ability of property holders to resist the admittedly half-hearted efforts of a number of governments to redistribute large fortunes among the community at large.

In the matters of income and conveyance then, the position of private property owners remains in reality substantially what it was before the large-scale spread of the joint stock form of organisation and divorce of ownership and control. Although this latter has meant that the bulk of owners of certain assets have no direct control over the use to which their investments are put, the point must be made that the relatively propertyless controllers are not unacquainted either with the pressure to create profit, or the ensuing ideological self-legitimation that were characteristic features in the experience of the capitalist class of old. It is known that most directors, and particularly those of the large corporations, have attended public schools and come, therefore, from relatively privileged social backgrounds.[39] Just as the abolition of purchase in the armed forces failed to open up the elite of the officer corps to all comers,[40] so too the emphasis on 'technical and managerial' skills has failed to 'democratise' the boards of large industrial commercial and financial organisations to any dramatic extent. Secondly, although the shareholdings of directors in the firms on whose boards they sit are only a small proportion of total shares, the market value of these shares and the income they yield is considerable,[41] and it must remain an open question as to whether there is much difference between the commitment of present-day business leaders to private property and that of the Victorian captains of industry. It can be demonstrated that most directors of large companies are substantial property owners in their own right even if only the shareholdings as noted in the relevant company reports are taken into account. This factor alone differentiates them from the ordinary company employees with whom they often compare themselves for the structural contingencies operating on the

254

TABLE 1: *The Distribution of Directorial Shareholdings* (*ordinary shares only*) *in the top seventy-five companies*

Value	Beneficial interest	Beneficial plus other interest	Distribution of wealth among male population
£	%	%	%
Up to 1000	18·9	15·9	23·4
1000–3000	19·8	18·5	30·8
3000–5000	9·8	9·2	19·2
5000–10,000	13·9	13·6	17·4
10,000–25,000	11·7	11·5	6·7
25,000–100,000	12·4	13·2	2·2
Over 100,000	13·5	18·1	0·3

Information on directorial shareholdings was drawn from the 1971 annual reports of the companies. The values of shareholdings are based on the average market value of the relevant shares from 1966–70 as given in Moody's *Investment Handbook 1971*.

The top seventy-five companies were selected according to the size of Capital Employed in 1971 are given in *The Times 1000*.

The figures for shareholdings refer to the value of ordinary shares only, and do not, of course, include shares these directors may hold in other companies. They therefore represent their minimum disposable wealth.

The figures for the male population as a whole refer to all forms of wealth and were drawn from *Social Trends No. 2*, H.M.S.O., London, 1971, p. 81.

director who owns a stake in his company with a considerable market value differs significantly from those experienced by workers. As Weber commented in his preliminary statement on class, ' "property" and lack of property are the basic categories of all class situations'.[42] Therefore it is worthwhile emphasising that the directors of those firms that dominate the British economy appear to have a long way to go before they can be meaningfully described as propertyless. Any analysis which proceeds on that assumption is profoundly misleading for it cannot be maintained that senior executives and directors stand outside the interests of private property.

These comments on the corporate elite and their relationship to property raise certain issues regarding the association of the distribution of power to class structure and elite formation. Class structure is, of course, very significant in this respect for as Weber was at pains to point out, 'Classes are a phenomenon of the distribution of power in a community.'[43] Yet it is unfortunately the case that that sector of British society which constitutes the apex of the class structure and the most important repository of class power, the upper-class, has been subject to little systematic research. Studies of power have tended far more often to focus on the activities of various elites, though again in the case of Britain there has been remarkably little work done if the political elite is excepted.

Thus the few studies which have addressed the problem of ascertaining the distribution of power between elites and non-elites, and within elite circles, have generally adopted an approach which emphasises decision-making and the formal structure of authority. Barely has systematic consideration been given to the context of class structure as a significant phenomenon of power.

There is no point in denying the centrality of decison-making but in the absence of an analysis of other aspects of power the particular elite in question may be viewed out of context and its autonomy and power overestimated. Bachrach and Baratz point out that 'It is possible for a group to be in a position to create the illusion of consensus by limiting debate to the non-controversial . . . all forms of political organisation have a bias in favour of the exploitation of some kinds of conflict and the suppression of others because organisation is the mobilisation of bias.'[44] Paradoxically, therefore, power is manifested both in the making of decisions, and, also in the ability to manage a situation such that certain issues rarely become matters for public discussion and arbitration. The management of consensus is thus an important aspect of power by whatever means it is achieved, although the means used will, of course, be particularly revealing of the relationship between the dominant and subordinate groups. This line of thinking can be taken further. Merton has pointed out 'institutions are differentially supported throughout society.'[45] In this respect they often represent the crystallisation of certain interests. They are rarely neutral. Thus the degree to which social institutions encompassing particular sectional interests survive, and are 'accepted', is an expression of the power of those who maximise their life chances and a life style by the continued existence of the institution in question.

Private property is such an institution, and property relationships are power relationships. To the extent that owners of property have successfully resisted the efforts of governments to curtail the rights of property and have successfully adopted strategies to avoid the compulsory redistribution of wealth through taxation property remains a potent social force. Property has, of course, been shorn of its legal electoral privileges and certain types of property have become more widely distributed among the population. However, as noted above, the general pattern of concentration of wealth has remained remarkably stable since the First World War, and yet has, at the same time, rarely been a political issue of first-rank importance. Even nationalisation, seen by many at the time as creating a socialist enclave in a capitalist economy, has taken place within the general framework of the assumptions of private property except that it was accomplished through compulsory purchase. But it was *purchase* by the State not expropriation, and there is evidence to suggest that the 'fair' compensation received by the former owners was channelled into rather more profitable enterprises with better long-run prospects.[46] Thus in a number of important respects private property and the power that flows from ownership remains intact. This is not to deny that there is a corporate elite whose sphere of control extends far beyond any property owned by the individuals of which it is constituted. Although the general parameters of the development can be discerned, the details such as the degree of internal integration and its power relative to other groups in society remain matter for research. Especially important is the clarification of the relationship between the State, or those who control the State apparatus, and the corporate elite.[47] Despite the emergence of this elite it appears that the assumptions and social relationships associated with property provide the general framework within which the corporate economy, and perhaps even major publicly owned enterprises, continue to operate. The corporate elite acts within the context of the norms and values associated with private property relations.[48] Thus while the forms in which property is held have changed and this had led to important modifications in the distribution of certain aspects of power, property relations remain a fundamental component of advanced capitalist societies. In Britain technocratic and meritocratic influences may have tempered the predominant position of property in regard to the distribution of power. Furthermore the relationship between the State and the upper-class is certainly more problematic than in the past. However, in the absence of systematic research on the British upper-class and in the light of gross evidence of the continued concentration of property ownership, it would appear that those views of industrial society which encompass the idea of the emasculation of property stand on insecure ground. This rise of the corporate elite has not demonstrably involved the transcendence of property and investigations of elites and their power should take this into consideration. Bottomore has stated 'an historical analysis of the changing class of structure modern societies . . . remains one of the most important unfulfilled tasks of sociology today'. Not the least benefit of such a study will be the light it casts on the ignored and obscured relationship of class structure to elite formation.

NOTES

1. Vilfredo Pareto, *The Mind and Society*, A. Livingstone and A. Bongiorno (trans.), Harcourt & Brace, London, 1963. A useful collection of Pareto's work can be found in S. E. Finer (ed.), *Vilfredo Pareto: Sociological Writings*, Pall Mall Press, London, 1966. An excellent account of the development of Mosca's ideas is contained in J. H. Meisel, *The Myth of the Ruling Class*, University of Michigan Press, Ann Arbor, 1962.

2. '. . . No credit is due to me for discovering the existence of classes in modern society. . . .', Marx to Weydemeyer quoted in T. B. Bottomore and M. Rubel (eds.), *Karl Marx: Selected Writings in Sociology and Social Philosophy*, Watts, London, 1961, pp. 3–4.

3. A notable exception in the case of Britain is W. L. Guttsman, *The British Political Elite*, MacGibbon & Kee, London, 1963.

4. Nicos Poulantzas, 'The Problem of the Capitalist State', in R. Blackburn (ed.), *Ideology in Social Science*, Fontana/Collins, London, 1972. Miliband's reply to the criticisms of Poulantzas is contained in the same collection.

5. Ralph Miliband, *The State in Capitalist Society*, Weidenfeld & Nicolson, London, 1969.

6. Raymond Aron, 'Social Class, Political Class, Ruling Class', in

R. Bendix and S. M. Lipset (eds.), *Class, Status and Power*, 2nd edition, Routledge & Kegan Paul, London, 1967; T. B. Bottomore, *Elites and Society*, Pelican Books, London, 1966, p. 44; A. Giddens, 'Elites in the British Class Structure', *Sociological Review*, Vol. 20(3), 1972.

7. 'A Discourse on the Origin of Inequality', in J. J. Rousseau, *The Social Contract and Discourses*, G. D. H. Cole (trans. and ed.), Everyman, London, 1958, p. 192; John Millar, *Origin of the Distinction of Ranks*, Edinburgh, 177.

8. Marx is somewhat ambiguous on this matter:

. . . although private property appears to be the basis and cause of the alienated labour, it is rather a consequence of the latter . . . Only in the final stage of the development of private property is its secret revealed, namely, that it is on the one hand the *product* of the alienated, and on the other the *means* by which labour is alienated, *the realisation of this realisation*.

T. B. Bottomore (ed. and trans.), *Karl Marx: Early Writings*, McGraw-Hill, New York, 1963, p. 131.

9. C. A. R. Crosland, *The Future of Socialism*, Jonathan Cape, London, 1956; Joseph A. Schumpeter, *Capitalism, Socialism and Democracy*, Allen & Unwin, London 1943.

10. R. Dahrendorf, *Class and Class Conflict in Industrial Society*, Routledge & Kegan Paul, London, 1959, Chs. VII and VIII.

11. J. K. Galbraith, *The New Industrial State*, Signet Books, New York, 1967.

12. Frank E. Manuel, *The New World of Henri Saint Simon*, Harvard University Press, Cambridge, Mass., 1956. The relevant section of Saint Simon's work is Volume IV of *L'Industrie*, 'Vues sur la propriete et la legislation'.

13. Raymond Aron, *Main Currents in Sociological Thought*, Vol. I, Pelican Books, London, 1969.

14. Durkheim's extended critique of Saint Simon is contained in his *Socialism and Saint Simon*, Alvin W. Gouldner (ed.), Collier/Macmillan, London, 1962.

15. A. Giddens (ed.), *Emile Durkheim: Selected Writings*, Cambridge University Press, Cambridge, 1972, pp. 11, 182.

16. This passage comes from 'La Famille conjugale', quoted in Kurt H. Wolff (ed.), *Essays on Sociology and Philosophy by Emile Durkheim et al.*, Harper Torchbooks, New York, 1960, p. 70. Ironically Durkheim's descendants are reported to have received considerable royalties from the sale of his work, and continue to do so.

17. A useful summary of the ownership and control debate is contained in John Child, *Business Enterprise in Modern Industrial Society*, Collier/Macmillan, London, 1969. For a good extended treatment, which also examines the impact of managerialist theories on Labour Party policy see Theo Nichols, *Ownership, Control and Ideology*, Allen & Unwin, London, 1969.

18. C. S. Beed, 'The Separation of Ownership and Control', *Journal of Economic Studies*, Vol. I(2), 1966.

19. James Burnham, *The Managerial Revolution*, John Day, New York, 1941.

20. ibid., pp. 92–3.

21. Peter Drucker, 'The Employee Society', in Peter Rose (ed.), *The Study of Society*, Random House, New York, 1967, p. 572.

22. Talcott Parsons, 'The Distribution of Power in American Society', in his *Structure and Process in Modern Society*, Free Press, New York, 1965, pp. 210–11.

23. The 'end of ideology' thesis has a number of variations. Among those associated with the general theme have been Raymond Aron, Daniel Bell, and S. M. Lipset. The latter has recently restated his position claiming the wilful misrepresentation of his views by some of his critics. See S. M. Lipset, 'The Controversy Till Now', *Encounter*, Vol. 39(6), 1972.

24. J. K. Galbraith, op. cit., Ch. 6. A trenchant criticism of Galbraith's argument is made in R. Miliband, 'Professor Galbraith and American Capitalism', in J. Saville and R. Miliband (eds.), *Socialist Register 1968*, Merlin, London, 1968.

25. The convergence thesis is discussed by John H. Goldthorpe, 'Social Stratification in Industrial Society', in Paul Halmos (ed.), *The Development of Industrial Society*, Sociological Review Monograph No. 8, 1964, and Ian Weinberg, 'The Problem of Convergence in Industrial Society: a critique', *Comparative Studies in Society and History*, Vol. XI(1), 1969.

26. Joseph A. Schumpeter, op. cit., p. 142.

27. Theodor Geiger, 'Class Society in the Melting Pot', in C. S. Heller (ed.), *Structured Social Inequality*, Collier/Macmillan, London, 1969.

28. For evidence of the notable increase in industrial concentration in Britain during recent years, and the role of mergers and take-over in this development, see M. A. Utton, 'Mergers and the Growth of Large Firms', *Bulletin of Oxford University Institute of Economics and Statistics*, Vol. 34(4), 1972; M. A. Utton, 'The Effect of Mergers

on Concentration: UK Manufacturing Industry 1954–65, *Journal of Industrial Economics*, Vol. XX(1), 1972; K. D. George, 'Changes in British Industrial Concentration 1951–8', *Journal of Industrial Economics*, Vol. XV(3), 1967.

In 1957 the 'top 80' companies held 53 per cent of total net assets.
In 1967 the 'top 80' companies held 62 per cent of total net assets.

29. Power is, of course, a notoriously difficult concept. The general distinction between decision-making dimensions of power and more general structural aspects is made by Giddens: '. . . "the institutional mediation of power" . . . refers to the general framework of the state and economy within which elite groups are recruited and structured . . . "the mediation of control" . . . refers to the power of policy formation and decision-making held by members of particular elite groups. . . .' Anthony Giddens, 'Elites', *New Society*, 16 November 1972.

30. A. B. Atkinson, *Unequal Shares*, Penguin, London, 1972. Atkinson has brought together most of the work on wealth-holding in Britain in this book.

31. This is most likely to be the case for the 'Clarendon' schools and other similarly expensive schools. They are, as Bamford says, 'consequently very exclusive from the purely financial point of view'. See T. W. Bamford, *The Rise of the Public Schools*, Nelson, London, 1967, Ch. 10. The Public Schools Commission reported in 1967 that the average annual fee for boarding boys at Headmasters' Conference Schools was £510.

32. For figures on the proportion of ex-public school pupils in various elites see D. Rubinstein and C. Stoneman (eds.), *Education for Democracy*, 2nd edition, Penguin, Harmondsworth, 1972, p. 84.

Evidence on the social origins of public school pupils is contained in T. H. J. Bishop and R. Wilkinson, *Winchester and the Public School Elite*, Faber, London, 1967; R. Hall, 'The Family Background of Etonians', in R. Rose (ed.), *Studies in British Politics*, Macmillan, London, 1967.

33. 'The primary significance of a positively privileged property class lies in
   (a) its exclusive acquisition of high-priced consumer goods,
   (b) its sales monopoly and its ability to pursue systematic policies in this regard,
   (c) its monopolisation of wealth accumulation out of unconsumed surpluses,
   (d) its monopolisation of capital formation out of saving . . .,

(e) its monopolisation of costly (educational) status privileges.' Max Weber, *Economy and Society*, G. Roth and C. Wittich (eds.), Vol. I, Bedminster Press, 1968, p. 303.

34. J. Wedgewood, *The Economies of Inheritance*, Routledge, London, 1929; C. D. Harbury, 'Inheritance and the Distribution of Personal Wealth', *Economic Journal*, Vol. 72(4), 1962; A. B. Atkinson, op. cit., and 'The Distribution of Wealth and the Individual Life Cycle', *Oxford Economic Papers*, Vol. 23(2), 1971.

35. 'The class system operates largely through the inheritance of property, to ensure that each individual maintains a certain social position, determined by his birth and irrespective of his particular abilities'. T. B. Bottomore, *Classes in Modern Society*, Allen & Unwin, London, 1967.

36. L. T. Hobhouse, *Liberalism*, Williams & Norgate, London, n.d., pp. 197–8.

37. Sir Josiah Stamp, 'Inheritance as an Economic Factor', *Economic Journal*, Vol. 36(3), 1926.

38. Concentration of personal wealth in England and Wales:

% of population	% of total personal wealth				
Over 25	1911–13	1924–30	1936–38	1954	1960
1	69	62	56	43	42
5	87	84	79	71	75
10	92	91	88	79	83
Rest	8	9	12	21	17

These figures are taken from Jack Revell, *Changes in the Social Distribution of Property in Britain During the 20th Century*, Department of Applied Economics, University of Cambridge, Reprint 295. The apparent discrepancy between these figures and those which appear in *Social Trends*, No. 3, CSO, 1972, p. 86, almost entirely disappears if note is taken of the fact that they relate to the different populations. The Government figures relate to the distribution of wealth among 'wealth-holders', while those of Revell concern the distribution of wealth among those over the age of twenty-five.

39. In 1966, 71 per cent of the directors of 102 leading companies attended public school. The dominance of public schools, and Eton in particular, is particularly pronounced in the City. See R. Heller, 'Britain's Top Directors', *Management Today*, March 1967.

There are few studies of the leaders of an industry as a whole taken over a long period of time. However Ericson's excellent work on the leaders of the steel industry shows that over 80 per cent have consistently come from Social Class 1 during the period 1850–1950. C. J. Erickson, *British Industrialists Steel and Hosiery, 1850–1950*, Cambridge University Press, Cambridge, 1959.

40. A. V. Tucker, 'Army and Society in England 1870–1900', *Journal of British Studies*, Vol. 2(2), 1963; C. B. Otley. 'The Social Origins of British Army Officers', *Sociological Review*, Vol. 18(2), 1970.

41. The information on directorial shareholdings was gleaned from the relevant company reports for 1971. The average share price for 1966–70 was calculated from the relevant Moody's Industrial Handbooks. A detailed analysis of directorial shareholdings is contained in Steven Nyman (Nuffield College, Oxford), 'Managerial Shareholding', unpublished paper, 1972. The median remuneration of the members of the boards of companies with assets in excess of £250 million was £16,490, and that for senior executives £9,090. NBPI, Report No. 107, Cmnd. 3970, 'Top Salaries in the Private Sector and Nationalised Industries'.

42. Max Weber, 'Class, Status, and Party', in H. Gerth and C. Wright Mills (eds.), *From Max Weber*, Routledge & Kegan Paul, London, 1961, p. 182.

43. Gerth and Mills, op. cit., p. 181.

44. P. Bachrach and M. Baratz, 'Two Faces of Power', *American Political Science Review*, Vol. LVII(4) 1962.

45. R. K. Merton, *Social Theory and Social Structure*, Free Press, New York, 1968, p. 176.

46. C. Jenkins, *Power at the Top*, MacGibbon & Kee, London, 1952, Ch. 2.

47. For an article which argues the weakness of business in its relations with the State see J. P. Nettl, 'Consensus or Elite Domination', *Political Studies*, XIII(1) 1965. For the contrary point of view see M. B. Barrat-Brown, 'The Controllers', *Universities and New Left Review*, Nos. 5–7, 1958, and R. Miliband op. cit.

48. As Friedmann states: 'Although many of the major powers flowing from property rights have now passed from the property owners to others, notably the managers of corporations, such power still *derives* from property' (Friedmann's italics). Wolfgang Friedmann, *Law in a Changing Society*, Penguin Books, 2nd edition, London, 1972, p. 102.

9. Elite Theory:
Ideological, Tautological, or Scientific?

MALCOLM JACK

In his *Teorica dei governi e governo parlamentare*, Gaetano Mosca, a leading exponent of elite theory among the nineteenth-century 'classicists', expresses great enthusiasm for the advent of a new science of society, saying: 'If no social science did exist up to the present moment, it can now come into being.'[1]

As he saw it, the time had come for the sweeping away of old value-ridden philosophics of obligation in favour of a new, empirically-founded science of society. Elite theory was to have provided the conceptual framework for such a science.

Late nineteenth-century elite theory was thus placed in a methodologically aggressive position by Mosca and his views were shared by the other great exponents of the theory, Vilfredo Pareto and Robert Michels.[2] From the largely theoretical writings of these 'classical' exponents, a diverse socio-political literature has arisen around the basic concepts of elite theory. Modern writers, such as Dahl and Hunter, have tried to investigate empirical methods of supporting some of the hypotheses of the earlier theorists. I shall not attempt in this paper to survey this extensive field but rather I will consider what I see as the main features of the classical theory[3] and the problems which they give rise to, bearing in mind the basic methodological preconception I have alluded to. The method I shall adopt will be to begin by considering what I think are the broad assumptions which classical elite theories make about the structure of society, especially as to the nature of power; as well as what I think are its psychological claims about human nature. I shall then consider in the light of these assumptions and the implications to which I claim they give rise, to what extent classical elite theory is purely prescriptive or ideological and whether it is tautologous, as some critics have claimed; I will also consider whether its concepts can be regarded as being scientific, in the sense of being susceptible to empirical validation, as some modern elite theorists have tried to demonstrate and finally I shall consider its influence upon, and utility for, socio-political theory.[4]

At its simplest, elite theory is a claim that in society, there is always a division between those who rule and those who are ruled and that the former group necessarily constitute a minority whilst the latter constitute the majority.[5] In this simple form, elite theory makes an assertion about the distribution of power in society, and also implies a view of human nature and a theory of history. However, if the elite claim amounted to no more than this, it could almost be said without further discussion that at best it was a truism, at worst, a tautology. But the elite claim is not so limited. In the first place its assertion that the division of society is necessary and not merely contingent is philosophically interesting. In the second place, it elaborates at great length what characterises this division and both explicitly and by implication commits itself to a view of the structure of society and the nature of politics.

Central to the elite theorists' understanding of society and politics is their notion of power. Power they interpret as the control and enjoyment of societal resources and in all societies it is to be found in the hands of an organised minority. Mosca states their position boldly:

> In all societies – from societies that are very meagrely developed and have barely attained the dawnings of civilisation, down to the most advanced and powerful societies – two classes of people appear – a class that rules and a class that is ruled. The first class, always the less numerous, performs all political functions, monopolises power and enjoys the advantages which power brings, whereas the second, the more numerous class, is directed and controlled by the first, in a manner that is now more or less legal, now more or less arbitrary and violent . . .[6]

Mosca's ruling class in the modern state are the owners or managers of production, but they may be part of a professional hierarchy (such as Michels' party leaders) or consist of men of a certain psychological type (such as Pareto's 'foxes' and 'lions'). Whatever is said of the elite, it is held to be self-consciously aware of its special position, 'conspiratorial' in this sense of having a common will to action and is, from the point of view of any observer, a coherent and organised minority, clearly discernible in society. This general position is held to by all elite theorists from the classical writers to modern exponents of the theory, although these latter have sometimes insisted upon the particularity of the elites they claim to have exposed.[7]

The classical elite theorists tended to concentrate on a particular aspect of this general theory. Michels, for example, concerned himself with the structure of leadership and organisation which he saw as the very basis of advanced society and which, in his view, necessarily entailed the existence of elites. In *Political Parties* he says:

The technical specialisation that inevitably results from all extensive organisation renders necessary what is called expert leadership. Consequently the power of determination comes to be considered one of the specific attributes of leadership, and is gradually withdrawn from the masses to be concentrated in the hands of the leaders alone. Thus the leaders, who were at first no more than the executive organs of the collective will soon emanicipate themselves from the mass and become independent of its control. Organisation implies the tendency to oligarchy . . .[8]

Michels' contention is that with the growth of a sophisticated economy, characterised by the division of labour, the skills needed to organise and maintain society become highly specialised and only a small group come to be seen as capable of exercising them. This is true of all advanced societies, including democratic ones, and leads to the establishment of elites who acquire and retain such skills.

Pareto, defining the elite simply as the best in any particular field (it can be an aristocracy of saints or an aristocracy of brigands), concerns himself more with the relation between the small, governing elite and the rest of society. In his account the elite is divisible into a governing and a non-governing section, the rest of society forming the non-elite or mass. Pareto's understanding of the structure of society in terms of these categories is closely linked to his analysis of human psychology, which I will consider later; at this point it suffices to say that the governing elite comprises those with the predominant psychological characteristics of leaders (which may vary historically) and that power resides with this group. The non-governing elite forms the broad class basis from which the smaller, effective political elite arises; its function is both to execute the decisions of the governing elite and to form a link between that group and the mass. Pareto was particularly interested in the composition of both the elite proper and the non-governing elite — the circulation of individuals from one to another and the gradual replacement of a governing elite by another became a method by which he explained how power is transferred or transmitted in society; in his own words:

> In conformity with a law which is of great importance and is the principal explanation of many social and historical factors, these aristocracies do not last but are continually renewed. This phenomenon may be called the circulation of elites.[9]

In an ideal society such changes would take place peacefully and need not be accompanied by vast social upheaval — the demise of one governing elite and the rise of another usually meant the replacement of one dominant type of individual by another (foxes by lions or vice-versa) as the old regime had become too rigid or the political formula which had held society together, no longer proved effective.[10]

In Mosca, the idea of the ruling elite is united with that of a ruling class[11] (e.g. see quotation above, p. 265). Like Michels he emphasises the need for organisation, especially in the modern state. Even in the case of monarchic or despotic rule, the individual in charge needed to rely on the backing of such a class and if it were deposed

> there would have to be another organised minority within the masses themselves to discharge the function of a ruling class. Otherwise all organisation, and the whole social structure, would be destroyed.[12]

Mosca's ruling class is a political class or a group of people in society, self-conscious of their distinctness and identifiable by their social and economic pre-eminence. Like Pareto he linked their position to their having certain psychological qualities. So he says:

> in addition to the great advantage accruing to them from the fact of being organised, ruling minorities are usually so constituted that the individuals who make them up are distinguished from the masses of the governed by qualities that give them a certain material, intellectual or even moral superiority; or else they are the heirs of individuals who possessed such qualities. In other words, members of a ruling minority regularly have some attribute, real or apparent, which is highly esteemed and very influential in the society in which they live.[13]

267

Mosca thus tended to view the elite as a class in society which performed all political functions of importance and such a class existed in democratic as well as in aristocratic societies. Like Michels he emphasised the fact that organisation made such a structure inevitable in modern society. Before the organised minority, each single individual in the majority stood alone.

Modern elite theorists have developed these postulates in different ways. C. W. Mills in *The Power Elite* abandons the wide-sweeping claim of the 'classicists' to uncovering an historical or sociological law, confining his claims to the structure of one society, namely the United States. According to Mills the elite are those who have most of what there is to have – wealth, power and prestige – which they gain through the institutional hierarchies of society such as the army, business and politics. In his analysis the elite are a 'compact social and psychological entity' made up of the 'top men' of these various hierarchies who collectively decide what needs to be decided and thus control the lives of everyone living in their country. In Mills the elitists' assumption that power, that is the ability to direct action in society, is cumulative, is manifest. For them economic power implies political power and they would endorse Hobbes' words:

> For the nature of power, is in this point, like to fame, increasing as it proceeds; or like the motion of heavy bodies, which the further they go, make still the more haste.[14]

The more limited analysis aimed at demonstrating the existence of an elite in a particular society was also adopted by F. Hunter in his work *Community Power Structure*. Hunter makes the effort to answer critics of elite theory who have said that the theory is never substantiated by empirical evidence. He uses what he calls his 'reputational method' which consists of drawing up lists of people of influence in the particular town he studies ('Regional City') on the basis of names supplied to him by the leading institutions of the town (such as the Chamber of Commerce). He then interviews numbers of 'judges' (people who had lived in the community for some years and who had some knowledge of its affairs) and tries to decide in the light of their opinions, which people on the lists might be members of the Regional City elite. Hunter is concerned to try to bring some empirical evidence to bear on the elite hypothesis rather than relying on historical or psychological generalisations as Mosca and the others had done. There are, of course, particular difficulties involved in both the

268

accounts of Hunter and C. W. Mills but I have introduced them here to illustrate the kind of modern studies which have followed the classical tradition of Mosca, Pareto and Michels and which share its assumption about the distribution of power in society. I shall now consider what I understand the classical theorists assume about human nature before discussing difficulties which the theory as a whole gives rise to.

CLAIMS ABOUT HUMAN NATURE

Elite theorists have two main and closely related assumptions about human nature – the first is that it remains constant, the second that man is not rational, in the sense that his behaviour is not seemingly directed to the attainment of ends, nor appropriate to any such attainment. Pareto begins his *Cours d'Economie Politique* of 1896 with these words:

> Human nature reveals uniformities which constitute natural laws. If these uniformities did not exist, then there would be neither social science nor political economy, and even the study of history would be largely useless.[15]

For Pareto the 'uniformities' which are constant are basic human instincts. Although he does distinguish rational from non-rational action (using the terms 'logical' and 'non-logical') in the sense I have indicated above, for him and other elitists, most human behaviour is of the latter type.

However, despite the fact that their behaviour is basically instinctual, men feel the need to justify their actions in rational terms. This they do by inventing theories which rationalise these actions and make them seem justified to themselves and to other men. Theories consist of an instinctive element – that is the action to be justified, which Pareto calls the 'residue' and which reflects some particular human instinct; and an 'ideological' element, that is the justifying-part of them which he defines as the 'derivation'. It is the 'residues' which remain constant and constitute the 'uniformities' which Pareto claims have existed throughout history. Thus he analyses historical epochs with a view to demonstrating the continued existence of certain 'residues' in the elite or the masses, these 'residues' reflecting constant characteristics of human nature. At first Pareto identified a great number of 'residues', reflecting the many complex instinctive patterns of behaviour revealed in the course of history; finally he reduced the large number to sets of six main classes of which two classes were especially important in the psychological make-up of individuals forming elites. The first of the two classes of 'residues' corresponds to the 'instinct of combinations' which is very strong in the human species and according to Pareto, '(it) has been and still is, a powerful activating cause of civilisation.'[16]

This is the instinct men have for combining – whether ideas, events or things – with a view to giving a form or coherency to their experience. Thus Pareto says that for a long period in European history, all fortunate events were ascribed to the protection of the wisdom of ancestors, whereas latterly, in modern times, all such events are ascribed to progress. The various concepts – the wisdom of ancestors and the idea of progress – are the typical products of the 'instinct of combinations'. The instinct in general leads men to theorise, to hypothesise, to combine sets of unrelated ideas into a pattern or scheme. Important results of this combining include the invention of social myths, vital to the survival of a society. If an elite consists of men in whom the 'instinct of combinations' predominates, then one could expect a society led by sophisticated ideologists and political manoeuverers. These men are political 'foxes', their methods tending to be those of expediency and pragmatism.

By contrast to an elite formed of men basically dominated by this 'instinct of combinations', is that formed by men in whom a second main class of 'residues', reflecting a second main class of instincts, prevails; namely 'residues' reflecting the instinct of the 'persistence of aggregates'. This set of instincts makes men try to preserve whatever forms of organisation, state of affairs or relationships have arisen. It is an instinct that will make men seek to preserve the form of a political organisation (such as the Roman Empire) or a family unit. It is also used, interestingly, by Pareto to explain the relationship between a living and a dead generation, to explain, in other words, the rites and ceremonies attached to burial etc. Where this instinct prevails, members of the elite will be conservative ('lions' in Paretan terminology) preservers of law and order, who believe in conservation of the *status quo*, if necessary by force rather than persuasion.

According to Pareto, all societies in history tend to be governed by elites in which one or other of these two categories of 'residues' predominates. In this all-inclusive manner, Pareto's claim may be criticised as being too simplistic – not only in its ignoring of the possibility of rational action based on free will but also in its subordinating all

270

factors (such as economic or other environmental factors) to considerations of human psychology. The psychological generalisations may themselves be criticised as being far too broad to include the many and diverse facets of human behaviour. Yet, having said this, it is difficult not to appreciate the range and dexterity of Pareto's analysis. He faces the problem of any scientist – namely how to account for a vast and diverse body of information and observation within a framework of simple and succinct explanations. And in dealing with a complexity of the magnitude he does, Pareto consistently makes interesting and important observations about the structure of society, about revolutions, propaganda and social mobility based upon his all-inclusive theory of psychology.

Neither Mosca nor Michels attempt anything on the vast, metaphysical, Paretan scale. In both cases, the assumptions about the unformity of human nature and the irrationality of human behaviour are maintained but a theory of human psychology is not systematically presented.

Thus Mosca says that:

Anyone who has travelled a good deal ordinarily comes to the conclusion that underneath superficial differences in customs and habits human beings are psychologically very much alike the world over; and anyone who has read history at all deeply reaches a similar conclusion with regard to the various periods of human civilisation.[17]

However, although Mosca does not offer a systematic analysis of human behaviour in the way Pareto does in his sociological consideration of institutions and social phenomena, he constantly alludes to the two basic premises I have mentioned and human psychology is often foremost in his mind. Thus when considering propaganda, he says:

. . . it is very hard to lead the masses in a given direction when one is not able as need requires to flatter passions, satisfy whims and appetites and inspire fear.[18]

Talking of revolution in another section of *The Ruling Class*, he alludes to the type of individual who emerges at times of crisis and change – one whose psychological make-up enables him to exploit the situation. He then considers the needs and feelings of the mass of

271

people at such a time – again in terms of their psychology. Indeed the numerous references to the mental states and attitudes of people in *The Ruling Class* is adequate testimony that Mosca's theory is as much psychological as sociological.

In the same way, although Michels does not offer a systematic theory of human behaviour, *Political Parties* is replete with allusions to the psychological states of elite and non-elite members. So

> In the trade union movement, the authoritative character of the leaders and their tendency to rule democratic organisations on oligarchic lines, are even more pronounced than in the political organisations;[19]

whilst the need for (authoritarian) leadership

> common to all classes not excepting the proletariat, furnishes a psychological soil upon which a powerful directive hegemony can flourish luxuriantly.[20]

Thus whilst Pareto's theory is the most elaborately developed one in terms of human psychology, the other elite theorists share his assumptions of human nature being constant throughout history and of human behaviour being instinctive rather than rational. They are also, though less systematically, concerned with relating their political and sociological observations to psychological features such as these. With these assumptions about human nature and those about society which I have mentioned in mind, I turn to consider the question of whether elite theory is mere ideology.

IS ELITE THEORY IDEOLOGICAL OR SCIENTIFIC?

Historically elite theory rose as a response to Marxism, a challenge to its ideology of equality. At the same time we are reminded that Mosca and Pareto were writing at a time when the political institutions of the liberal democratic state were seen to be disintegrating. Classical elite theory was thus at once anti-Marxist and anti-democratic for elite writers regarded both these ideological views as being less than adequate to explain political phenomena. It was their view that both political doctrines misunderstood the necessary distribution of power in any society – the Marxists being led to believe in the possibility of the withering away of the state and the liberal democrats into the equally mistaken notion of the possibility of popular sovereignty. Like many writers who regard themselves as *exposeurs*, the classical elite theorists insisted on the realism of their case in the face of absurd dogmas which misunderstood basic facts – in this case the facts of human nature and of political life.

Criticising Marxism, the elitists said it had been wrong even in areas where it had produced useful analyses, as in its contribution to the understanding of ideology. Instead of recognising that political myths ('illusions of the epoch') were a constant feature of political life, the Marxists had interpreted ideology as a feature of capitalist society, which would disappear with the disappearance of the state. The disappearance of the state was itself an absurdity in the eyes of the elitist writers and while it existed, they held it as axiomatic that it would be divided among a governing elite and a mass. Utopianism had entered the Marxist analysis and entirely distorted what for the elitists was a first lesson in political reality – it thereby discredited any claims that Marxists made to being scientific. However the exposure of Marxism as nothing more than an ideology for the proletariat and a dismissal of its utopianism was not the end of the elitist criticism of Marxism. There remained their rejection of the Marxist interpretation of social phenomena in terms of economic forces. Neither Mosca nor Pareto had any doubt that wealth and economic factors needed to be accounted for in any theory about society but they rejected the view that all other social phenomena could be explained in terms of them. For the elitists any society was to be explained in terms of its power structure and this depended upon the quality and competence of political leadership. Thus they insisted on the autonomy of politics and looked for psychological rather than economic explanations of the state of society.

Despite these considerable differences and the overtly antagonistic position the classical elite theorists took up against Marxism, there were certain things common to the two approaches and certain writers, such as Burnham and more recently Djilas, have combined both Marxist and elitist elements in their theses. Both theories claimed to have exposed the myths of modern liberal societies by advancing scientific analyses, Marxism concentrating on an economic theory, elitism on a psycho-political one. Both emphasised the importance of ideology and both regarded each other as mere ideologies. Both recognised the division of society into hierarchies, Marxism forecasting the eventual end of such division with the end of the state. Both regard the possibility of uncovering 'laws' which underlie the historical process although these 'laws' are necessarily different.

Historical factors have abetted the illicit relationship between Marxism and elitism. Burnham, though insisting that the elite derived its dominant position in society through its control of the means of production, nevertheless finds himself having to account for the continuance of a ruling class after the Bolshevik revolution in Russia. His conclusion is that in the modern conditions of advanced society, a small minority must govern, or, in other words he accepts Michel's 'iron law of oligarchy'. Another interesting progeny of this intercourse is Djilas, whose book *The New Class* is an analysis of Communist society from within on the basis of elitist postulates. Djilas says that the 'new class' are not identical with the Communist Party in Yugoslavia, although the party is the core of this class. Rather the class are 'those who have special privileges and economic preference because of the administrative monopoly which they hold'.[21]

Indeed, according to Djilas, the rise of the 'new class' is at the same time the demise of the all-powerful control of the party, since as the new class becomes more powerful it is less inclined to use the party's network. The party, in effect, is by-passed and begins to lose what I have remarked as being an important characteristic of an elite in the classical account, namely its self-consciousness as a unit. The members of Djilas' 'new class' are professional men – administrators and Burnham-type managers of state industries. Their social origins may have been working-class and indeed they and their fathers championed the revolutionary cause of the proletariat, but in course of time they developed into a group with its own interests and identity and their monopoly of nationalised ownership only helped this development. Djilas thus seems to offer corroboration for the classical elitists' insistence on the inevitability of a ruling class (what happens to his 'new class' is very similar to what Michels said was happening to the trade union leaders of his day) and for their dismissal of the classless society as mere utopian fancy.

However, the relationship between Marxism and classical elitism also suggests the extent to which the latter was itself an ideology. One critic has expressed this rather forcefully, saying:

The theorists of elites defend . . . the legacy from the inegalitarian societies of the past, while making concessions to the spirit of equality . . . They accept and justify the division of society into classes, but endeavour to make this division more palatable by

274

describing the upper classes as elites, and by suggesting that the elites are composed of the most able individuals, regardless of their social origins.[22]

Nor is the ideological nature of elite theory lessened when it is considered in relation to liberal democracy. It may be that in later years Mosca became more favourably disposed to liberal democracies, but in *The Ruling Class* he wrote 'Social democracy is more than anything else the intellectual malady of our age.'[23]

Pareto is even more extreme in his strictures against humanitarians and other 'degenerate individuals' of liberal or democratic persuasion.

The basis of the theoretical objection of elite theorists to democracy is in their rejection of any possibility of popular sovereignty. Thus S. M. Lipset has said even of Michels' *Political Parties*: 'From the perspective of a concern with a more democratic and egalitarian society, *Political Parties* is a pessimistic book.'[24]

In modern times various writers such as Mannheim have tried to show that the elite hypothesis need not be inimical to democrats, that a democracy can consist of competing elites. This was not the context in which the classical theorists envisaged the operation of elites – they were avowedly anti-democratic as they were anti-Marxist.

Thus elite theory, in its classical form, is a distinctively normative theory of politics. Elite theorists attacked the egalitarianism of Marxism and of liberal democracy; they defended, if even in the guise of a new realism, the values of hierarchy, order and excellence.[25] In saying this I do not mean to suggest that the theory in its classical form has not been of importance for social and political analysis; indeed my contention is the very opposite, that for the very reason of its ideological character, the theory has been influential. In his consideration of this aspect of the subject, Bottomore has said:

> To criticise a conceptual scheme or a theory in its ideological aspect is not, therefore, simply to show its connection with a broader doctrine of man and society and to oppose another social doctrine to it; it is also, or mainly, to show the scientific limitations of the concepts and theories, and to propose new concepts and theories which are truer or more adequate to describe what actually occurs in the sphere of society.[26]

I hope to have already shown in a general way the 'broader doctrine of man and society' to which elite theory can be related but

275

in addition it is my contention that to indicate the ideological nature of a theory is not necessarily to show us the limits of its scientific applicability nor to lead us to search for 'theories which are truer or more adequate'.[27]

CONCLUSION

Modern developments in political science would tend to substantiate the view that attempts to elucidate and develop some of the concepts and ideas of classical elite theory have led to interesting and fruitful results. I have referred to the work of C. W. Mills and Hunter in the United States and to such Marxist writers as Burnham and Djilas. These are works which can be said to have arisen on the basis of trying to develop, synthesise or amend some of the concepts of Mosca, Pareto and Michels. Similarly the studies of writers such as Dahl and Polsby, where attention has been focused on the possible ways in which elite hypotheses may be empirically substantiated, can be seen in this tradition.[28] Yet another area where elite concepts have been influential is in that of democratic theory where there have been attempts to revise analyses of democratic societies in the light of elitist concepts or to incorporate them in democratic ideology. Mannheim provides an interesting illustration of this in such passages as the following:

the actual shaping of policy is in the hands of the elite, but this does not mean to say that society is not democratic. For it is sufficient for democracy that the individual citizens, though prevented from taking a direct part in government all the time, have at least the possibility of making their aspirations felt at certain intervals.[29]

Other applications have been made of elite hypotheses. Thus Kornhauser has used the elite model to compare ideological systems and to ascertain the degree of the 'openness' of communication between the elite and the mass in modern, mass society. From a consideration of this relationship, he develops a typology applicable to all mass societies.

Elite theory in its classical form did not achieve the sweeping away of the normative element as Mosca had hoped, but it did lead to much useful and significant social and political analysis.

276

1. Quoted in J. H. Meisel, *The Myth of the Ruling Class*, Ann Arbor, Michigan, 1962, p. 31.

2. Thus in the *Cours d'Economie Politique*, Pareto considers the possibility of a science of society at some length, particularly comparing social with mechanical phenomena.

3. In following this method I am aware of the danger of underestimating the differences between the various elite theorists, but my contention is that at a certain level of generality there are facets common to all of them and that it is thus possible to talk of elite theory as a unified doctrine.

4. Although much concerned in this paper with the impact elite theory has had upon the development of empirical and analytic political science in a more value-free sense, I do not mean to ignore its influence upon or relation to, normative theories, such as Marxism and liberal democratic theory. Moreover it is my contention that even allowing for a normative/positive distinction in our interests as ideologists or social scientists respectively, we can seldom discuss important social and political theories which relate exclusively either to the world of value or of fact.

5. See T. B. Bottomore, *Elites and Society*, Pelican, London, 1966, p. 19, where he points to the determinism inherent in this position.

6. G. Mosca, *The Ruling Class*, Livingston (ed.), McGraw Hill, New York, 1939, p. 50.

7. See C. W. Mills, *The Power Elite*, Oxford University Press, New York, 1956, and F. Hunter, *Community Power Structure*, Anchor Books, Garden City, New York, 1963.

8. R. Michels, *Political Parties*, The Free Press, New York, 1966, p. 70.

9. V. Pareto, *Sociological Writings*, S. E. Finer (ed.), Pall Mall, London, 1966, p. 155.

10. Kolabinska, a disciple of Pareto's, continued her work in *La Circulation des elites en France*, Imprimeries Reunies, Lausanne, 1912.

11. See Bottomore, op. cit., p. 36 et seq. for a discussion of the terms 'ruling class' and 'governing elite'.

12. Mosca, op. cit., p. 51.

13. ibid., p. 53.

14. T. Hobbes, *Leviathan*, Oxford University Press, Oxford, 1909.

15. V. Pareto, op. cit., p. 97.

16. ibid., p. 224.

17. Mosca, op. cit., p. 39.

18. ibid., p. 193.

19. Michels, op. cit., p. 159.

20. ibid., p. 88.

21. M. Djilas, *The New Class*, Unwin Books, London, 1966, p. 49.

22. Bottomore, op. cit., p. 148.

23. Mosca, op. cit., p. 235.

24. S. M. Lipset in Michels, op. cit., Introduction, p. 25.

25. The notion of hierarchy is closely linked to that of the superiority (of the elite) in elitist thought. Some elitists have insisted that this superiority is necessary for the maintenance of culture and indeed of civilisation, this being the special function elites perform in society. See T. S. Eliot, *Notes Towards the Definition of Culture*, Faber and Faber, London, 1948, and Ortega y Gasset, *The Revolt of the Masses*, Allen and Unwin, London, 1932.

26. Cf. Bottomore, p. 20, where he also says: 'every sociological concept and theory has an ideological force by reason of its influence upon the thoughts and actions of men in everyday life.'

27. ibid.

28. In an earlier work, '*The Critique of the Ruling Elite Model*', *American Political Science Review*, Vol. 52(2), 1958, pp. 463-9, R. Dahl had cast aspersions upon the scientific status of elite theory (see especially pp. 463-8), a theme raised by N. W. Polsby in his work *Community Power and Political Theory*, Yale University Press, New Haven, 1963 (see p. 5). This allegation has been associated with the further view that elite theory is tautologous (see W. G. Runciman, *Social Science and Political Theory*, Cambridge University Press, Cambridge, 1963, p. 69). Empirical evidence in the form of historical research and sociological investigations (some undertaken by Dahl himself) can be said to have answered these charges by showing (as in Hunter) the possibility of validation of the elite hypothesis.

29. K. Mannheim, *Essays on the Sociology of Culture*, Routledge & Kegan Paul, London, 1956, p. 179.

10. Models of Political Party Organisation and Strategy:
Some Analytic Approaches to Oligarchy

E. SPENCER WELLHOFER AND
TIMOTHY M. HENNESSEY*

Political scientists have long been fascinated with the behaviour of political parties in democratic political systems. Yet with years of effort and a plethora of studies few models exist which adequately explain why political parties operate the way they do. Part of the difficulty which underlies such theoretical paucity is that most of the extant models are closely related to the particular cultural and political tradition of the researchers and are normatively laden.

The basic features of the two most prominent models were summarised recently by William Wright.[1] He groups the features into two broad types which he terms the Rational–Efficient model and the Party Democracy model.

Wright associates the Rational-Efficient model with current research on the United States and the Party Democracy model with the European tradition of scholarship. It is interesting to note, however, that the basic differences between the two models, apart from the fundamental structural distinctions, concern goals and characteristics which are not easily susceptible to analysis and empirical test. But to impute such goals to parties does not move us ahead in the analytic task of explaining the basic processes and behaviour which characterise parties, although it may clarify the scholar's normative commitments as well as the stated goals of the party. If we take Wright's

* We wish to acknowledge our gratitude for the financial support of the Department of Political Science and the Office of International Studies and Programmes at Michigan State University. In addition, Professor Hennessey wishes to thank the Ford Foundation and Professor Wellhofer, the Fulbright Fellowship programme for additional financial support. Finally, we both wish to acknowledge our intellectual debt to Professors Joseph Schlesinger and Albert Hirschman for their encouragement and stimulation. Any errors which are present are, of course, our own.

FIGURE 1. Party Functions

Functional Characteristics	Rational-Efficient Model	Party Democracy Model
1. Manifest functions	Narrow range of functions; almost exclusive emphasis on electoral function; any other functions subordinate.	Broad range of functions: ideological, electoral, and governing; other functions subordinated to ideological function.
2. Activities	Limited and intermittent, geared to election cycle.	Extensive and continuous.
3. Prime beneficiary	Voters (actually elected public officials).	Members.
4. Organisational incentives	Material (patronage).	Purposive (especially policy-ideological).
5. Operational style	Pragmatic.	Ideological.

Wright, op. cit., p. 32.

distinctions seriously, we are faced with a dichotomy which constrains those who seek to explain the possible development of political parties from one model to the other (e.g., from Party Democracy to Rational–Efficient). To avoid this problem what is needed is to develop analytic concepts which capture the interface between the two models. Such a task is the purpose of this paper and we will seek to isolate the dimensions of party development which capture the transformations and accompanying tensions in socialist working-class parties as they tend to move from the Party Democracy strategy to the Rational–Efficient strategy.

PARTY TRANSFORMATION: THE INSIGHTS OF MICHELS

While the important normative issues which divide these two models must be kept clearly in mind, the fundamental task facing scholars attempting to construct general models of party development is to ensure that their assumptions incorporate relevant strategies and structural differences between different types of parties. Indeed, Robert Michels many years ago alerted us to the dangers of using imputed party goals as analytic givens and his own work is testimony to the potential analytic richness which one can derive when these normative characteristics are taken as problematic.[2]

It is especially ironic that most studies of political parties by Europeans which employ the party democracy model as a point of departure tend to ignore the warnings of Michels concerning the fundamental transformations in such parties which lead them away from their stated goals. Now this may be because Michels is far from clear in his argument at a number of critical points and much scholarly effort has been expended in attempting to explain his argument.[3] Yet a number of his insights are important for our purposes when they are related to the recent advances by political scientists of the political economy school of thought. The aspects of Michels' work which will specifically concern us begin with his fundamental assumption that if democracy is to be achieved, it must be through the development of a 'democratic party'. Now as Gordon Hands rightly observes, Michels does not make a clear distinction between, '(a) a party which aims at setting up, or supports, a democratic state government and (b) a party which has a democratic internal structure.'[4] While this is true, the distinction is one that proponents of the party democracy model, as well as practising politicians in socialist working-class parties, have found particularly troubling. Hence, the fact that Michels was not clear on this point in no way diminishes the fundamental tensions which exist in many socialist working-class parties over these two, often conflicting, goals.

From these assumptions about the democratic party, Michels derives a number of other notions about democracy which are also central to discussions by political scientists and socialist leaders about the nature of such parties. As Hands points out, there are three senses in which Michels conceives of party democracy. First, Michels uses democracy in a 'Marxist manner in which democracy is seen as being fundamentally impossible within the capitalist state. Sometimes this seems to be a matter of saying that the absence of the private ownership of the means of production is a necessary practical condition for democracy, but at other times he equates it with socialism.'[5] We would argue that this lack of clarity in Michels' argument is, again, indicative of the tension in socialist parties between a desire to see a fundamental transformation in the economy and society on the one hand, and the desire to have socialist reform within the context of existing structural arrangements, on the other.

Secondly, Michels uses the term democracy in Rousseau's sense of 'direct democracy', 'in which policy initiatives come from, and policy decisions are made more or less by, the rank and file. . . . The meeting of the whole membership is seen as the central democratic mechanism, although some form of delegation may also be possible.'[6]

281

Thirdly, Michels speaks of 'democracy' in relation to representation.

The essential element here is seen as a certain degree of agreement between the wishes of the rank and file and the policies actually pursued by the leadership. A system of government is democratic in this sense if it incorporates institutional arrangements which ensure such agreement; for example, the determination of policy by elected representatives, or perhaps the selection of leaders by a process of electoral competition between elites.[7]

It is in terms of these basic assumptions about democratic parties that Michels began to specify the tendencies which serve to destroy such democracy; namely, oligarchic tendencies. For Michels, such factors contribute to a separation of leaders from followers and undermine the basic requirement that party policies correspond with the wishes of party members. These oligarchic tendencies are a function of a set of factors which relate to (a) the origins of leadership and (b) why leadership *must* become more and more separated from the membership. Michels' treatment of the origin of leadership is basically a psychological explanation which seeks to demonstrate that the masses will inevitably exhibit a 'need' for leadership – a predisposition for hero worship. Many scholars have concentrated on his psychological explanations but these seem to be of secondary importance to his overall argument concerning the constraints on the achievement of democracy. As Juan Linz notes:

Michels was dissatisfied with 'psychological' (i.e. motivational) explanations of the oligarchic tendencies in organisations. His whole analysis emphasised the constraints derived from organisational needs, the growth of the organisation, the need to make rapid decisions, the difficulties of communicating with the members, the growth and complexity of the tasks, the division of labour, the need for full-time activity and from the consequent processes of selection of leadership and development of knowledge and skills. These processes, in turn, lead to the emergence of stable leaders, whose professionalisation, combined with their consciousness of their own worth, leads to oligarchy. The impor-

282

tant point is that the leaders'deviation from norms they themselves accept is not the result of their motivation. The fact that
conformity to certain norms may indirectly lead to deviation
from other norms accepted by the same person has, of course,
been emphasised by social scientists since Marx. Michels studied
the special case of men who despite their commitment to democracy, often acted in ways not conforming to their values because
of the demands of organisation and other factors of political life.
While Michels often referred to the 'psychological predisposi-
tions' of both the masses and the leaders, he saw these predis-
positions as fundamentally serving to reinforce or, occasionally,
to weaken the organisational factors, even though at times they
also seemed to him to function independently. Significantly,
when he presented his theory schematically in a chart, he did not
stress the manipulative or illegitimate actions of the leaders
(which he discussed at length elsewhere in *Political Parties*), but
concentrated instead on the factors influencing active and effective participation of the members in decision-making.[8]

This feature of Michels' argument proceeds from a form of primi-
tive democracy which is eventually transformed into an oligarchic
pattern by the problem of size, and the need for specialisation and
parliamentary representation. The latter problem was of particular
importance for Michels, as it is for our analysis. As Linz observes,
'Michels deplored the way calculations of parliamentary advantage
dominated party life and led to the abandonment of every vigorous
idea and every energetic course of action.'[9] Indeed, the latter concern strikes to the heart of the nature of representation to be adopted
by socialist working-class parties in a democratic political system.
Michels was not satisfied with electoral accountability as a criterion
of democracy. He was concerned with the responsibility or responsiveness of the leaders to their members rather than to the larger
society.

Michels conceived of an ideal party as a purely ideological
group, open only to those who share the goals of the founding
members and identify their interests with the original conception
of the interests of the group. According to Michels, the sole cause
of deviation from party ideology is oligarchy. It is in the nature

283

of oligarchy to sacrifice ideological purity to the methodical organisation of the masses for electoral victory.[10]

This latter tendency was of great importance to Michels and represented an 'omnibus' tendency of socialist parties to shift their appeals from the membership to the general electorate, 'from appeals to the class electorate to appeals to a broader electorate – such shifts may produce a more moderate programme, while opposition as a matter of principle is replaced by competition with other parties and disloyal opposition to the social and political system is replaced by loyal opposition and even by participation in governing.'[11] Michels was asking:

> are leaders responsible only to their constituency, or are they responsible also to the larger whole of which their constituency is a part? Are they responsible to the party membership or to the electorate? The problem of responsibility to a larger unit – the society as a whole – rather than to a particular constituency becomes especially acute when a party is in power, rather than in the opposition; this was a problem socialist leaders had not faced at the time *Political Parties* was written.[12]

Yet, this is a problem students of political parties face today as the changing role of socialist working-class parties in Western Europe and Britain becomes the subject of considerable scholarly speculation. Many would agree, for example, that there are sound theoretical and empirical reasons for rejecting Maurice Duverger's prediction that the working-class, multi-nuclear party is the wave of the future,[13] at least in the pure form he outlined. Indeed, some like Leon Epstein reject Duverger's argument by carefully noting that such parties have undergone a stark transformation by placing a higher priority on electoral success than ideological consistency and responsibility to their membership and, as a result, are coming to resemble American political parties.[14]

While debates like these over the changing nature and strategy of such parties are particularly provocative, they can ultimately only be useful to those scholars committed to systematic theorising when the discussion is grounded in some theory of political party development. In turn, such theories must be composed of sound analytic elements which permit one to say *why* it may be the case that party elites begin to change their strategies over time. In the paper which follows we shall attempt to integrate some of the insights from the rational school of thought, principally the work of Anthony Downs, Mancur Olson, Joseph Schlesinger and Albert Hirschman in order to make such an analytic specification, albeit a preliminary one.[15] This specification will be undertaken in the light of questions raised by Michels, as well as current empirical evidence on political party development.

I THE DEVELOPMENT OF SOCIALIST WORKING-CLASS PARTIES

A The Early Years and Olson's Problem

The primary strategic consideration for the leadership of embryonic socialist working-class parties is to isolate a social group of potential members and supporters and to design an ideology and programme which will appeal to such a group, in this case the working-class. But the survival of such parties during their early years is fundamentally dependent on their ability to solve the problem of rational non-involvement raised by Olson whereby prospective members find it 'irrational' to join and, as a consequence, such organisations collapse.[16]

Olson questions whether the widely held idea that groups tend to act in support of their group interests is *logically* connected with the premise of rational self-interested behaviour. He argues that most organisations produce what economists call 'collective goods' – goods that are available to all members of the group whether or not they have borne any of the costs of providing them. And, since individuals will get the benefits in any case, there is no incentive for them to bear the costs of organisation, and for this reason groups frequently fail in their organisational efforts. As he observes:

If the members of a large group rationally seek to maximise their personal welfare, they will *not* act to advance their common good or group objectives unless there is coercion to force them to do so, or unless some separate incentive, distinct from the achievement of the common interest, is offered to the members of the group on the condition that they bear the costs or burdens involved in the achievement of group objectives.[17]

285

It is this fundamental problem which embryonic socialist working-class parties face and which their organisational strategies must be designed to overcome. After examining these strategies, we shall attempt to show how each seeks to overcome Olson's dilemma.

B *Types of Organisational Structure and Strategy: Direct and Indirect*

In order to obtain sufficient operational resources, socialist working-class parties have traditionally adopted two different organisational strategies: what Duverger terms *Direct* and *Indirect*.[18] Duverger argues that the adoption of one type of structure over and against another basically originated in problems of development.[19] He notes that indirect structures were the result of trade unions developing before the party, the opposite situation pertaining to the development of a direct structure. In certain countries, through the absence of universal suffrage (Belgium and the Scandinavian countries) or special conditions of the electoral struggle (the two-party system in England), there was little possibility at the end of the nineteenth and beginning of the twentieth centuries of any parliamentary representation of the proletariat nor of any influence on the elections other than locally. Consequently, working-class action developed first of all in the occupational sphere by means of trade unions or co-operatives which became powerful and organised *before* the existence of socialist parties. When political and electoral evolution allowed the development of the latter, the trade union organisations already in existence provided them with a ready-made framework as well as with solid support: hence, the tendency to indirect structure.[20] A good example of this strategy is the British Labour Party of 1900.

The structure of the socialist working-class parties in continental Europe (e.g., the German Social Democratic Party), is an example of direct structure and is a 'pure' form. It was directed to organising as large a proportion of the masses as possible and involved a definite scheme of affiliation complemented by a very strict system of individual subscriptions upon which the party was dependent for its resources: hence, its direct structure.

Yet, while acknowledging the merits of Duverger's argument, one must also note the 'rationality' of the strategy; that is, leaders might conceivably have chosen a different strategy had they not been predisposed to approach the problem as one of resource scarcity and the consequent necessity of elite-elite bargaining between the powerful unions and their political wing—the Labour Party—to gain such

286

scarce resources. For example, it could hardly be lost on the leaders of the embryonic Labour Party that there were one and a half million trade union members in 1895, a fifth of the total number of adult workers. At the same period the Independent Labour Party, founded by Keir Hardie, gained only 45,000 votes and not a single seat in Parliament because of the two-party system. The trade union organisation alone made it possible to form a political party capable of taking its place between the Liberal and Conservative giants.[21]

The strategy for direct parties was also 'rational'. In a variation on Anthony Downs, we might say that the leaders attempted to 'sell' services and an ideology to prospective members in order to obtain sufficient resources to carry out their programmes and to gain party offices for themselves.[22] We would argue that, in the direct case, such resources are needed to construct the multi-nuclear organisational infrastructure required to: (a) mobilise prospective members; (b) provide channels through which the preferences of the social base can become known; (c) deliver the promised services; and (d) provide the rewards of party office for ambitious members.

By contrast, the indirect strategy was basically a question of profitable exchange between two sets of elites; namely, union leaders and party leaders, and did not directly involve the membership until much later. The system basically consisted of trade unions, co-operative societies, friendly societies and groups of intellectuals who united to establish a common organisation; there were no individual party supporters or members but, rather, only members of the component groups.

Moreover, unions tended to be the most powerful component group in the party since under British law, except between 1927 and 1945, unions could affiliate any number of members they wished (providing the members did not contract out by specifying that their union dues not go to the Labour Party). But even when the unions functioned under the more restricted legislation that permitted affiliation only by members who 'contracted in' (those who specified they wanted a portion of their union dues paid to the Labour Party), the unions were in a position to make sufficient contributions available so as to dominate party councils if and when they wished to do so.[23]

287

But as Duverger correctly notes, the Reform of 1918 in the Constitution of the party fundamentally transformed the party from indirect to more direct. Along with the collective membership of trade unions, co-operatives, and other socialist groups the Labour Party permitted the individual membership of men and women not belonging to these organisations.

Thus a real 'direct' party community was established alongside the trade unions and other corporate communities united with the party by federation. The party has continued to grow in importance; with its 729,624 individual members the Labour Party was in 1949 the most powerful socialist party in Europe, even without taking into account the support of the trade unions. Nevertheless, the latter continued to wield a large majority in the directing bodies of the party at all levels. The general picture then is a purely indirect party being transformed into a mixed party in which individual members are found side by side with affiliated members.[24]

Party decisions to organise in a direct and indirect fashion are closely related to the dilemma of rational non-involvement raised by Mancur Olson and both the direct and indirect strategies contained features which surmounted the problem. In the case of a party with direct organisational structure, the group to which appeals were made was the working-class, but the individuals of this class were offered services in exchange for membership dues and organisational burdens. These services typically took the form of goods and services offered at below market prices, e.g. mutual benefit societies, housing and consumer co-operatives, educational opportunities, specialised publications, libraries, medical care, etc. Such services acted as selective incentives designed to benefit party members *only* and were not collective goods for the working-class as a whole; that is, every member of the working-class could not avail himself of these programmes unless he paid dues. The multi-nuclear nature of the party and the multitude of services offered made for the development of meaningful social and recreational units, which served as non-collective social benefits to attract members. Examples of such units are sporting clubs and teams, youth organisations, hobby clubs, student organisations, co-operatives etc. which act as agents to dispense services and a focal point for social solidarity (another incentive). These units tend

288

to generate social solidarity which may be very significant in the development of such parties, and we shall have reason to return to this point later in the paper.[25] Finally, additional selective incentives existed; namely, offices in the organisation, which were offered to those members who bore the largest burden of organisation 'costs' and these individuals were expected to move the organisation forward.

The 'indirect' socialist working-class party, such as the British Labour Party also avoided Olson's dilemma, but for quite different reasons. The trade unions became the principal resource base of the party. And since the unions effectively coerced union members to contribute, the party was able to obtain resources without having to serve the membership directly, although as we have just observed, as the Labour Party became more direct in character, it began to provide many of these services through the constituency organisations. Thus, the early organisational crisis for the Labour Party was solved through mechanisms of coercion rather than voluntary membership and leadership-mass exchanges.

In sum, then, we have noted that the socialist working-class party with a direct organisational structure tried to obtain sufficient resources from members, to create an infrastructure to integrate potential members, to offer services as well as party offices which acted as selective incentives not obtainable elsewhere at lower cost and the creation of an ideology which acted as a rationale for party policies. By contrast, the party with indirect structure frequently entered into a coalition with the trade unions and other groups to obtain the resources necessary to operate, in exchange for a guaranteed powerful position in the Labour Party of union leaders and other affiliated groups. It is important to note that union member contributions were not arrived at 'rationally' by the membership since they were 'coerced' by the union leadership.

Olson's dilemma was avoided initially by these two types of socialist parties but by different strategies. As we shall see, however, both types of parties were again forced to surmount Olson's problem at later points in their development when they begin to play the competitive electoral game seriously.

c *Organisational Structure and Party Democracy*

These structural strategies also have important implications for theories of party democracy. Here we shall specify the necessary, although far from sufficient conditions for party democracy *to be an organisational condition the properties of which consist of incentives and decision-rules for the membership to make their 'claims' known to the leadership and incentives and decision-rules for leaders and prospective leaders to take these membership preferences or claims into account in designing their ideology and policies so as to gain operational resources as well as their own goal of office.*[26]

During the early period of development, both of these conditions are theoretically present in socialist parties with direct organisational structure whereas they are not readily apparent in parties with indirect structure. In the former, the membership can only rationally respond to the selective incentives offered by the party if their preferences for *provision of services correspond to some degree to the services offered.* The wide range of services offered by the German SPD is indicative of the efforts to raise membership without the benefit of indirect membership via trade unions. The party even found it necessary to compete with the unions for supplying direct benefits to members.[27] There is an incentive for members to make their preferences known by making 'claims' on the leaders at all levels of the multi-nuclear organisation, for otherwise the 'costs' they have suffered for membership may be in vain if the provision of services is inappropriate (i.e. ones they do not prefer). Leaders have incentives to respond to these member claims in order to increase their chances of gaining party office.

In parties with indirect structure, however, the members are dues payers by default and in this sense are 'coerced' and thus have few incentives to make their preferences known to the party, although they do have incentives to make 'claims' on the parallel union structure with respect to the provision of occupational services.[28] At the leadership level, there are few incentives to give direct attention to the claims of members since they can gain a large number of resources without doing so. Instead, they must give their attention to the preferences of union leaders and leaders of other affiliated groups lest these units curtail their provision of resources to the party. This is basically an elite-elite bargaining relationship, even if the ideological content of the exchanges is directed to the interests of the working-class. As indirect parties approach a more 'mixed' strategy of voluntary members *and* 'coerced' union contributors, however, party leaders can be expected to develop incentives and corresponding decision-rules appropriate to the 'claims' of voluntary members and they will behave in this manner in order to attain offices in the

290

emerging party instead of the trade unions. In short, to the extent that indirect structures evolve into direct structures, the conditions of party democracy previously specified are more likely to emerge. The increased reliance of the Labour Party on funding from the constituency organisations constituted a shift to a more direct membership, the result being an increased efficacy of constituency claims on the party leaders.

Given the differences associated with these two types of party organisation, we would expect that not all party members will participate with equal fervour or bear equal organisational burdens, since individual preference schedules differ, as do personal resources (education, skill, etc.). This inevitably leads to differing degrees of participation by members in party matters. But the possibility of 'claims' is still present in both structures, although less so in indirect ones, since leaders must remain 'open' to such claims owing to the necessity of gaining resources to carry out their policies, the success of which permits them to gain or retain office. This *natural stratification in participation* is itself a condition which encourages the leadership to be receptive to claims and these incentives are closely related to processes of elite recruitment.

D *Party Office Incentives and Leadership Selection: The Adjusted Schlesinger Model*

Joseph Schlesinger has argued that politicians are creatures of ambition and respond to the goals of office.[29] As he notes: 'Office remains the one observable goal that we have in politics, a fact upon which the political system itself rests, and which, for that reason, can provide a theoretical basis for the understanding of politics.'[30] But ambition for office develops within a specific situation, that is in response to the possibilities that lie before the politician. Schlesinger argues that political scientists ought to examine the structure of opportunities that condition the incentives of politicians. Political parties are essential to his approach because they serve to 'tie men's ambitions together, linking their fate over time'.[31]

Schlesinger is concerned primarily with ambitions that are structured in the context of the electoral market in the American political system. Yet the essential elements of his argument would seem to apply as well to parties outside the American system with complex organisational structures which provide a range of *party offices* as well as the potential for public offices.

291

In this sense, the opportunity structures to which ambitious members respond are closely associated with the expanding and developing infrastructure of the party and most of the leaders selected during these early years will be recruited from those members who have gained experience in one or more of the party's sub-units and particularly the units which provide the bulk of resources.

This observation on the recruitment process can be clarified by noting Schlesinger's *manifest-office hypothesis*. This hypothesis states that ambitious individuals will make rational calculations to advance as efficiently as possible and these calculations will be influenced by the character of the office hierarchy. Offices which share similar constituencies, demand similar skills and engage similar antagonists will be used, in combination, for advancement. In other words, the more lower level offices are similar to higher level offices in terms of membership, the formal rules of selection and office functions and skills, the more these will be used as stepping stones to the top.[32] In the case of the embryonic parties in question, the more previous offices and skills in the sub-units resemble or come to resemble higher level offices in the party, the more accurately the ambitious member will be able to calculate his opportunity structure and act accordingly to achieve his ends.

In the light of the manifest-office hypothesis, it seems reasonable to assume that when success in reaching party office is tied to successful performance of duties in the sub-units, then the leaders who make it to the top should also be those who were the most 'successful' in delivering preferred goods and services to members via the sub-unit organisation and that, in the process, they will be, to some degree, receptive to 'claims' made by members in these 'sub-units'. The recruitment process should reinforce incentives for leaders to be responsive to claims made by members and this, in turn, should contribute to their own chances of office success. Thus office incentives and leadership recruitment processes reinforce the conditions necessary for party democracy. But there are still other analytic considerations concerning the behaviour of members and leaders which either reinforce or constrain democratic possibilities.

E *Modes of Response: Hirschman's Model*

Since it would be naive to assume that the members' preferences will be the same as the party's provision of services, it is to be expected, as we have already observed, that 'claims' will be made by members on the leadership to move programmes closer to their own preference schedules. Indeed, this expression is fundamental to the dynamics of democracy. But how can we isolate the analytic dynamics of such claims? Here the work of Albert Hirschman in his recent volume, *Exit, Voice, and Loyalty*, is particularly instructive.[33]

Hirschman's thesis proceeds from a fundamental pessimism in which organisations are viewed as

permanently subject to decline and decay; that is to loss of rationality and efficiency and surplus producing energy, no matter how well the institutional framework within which they function is designed.[34]

Such deterioration in organisational performance is reflected in two basic behaviours. First, customers (i.e. members) stop buying the organisation's products and so revenues or membership decline. As a result, managers (i.e. leaders) search for causes in order to recuperate. Secondly, the organisation's members express their dissatisfaction with the 'quality' of its product and make this dissatisfaction known to the leadership through general protest, that is, by the *Voice* option, or if this fails, resort to leaving the organisation—the *Exit* option. Hirschman recognises the theoretical potential of applying his concepts to political parties. As he notes:

One way of catching that rare bird, an organisation where exit and voice both hold important roles, may be to look for groupings from which members can both exit and be expelled. Political parties and voluntary organisations in general are excellent examples.[35]

His third central concept, *Loyalty*, is also useful for understanding party strategy and behaviour, and we shall turn to this point in the discussion which follows.

According to Hirschman, *voice* comes about when the buyers (members) attempt to change the practices, policies and outputs of the firm (party) to which they belong.

Voice is here defined as an attempt to change, rather than escape from, an objectionable state of affairs, through individual or collective petition to the management (leaders) directly in charge, through an appeal to higher authority.[36]

In this sense, voice has the function of alerting an organisation to its failings.

The decision to leave the organisation, or *exit*, comes about in relation to voice. As Hirschman argues: 'The decision whether to exit will often be taken *in light of the prospects of effective use of voice*. If customers (i.e. members, activists) are sufficiently convinced that voice will be effective, then they will *postpone* exit.'[37] The decision to remain with the organisation, which is perceived as deteriorating, is based on two calculations: '(1) an evaluation of the chances of getting the organisation "back on the track" through one's own action or through that of others or (2) a judgement that it is worthwhile, for a variety of reasons, to trade the certainty of joining another organisation which is available here and now against these chances.'[38] He argues that account must also be taken of the direct costs of voice incurred as organisation members spend time and money in an attempt to achieve changes in current policies and practices.

As voice tends to be costly in comparison to exit, the member will be less able to afford voice. That is, the discontented member will leave when the costs of devoting even a modicum of his time to correcting faults in the organisation is exceeded by his estimate of the expected benefits.

In general, Hirschman views exit as the province of economics and the competitive market and voice as the province of politics and qualitative judgements, since exit requires nothing but a clear-cut either/or decision regarding the opportunities *vis-à-vis* one's own, whereas voice is essentially an art evolving in new directions. Voice involves 'the possible *discovery* of lower cost and greater effectiveness and the presence of the exit alternative can, therefore, tend to atrophy the development of the art of voice'.[39]

The concepts of voice and exit are rendered particularly meaningful for political scientists through the introduction of his third concept — *loyalty*. This is so owing to the fact that political organisations devote a great deal of time and effort *via* the manipulation of selective incentivies (e.g. social solidarity incentives), and socialisation, in order to instil loyalty. The most significant aspect of Hirschman's concept of loyalty is that it can:

neutralise within certain limits the tendency of quality-conscious members to be the first to exit[40] . . . As a result of loyalty, these individuals will tend to stay on longer than they would ordinarily in the hope or, rather, reasoned expectation that improvement or reform will be achieved 'from within'.[41] Thus, loyalty, far from being irrational, can serve the socially useful purpose of preventing deterioration from becoming cumulative, as it often does when there are no barriers to exit.[42]

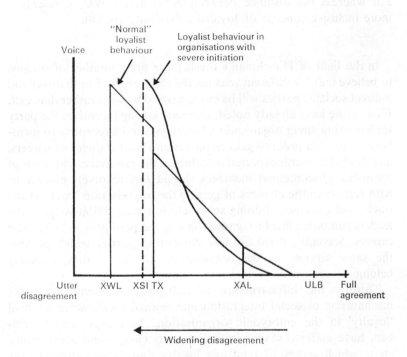

FIGURE 2.   Loyalist behaviour in the face of increasing disagreement with an organisation

In short, loyalty may help the organisation retain its most quality-conscious members by raising the costs of exit. Loyalty influences both exit and voice when organisational members experience increasing disagreement with the organisation's policies in the following manner (see Figure 2).

'The horizontal axis measures the level of agreement or disagreement [of party leaders or members] with the policies of the party.

The vertical axis represents the amount of protest that comes about as a reaction to this disagreement. There comes a point in the process at which exit takes place if loyalty is not present (XAL). Then as disagreement widens further, the member will think of exit and threaten it (TX-point of threat). Finally, loyalty reaches its breaking point and exit takes place (XWL-exit with loyalty). The strength of loyalty is then either the distance between XAL and TX or between XAL and XWL. The former represents loyalty with no thought of exit whereas the distance between XAL and XWL represents a more inclusive concept of loyalist behaviour.' (p. 88).

In the light of Hirschman's thesis there are a number of reasons to believe that for different reasons the early years of both direct and indirect socialist parties will be characterised by voice rather than exit. First, as we have already noted, there are strong incentives for party leaders using direct organisational strategies to be receptive to members' 'claims' in order to gain resources and further their own careers, and this behaviour is expected to influence the rational calculations of members. Discontented members should feel relatively efficacious with respect to the chances of getting the organisation 'back on the track' and the costs of doing so should not be prohibitive since the leaders can only afford to ignore them at the peril of damaging their careers. Secondly, there are few competing parties which provide the same services as the organisation to which they currently belong.

Thirdly, the infrastructure of the party frequently provides mechanisms of social integration and reward which serve to instil 'loyalty' in the embryonic organisation. Moreover, many members have suffered severe initiation costs (jail, social approbation etc.), which serves to reinforce loyalty and thereby diminish the chances of severe voice and ultimately, exit, as Hirschman's diagram suggests. As a consequence of these considerations we would expect the early years of the direct party to be characterised by voice rather than exit.

Equally true during the early years in parties of indirect structure, the exit option is costly for members owing to their membership in the unions and therefore the possible occupational sanctions which can be brought to bear on members. As Hirschman notes, unions establish rules so as to make exit as costly as possible in order to retain support.[43] Particularly during periods of militancy it is likely that the occupational sanctions make the costs of exit from the Labour Party prohibitive and hence members, in so far as possible, will voice to make their preferences known because the exit option is not a viable choice.

Finally, as we have noted, Hirschman sees exit as the province of economics and voice as the province of politics, but we shall see in the section which follows that there are powerful forces in the later years of party development which tend to reinforce exit rather than voice and which diminish the potential for party democracy.

II FORCES FOR TRANSFORMATION: THE EMERGING ELECTORAL GAME

During its early years the party makes the building of a large membership its top priority and is not in a position to design strategies appropriate to *victory* in the larger electoral arena, although candidates are run and some success may already have been attained. Once it is successful in obtaining membership resources, however, it becomes feasible to begin to design strategies of competition for electoral victory as well. This choice to conduct a 'mixed' strategy of membership *and* electoral success, while perhaps inevitable, is fraught with risks and many of the problems plaguing socialist working-class parties stem from this critical juncture in their development.

There are a number of strategic reasons why leaders in both types of socialist working-class parties should begin to consider the advantages of entering the electoral game, in addition to the obvious benefits of government control and the opportunity to translate party programmes into public policy. First, as the working-class begins to change from unskilled to skilled and many formerly working-class people become lower middle-class, it becomes increasingly difficult for the party to calculate precisely the changing parameters of their traditional bases of support (i.e. their information costs tend to increase as the composition of the working-class changes). In direct parties and in the later stages of indirect parties, this creates problems with respect to the appropriate posture to assume in order to maintain sufficient membership resources so as to operate the party infrastructure and provide the necessary goods and services to members. Moreover, the costs of members' 'claims' on leaders are high; that is, the 'costs' of party democracy place constraints on the leader's 'room to manoeuvre' in order to design policies to meet these changing social conditions. And while the indirect party has a relatively more 'fixed' resource base in the unions which gives them more 'freedom to manoeuvre', the party still has rising costs of information and infrastructure as well as claims as they become more direct in structure.[44] In other words, leaders face a problem of marginal substitutability of members and of the costs of voters' claims: with the high costs of the membership's claims the possibility of reducing membership while increasing voters is appealing since voters are less able to make claims on the party than members. Thus, as the costs of exit for members decline and the costs of organisational maintenance increase, leaders face a choice of becoming more responsive to members' claims to retain membership or of providing public policy to pay off voters who are not members. *In short, the costs of information, infrastructure and claims as well as the obvious multiple benefits of public office serve as incentives for the leadership to give serious consideration to the opportunities present in an electoral strategy over and against a party strategy.*

A *Party Systems and Strategies: The Two-Party Case*

Once the decision to enter the electoral arena seriously is made, several important consequences follow for socialist working-class parties in *two-party systems*. After establishing the party structure, socialist working-class parties are concerned with capturing votes from the newly enfranchised working-class and their appeals are designed accordingly. Downs suggests that the situation for the Labour Party in England, for example, was located at C in the diagram below, which was a strategy designed to outflank the Liberals and Conservatives.[45]

But when the Labour Party gained substantial support and the Liberal Party was relegated to a minor position, the party could begin to think of *winning* the government in competition with the Conservatives. This called for a different strategy. Once they entered the two-party (or more accurately, the two-and-one-half party) system as in England and post-war Germany, their ideology and promises had to be adjusted accordingly.[46] No longer could the party be viewed as a strictly working-class party but one whose policies were attractive to a number of voters in the centre of the political spectrum. As Downs points out, this strategy requires some 'beclouding' or adjustment in previously clear ideological positions in order to appeal to the larger electorate.[47] These analytic considerations are reinforced by political

298

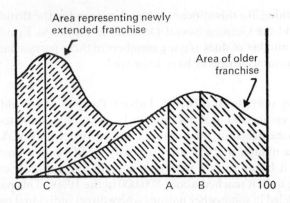

Area representing newly
extended franchise

Area of older
franchise

O   C   A   B   100

FIGURE 3
Anthony Downs, op. cit., p. 129.

scientists who refer to the 'changing character' of socialist working-class parties. As Epstein observes: 'Much of the shift in party posture in Britain and in other nations has been in the form of a continued dilution, now almost liquidation, of traditional socialist doctrine. This is most plain in Britain, West Germany and other nations where there is a large unified socialist working-class movement.[48]

The problem for party leaders once the decision to win is made is the 'uncertainty' and risk concerning the extent to which voters can actually be convinced to vote for their party and the possible effects such a shift in party position may have in diminishing their traditional base of support. Hence, information and risk costs are still high although these may not be so high as to forgo the chance to reduce the costs of membership, infrastructure and claims as well as the opportunity to gain the rewards of public office. But once the leadership makes public promises to deliver goods and services to the voters, which were previously restricted to members, this should reduce the incentives for prospective members to join the party or individuals who are already members to remain, since these same goods and services can now be obtained through promised public policy, whether one is a member or not. In other words, as Olson would argue, the policies of the party become public goods and accrue to any member of the class (i.e. working-class voters and the public in general) irrespective of membership in the party, which reduces incentives to join or remain. This may have the effect of reducing the number of party members as well as the quantity of resources they represent, while electoral support may increase.

299

Something like this appears to have happened in the British Labour Party and the German Social Democratic Party. As Epstein points out, the number of dues-paying members in these parties has declined while electoral prospects have improved.

Noting only its (the British Labour Party's) direct individual membership and not its differently responding affiliated trade union membership, the number enrolled reached its peak of just over a million in 1952 after a nearly steady climb from 1945. Then it began to fall, with only a small and sporadic counter-trend, until it reached about 800,000 in the 1960s. This pattern is paralleled in some other nations where direct individual membership can be distinguished from indirect affiliated membership (local or national). The German Social Democrats have lost members, going from 875,000 in 1947 to a low of 585,000 in 1954 before climbing back to 624,000 in 1958 and 664,000 in 1961. The lower levels of membership, it should be noted, coincided with fairly substantial electoral gains. It may fairly be suggested that the Social Democrats are thus becoming a party with a broader but less intense appeal. In accord with this suggestion is the party's tolerance of a looser membership. Certainly the mass-membership base is becoming less significant.[49]

If membership declines while support from voters increases, this may make the 'claims' of members less viable with the leadership, since in the long run they can be replaced by voters to provide electoral support for the party. Of course, in the short run, under the high-risk conditions associated with this period, remaining members may still be able to make their 'claims' viable by insisting that any electoral success was a consequence of their continued support. However, as the party gains more and more success in the electoral arena, one can expect such an assertion to be less credible with the leaders.[50]

Decline in membership is also a good indicator of the extent to which the party leaders have chosen to use the organisation as a campaign vehicle rather than as a means of creating *social solidarity incentives* for members.[51] If, as we have assumed, organisational activity was once the main source of such social solidarity incentives then it follows from Hirschman that 'loyalty', which is closely related to such incentives, will be decreased accordingly. This should further

300

reinforce the tendency for party members to 'voice' strenuously and then exit. The latter mode of response will become increasingly the case since members will come to perceive leaders as less receptive to their 'claims' and the costs of getting the party back on the track to be too high. Moreover, as we have already observed, the attractiveness of simply becoming a voter, which involves few costs and the similar rewards via public policy, increases the probability of exit to voter status from membership status. This is more true of the direct rather than indirect affiliates to the party since while the direct affiliate need merely stop paying his dues by default, the indirect affiliate must consciously decide to 'contract out'.

Finally, to the extent that leaders can substitute voters for members, and thereby reduce the viability of members 'claims' on them, *party* democracy is diminished since it is clear that voters do not have the same *direct* claim on party leaders that members do: voters can only make their preferences known at elections, which makes their influence over party programmes minimal. This, in turn, reduces the incentives of party leaders to design their programmes specifically to fit the preferences of their members, over and against voters.

B *Elite Responses as Constraints on the 'Pure' Electoral Strategy*

The opportunities and offices to which ambitious members are expected to respond rationally will also undergo change once the electoral strategy is emphasised. Instead of careers built in the sub-units with measures of success being determined by membership satisfaction, career opportunities will increasingly shift to successful performance in constituency organisations and the ability to win elected office in the wider electoral arena. That and electoral success and parliamentary skills will begin to be valued as requirements for leadership. In short, opportunity structures and the manifest office hierarchy come to be associated with the electoral strategy rather than the party strategy and ambitious members are expected to act accordingly.[52]

But the new strategy is expected to have serious consequences for some ambitious members as well as some established leaders. They too must make exit-and-voice calculations under conditions of quality deterioration. They will see part of such quality deterioration as disruption in the opportunity structures which makes their rational calculations for advancement increasingly fraught with risk. During this period they will be forced to undertake iterative calculations which will oscillate between the party and electoral strategy.[53]

But since many of these prospective leaders as well as established leaders have heavy sunk costs in the party and have suffered severe initiation in Hirschman's terms, they will more than likely remain loyal, but when they do begin to voice it will be of a severe kind. This should lead to extreme disputes in the party which will usually be cast in ideological terms in order to gain membership and voter support for the intra-elite struggle.

In the light of these observations, it is critical to note that the opportunity structures and the manifest office hierarchy to which party leaders respond on their way to the top have important ideological implications which serve to constrain those in the party who seek to adjust their ideology and programme to the 'pure' electoral strategy This is so owing to the fact that a significant proportion of the leadership is expected to have been recruited during a period in which a party strategy was dominant and they have heavy sunk costs in the ideological programmes associated with such a strategy (e.g. commitments to working-class interests, length of membership, the creation of communication networks and contacts and commitments to the ideals of party democracy). Leaders 'socialised' in such a manner are expected to resist the allocation of party resources to a purely electoral strategy or at least demand what they consider to be an equitable distribution of resources to both the party and the electoral strategy.

This situation may perhaps best be conceptualised by viewing the preferences of party leaders as a set of indifference functions as between the electoral and party strategies since it is unlikely, except in extreme cases, that they will prefer one strategy to the total exclusion of the other; that is a block of electoral zealots on the one hand and party zealots on the other. Rather they will prefer some allocation of resources to both strategies. Moreover, we might conceptualise the problem as a difference of opinion with respect to the allocation of resources by specifying a set of hypothetical budget lines with the party goals on the B axis and the electoral goals on the A axis, as we have in Figure 4 below.

During the very early periods of development we would expect the allocation of resources roughly to resemble the budget line for period one. But the general *tendency over time* is for the party to increasingly allocate more resources to the electoral game which moves the budget line upward and to the left culminating in period four with a complete reversal of allocations.

302

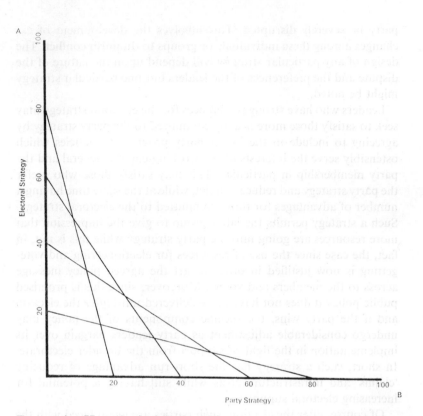

FIGURE 4. Hypothetical Budget Lines

Resource Allocation Schedules Over Time

Period	A	B	
Period 1	20	80	Base Resources = 100 units
Period 2	40	60	The resources available to the party is ex-
Period 3	60	40	pected to increase over time but, for pur-
Period 4	80	20	poses of argument, we have assumed that
			they have a base of 100.

This hypothetical pattern is simply illustrative and represents certain general tendencies. Actual allocations are expected to fluctuate upwards and to the left, or downwards and to the right, depending on a number of factors, especially the electoral success of the party.

Since the party leadership is composed of individuals who prefer one type of allocation over another, some disputes are inevitable, and means must be found for resolving these lest the operation of the

303

party be severely disrupted. This involves the development of exchanges among these individuals or groups to diminish conflict. The design of any particular strategy will depend upon the nature of the dispute and the preferences of the leaders but one particular strategy might be noted.

Leaders who have strong preferences for the electoral strategy may seek to satisfy those more heavily committed to the party strategy by agreeing to include in the broad party programme policies which ostensibly serve the interests of the working-class in general and the party membership in particular. This may satisfy those who prefer the party strategy and reduce conflict, while at the same time having a number of advantages for those committed to the electoral strategy. Such a strategy permits the latter group to give the impression that more resources are going into the party strategy while this is not, in fact, the case since the use of resources for electioneering and vote-getting is now justified in order to get the agreed policy message across to the members and voters. Moreover, since this is promised public policy it does not have to be delivered until *after* the election and if the party wins, the specific components of the policy may undergo considerable adjustment as party leaders bargain over its implementation in the light of support from the broader electorate. In short, such a strategy has the short-run advantage of reducing 'claims' and infrastructure costs while still having a potential for increasing electoral support.

Of course, after the election, such parties are again faced with the problem of disagreement amongst the leadership. For if the party loses, some leaders may claim that this resulted from a failure to allocate sufficient resources into the party strategy in order to gain support from that traditional sector, whereas those committed to the electoral strategy may feel that the leadership was too severely constrained in their ability to adjust policies to appeal to the general electorate.

The preceding observations are simply intended to show that so long as the careers, sunk costs and preferences of leaders differ, ideological disputes over party purpose and mission, as well as the allocation of resources appropriate to these differing visions are perhaps inevitable in socialist working-class parties. In this sense, one cannot anticipate an 'end to ideology', albeit there may be a dimunition in this feature as compared with earlier periods of development.[54]

Finally, it is to be expected that segments of the party leadership will seek to reduce the probabilities of deep ideological disputes by

304

recruiting new leaders whose careers and preferences closely correspond to the changing priorities of the party. Patterns of recruitment and the characteristics of those recruited are important indicators of shifting strategies. Indeed, many scholars have noted a relationship between the types of leaders recruited and the increasing propensity for such parties to adjust their ideological commitments in order to play electoral and parliamentary politics more effectively.

SUMMARY AND CONCLUSION

We began our inquiry by noting that William Wright's distinction between rational efficient models and party democracy models was in one sense a false dichotomy in that it implied that analytic approaches appropriate for one type of party were not appropriate for the other. Using the insight of Robert Michels as a point of departure, we sought to argue that when certain rational models of behaviour incorporate the appropriate structural characteristics and strategies into their assumptions they can provide a number of insights into the development of parties which are normally thought to fall under the party democracy rubric; namely, socialist working-class parties in two party systems.

In our discussion we employed the theories of Olson, Schlesinger, Hirschman and Downs to specify some of the factors which tend to transform the strategies and functions of such parties from party democracy behaviour to rational-efficient behaviour (Figure 2). In the course of our discussion we considered the differing structural strategies chosen by such parties in their early years as they sought to solve Olson's problem of rational non-involvement in order to secure operational resources. We also examined the extent to which such parties initially met our conditions of party democracy as well as noting the relationship between these conditions and the structure of opportunities available to ambitious members and the process of leadership recruitment. Using Hirschman's model we investigated the domain and modes of response which are present in socialist working-class parties with different organisational structures and then attempted to relate these responses to our previous discussion of the Olson and Schlesinger models.

After considering the problems which face such parties during their formative stages we turned our attention to the impact on party strategy and function when a significant proportion of the leadership makes a commitment to allocate resources to electoral politics in

305

order to *win*, not simply compete. We noted that this decision is made and implemented owing to certain rational calculations which make electoral politics more attractive than commitments to the party membership. This, in turn, sets in motion a series of considerations which begin to transform many of the conditions which encouraged party democracy in the embryonic party. As far as possible, voters are often substituted for members, ideological purity is diminished, and party activity is less continuous and extensive. But we also noted that such transformation is far from complete, since there are a number of countervailing forces in socialist working-class parties which constrain, and will probably continue to constrain, the movement to pure rational-efficient behaviour. These constraints are related to a number of factors including the changing nature of industrial society, its impact on mass preferences and the electoral success of the party. While keeping these factors in mind we chose to concentrate on the constraints imposed on a complete transformation by conflicting leadership preferences regarding the mission of the party. We viewed these differing preferences as related to their social background, organisational experience and career patterns. These represent heavy sunk costs for the leaders and influence their view of the party's appropriate role *vis-à-vis* the party strategy and electoral strategy. And since leaders and ambitious members have heavy sunk costs, they will usually have correspondingly high commitments of loyalty in Hirschman's terms, hence policies with which they disagree are expected to encourage the creative use of the art of voice and general protest in order to get the party 'back on a track' closer to their preferences. This, of course, necessitates a complex configuration of creative bargaining and exchange among and between leaders and activists with differing preferences. The critical question for scholars is the theoretical isolation of the factors which influence the predominance of one set of leadership preferences over another. Finally in parties which have made substantial commitments to winning elections, such bargaining is not likely to involve the mass membership; thus the problem of party democracy.

Our general discussion has been limited to socialist working-class parties in two-party systems and much additional work needs to be done on the implications of the electoral strategy on such parties in multi-party systems. Here we have only been able to touch on this question in a footnote (36) and in another article referred to there. But there seems to be some evidence that ideological purity must be sacrificed in coalition-making and this has the effect of reducing both

306

the reliability and responsibility of leaders to members. Important consequences follow from this for conflict and coalition-making within the leadership of such parties. In these cases, rational models of political behaviour have proved useful, as is demonstrated in the work of Leiserson, Axelrod and Rosenthal.[55]

All debates about the functions of political parties proceed from some concept of representation. As Epstein observes, there are really two conflicting theories: (1) elected public office holders, individually or collectively, decide policy: they may or may not respond to voters or members; and (2) the office holder is considered the party agent. The core of the second theory, which is presumably fundamental to socialist working-class parties, is that elected representatives reach agreement as a result of decisions by the organised party membership.[56] The first roughly corresponds to the rational-efficient model and the second to the party democracy model.

These two forms of representation were discussed at some length by theorists such as Ostrogorski, Michels and Duverger: Ostrogorski subscribes to the first while Michels and Duverger prefer the second.[57] Michels in particular was critical of the tendency of parliamentary representatives of social democratic parties to act independently from the wishes of their membership in order to respond to voters. The current evidence would seem to have confirmed Michels' fears. Socialist working-class leaders appear to have adopted a strategy closer to the first concept of representation than to the second, although a number of important constraints limit their movement in this direction. These developments suggest a fundamental paradox for socialist parties: the more they seek to win the competitive electoral game in two-party systems in order to translate their ideological preferences into public policy, the less chance they have of achieving 'pure' party democracy.[58]

NOTES

1. William E. Wright, *A Comparative Study of Party Organisation*, Charles E. Merrill, Columbus, Ohio, 1971, Ch. 1.

2. Robert Michels, *Political Parties: A Sociological Study of the Oligarchic Tendencies of Modern Democracy*, Crowell-Collier, New York, 1962.

3. For several excellent treatments of Michels' work see the following: C. W. Cassinelli, 'The Law of Oligarchy', *American Political*

Science Review, vol. 67, no. 3, September 1953, pp. 773–84; John D. May, 'Democracy, Organisation and Michels', *American Political Science Review*, vol. 59, no. 2, June 1965, pp. 417–29; Giovanni Sartori, 'Democrazia, burocrazia e oligarchia nei partiti', *Rassegna Italiana di Sociologia*, vol. 1, Luglio-Settembre 1960, pp. 119–36; and Juan Linz, 'Leadership democrazia e oligarchia: in margine alla "Sociologia del partiti politici" di R. Michels', *Rassegna Italiana di Sociologia*, vol. 6, Luglio-Settembre 1965, pp. 361–86; Juan Linz, 'Robert Michels', *International Encyclopedia of the Social Sciences*, Macmillan, New York, 1968, pp. 265–71; I. M. Zeitlin, *Ideology and the Development of Social Theory*, Prentice-Hall, New Jersey, 1968, Ch. 14; Gordon Hands, 'Robert Michels' *Political Parties*', *British Journal of Political Science*, Vol. 1, part 2, April 1972, pp. 155–72.

4. Hands, loc. cit., p. 156.

5. ibid., p. 158.

6. ibid.

7. ibid., p. 159.

8. Linz, 'Robert Michels', *International Encyclopedia of the Social Sciences*, pp. 266–7.

9. ibid., p. 266.

10. ibid., p. 268.

11. ibid., p. 269.

12. ibid., p. 267.

13. Maurice Duverger, *Political Parties: Their Organisation and Activity in the Modern State*, John Wiley, New York, 1963, pp. 422–7.

14. Leon Epstein, *Political Parties in Western Democracies*, Praeger, New York, 1967, *passim*.

15. See Anthony Downs, *An Economic Theory of Democracy*, Harper & Row, New York, 1957; Mancur Olson Jr., *The Logic of Collective Action: Public Goods and the Theory of Groups*, Harvard University Press, Cambridge, 1965; Joseph Schlesinger, *Ambition and Politics*, Rand McNally, Chicago, 1966; Albert O. Hirschman, *Exit, Voice and Loyalty: Responses to Decline in Firms, Organisations and States*, Harvard University Press, Cambridge, 1970.

16. Olson, op. cit., Ch. 1.

17. ibid., p. 2.

18. Duverger, op. cit., pp. 13–22. Direct affiliation is the position of the member when no intervening organisation other than the party stands between himself and the leadership. Indirect membership is the condition in which party membership, in part, is a consequence of membership in a secondary organisation such as a trade union.

308

19. ibid., p. 15.

20. ibid., p. 16.

21. ibid., p. 15.

22. Downs, op. cit., Ch. 2. Downs argues that parties 'sell' policies to voters in exchange for votes.

23. Epstein, op. cit., p. 147.

24. Duverger, op. cit., p. 15.

25. See Olson's treatment of social solidarity incentives in trade unions, op. cit., p. 67.

26. The concept of 'claims' was suggested by Joseph Schlesinger in his 'Riker vs. Downs and the Definition of Political Parties', pp. 9–11, paper delivered at the First Annual Conference On Political Party Organisation and Behaviour, Michigan State University, 8–9 May 1972. The concept refers to the predisposition of individuals or groups of individuals for making their preferences binding on leaders.

27. Robert Michels, op. cit., pp. 138–9, pp. 188–91.

28. We shall confine our discussion to the Labour Party proper and not to the unions. Issues of union democracy, while important, cannot be adequately treated here. For a systematic study of this question see Martin Harrison, *Trade Unions and The Labour Party*, Allen & Unwin, London, 1960, and Seymour Lipset, Martin Trow and James Coleman, *Union Democracy*, The Free Press, Glencoe, 1952. Changes in party finance from unions to constituency organisations in the British Labour Party can be found in Martin Harrison, 'Britain', in Richard Rose and Arnold J. Heidenheimer (eds.), 'Comparative Political Finance', *Journal of Politics*, vol. 25, No. 4, November 1963, p. 675.

29. Schlesinger, *Ambition and Politics*, pp. 1–21.

30. ibid., p. 8.

31. ibid., p. 3.

32. ibid., pp. 99–101.

33. Hirschman is an economist who attempts to use microeconomic analytic techniques to investigate the responses of organisations to decline. His work is particularly suggestive for scholars concerned with *qualitative* decline *vis-à-vis* the more easily measurable quantitative indicators of decline.

34. ibid., p. 1.

35. ibid., p. 77.

36. ibid., p. 30.

37. ibid., p. 37.

38. ibid., p. 38.

39. ibid., p. 43.

40. ibid., p. 39.

41. ibid., p. 79.

42. ibid., p. 79. Schlesinger, drawing on Hirschman, notes the differing potential for exit and voice present in various types of political parties. See his 'Riker vs. Downs', pp. 12–13.

43. ibid., p. 34.

44. Infrastructure costs refer to the allocation of scarce resources to build and maintain a multi-nuclear organisation to deliver services and create social solidarity incentives for members. This is always costly and there is a strong tendency for parties to convert such infrastructures into machinery to get out the voter rather than to continue to provide information, services, and social solidarity incentives to members. Claims and infrastructure costs can be reduced by appealing to voters rather than members. The former, who can make few direct claims on leaders, are substituted for members who *can* make such claims. Moreover, the infrastructure can be converted to a vote-getting machine while curtailing other services.

45. Downs observes that new parties are most likely to appear and survive when there is an opportunity for them to cut off a large part of the support of an older party by sprouting up between it and its former voters. This applies to the Labour Party in 1900 since the enfranchisement of the working-class in the late nineteenth century had shifted the centre of voter distribution far to the left of its old position. 'And the Liberal Party, even after it moved to the left, was to the right of the new centre of gravity, although it was the more left of the two major parties. The Labour Party correctly guessed that they could outflank the Liberals by forming a new party to the left of the latter and they did. This trapped the Liberals between the two modes of the electorate and their support rapidly diminished to insignificant size.' Downs, op. cit., pp. 128–9.

46. We have chosen to confine our discussion to the strategic considerations faced by socialist working-class parties in two-party systems. This in no way should be interpreted as a severe limitation on our general argument since such parties in multi-party systems, such as Italy and France, are also confronted with certain benefits and burdens once they seek to win, except winning in these cases usually means becoming a partner in a government coalition. The problem in such systems does not spring from an adjustment in their ideological purity to gain more voters at the centre, since they will usually attempt to remain as distinct as possible from other parties,

310

but rather at the government level. Once they become members of a coalition and enter into exchanges with other parties to their right, they must give up some of their ideological purity in order to make public policy. But if they do so, they face charges by party leaders and supporters that the government in which they are a partner is producing policies which do not go far enough towards meeting their ideological preferences and, in any case, they were not the ones promised during the electoral campaign. This may cause some members to consider exiting from the party. Moreover, such charges from members and some leaders outside the parliament can lead to severe disputes in the party as ambitious members use such issues to charge parliamentarians of their party with betrayal and seek to remove them in order to fulfil their own office ambitions. For a study of the question of transformation in socialist working-class parties once they seriously seek to gain governmental power in France and Italy, see Timothy M. Hennessey and Jeanne Martin, 'Exchange Theory and Parliamentary Instability', in Alan Kornberg (ed.), *Legislatures in Comparative Perspective*, McKay, New York, 1972.

It is important to note that when the German Social Democratic Party began to compete seriously in the electoral market-place, they did so in what was, at that time, a multi-party system. Our discussion, however, is confined to their changing strategy and behaviour in the period since World War II when a two-and-a-half party system existed in West Germany.

47. The convergence hypothesis suggested by Downs does not stand unqualified. As he points out, the possibility of convergence toward the centre in a two-party system 'depends upon the refusal of extremist voters to support either party if both become alike – not identical but merely similar. In a certain world – where information is complete and costless, there is no future-oriented voting, and the act of voting uses up no scarce resources – such abstention by extremists would be irrational. As long as there is even the most infinitesimal difference between A and B extremist voters would be forced to vote for the one closest to them, no matter how distasteful its policies seemed in comparison with those of their ideal government.

'It is always rational *ex definitione* to select a greater good before a lesser, or a less evil before a greater; consequently abstention would be irrational because it increases the chances of the worse party for victory. In an uncertain world, however, abstention is rational for extremist voters who are future-oriented. They are willing to let the worse party win today in order to keep the better party from moving towards the centre, so that in future elections it will be closer to them. Then when it does win, its victory is more valuable in their eyes. Abstention thus becomes a threat to use against the party nearest one's own extreme position so as to keep it away from the centre.'

Moreover, for Downs, uncertainty increases the possibility that rational extremist voters will abstain because, given information costs, 'even significant differences will pass unnoticed to the radical whose own views are so immoderate that all moderates look alike.' (Downs, op. cit., pp. 118–9). Thus, as socialist working-class parties move toward the centre they not only experience an exit of members but an abstention by radical supporters and this forces them to seek to compensate for this by picking up voters from other sectors of the population.

48. A leading example of a retreat from pure socialist ideology is the case of the German Social Democratic Party. After 1949 there was a stark change in the party's programme. As Epstein observes, 'Its socialism ceased to be socialism in any formally accepted meaning of the term. The capitalist economy was frankly and openly accepted when the party adopted its new basic programme in 1959. At the Bad Godesberg conferences at the time, the Social Democrats voted that "the consumer's freedom of choice and the worker's freedom to choose his job are fundamentals of a socialist economic policy, while free enterprise and free competition are important features of it".' And in 1964, the party paid tribute to the dynamics of the market economy. Entering the grand coalition of 1966 'required no new doctrinal concessions'. Epstein, op. cit., p. 158. See also: Lewis J. Edinger, *Kurt Schumacher*, Stanford University Press, Stanford, 1965; V. Stanley Vardys, 'German's Postwar Socialism: Nationalism and Kurt Schumacher', *The Review of Politics*, Vol. XXVII, no. 2, April 1965, pp. 220–44; Otto Kirchheimer, 'Germany: The Vanishing Opposition', in Robert Dahl (ed.), *Political Oppositions in Western Democracy*, Yale University Press, New Haven, 1966, p. 245 and Douglas A. Chalmers, *The Social Democratic Party of Germany: From Working-Class Movement to Modern Political Party*, Yale University Press, New Haven, 1964. The British Labour Party, like the German Social Democrats, has also come to accept capitalism. Electorally it has come to be assumed that any commitment to nationalisation is an electoral liability. But it cannot be abandoned altogether because of internal party reasons. As Epstein observes, 'what is different about the Labour Party in the 1960s is that any nationalisation... will be justified only under particular circumstances

and not as the beginning of a new order.' Epstein, op. cit., p. 159.

49. Epstein, op. cit., p. 164.

50. The viability of claims by members will vary depending on the closeness of election victories. If they are particularly close, members will have incentives to make 'claims' on leaders by arguing that it was their support which pushed the party 'over the top'. Such claims may be difficult to ignore and leaders may be especially vulnerable under these conditions. See Schlesinger, 'Riker v. Downs', pp. 4–5, for a similar observation concerning voters in close elections.

51. Some of the usual social solidarity incentives may be undermined by the success of government welfare programmes in any case.

52. During the 1950s and 1960s there was a noticeable drop in the trade union sponsorship of MPs and in the working-class character of Labour's top parliamentary leadership. This was evidenced by the decline in trade union sponsored MPs from 80 per cent in 1918 to 37 per cent in 1966. That is, parties will attempt to recruit candidates for office who are more appealing to the general electorate. This is also shown by the Labour Party's increasing recruitment from the professional classes. Labour MPs of professional class background increased from 35 per cent in 1951 to 40 per cent in 1970 and there was a decline of workers from 37 per cent to 26 per cent in the same period. Among new Labour MPs in the 1970 Parliament, just over half were professional people, and only 18 per cent could be called workers. Moreover, candidates of professional class background have greater electoral success than those of working-class background. See David Butler and Michael Pinto-Duschinsky, *The British General Election of 1970*, Macmillan, London, 1971, pp. 299–304. For additional data on these changes see Z. Bauman, *Between Class and Elite*, Manchester University Press, Manchester, 1972; W. L. Guttsman, 'The Changing Structure of the British Political Elite, 1886–1935', *British Journal of Sociology*, vol. II, No. 2, June 1951, pp. 122–34, and his 'Changes in British Labour Leadership', in Dwaine Marvick (ed.), *Political Decision-Makers*, The Free Press, Glencoe, Ill., 1961 and *The British Political Elite*, MacGibbon & Kee, London, 1963. For another such analysis consult Jean Bonnor, 'The Four Labour Cabinets', *Sociological Review*, vol. 6, No. 1, July 1958, pp. 37–48; and David E. Butler and Richard Rose, *The British General Election of 1959*, Macmillan, London, 1960, pp. 128–30; David E. Butler and Anthony King, *The British General Election of 1964*, Macmillan, London, 1965, p. 237 and their *The British General Election of 1966*, Macmillan, London, 1966, p. 210.

53. That is, as increased emphasis is placed on electoral victory, aspirants in the party and trade union organisation are at a disadvantage to the degree they can not shift their careers to electoral politics. Nor is this situation endemic solely to the early years of a new electoral strategy. See D. E. Butler and Anthony King, *The British General Election of 1966*, pp. 30–43, for a discussion of the conflicts between elected officials and party and trade union officials. The authors note the resentment of Transport House staff members over their reduced influence on party policy during the Labour Government and the succeeding electoral campaign. In addition, party officials resented the use of market research to gauge public opinion rather than through consultation with Transport House.

54. The recurring nature of such disputes is, of course, not simply a function of age, that is, of those socialised at an earlier period of party development. Indeed, much of the ideological dispute in the SPD as they pursue an electoral strategy comes from a combination of the 'New' and 'Old' left. As Conradt notes:

> The Social Democrats, in spite of electoral gains, are still faced with the dual problem of maintaining their newly won support in middle-class areas, without thereby alienating its left wing. The changes in the party's policies, tactics, leadership, and style that have been especially noticeable since the late 1950s and subsumed under the general strategy of 'embracing the middle', have not occurred without internal opposition, especially from the party's new and old Left. The SPD Left has argued that the party by 'embracing the middle' has in fact adapted to the economic and sociological givens of West Germany and has essentially taken the easy road to political power. The party's entrance into the Grand Coalition and its 1969 alignment with the middle-class Free Democrats are cited as evidence that the party has sacrificed its principles and commitment to social and political change. Instead of attempting to convince the electorate of the need for an extensive restructuring of the economy and society, the party has restructured itself to the function of representing diverse social groupings without thereby changing the power relationships between them. The Left's *bête noire* in this regard is Schiller who has steadfastly refused to consider programmes such as steeper inheritance taxes and an extension of co-determination. In terms of internal party equilibrium, however, there is little doubt that the election results strengthened

and consolidated the position of the party's moderate 'Establishment', i.e. that group within the SPD drawn largely from the ranks of party functionaries and office holders at local, state, and national levels who conceive of the SPD as a centre-left, yet broadly based party of reform. The classic 'proletarian core' of the party, still based in some trade unions has been in continuous decline since the 1950s and the 1969 election, to the extent that it justified the Grand Coalition and indeed the entire Brandt-Wehner strategy, weakened it still further. In the future the most significant intraparty opposition to the present course will come from the party's new Left, largely centred in the SPD's youth organisations. This group conceives of itself as the SPD of the 1980s and supplements its class conflict pronouncements with a vigorous generational struggle. Its ranks appear to be growing; between 1960 and 1969 the percentage of new SPD members under 30 rose from 27·5 per cent to 47·6 per cent. Although weakly represented in the party's national leadership bodies, i.e., Federal Praesidium and Executive, the Young Socialists have become increasingly active and influential in the party's local organisations where they capitalise on the relative inactivity of the rank and file. To the extent that the national success of the party has increased their own notoriety, the Young Socialists since 1969 have profited from a strategy they in principle opposed. David P. Conradt, 'The West German Party System', *Sage Professional Papers In Comparative Politics*, Vol. 3, 1972, pp. 43–4.

55. See Michael Leiserson, 'Factions and Coalitions in Japan: An Interpretation Based on the Theory of Games', *American Political Science Review*, vol. 62, No. 3, September 1968, pp. 770–87; Robert Axelrod, *Conflict of Interest: A Theory of Divergent Goals with Applications to Politics*, Markham, Chicago, 1970; Howard Rosenthal 'Voting and Coalition Models in Election Simulations', in William Coplin (ed.), *Simulation in the Study of Politics*, Markham, Chicago, 1969, pp. 237–85.

56. Epstein, op. cit., p. 292.

57. ibid., pp. 292–3. M. Y. Ostrogorski, *Democracy and the Organisation of Political Parties*, Vol. I, Macmillan, London, 1902, Chs. 4–5. Robert Michels, op. cit., p. 181, and Duverger, op. cit., p. 185.

58. Throughout this paper we have chosen to concentrate on changing party *strategies*. This approach is in no way intended to

overlook the important constraints on party democracy which result from the general problem of organisational development. The transition in party organisations from ideological concerns to bureaucratic, operational functions, can also be approached from the point of view of organisational theory. For an empirical study of the constraints on party democracy which come about as a result of the process of institutionalisation see E. Spencer Wellhofer and Timothy M. Hennessey, 'Political Party Development: Institutionalisation and Leadership Recruitment', *Midwest Journal of Political Science*, forthcoming, 1974.

11. When is a Decision not a Decision?

GERAINT PARRY AND
PETER MORRISS

Perhaps the major contribution to political science made by the many studies of community power has not been the portrayal of local communities so much as the extra refinement they have brought to the analysis of political power in general. In this the work of Floyd Hunter and of Robert A. Dahl must take pride of place not merely for the quality of their own analyses but for the informative debate which their rival conclusions and methodologies aroused. The community studies of Presthus and of Agger, Goldrich and Swanson brought further evidence and methodological refinement. But of equal significance have been two short, theoretical articles which have come to play a major part in controversies not merely about the analysis of power but also about American society and its malaise. They were written by Peter Bachrach and Morton Baratz and appeared in the *American Political Science Review* in 1962 and 1963 and are now reprinted as chapters of their recent book *Power and Poverty: Theory and Practice*.[1]

To this linked debate on community power and American policy these seminal articles contributed the notion of a 'non-decision'. The significance of what is, as we shall see, an unfortunate term lies in the fact that what has been called the 'decisional approach' had come to dominate the analysis of political power amongst American political scientists. In turn this approach was associated with what was also termed a 'pluralist' analysis of American power relations. The method was to isolate within any given community certain key 'decisions' which were thought likely to illustrate the power relations which prevailed. These key decisions were chosen from a range of different issue areas. The object was of course to test whether the same groups took the 'key decisions' in all or many of these different issues. If they did the community could be said to be ruled by an elite. If they did not, but instead different persons made decisions in each issue area, the community was said to be 'pluralist' in its decision-making process. The conclusions of research conducted along these lines were

317

almost invariably that the communities were pluralist and this invited the hypothesis that America too was pluralist or, as Dahl termed it, 'polyarchal'.

This approach and its different attendant conclusions threatened to become an orthodoxy amongst political scientists – part of 'normal politics' as both sides proclaimed, turning Kuhn's terminology to suit their differing purposes. The pluralist position came under attack quite early particularly from avowedly radical writers[2] but it was perhaps the twin explosions of the urban riots and Vietnam which brought pluralist orthodoxy most into question. For a prime conclusion of the pluralist analysis had been the 'permeability' of American democratic institutions. The study of decision-making showed that any group with a grievance could make itself heard by conducting itself in conformity with the established decision-making procedures. A lack of protest indicated satisfaction. Yet the cities were in turmoil, apparently overnight and inexplicably if one were to accept the pluralist conclusions and the pluralist methodology.

It was almost certainly this crisis which gave the Bachrach and Baratz articles such currency after they had caused little impact on their first appearance. The authors suggested that the decisional approach was inadequate because it had failed by its very methodology to identify and describe 'non-decisions'. These 'non-decisions' occur when issues are prevented – for various reasons which will be examined later – from ever reaching the 'agenda' of a community. It then follows that a study of 'decisions' will not identify matters upon which there have never been any decisions. And equally clearly it seemed a plausible hypothesis to suggest that the crisis of the cities was the outcome of 'non-decisions' which had therefore been overlooked by the pluralists. It was also a hypothesis which was in line with what so many critics had long alleged about American urban policy, that it was a policy of neglect of public functions – that it formed part of a general picture of private affluence and public squalor. The concept of a non-decision was then an intuitively plausible idea which fitted in with what seemed to be frightening empirical confirmations of the most pessimistic critical analyses of American society. And indeed the 'non-decision' threatened itself to become a part of a new critical orthodoxy applied to any policy outcome with which the critic disagreed. But despite this success – or perhaps because of it – the idea of non-decisions is extremely difficult to pin down. A critical examination of the idea was due and indeed has been forthcoming in a recent article by Raymond Wolfinger – one of

318

Dahl's original associates on the New Haven project – and in a reply to Wolfinger by Frederick W. Frey who attempts to mediate between the sides.[3] But, for reasons which we shall indicate, the restatement of the pluralist decisional approach is unsatisfactory. Accordingly, whilst pointing out some of the difficulties of the original account of non-decisions, we wish to suggest another way in which the problems raised by non-decisional analysis might be tackled. In particular, we want to argue that although primacy should be given to a 'decisional' approach to the study of power, not all exercise of power in society can be explained in terms of an actor 'A' *causing* another actor 'B' to act in a manner which he did not originally intend. Very often 'A' gains advantages and 'B' is disadvantaged by the performance of social 'routines' which go largely unquestioned. In this way 'A' acquires 'consequential' power although he may not have brought the routine into being and although he may be in no direct causal relationship with 'B'.

But before we go on to examine these problems in detail, it might be useful to place the study of power and decisions in a wider context of the study of politics.

If the idea of a 'non-decision' seems intuitively plausible so does the study of politics by the study of political decisions. For is not this what politics is about? Political power is a matter of making key decisions. Let us then study these key decisions and see how they are taken – either proceeding as a historian does or as Dahl's team were fortunate enough to do by watching the decision-making process as it happened. What makes this approach the more understandable is that politics is widely thought of as concerned with the resolution of conflict. This is a view taken by political sociologists and traditional political philosophers. Compare two remarkably similar utterances. First Robert A. Dahl:

> If everyone were perfectly agreed on ends and means, no one would ever need to change the way anyone else behaved. Hence no relations of influence or power would arise. Hence no political system would exist.[4]

And secondly Sir Isaiah Berlin opening his celebrated Inaugural Lecture on 'Two Concepts of Liberty':

> If men never disagreed about the ends of life, if our ancestors had remained undisturbed in the Garden of Eden, the studies to which the Chichele Chair of Social and Political Theory is

319

dedicated could scarcely have been conceived. For these studies spring from, and thrive on, discord.[5]

Such descriptions of politics would gain a wide measure of acceptance amongst political scientists even if some would wish to make some modifications, in particular to specify more particularly what kind of conflict counted as political.[6] Political conflicts are resolved by political decisions—the exercise of choice between conflicting policies, groups or persons. The 'key' decisions relate to the 'key' conflicts—those which have the greatest significance to the political unit, its members and its leaders.

Given this picture of politics as problem-solving then the study of decision-making will seem the correct path to an accurate description and explanation. This is probably in line with the popular image of politics as the sphere of action where individuals and groups conflict and where decisions are taken. It also permits the researcher to present his study in a narrative form, telling the story of the victories and reversals of the rival protagonists, and though this is not a major consideration in scholarly investigation it adds interest and conviction to the results.

It is not, of course, to be denied that much politics is of this sort. Decisions are taken, significant conflicts do occur. Politics includes the activity of authoritative community integration and this is why politics is of such importance, whether its importance lies in its being the supreme activity of man or in its being a necessary evil. The sense of being involved in the 'centre of things' constitutes the 'charm of politics' and its vocation for participants and theorists from Machiavelli to Weber or R. H. S. Crossman.

But there is another way of looking at politics which lays far less stress on conflict and its resolution through decisive action. Politics is also 'ruling'. 'Ruling' does of course imply the attempted resolution of conflicts but it implies, even more, regulation. A great deal of ruling consists in the performance of routines. Now, as Sharkansky has pointed out in one of the rare attempts to study this neglected yet essential part of politics, routines may be procedures leading up to decisions or may be decisions themselves.[7] The routine may indicate the criteria to consider, as in Sharkansky's example of the percentage increment from one year's budget to the next. Or the routine may lay down exact formal procedures for certain types of decision or the decision may itself be specified as when there is a routine answer to certain kinds of claim.

320

So politics is the application of fairly standard procedures to recurrent problems rather than the settlement of 'world-historical' conflicts. The regular meetings of government consultative committees involving unions, business and government are as much a part of ruling as the confrontation of unions and government over new industrial legislation. Indeed the consultative committees are far more numerous and frequent and are indubitably indicative of power relations in the society. More broadly, government routinely works within the prevailing mode of economic production and exchange. This is not to say that government cannot change this predominant mode, nor is it to say that governments never do fundamentally challenge it. Governments can and, on occasion, do. It is to make the more modest claim that governments ordinarily spend more time in administering an on-going political system than in making fundamental changes in it.

This is the sense in which Oakeshott is right in describing politics as *'attending* to the arrangements' of a community rather than as *making* the arrangements. The bulk of the 'arrangements' are there before the advent of any particular government and are still there after its departure. This is true of the basic institutions – parliament, the courts. It is true of the economic institutions, whether the planning system of socialist countries or the banking system of capitalist countries. It is also true of the ordinary legislation. A striking feature of democracies is the continuity of legislation and treaties from one government to the next. This is a basic fact of political life and a major presupposition of legal theory and of political obligation.

Politics conceived of as ruling has thus an inbuilt conservatism. As Sharkansky says 'routines are conservative mechanisms'.[8] The routines Sharkansky studies involve incremental changes from previous standards and keep change under considerable control. The recognition of the conservative nature of 'ruling' need not commit one to the more prescriptive mood of some of Oakeshott's utterances:[9]

In any generation, even the most revolutionary, the arrangements which are enjoyed always far exceed those which are recognised to stand in need of attention, and those which are being prepared for enjoyment are few in comparison with those which receive amendment: ... the greater part of what we have is not a burden to be carried or an incubus to be thrown off, but an inheritance to be enjoyed.

Despite Oakeshott, for many people existing arrangements are matters for endurance rather than enjoyment but it remains true that 'the new is an insignificant proportion of the whole'. And that this understanding of politics may be viewed in a quite different light may be recognised by the analysis of 'non-decisions' by many of the more radical critics. They acknowledge the significance of routines and, like the conservatives, hold that the study of decision-making, isolated from the wider cultural, ideological and economic contexts, is inadequate. But their emphasis is on what they hold to be the disproportionate power in the hands of the few — power which is best indicated by the routine, unquestioned and unspectacular activities of governments and of economic leaders. The implication is that the routinely powerful is the truly powerful.

To understand this process they employ two related concepts — 'non-decisions' and 'mobilisation of bias', the latter term being adapted from Schattschneider's study *The Semi-Sovereign People*. Despite its growing popularity the term 'non-decision' is by no means clearly defined. In their original articles Bachrach and Baratz did not offer a formal definition but their usage indicates what they had in mind. Non-decisions are acts which help support the 'mobilisation of bias' which in turn gives legitimacy to the non-decisions. Mobilisation of bias is defined in *Power and Poverty*. It is 'a set of predominant values, beliefs, rituals, and institutional procedures ("rules of the game") that operate systematically and consistently to the benefit of certain persons and groups at the expense of others'.[10] Consequently

> when the dominant values, the accepted rules of the game, the existing power relations among groups, and the instruments of force, singly or in combination, effectively prevent certain grievances from developing into full-fledged issues which call for decisions, it can be said that a none-decision-making situation exists.[11]

These usages indicate a process by which opposition is thwarted before it reaches the formal stages of authoritative decision-making. The opposition's proposals do not reach the 'agenda'. But in *Power and Poverty* Bachrach and Baratz add an explicit definition which, while including these situations, goes still further and renders the concept too all-embracing to be useful. It is

A decision that results in the suppressing or thwarting of a latent or manifest challenge to the values or interests of the decision-maker. To be more nearly explicit, none-decision-making is a means by which demands for change in the existing allocation of benefits and privileges in the community can be suffocated before they are even voiced; or kept covert; or killed before they gain access to the relevant decision-making arena; or, failing all these things, maimed or destroyed in the decision-implementing stage of the policy process.[12]

Wolfinger being dismissive of the whole notion of non-decisions does not offer any definition but Frey in his more mediatory article does:

A non-decision occurs when a choice among alternatives by one actor is either not perceived by him or, if perceived, is not made, and always, in either case, because of some exercise of power by another actor.[13]

The general upshot is that non-decision-making procedures ensure that only those issues which are 'safe' in the sense of posing no fundamental threat to the existing decision-making elite are permitted to reach the community's agenda.

From these definitions and from the list of activities characterised as non-decisions it is clear that the term itself is by no means satisfactory and is misleading even if one acknowledges that the procedures described do require analysis.

One apparent meaning of 'non-decision' is any political activity which is not a 'decision' — i.e. that 'non-decision' stands to 'decision' as *non-p* to *p*. The wider the term non-decision is made the more it approaches this clearly useless notion. This is not, however, an insignificant quibble. One refrain of pluralist responses to non-decision analysis is to say, as Nelson Polsby does, 'For every event... that occurs there must be an infinity of alternatives. Then which non-events are to be regarded as significant?'[14] And the reply this receives from Matthew Crenson:[15]

From the infinity of non-events available, why should we pick those related to air pollution instead of those related to the prevention of elephant stampedes or the persecution of witches?

323

begs the question of how to construct criteria of significance for distinguishing within a range of *possible* alternatives.

Nor can non-decision be regarded satisfactorily as the contradictory of decision. A decision is best seen as, to adapt Hobbes, an act of will which ends deliberation. It is a choice between alternative courses of action. There is therefore in principle a point of choice or of decision. There is a 'performative utterance'[16] such as 'I decide' or 'it is hereby decided' which indicates at least the formal decision and there are criteria embodied in the 'speech act' whereby one can discern who has the authority to make these utterances. This may be very difficult to study but it does seem to be what is involved in principle in the concept of a 'decision'.

To say that a 'non-decision' is the opposite of such a decision would imply that no point of choice had been reached, no performative utterance or 'illocutionary act'. There would be a continuing process of deliberation without formal termination. This may come close to one of the situations described by Bachrach and Baratz – the condition of 'drift' or the 'decisionless decision' as they call it. Yet even this situation where 'history is made behind men's backs,' as Wright Mills so perceptively put it, is not adequately portrayed as the contradictory of a 'decision'. What happens is a series of lesser decisions or choices each of which forecloses other courses of action and commits the actor or others, superiors and inferiors, to directions they might not have taken if starting *de novo*. But this is not to say that there has been no 'decision' since there have been many decisions. What it means is that 'big events' are not necessarily produced by 'big causes' – a view which many a historian would share. So, to accept Bachrach and Baratz's example, the Bay of Pigs may not have been the consequence of one major decision but it was the outcome of many lesser ones and even in this case someone with authority has to give the final go-ahead even if this is a mere *imprimatur*.

What we wish to argue is that in many cases non-decisions *are* decisions. They are not, however, necessarily the sorts of 'key decisions' studied by the 'decisional approach' associated with the work of Dahl and his associates. Many are lesser decisions which are component parts of a routine and the power which a routine reflects may be of a different kind to that discovered by the analysis of decisions. Bachrach and Baratz's own language gives support to this version of a 'decisional approach' to non-decisions. The definition of a non-decision cited above begins by saying that it is a decision. Unless non-decisions are approached in this way there will be the continuing danger that the notion will be devalued by the inclusion of what are very different political techniques. It is a danger present in Bachrach and Baratz's own study.[17] Both action and inaction are described as non-decisions. Some non-decisions appear to involve conscious choices, others to be the outcome of the unconscious acceptance of community values. Still others are identifiable only by their social and political consequences. To understand the power and the penetrability of any community it is better to replace blanket terms like 'non-decision' with a more precise analysis of the many different patterns decision-making can take.

Firstly one must try to sort out the 'chinese box' of decisions. We have suggested that a decision is a performative utterance discernible according to certain rules. This can be a highly formal definition of decision—the signature of the President or the announcement by a board of directors. This is *the* decision. But clearly this may be a mere *imprimatur*. *The* decision is thus the large 'box' which contains the lesser decision 'boxes'. What is being said here, and also in some of the non-decisional literature, is that there is a distinction between the formal structure of power and informal power relations. Clearly the more the 'decisional' approach confines itself to formal decisions the more it overlooks the informal. But it is also the case that the more the 'non-decisional' approach confines the term 'decision' to the formal procedures the more it will attribute power to 'non-decision'-making, to the greater confusion of all.

Moreover it is difficult to lay down a sensible universal definition of 'formality'. If one selected the moment of presidential or monarchical signature it would, absurdly, exclude the 'decisional' activities of legislators. If instead one chose to define the legislative process as 'the decision' and all else as non-decision stages this would have almost equally absurd consequences for the study of, say, British policy-making. It would place the relations between pressure groups and civil service, which is so crucial to British government, in the 'non-decision' category. Certainly these discussions do much to decide what is on the agenda for cabinet and parliamentary consideration but it would clearly be wrong to designate so regular a part of the governmental process as semi-legitimate. 'Non-decision' is not, then, just a temporal term, but an evaluative one as well.

When we in fact look at examples of so-called 'non-decision-making' we see how important it is to distinguish between them. Bachrach and Baratz distinguish four different forms of 'non-decisions'[18] and a couple of cognate types. Firstly there is the use of force. They list harassment, imprisonment, beatings and murder. Now, even if they have the same purpose of preventing an issue being raised, this is a rather mixed list which includes both criminal acts such as murder and constitutional acts such as imprisonment. However cynical one may be about some of the legal procedures of courts in the southern states of the USA – the example discussed in these pages – it is essential to take due note of the differences involved. Imprisonment does imply a formal decision procedure.

Secondly they cite the threat of sanctions against the reformer. Their list of sanctions again ranges widely from threats of dismissal to co-optation in a participatory democracy. Once more we would prefer to regard these as 'decisions' and decisions, moreover, which involve very different procedures, different degrees of legitimacy and different consequences for both agent and patient. The process of co-optation has, of course, been a long-standing technique of limiting opposition – almost a tradition in Britain – but it does involve costs for the elite who have at least to surrender exclusivity and usually have to make some concessions on policy. In the same category one should perhaps include the technique of the pre-emptive strike of 'stealing the Whigs' clothing'. This step, when taken by the Mayor of Baltimore in his dealings with CORE organisers, is termed by Bachrach and Baratz a 'direct case of none-decision-making.'[19] Yet, if ever there was one, here was a *decision*, taken by the authoritative political leader in a constitutional manner. He acted in a way he would not otherwise have done and in a direction which would benefit the poorer sections of the society. Certainly this also had the effect of keeping the initiative in his own hands rather than those of the CORE organisers but this consequence is scarcely enough to designate it a non-decision, any more than it would have been if an established party had been beaten to the gun. In politics someone gains and someone else loses but everyone has to bear some costs.

Bachrach and Baratz's third category of non-decision is the invocation of procedures to thwart or redirect innovation. The example given is the frequent practice of referring demands to committees of enquiry. The final category is strengthening and reshaping the 'mobilisation of bias'. Two instances are offered. One involves the introduction of new procedural barriers to change. The other involves calling on the norms of the society to limit demands or even render them illegitimate by regarding the control of business as outside the realm of politics and as part of the free-enterprise system. Once again

326

these cases are different and some involve clear decisions. Shelving a policy may be a ploy but it is also a decision, as is the introduction of new procedural barriers.

The final instance of the effect of social norms in thwarting demands is rather different and raises many problems precisely because this is less obviously an assignable decision. It belongs with a cluster of problems associated with routines, ideologies and what Banfield once termed 'steady state' situations.

Political routines and 'decisionless decisions'[20] are perhaps the easiest to deal with. The latter are situations of drift where a series of smaller decisions commits each actor towards a bigger decision which he would not have independently contemplated. Routines tend to display a type of decision-making, termed 'disjointed incrementalism'. This is far nearer a conscious political style.[21] The decision-maker follows a pattern of changing policy only at the margins. He does not think out every policy *de novo*. This would be an impossible undertaking. He operates instead within a framework of reference – not of his own making – which is largely composed of the precedents for his present decision and for comparable decisions[22] and by the minor amendments which most claimants press for. This description, undoubtedly accurate for most forms of ruling, has been upheld by some pluralists[23] as illustrative of the fallacies of the non-decision analysis. Since decision-makers cannot consider all conceivable policies they cannot be condemned for thwarting some conceivable reformist policies. But this assumes that this is a conscious decision whereas, in fact, the concept of the mobilisation of bias admits of a more subtle interpretation fully in accordance with Lindblom's and Sharkansky's analyses of routines. The decision-maker excludes possible options because he works within an established framework of ideas and procedures which may eventually rub off on the clients. They may then either only put in claims which are in line with established practices or may abandon their pressure since they are convinced it does not fit in with established precedent and is likely to be rejected as a consequence. Such anticipated reaction or 'renunciation' as Wolfinger calls it is, rather curiously and inconsistently, not treated by the authors of *Power and Poverty* as an example of non-decision-making – whether it is the mass anticipating the elite or the elite anticipating the mass. It is curious in that such anticipations are of the stuff of politics. Once again we should wish to treat them as decisions – though in this case it is the patient and not the agent whose performatives are at issue. The difficulty consists in knowing if they happened where no

327

evidence is available of a kite being flown or of a minute which is not proceeded with or of a proposal hastily withdrawn.

Even graver difficulties of observability and identification face that familiar yet still problematic notion of 'false consciousness'. When faced with non-participation, why, asks Wolfinger, do neo-elitists attribute this to satisfaction and complacency when it is the elite which does not participate and to false consciousness when it is the poor or the masses who abstain?[24] The reply is that it is the elite which reaps the benefits from inaction and the poor which stands to gain by reform. But this, whilst plausible at first glance, raises difficulties which have been very readily pointed out by the critics of the Bachrach and Baratz approach. To suppose that the poor are subtly but deliberately prevented from participating ignores too hastily the possibility that such social consequences may not be intended even by those who benefit. More importantly it is alleged that the reply involves the insertion by the political scientist of his own bias. The failure by a group to conform to the commentators' independently premeditated expectations is attributed to a 'non-decision' by some other group or else to 'false consciousness'.

The problem may be examined by turning our attention to the other side of the non-decision coin – the 'non-issue'. The alleged effect of a so-called none-decision is to prevent an issue being formally decided by nipping it in the bud before it becomes an issue. As with (non)-decisions so with (non)-issues it is necessary to differentiate between cases. Much seems to turn on what counts as a fully fledged issue. An 'issue' is a matter which is to be decided. But this supposes that someone recognises that it is to be decided and for this there are several candidates – authorised legislatures, pressure groups, ordinary citizens or outside observers.

Clearly there is no problem where all these groups recognise that a matter is to be decided. This is an issue and is likely to reach the authoritative decision-making stage. The problems arise when the situation falls short of this. Firstly it could happen that all parties recognise that a matter must be decided sooner or later but the political elite (assuming its existence for purposes of argument) would prefer to defer decision since it involves awkward commitments which could cost support. That part of the political elite currently in a position to deal with the matter would sooner see someone else burn his fingers. Such a situation should be observable by interviews, access to records and so on. It seems proper to call this an issue just as we suggested it was proper to describe the attempt to shelve the matter as a

decision. Secondly it is possible for some groups to recognise something as an issue while others do not. Agger and his associates describe
such situations in one of the cities in the southern USA which they
studied.[25] Once again there is public evidence of both concern and
lack of concern and, usually, of some efforts to make the other side
show concern. Here once more we would wish to say that the issues
had been raised even though one might wish to add that the 'issue
had not been joined'. Whilst it is tempting to think, as Frey notes,[26]
that an 'issue' implies controversy this is not so as is suggested by the
qualifying phrases 'at issue', 'join issue' or 'take issue'.

All these examples are overt and can perfectly well be described in
terms of 'decisions' and 'issues'.

The next examples raise more difficulties. Firstly the elite may seek
to prevent an issue being raised by techniques ranging from rewards
to legitimate and illegitimate sanctions. We have already noted that
these techniques are themselves very different. They do moreover
assume that the elite can recognise an issue on the horizon and to the
extent that the evidence for this is fairly public it fits, in all its variations, into the overt issue category. It is when the stifling procedure is
covert that the difficulties arise. There is little, short of a 'lead', that
can uncover the discreet telephone call and without it the investigator
is left with nothing but surmise. One would wish to say that there was
an issue but it was suppressed before it received a public airing.

As ever the more one approaches the 'anticipated reactions' and
'false consciousness' end of the continuum the greater the problems of
observability. Some anticipated reactions can be traced and can be
described in terms of decisions. Some evidence in other cases may be
available if, say, grievances can be elicited by means of interview and
then these grievances contrasted with the apparent inaction of the
aggrieved. If the contrast is put to the subject one may well receive
answers couched in terms of 'rational apathy' which would do credit
to Downs's voter.[27] Why bother to participate if the chances that one
will fail are so high?[28] Antipathy and apathy must not be confused.
It is true of course that one must take care with such evidence that it
is not itself coloured by either later events or by the investigation
itself. The investigator would today get far more politicised replies to
questions about grievances, apathy, alienation and non-participation
in Northern Ireland than he would have received in the 1960s.

Nevertheless it is when the grievances cannot be readily elicited
that the most vigorous opposition to 'non-decision' analysis arises
and it must be acknowledged straight away that some of the doubts

of the critics are justified. The opportunity to interpret the situation in the light of what the commentator would expect to find does exist. But there are still some steps one can take to investigate the reason for apparent satisfaction with what others might think unsatisfactory conditions. It is acknowledged even by Wolfinger that there are cases where such satisfaction is *prima facie* surprising—the Negroes in the southern USA are always safely cited.

Firstly it might be that a person's expressed satisfaction with his society and its social and economic relationships was inconsistent with his continued but frustrated attempts to marginally improve his situation by, say, wage demands.[29] Once made conscious of the limits of his 'trade unionism' he might in the classic Leninist manner turn his attention to the overall political system and be aroused from his inertia. This might give retrospective evidence of the state of 'false consciousness' which previously existed (though one must again beware of retrospective reanalysis).

Secondly if we adopt Brian Barry's view that a policy is in a person's interests if it increases his opportunities to get what he wants[30] then we can justify our saying what we frequently do say, namely that X has mistaken his interests. Wealth and power are evidently in a person's interests and his failure to put forward demands which would promote such interests is at least a phenomenon that demands explication. The comparative silence of the American ghettoes in the 1950s in the face of inadequate housing and jobs can thus be seen as a portent of disaster rather than as broad satisfaction with the social and political system. That said, it must immediately be acknowledged that such assertions cannot be so readily made where one is, as is so often the case, trying to explain the failure of one issue to appear rather than others, all of which would fit the criteria for being in the interests of, say, the ghetto poor. Why does education surface as an issue in some cities and not in others, or urban renewal or air pollution? The non-decisional answer is that only the 'safe' issues are permitted to become full issues. But this can be dangerously close to self-confirming when the definition of a 'safe issue' is also one which has been allowed to surface.

More promising are the attempts of Crenson to examine comparable communities in order to explain their varying performances on one issue—in this instance the issue was pollution. Failure in one community to deal with an issue becomes all the more striking and in need of explication if several other comparable communities face up to it. Another approach is to examine policy outputs in comparable communities. No doubt this is easier said than done. It is difficult to ensure comparability. It is fallacious to argue directly from outputs to intended use of power even if one can say something about the 'consequential' distribution of resources.[31]

One of the major difficulties in research into power is how one can identify the power agent—the 'A' in the examples of A getting B to do what he does not wish to do. There can be argument as to whether A acted or even, when dealing with the 'mobilisation of bias' or with certain kinds of routine, as to whether A exists as an identifiable person or group. But in these situations it may be possible to recognise the patient—the B who is doing something he does not want to do or who is getting considerably less than he wishes and much less than others in the system. One might then begin at the 'bottom'—with grievances—and study the decisions (performative utterances or illocutionary acts) of B. Primacy should be given to the causal approach which attempts to trace some identifiable person or group acting to alter the balance of choices and advantages open to others. But often this causal chain will arrive back at a routine and the analysis of routine raises different problems of analysis.

The pluralist model of power is a causal one. It requires that one shows that A is able to make B do something he would not otherwise do—which has to be illustrated by some actual decision. In the case of 'non-decisions' A must be shown preventing B raising an issue. If this is not shown then A does not possess power over this issue at least. Several community-power studies have examined the exercise of power in this way. There are cases of A getting his way constitutionally, by force of reputation and by covert, illegitimate threats. And there have been studies such as Dahl's which have failed to reveal any such success—or even attempts—at stifling threats to established interests.

But power need not be seen in this causal manner. Power can also be understood as resources which may then be used to acquire the power-holder's 'future apparent good'. Discovering the 'decision-makers' in a routine does not necessarily indicate the 'men of power' if by this one means either the persons who ultimately determine another person's range of choices or those who gain in resources as a consequence of the routine. The routine decision may be taken by an official who has not himself laid down the procedure he follows and who does not gain in any significant way from the decisions taken. Routines may however routinely grant resources or powers to some and deny them to others. They routinely ignore certain inputs and

331

they routinely distribute the outputs.[32] As Parenti points out, rules in politics are seldom neutral but are 'the embodiment of past political victories'.[33] It can thus be difficult for certain demands to penetrate the system and be fully recognised as issues. But this does not necessarily mean that the powerful have to be, or can be seen to be, consciously acting to thwart such demands. They may be the unconscious beneficiaries of the bias which does not have to be consciously mobilised by the system. Nor do the various elite groups have to act conspiratorially. One of the consequences of elite consensus is to confirm elite position without the necessity of any power display in a causal sense. This is what Crenson means when he suggests that 'a polity that is pluralistic in its decision-making can be unified in its none-decision-making'[34] — though this, as has been seen, is not the terminology favoured here. It would also be misleading to describe those who support and maintain the routines — administrators, judges, police — as the 'agents' of the powerful. This implies more conscious direction than is always the case in social affairs.

What the existence of routines suggests is that there are at least three kinds of power to consider. Firstly there is the power to initiate the routine. Secondly there is the power by which the routine is maintained. Thirdly there is the distribution of power which is consequential upon the performance of the routine. These should not be confused and it does not follow that the same persons possess all three forms of power. The initiatory power is of course causal in nature. It is analysable in principle as a decision whether it is overt or covert. The power to maintain the routine is similarly analysable in terms of decisions but not, this time, 'key decisions'. Rather these are the lesser decisions, limited by precedent and custom, which have been analysed in the work of Lindblom and of Sharkansky. Their analysis involves a study of incremental procedures, of the range of options considered by those involved in ruling, the impact these procedures in turn have upon the inputs. But this approach will rarely trace the resultant distribution of power resources to a specific command of a 'ruling elite'. The third type of power is not causal but 'consequential'. Though different in its nature it does not seem unreasonable to accept the ordinary usage by which those who benefit are termed 'powerful' even if they have not acted directly to secure such benefits. Indeed if two types of power were comparable one might be tempted to say that those who could rely on established routines to get what they wanted were more powerful than their ancestors who had to fight to establish such routines. But the real point is that these powers are not the same. And nothing in the analysis of the routines of ruling commits one to the belief that the 'elite' who benefit from a routine will be able to resist a challenge to the routine. They have what Mosca termed the advantages of *positions déjà prises* but these are not insurmountable. Some routines are democratically established and in principle subject to democratic control. The beneficiaries are therefore themselves dependent. One difficulty with such control is that routines by their nature tend to be conservative, that they have their own momentum. Their overthrow is hence more difficult. An extreme instance would be the difficulty of democratically altering the routines and expectations resulting from political boundaries. Both majoritarian and pluralist democratic theory have difficulties in dealing with secessionist movements.[35] The existence of routines may thus indicate the degree of 'openness' or 'permeability' of the polity.[36]

The case of Ireland may illustrate in rough and ready fashion the distinctions we have in mind. We might then say, for sake of argument, that those who drew up the present borders between the North and Eire had the power to establish the various governmental and constitutional routines. They are not the same persons as those who now maintain these routines. Nor are they the beneficiaries of the routines (though some of their descendants may be). But as a consequence of the routines some groups in the North, notably the Orange Order, have gained in power, and others, notably the Catholics, have been relatively powerless. This distribution of resources may be seen as by now embedded in the routines of Northern Ireland politics and society rather than as directly attributable to the 'key decision-makers' of fifty years ago.

In conclusion, we suggest that a sensible procedure in the analysis of political and social power would be to treat it in the first place as the taking of decisions. We propose to discard the notion of 'non-decision'. Most — though not all — so-called 'non-decisions' can be seen to fit into the category of decisions. Such as are not explicable as decisions are primarily examples of 'false consciousness' which remains a problem to be elucidated. The 'decisions' are those of both agent and patient — both A and B — since the performative utterances of both 'sides' are some indication of the conduct or the anticipated conduct of the other. The next task would be to distinguish between the very many types of decision from the 'key decision' of the pluralist analyses to the 'routine decision' and to the 'decisionless decision'. One would then be in a position to distinguish the types of power in each case – whether initiatory, routine or, for want of a better term, 'consequential'.

Primacy is then given to the 'decisional' approach since this is in principle the most economical explanation couched in historical terms. But it is not regarded as the only possible explanation of a given distribution of social resources. Politics is a matter of speaking and acting, of decisions and choices. But it is also a matter of customs and regulations, of traditions and of ruling. If politics is so 'pluralist' in its methods it perhaps ought to admit of a certain eclective 'pluralism' in its analysis. Different styles of governing demand different styles of explanation. Put together they may also help explain how 'non-issues' may become issues, how today's new demands are transformed into tomorrow's routines and what forms effective participation must take if today's routines are to be challenged by tomorrow's decisions.

NOTES

1. Oxford University Press, New York, 1970.

2. e.g. Todd Gitlin, 'Local Pluralism as Theory and Ideology', *Studies on the Left*, vol. 5, No. 3, Summer 1965, pp. 21–45 and reprinted in A. McCoy and Playford, *Apolitical Politics*, Crowell, New York, 1967, a collection of much of this critical literature.

3. R. Wolfinger, 'Nondecisions and the Study of Local Politics', and F. Frey, 'Comment: On Issues and Nonissues in the Study of Power', both in *American Political Science Review*, Vol. 65, no. 4, December 1971, pp. 1063–80 and 1081–1101 and a 'Rejoinder' by Wolfinger, pp. 1102–4.

4. *Modern Political Analysis*, Prentice-Hall, Englewood Cliffs, 1st edition, 1963, p. 72.

5. *Four Essays on Liberty*, Oxford University Press, Oxford, 1969, p. 118.

6. e.g. Bernard Crick, *In Defence of Politics*, Weidenfeld & Nicolson, London, 1962 and D. D. Raphael, *Problems of Political Philosophy*, Pall Mall and Macmillan, London, 1970.

7. Ira Sharkansky, *The Routines of Politics*, Van Nostrand Reinhold, New York, 1970, Ch. II and *passim*.

8. *The Routines of Politics*, p. 9.

9. 'Political Education' in *Rationalism in Politics*, Methuen, London, 1962, pp. 112–13.

10. *Power and Poverty*, p. 43.

11. 'Decisions and Nondecisions: An Analytical Framework', *American Political Science Review*, Vol. 57, no. 3, September 1963, p. 641. This passage is not reprinted in *Power and Poverty*.

12. *Power and Poverty*, p. 44. See Wolfinger's comment on this passage, loc. cit., fn. 22, pp. 1065–6.

13. Frey, loc. cit., p. 1092.

14. *Community Power and Political Theory*, Yale University Press, New Haven, 1963, p. 97.

15. Matthew A. Crenson, *The Un-Politics of Air Pollution: A Study of None-Decision-making in the Cities*, Johns Hopkins Press, Baltimore, 1971, p. 26.

16. See J. L. Austin, 'Performative Utterances', *Philosophical Papers*, Oxford University Press, Oxford, 1961, pp. 220–39, and *How to Do Things with Words*, Oxford University Press, Oxford, 1962. See also W. J. M. Mackenzie, 'Models of Collective Decision-Making', *Social Sciences: Problems and Orientations*, Mouton for UNESCO, The Hague, 1968, pp. 356–70.

17. See the examples cited in *Power and Poverty*, pp. 70–3.

18. *Power and Poverty*, pp. 43–6.

19. *Power and Poverty*, p. 71.

20. See also above, p. 324.

21. On such styles see A. F. Davies, 'The Concept of Administrative Style', *Australian Journal of Politics and History*, Vol. 12, no. 1, 1966.

22. See Charles Lindblom, 'The Science of "Muddling Through" ', *Public Administration Review*, Vol. XIX, no. 2, Spring 1959, pp. 79–88.

23. e.g. Wolfinger, loc. cit., pp. 1066–70.

24. Wolfinger, loc. cit., pp. 1070–7.

25. *The Rulers and The Ruled*, p. 307.

26. Frey, loc. cit., p. 1087.

27. Downs argued in *An Economic Theory of Democracy*, Harper & Bros., New York, 1957, that in an election with a large electorate it is rational for an individual not to vote, since the chances of his vote swaying the result is very small, and does not outweigh the costs involved.

28. Some of Parenti's subjects fall into this category. See 'Power and Pluralism: A View from the Bottom', in M. Surkin and A. Wolfe, *An End to Political Science*, Basic Books, New York, 1970, pp. 129–31.

29. Steven Lukes drew our attention in discussion to this possibility.

30. *Political Argument*, Routledge, London, 1965, p. 176.

31. See later, pp. 333–4.

32. See Sharkansky, *The Routines of Politics*, p. 9.

33. Parenti, loc. cit., p. 135.

34. Crenson, *The Un-Politics of Air Pollution*, p. 179.

35. See, e.g., John Locke, *Second Treatise*, section 117, and R. A. Dahl, *A Preface to Democratic Theory*, University of Chicago Press, Chicago, 1963, Phoenix Books edition, pp. 96–7.

36. That this problem has been recognised for a very long time is shown by J. G. A. Pocock, when discussing the doctrine of Han Fei, an ancient Chinese philosopher. He writes: 'Where A has power and B has not, it is a sign of weakness for either to take the initiative; but B must take it and A need not. How power is acquired in the first place, Han Fei does not tell us here; but once acquired, it is maintained not by exertion but by inaction; not by imposing norms, but by being prerequisite to their imposition; not by the display of *virtu*, but by the characterless force of its own necessity. The ruler rules not by solving others' problems, but by having none of his own; others have problems — i.e., they desire the power which he has — and by keeping these unsolved he retains his power over them.' J. G. A. Pocock, 'Ritual, Language, Power: An Essay on the Apparent Political Meaning of Ancient Chinese Philosophy', in his *Politics, Language, and Time*, Methuen, London, 1972, p. 69.

12. Bibliography of Studies on British Elites

Within the rigorous limits listed below, what follows is as complete a bibliography on social and political elites in twentieth-century Britain as the short period of time available for its compilation could allow. It is restricted to scholarly studies on the origins, recruitment, circulation and ideology of incumbents of powerful institutional offices in Britain. With a few noteworthy exceptions, the following have therefore been deliberately excluded: (1) biographies and memoirs; (2) works on foreign elites, unless they contain substantial references to Britain; (3) works not written in English; (4) studies of elites in the nineteenth century or earlier; (5) 'elitism' as normative political theory; (6) work on the concept of power; (7) empirical studies of decision-making and pressure groups; (8) analyses of the structure, operation and relations of powerful institutions, e.g. the higher civil service.

References marked with an asterisk contain extensive bibliographies which include (but range beyond) studies of a particular type of elite.

General Works on Elites in Industrial Society

Beck, C. and McKechnie, J. T., *Political Elites: a Select Computerised Bibliography*, MIT Press, Cambridge, Mass., 1968.

Lasswell, H. D., Lerner, D. and Rothwell, C. E., *The Comparative Study of Elites: an Introduction and Bibliography*, Stanford University Press, Stanford, California, 1952.

Bottomore, T. B., *Elites and Society*, Watts, London, 1964.

Burnham, J., *The Managerial Revolution*, Day, New York, 1941.

Edinger, L. J., *Political Leadership in Industrial Societies*, John Wiley and Sons, New York, 1967.

Keller, S., *Beyond the Ruling Class*, Random House, New York, 1963.

Linz, J., Dogan, M. and Edinger, L. J., *Political Elite and Social Structure*, forthcoming.

Miliband, R., *The State in Capitalist Society*, Weidenfeld & Nicolson, London, 1969.

Parry, G., *Political Elites*, Allen & Unwin, London, 1969.

Thoenes, P., *The Elite in the Welfare State*, Faber and Faber, London, 1966.

Wilkinson, R., *Governing Elites: Studies in Training and Selection*, Oxford University Press, New York, 1969.

Young, M., *The Rise of the Meritocracy 1870–2033*, Penguin Books, Harmondsworth, 1958.

Aron, R., 'Social Structure and the Ruling Class', *British Journal of Sociology*, Vol. 1 (1 and 2), 1950.

Barkley, R., 'The Theory of the Elite and the Mythology of Power', *Science and Society*, Vol. 19(2), 1955.

Giddens, A., 'Elites', *New Society*, Vol. 22, no. 527, 16 November 1972.

Edinger, L. J. and Searing, D. D., 'Social Background in Elite Analysis: a methodological inquiry', *American Political Science Review*, Vol. 61(2), 1967.

Janowitz, M., 'Social Stratification and the Comparative Analysis of Elites', *Social Forces*, Vol. 35(1), 1956.

Nadel, S. F., 'The Concept of Social Elites', *International Social Sciences Bulletin*, Vol. 8, 1956.

Poulantzas, N., 'The Problem of the Capitalist State', *New Left Review*, No. 58, 1969.

Putnam, R. D., 'Studying Elite Political Culture: the case of "ideology",' *American Political Science Review*, Vol. 65(3), 1971.

General Works on British Elites

Guttsman, W. L. (ed.), *The English Ruling Class*, Weidenfeld & Nicolson, London, 1969.

Nicholson, E. M., *The System*, Hodder & Stoughton, London, 1967.

Sampson, A., *The Anatomy of Britain*, Hodder & Stoughton, London, 1962.

———, *The Anatomy of Britain Today*, Hodder & Stoughton, London, 1965.

———, *The New Anatomy of Britain*, Hodder & Stoughton, London, 1971.

Stacey, F., and M., *Who Rules Britain?* Fontana, London, forthcoming.

Thomas, H. (ed.), *The Establishment*, Blond, London, 1959.

Urry, J. and Wakeford, J. (eds.), *Power in Britain*, Heinemann Educational, London, 1973.

Chester, D. N., 'Who Governs Britain?', *Parliamentary Affairs*, Vol. XV (4), 1962.

Cole, G. D. H., 'Elites in British Society', in his *Studies in Class Structure*, Routledge & Kegan Paul, London, 1955.

Hewitt, C., 'National Policy-Making in Post-War Britain', *British Journal of Political Science*, Vol. 4(1), 1974.

Giddens, A., 'Elites in the British Class Structure', *Sociological Review*, Vol. 20(3), 1972.

Lockwood, D., 'The Distribution of Power in Industrial Society — A Comment', *Sociological Review Monographs*, No. 8, 1964.

Miliband, R., 'Who Governs Britain?', *Universities and Left Review*, No. 3, 1968.

Worsley, P., 'The Distribution of Power in Industrial Society', *Sociological Review Monographs*, No. 8, 1964.

Monarchy and Aristocracy

Abshagen, K. H., *Kings, Lords and Gentlemen: The Influences and Power of the English Upper Classes*, Heinemann, Toronto, 1939.

Bloomfield, P., *Uncommon People: A Study of England's Elite*, Hamilton, London, 1955.

Hardie, F., *The Political Influence of the British Monarchy 1868–1952*, Batsford, London, 1970.

Martin, K., *The Crown and the Establishment*, Penguin Books, Harmondsworth, 1963.

Perrot, R., *The Aristocrats: A Portrait of Britain's Nobility and their Way of Life Today*, Weidenfeld & Nicolson, London, 1968.

Sinclair, A., *The Last of the Best: The Aristocracy of Europe in the Twentieth Century*, Weidenfeld & Nicolson, London, 1969.

Thompson, F. M. L., *English Landed Society in the Nineteenth Century*, University of Toronto Press, Toronto, 1963.

Baltzell, E. D., 'Reflections on Aristocracy', *Social Research*, Vol. 35(4), 1968.

Birnbaum, N., 'Monarchs and Sociologists', *Sociological Review*, Vol. 3(1), 1955.

Shils, E. and Young, M., 'The Meaning of the Coronation', *Sociological Review*, Vol. 1(2), 1953.

Political Elites

Buck, P. W., *Amateurs and Professionals in British Politics 1918–59*, University of Chicago Press, Chicago, 1963.

Guttsman, W. L., *The British Political Elite*, MacGibbon & Kee, London, 1964.

Lieber, R. J., *British Politics and European Unity: Parties, Elites and Pressure Groups*, University of California Press, Berkeley, 1970.

Mathews, D. R., *The Social Background of Political Decision Makers*, Random House, New York, 1954.

Ranney, A., *Pathways to Parliament: Candidate Selection in Britain*, University of Wisconsin Press, Madison, 1965.

Richards, P. G., *Patronage in British Government*, Allen & Unwin, London, 1963.

*Rose, R. (ed.), *Studies in British Politics* (second edition), Macmillan, London, 1969.

————(ed.), *Policy Making in Britain: A Reader in Government*, Macmillan, London, 1969.

Roth, A. and Kerbey, J., *The Business Background of MPs*, Parliamentary Profile Services, London, 1972 (earlier editions in 1963, 1965 and 1967).

Rush, M. D., *The Selection of Parliamentary Candidates*, Nelson, London, 1969.

Thomas, J. A., *The House of Commons 1906–11: an Analysis of its Economic and Social Character*, University of Wales Press, Cardiff, 1958.

Abrams, M., 'British Elite Attitudes and the European Common Market', *Public Opinion Quarterly*, Vol. 29(2), 1965.

Alt, J., 'Continuity, Turnover and Experience in the British Cabinet 1868–1970' in Alt, J. and Herman, V. (eds.), *Cabinet Studies*, Macmillan, London, 1974.

Bonnor, J., 'The Four Labour Cabinets', *Sociological Review*, Vol. 6(1), 1958.

Brady, A., 'The British Governing Class and Democracy', *Canadian Journal of Economics and Political Science*, Vol. 20(4), 1954.

Buck, P. W., 'Early Start Towards Cabinet Office 1918–55', *Western Political Quarterly*, Vol. 16(3), 1963.

————, 'MPs in Ministerial Office', *Political Studies*, Vol. 9(4), 1961.

Crosland, C. A. R., 'Insiders and Controllers', in his *The Conservative Enemy*, Jonathan Cape, London, 1962.

Guttsman, W. L., 'Aristocracy and the Middle Class in the British Political Elite, 1886–1916', *British Journal of Sociology*, Vol. 5(1), 1954.

————, 'Changes in British Labour Leadership', in Marvick, D. (ed.), *Political Decision Makers*, The Free Press, New York, 1961.

———, 'The Changing Social Structure of the British Political Elite, 1886–1935', *British Journal of Sociology*, Vol. 2(2), 1951.

———, 'Social Stratification and the Political Elite', *British Journal of Sociology*, Vol. 11(2), 1960.

Headey, B., 'What Makes for a Strong Minister?', *New Society*, Vol. 16, no. 419, 8 October 1970.

Heasman, D. J., 'Parliamentary Paths to High Office', *Parliamentary Affairs*, Vol. 16(3), 1963.

Herman, V., 'Patterns of Governmental and Ministerial Stability in Western Parliamentary Democracies', in Alt, J. and Herman, V. (eds.), *Cabinet Studies*, Macmillan, London, 1974.

Johnson, R. W., 'The British Political Elite 1955–70', *European Journal of Sociology*, Vol. XV(1), 1973.

Laski, H. J., 'The Personnel of the British Cabinet, 1801–1924', *American Political Science Review*, Vol. 22(1), 1928.

Nairn, T., 'The British Political Elite', *New Left Review*, no. 23, 1964.

Rose, R., 'The Making of Cabinet Ministers', *British Journal of Political Science*, Vol. 1(4), 1971.

Wilkinson, R., 'Political Leadership and the Late Victorian Public School', *British Journal of Sociology*, Vol. 13(4), 1962.

Willson, F. M. G., 'Routes of Entry of New Members of the British Cabinet, 1801–1958', *Political Studies*, Vol. VII(3), 1959.

———, 'Entry to the Cabinet, 1959–68', *Political Studies*, Vol. 18(2), 1970.

———, 'Some Career Patterns in British Politics: Whips in the House of Commons, 1906–66', *Parliamentary Affairs*, Vol. 24(1), 1970.

McEwen, J. M., 'Unionist and Conservative Members of Parliament, 1914–39' (Institute of Historical Research, London, Ph.D. thesis, 1959).

Administrative Elites

Recruitment to the Administrative Class of the Home Civil Service and Senior Branches of the Foreign Office, Cmnd. 232, HMSO, London, 1967.

Report of the Committee on the Civil Service, Vol. 3, Part 1: Halsey, A. H. and Crewe, I. M., *Social Survey of the Civil Service*, and Part 2: *Other Surveys*, HMSO, London, 1969.

Campbell, G. A., *The Civil Service in Britain*, Gerald Duckworth, London, 1955.

*Chapman, R. A., *The Higher Civil Service in Britain*, Constable, London, 1970.

Dale, H. E., *The Higher Civil Service*, Clarendon Press, Oxford, 1941.

Fry, G. K., *Statesmen in Disguise: the Changing Role of the Administrative Class of the British Home Civil Service, 1853–1966*, Macmillan, London, 1969.

Griffith, W., *The British Civil Service*, HMSO, London, 1964.

*Kelsall, R. K., *Higher Civil Servants in Britain*, Routledge & Kegan Paul, London, 1955.

Robson, W. A. (ed.), *The Civil Service in Britain and France*, Hogarth Press, London, 1956.

Strauss, E., *The Ruling Servants*, Allen & Unwin, London, 1961.

Bottomore, T. B., 'The Administrative Elite', in Horowitz, I. L., *The New Sociology*, Oxford University Press, New York, 1964.

Brittan, S., 'The Irregulars', in Rose, R. (ed.), *Policy-Making in Britain*, Macmillan, London, 1969.

Campbell, G. A., 'Civil Service Recruitment', *Quarterly Review*.

Crossman, R., 'Scientists in Whitehall', *Encounter*, July 1964.

Dodd, C. H., 'Recruitment to the Administrative Class 1960–64', *Public Administration*, Vol. 45(1), 1967.

Fabian Society, 'The Administrators: Reform of the Civil Service', *Fabian Tract* no. 355, 1964.

Fry, G. K., 'Some Developments in the British Home Civil Service since the Fulton Report', *Public Administration*, (Sydney)), Vol. 19(1), 1970.

Greaves, H. R. G., 'The Structure of the Civil Service', *Political Quarterly*, 25(4), 1954.

Helsby, L. N., 'Recruitment to the Civil Service', *Political Quarterly*, 25(4), 1954.

Jeffries, M., 'Married Women in the Higher Grades of the Civil Service and Government Sponsored Research Organisations', *British Journal of Sociology*, Vol. 3(4), 1952.

Keeling, D., 'The Development of Central Training in the Civil Service 1963–70', *Public Administration*, Vol. 49(1), 1971.

Kelsall, R. K., 'The Social Background of the Higher Civil Service', *Political Quarterly*, Vol. 25(4), 1954.

Larner, C., 'The Organisation and Structure of the Foreign and Commonwealth Office', in Boardman, Robert and Groom, A. J. R., *The Management of Britain's External Relations*, Macmillan, London, 1973.

Milne, R. S., 'Has Britain an Economic General Staff?', *Public Administration*, (Sydney), vol. 12(1), 1953.

342

Nettl, J. P., 'Consensus or Elite Domination – the Case of Business', *Political Studies*, Vol. 13 (1), 1965.

Nightingale, R. T., 'The British Foreign Office and Diplomatic Service, 1851–1929', *Realist*, Vol. 3, 1929.

———, *The Personnel of the British Foreign Office*, Fabian Society Tract, 232, 1930.

Oppenheim, A. N., 'The British Diplomat', in Boardman, Robert and Groom, A. J. R., *The Management of Britain's External Relations*, Macmillan, London, 1973.

Parris, H., 'Recruitment and Training for the Civil Service: the French and British Tradition Compared', *Cahiers africains d'administration publique*, Vol. 4, 1968.

PEP, *Advisory Committees in British Government*, Allen & Unwin, London, 1960.

———, 'Government by Appointment', *Planning*, Vol. XXVI, 1960.

Putnam, R. D., 'The Political Attitudes of Senior Civil Servants in Western Europe', *British Journal of Political Science*, Vol. 3(3), 1973.

Robinson, K., 'Selection and Social Background of the Administrative Class', *Public Administration*, Vol. 33(4), 1955.

Sheriff, P. E., 'Outsiders in a Closed Career: the Example of the British Civil Service', *Public Administration*, Vol. 50(4), 1972

Smith, J. H. and Chester, T. E., 'Distribution of Power in Nationalised Industries', *British Journal of Sociology*, Vol. 2(4), 1951.

Subramaniam, V., 'Representative Bureaucracy: A Reassessment', *American Political Science Review*, Vol. 61(4), 1967.

Rickerd, P. E., 'Mobility Between the Administrative Elite and Outside Employment: A Study of the British Civil Service Against the Background of French Experience' (London, LSE, Ph.D. thesis, 1968).

Economic Elites

Aaronovitch, S., *The Ruling Class: A Study of British Finance Capital*, Lawrence & Wishart, London, 1961.

Acton Society Trust, *Management Succession*, London, 1956.

Clark, D. G., *The Industrial Manager: His Background and Career Pattern*, Business Publications, London, 1966.

Clements, R. V., *Managers, a Study of their Careers in Industry*, Allen & Unwin, London, 1958.

Copeman, G., *Leaders of British Industry*, Gee, London, 1955.

Erickson, C., *British Industrialists, Steel and Hosiery, 1850–1950*, Cambridge University Press, Cambridge, 1959.

Ferris, P., *The City*, Gollancz, London, 1960.

Jenkins, C., *Power at the Top: a Critical Survey of the Nationalised Industries*, MacGibbon & Kee, London, 1959.

Lewis, R. and Stewart, R., *The Boss: The Life and Times of the British Business Man*, Phoenix House, London, 1958.

———, *The Managers: A New Examination of the English, German and American Executive*, New American Library, New York, 1961.

Morgan, E. V., *The Structure of Property Ownership in Great Britain*, Clarendon Press, Oxford, 1960.

National Economic Development Council, *Managerial Recruitment and Development*, HMSO, London, 1965.

*Nichols, T., *Ownership Control and Ideology*, Allen & Unwin, London, 1969.

Parkinson, H., *Ownership of Industry*, Eyre & Spottiswood, London, 1951.

PEP, *Attitudes in British Management*, Pelican Books, Harmondsworth, 1966.

Stewart, R., *Managers and their Jobs*, Macmillan, London, 1967.

Barratt-Brown, M., 'The Controllers', *Universities and Left Review*, Vol. 1 (5–7), 1958.

Barritt, D. P., 'The Stated Qualification of Directors in Large Public Companies', *Journal of Industrial Economics*, Vol. V(3), 1956–7.

Bendix, R., 'The Self-Legitimation of an Entrepreneurial Class: The Case of England', *Zeitschrift für die gesamte Staatswissenschaft*, Tübingen, 1954.

The Director, 'The Anatomy of the Board', October 1959.

———, 'The Life and Times of a Director', January 1965.

———, 'The Director Observed', April 1966.

Finer, S. E., 'The Federation of British Industries', *Political Studies*, Vol. 4(1), 1956.

———, 'The Political Power of Private Capital', *Sociological Review*, Vols. 3(2) and 4(1), 1955–6.

Humblet, J. E., 'A Comparative Study of Management in Three European Countries: UK, France and Belgium. Preliminary Findings', *Sociological Review*, Vol. 9(3), 1961.

Lewis, R. and Stewart, R., 'The Men at the Top', *Encounter*, November 1958.

Lupton, T. and Wilson, C. S., 'The Social Background and Connections of "Top Decision Makers",' *Manchester School of Economic and Social Studies*, Vol. (1), 1959.

Musgrave, P. W., 'The Education Profiles of Management in two British Iron and Steel Companies with some Comparisons, National and International', *British Journal of Industrial Relations*, Vol. 4(2), 1966.

Macrae, N., 'The Faults in the Dynamos: a Probe into "Men at the Top",' *Encounter*, July 1965.

Mosson, R. M. and Clark, D. G., 'Some Inter-Industry Comparisons of the Background and Careers of Managers', *British Journal of Industrial Relations*, Vol. 6(2), 1968.

The Church

The Economist, 'The Bishops' Bench', Vol. CLXXXI, 20 October 1956.

Morgan, D. H. J., 'The Social and Educational Background of Anglican Bishops: Continuities and Changes', *British Journal of Sociology*, Vol. 20(3), 1969.

Simey, J., 'The Church of England and English Society', *Social Compass*, Vol. 11(3–4), 1964.

Smart, D. A., 'Who Are Made Diocesan Bishops?', *Theology*, Vol. XLVIII, no. 297, 1945.

The Times, 'Bishops in the Church of England', 28 March 1956.

Welby, P. A., 'Ecclesiastical Appointments, 1942–61', *Prism*, Vol. VI(5), 1962.

The Judiciary

Abel-Smith, B. and Stevens, R., *Lawyers and the Courts: A Sociological Study of the English Legal System, 1750–1965*, Heinemann, London, 1967.

Goldstein-Jackson, K., 'The Judicial Elite', *New Society*, 14 May 1970.

Zander, M., *Lawyers and the Public Interest*, Weidenfeld & Nicolson, London, 1968.

Richards, P. G., 'The Selection of Justices of the Peace', *Public Law*, 1961, (2).

The Military Elite

Abrams, P., 'Democracy, Technology and the Retired British Officer: A Study of the Activities and Standing of Retired Officers in

Britain', in Huntington, S. P. (ed.), *Changing Patterns of Military Politics*, Free Press, New York, 1962.

Barnett, C., 'The Education of Military Elites', *Journal of Contemporary History*, Vol. 2(3), 1967.

Otley, C. B., 'Militarism and the Social Affiliations of the British Army Elite', in Van Doorn, J. (ed.), *Armed Forces and Society*, Mouton & Co., The Hague, 1968.

——, 'Public School and Army', *New Society*, 17 November 1965.

——, 'The Social Origins of British Army Officers', *Sociological Review*, Vol. 18(2), 1970.

Razzell, P. E., 'Social Origins of Officers in the Indian and British Home Army, 1758–1962', *British Journal of Sociology*, Vol. 14(3), 1963.

Hayes, B., 'The Changing Social Origins of Entrants to the Royal Military College Sandhurst During the Nineteenth Century' (Manchester University, Dip. Ed. dissertation, 1959).

Otley, C. B., 'The Origins and Recruitment of the British Army Elite, 1870–1959' (Hull University, Ph.D thesis, 1965).

Local Elites

Moss, L. and Parker, S. R., *The Local Government Councillor*, Vol. II of the Report of the Committee on the Management of Local Government (Maud), HMSO, London, 1963.

Birch, A. H., *Small Town Politics*, Oxford University Press, Oxford, 1959.

Clements, R. V., *Local Notables and the City Council*, Macmillan, London, 1969.

Lee, J. M., *Social Leaders and Public Persons: A Study of County Government in Cheshire Since 1888*, Clarendon Press, Oxford, 1963.

Musgrove, F. J., *The Migratory Elite*, Heinemann, London, 1963.

Stacey, M., *Tradition and Change*, Oxford University Press, Oxford, 1960.

Biffen, J., 'The Constituency Leaders', *Crossbow*, Vol. IV, 1960 (reprinted as 'Conservative Constituency Leaders' in Rose, R. (ed.), *Studies in British Politics*, Macmillan, 1969).

Cavenagh, W. E. and Newton, D., 'Administrative Tribunals: How People Became Members', *Public Administration*, Vol. 49(2), 1971.

Harris, R., 'The Selection of Leaders in Ballypeg, Northern Ireland', *Sociological Review*, Vol. 9(2), 1961.

Headrick, T., 'The Town Clerk. His Training and Career', *Public Administration*, Vol. 36(3), 1958.

Kavanagh, D., 'The Orientations of Community Leaders to Parliamentary Candidates', *Political Studies*, Vol. XV(4), 1967.

Miller, D. C., 'Industry and Community Power Structure: A Comparative Study of an English and American City', *American Sociological Review*, Vol. 23(1), 1958.

Miller, D. C., 'Decision-Making Cliques in Community Power Structures: A Comparative Study of an English and an American City', *American Sociological Review*, Vol. 23 (1), 1958.

Morris, D. S. and Newton, K., *Chairmen and Non-Chairmen of Birmingham Council*, Discussion Paper, Series F, No. 4, Faculty of Commerce and Social Science, University of Birmingham.

————, *Profile of a Local Political Elite: Businessmen on Birmingham Council, 1920–66*, Discussion Paper, Series F, No. 6, Faculty of Commerce and Social Science, University of Birmingham, 1969.

————, *The Social Composition of Birmingham Council, 1930–66*, Discussion Paper, Series F, No. 2, Faculty of Commerce and Social Science, University of Birmingham.

Musgrove, F., 'The Educational and Geographical Background of Some Local Leaders', *British Journal of Sociology*, Vol. 12(4), 1961.

Newton, K., *The Recruitment of Councillors*, Discussion Paper, Series E, No. 8, Faculty of Commerce and Social Science, University of Birmingham.

————, *The Social Composition of Councils*, Discussion Paper, Series E, No. 9, Faculty of Commerce and Social Science, University of Birmingham.

Plowman, D. E. G., Minchinton, W. E. and Stacey, M., 'Local Status in England and Wales', *Sociological Review*, Vol. 10(2), 1962.

Ridley, P. F. C., 'Business Leaders and Civil Participation: a Study of Liverpool Businessmen and their Attitudes to the Local Community' (Liverpool University, MA thesis, 1970).

Sharpe, L. J., 'Elected Representatives in Local Government', *British Journal of Sociology*, Vol. 13(3), 1962.

Trade Union Elites

Hughes, J., *Membership Participation and Trade Union Government*, Research Paper no. 5 of the Royal Commission on Trade Unions and Employers' Associations (Donovan), HMSO, London, 1968.

Allen, V. L., *Power in Trade Unions: A Study of their Organisation in Great Britain*, Longmans Green, London, 1954.

———, *Trade Union Leadership*, Longmans Green, London, 1957.

———, *Trade Unions and the Government*, Longmans Green, London, 1960.

Clegg, H. A., Killick, A. J. and Adams, R., *Trade Union Officers*, Blackwell, Oxford, 1961.

Goldstein, J., *The Government of British Trade Unions*, Allen & Unwin, London, 1952.

Roberts, B. C., *Trade Union Government and Administration in Great Britain*, Bell, London, 1956.

Allen, V. L., 'The Ethics of Trade Union Leaders', *British Journal of Sociology*, Vol. 7(4), 1956.

———, 'The Reorganisation of the Trades Union Congress, 1918–27', *British Journal of Sociology*, Vol. 11(1), 1960.

Educational Elites and the Education of Elites

Report of the Committee on Higher Education (Robbins), HMSO, London, 1963.

Reports of the Public Schools Commission (Newsom), HMSO, London, 1968–70.

Report of the Committee of Inquiry, University of Oxford (Franks), Clarendon Press, Oxford, 1966.

Anderson, C. A. and Schapner, M., *Schools and Society in England: Social Backgrounds of Oxford and Cambridge Students*, Public Affairs Press, Washington, 1952.

Bishop, T. J. H. and Wilkinson, R., *Winchester and the Public Schools Elite*, Faber & Faber, London, 1967.

Craig, C., *The Employment of Cambridge Graduates*, Cambridge University Press, London, 1963.

Halsey, A. H. and Trow, M., *The British Academics*, Faber & Faber, London, 1971.

Kalton, G., *The Public Schools: A Factual Survey of Headmasters Conference Schools in England and Wales*, Longmans, London, 1966.

Kelsall, R. K., *et al.*, *Graduates: the Sociology of an Elite*, Methuen, London, 1972.

———, *Six Years After*, Higher Education Research Unit, Department of Sociological Studies, Sheffield University, 1970.

Ogilvie, V., *The English Public Schools*, Batsford, London, 1957.

PEP, *Graduate Employment*, Allen & Unwin, London, 1956.

————, *Graduates in Industry*, Allen & Unwin, London, 1957.

Rothblatt, S., *The Revolution of the Dons: Cambridge and Society in Victorian England*, Faber & Faber, London, 1968.

Wakeford, J., *The Cloistered Elite: A Sociological Analysis of the English Public Boarding School*, Macmillan, London, 1969.

Weinberg, I., *The English Public Schools: The Sociology of Elite Education*, Atherton Press, New York, 1967.

*Wilkinson, R., *The Prefects: British Leadership and the Public School Tradition*, Oxford University Press, London, 1964 (also published as *Gentlemanly Power*, New York, 1964).

Bamford, T. W., 'Public Schools and Social Class, 1801–50', *British Journal of Sociology*, Vol. 12(3), 1961.

Campbell, F., 'Latin and the Elite Tradition in Education', *British Journal of Sociology*, Vol. 19(3), 1968.

Collisson, P. and Millen, J., 'University Chancellors, Vice-Chancellors and College Principals: A Social Profile', *Sociology*, Vol. 3(1), 1969.

Crichton-Miller, N., 'The Mobility of Graduates', *Graduate Appointments Register*, 1966.

Eggleston, J., 'Secondary Schools and Oxbridge Blues', *British Journal of Sociology*, Vol. 16(3), 1965.

Hall, R., 'The Family Background of Etonians', in Rose, R. (ed.), *Studies in British Politics*, Macmillan, London, 1969.

Jenkins, H. and Caradog Jones, D., 'Social Class of Cambridge Alumni of the Eighteenth and Nineteenth Centuries', *British Journal of Sociology*, Vol. 1(2), 1950.

McQuail, D., O'Sullivan, L. P. and Quine, W. G., 'Elite Education and Political Values', *Political Studies*, Vol. XVI(3), 1968.

PEP, 'Salaries of Graduates in Industry, London', *Planning*, Vol. (1), 1961.

Szereter, R., 'A Note on the Staffing of Public Schools, 1939–64', *British Journal of Sociology*, Vol. 18(2), 1967.

Trow, M. and Halsey, A. H., 'British Academics and the Professorship', *Sociology*, Vol. 3(3), 1969.

Bishop, T. J. H., 'Origins and Achievements of Winchester College Pupils, 1836–1934' (University of London, LSE, Ph.D thesis, 1962).

Standley, C. C., 'Recruitment and Records of University Students in Great Britain' (Somerville College, Oxford, B.Litt., 1953).

Communications Elites

Report of the Royal Commission on the Press (Shawcross), HMSO, London, 1962.

Jenkins, C., *Power Behind the Screen*, MacGibbon & Kee, London, 1961.

*Seymour-Ure, C., *The Press, Politics and the Public*, Methuen, London, 1968.

*Tunstall, J. (ed.), *Media Sociology: A Reader*, Constable, London, 1970.

————, *Journalists at Work, Special Correspondents: their News Organisations, News Sources and Competitor-Colleagues*, Constable, London, 1971.

————, *The Westminster Lobby Correspondents*, Routledge & Kegan Paul, London, 1970.

Current Research on British Elites

Bell, C. R., 'Background and the routes to the top of the British elite in the nineteenth century', Department of Sociology, University of Essex.

Brook, J., 'The judiciary of the superior courts 1820–1968: a sociological study', Department of Sociology, Bedford College, London.

Campbell, P. W., 'Political elites in Britain and France', Department of Politics, University of Reading.

Giddens, A., Ingham, G. K. and Stansworth, P., 'Elites in the British class structure', Department of Economic Affairs, Cambridge.

Otley, C. B., 'Sociological, political and historical features of the role and position of the army in Britain', Department of Sociology, Lancaster University.

Scotford-Morton, M., 'British and French administrative training', Department of Sociology, University of Reading.

Wakeford, J., 'Cluster analysis of certain social and educational characteristics of 1500 members of selected British elites', Department of Sociology, Lancaster University.

Wright, M. W., 'Changes in the Civil Service 1960–70', Department of Government, Manchester University.

NOTES ON CONTRIBUTORS

COLIN BELL is Senior Lecturer in Sociology at the University of Essex. He is the author of *Middle Class Families* (1968), *The Disruption of Community Life* (1970) and co-author of *Community Studies* (1972) and *Persistence and Change: a Second Study of Banbury* (forthcoming). He is currently writing a book on the social situation of women in industrial societies.

DOUGLAS BENSON is a Research Associate in the Department of Sociology, Manchester University. He is currently working on a project on 'Community Reactions to Deviance' financed by the Social Science Research Council.

IAN BUDGE is a Reader in the Department of Government at the University of Essex. He wrote *Agreement and the Stability of Democracy* (1970) and was co-author of *Scottish Political Behaviour* (1966), *Political Stratification and Democracy* (1972) and *Belfast: Approach to Crisis* (1973). His present research (with Dennis Farlie) is on spatial models of voting and party competition.

IVOR CREWE is Lecturer in the Department of Government at the University of Essex. He is the co-author of *Social Survey of the Civil Service* (HMSO, 1969) and has written several articles on British electoral behaviour. He is currently engaged on a project on 'The Politics of the English Middle Classes' financed by the Social Science Research Council.

COLIN CROUCH is Lecturer in Sociology at the University of Bath. He is the author of *The Student Revolt* (1970) and two Fabian papers, *Politics in a Technological Society* (1970) and (with Stephen Mennell) *The Universities: Pressures and Prospects* (1972); and has contributed to M. Archer and S. Giner (eds.), *Contemporary Europe: Class, Status and Power* (1971); M. Archer (ed.), *Students, University and Society* (1972) and to P. Townsend and M. Bosanquet, *Inequality Under Labour* (1972). At present he is working on the implications of recent developments in incomes and industrial relations policies in Britain for theories of class structure.

351

DENNIS FARLIE is a Reader in Mathematics at the University of Essex. He has written articles for *Biometrika, Statistician* and the *Journal of the Royal Statistical Society (B)*. He is collaborating with Ian Budge on research into spatial models of voting and party competition; and is generally interested in multivariate statistical analysis, especially the presentation of multivariate statistics.

W. L. GUTTSMAN is the Librarian of the University of East Anglia. He wrote *The British Political Elite* (1965) and edited *The English Ruling Class* (1969). He is now engaged on a comparative study of Social Democratic parties.

VICTOR HANBY is a Lecturer in political sociology at the University of Stirling. He has written articles on electoral systems for *Comparative Political Studies* and the *British Journal of Political Science* and is now engaged on research into the recruitment of leaders in left-wing political parties.

TIMOTHY HENNESSEY is Associate Professor at the Department of Political Science, Michigan State University. He is the author of *Comparative Political Socialisation* (1973) and numerous articles on political socialisation, political culture and legislative behaviour in various journals of political science. He is now engaged with Spencer Wellhofer on a study of the organisation and recruitment of left-wing parties in England, Sweden, Denmark, Norway and Argentina since the turn of the century.

MALCOLM JACK is Clerk of the House of Commons and a Ph.D. candidate at the London School of Economics. His main interests are in political and social philosophy, especially 'elite theorists', and also the writings of Bernard de Mandeville.

PETER MORRISS is a Graduate Student in the Department of Government, Manchester University. He is interested in problems in the concept of political power and is the author of 'Power in New Haven: A Reassessment of *Who Governs?*' in the *British Journal of Political Science*, October 1972.

GERAINT PARRY is Senior Lecturer in Government at Manchester University. He is the author of *Political Elites* (1969) and editor of *Participation in Politics* (1972) as well as many articles on political sociology, political theory and the history of political ideas. He is currently working on a study of John Locke's political thought.

352

PHILIP STANWORTH is a Research Officer at the Department of Applied Economics, Cambridge University. He is engaged on a project on 'Elites in the British Class Structure', financed by the Social Science Research Council.

FRANCES WAKEFORD is an independent research worker and part-time lecturer in sociology at the Charlotte Mason College, Ambleside.

JOHN WAKEFORD is Senior Lecturer in Sociology at Lancaster University. He is the author of *The Strategy of Social Enquiry* (1968), and *The Cloistered Elite* (1969) and he is joint editor of *Power in Britain* (1973). His present research interests include power and deviance, the field of education generally, and relations between universities and elites.

E. SPENCER WELLHOFER is Assistant Professor in the Department of Political Science, Michigan State University. He has written numerous conference papers on the recruitment of party elites and the development of party organisations and is currently involved (with Timothy Hennessey) on a comparative study of the organisation and recruitment of left-wing parties in Britain, Sweden, Denmark, Norway and Argentina since the turn of the century.

INDEX

Dahl, R., 12, 34, 36, 317, 319, 331
Dahrendorf, R., 118, 171
datacrat, 19
decisions & decision making, 200, 256, 317–336; and business, 250; and class structure, 243–4; and trade unions, 70; by informal bodies, 17
democracy, 275–6; and political parties, 28, 289–91, 300, 314–15n; and power, 333
demographic data, 202–4, 230–32
Dennis, N., 32
d'Hondt system (German elections), 94
Dictionary of National Biography, 161–171; editorial policy, 165–9; exclusion from, 168; process of nomination for, 168–9
differentials, pay, 58–9; between skilled & semi-skilled, 60,
directories, use of for elites research, 161–71
directors, company, 255; social background, 254
division of labour, 247
Djilas, M., 274
Domhoff, G., 200–201, 204, 237
Donovan Commission, 69
Downs, A., 286, 298, 310–12n
Drucker, P., 248
Durkheim, E., 247
Duverger, M., 286–8

economic growth, 56
economic power, 19
Edinger, L. J., 21, 202–3, 207–8, 238
education: and elite groups, 171–98 *passim*; and social background, 101, 228; and social class, 128; *see also* grammar schools, public schools *and* universities
elections, 297–307; and ideology, 284; and two party systems, 288–301; 310–11n; strategy, 298–305
electoral system, British and German, 93–100
electorate, 30, 298–305; and the elected representatives, 118; issue preferences, 234
elite theory, 264–78; and Marxism, 272–6; classical, 244
elites: and decision making, 317–36; and issue preferences, 199–240; and property, 243–63; and the state, 78; background of, 20–27, 199–240; British studies of, 12–44; circulation of, 18–20, 266; comparisons between different ones, 14; connections between, 15–16; defined, 10–11, 266; disagreement on socioeconomic issues, 216; in political parties,

89–125, 279–315; legislative, 204; N.E.C. & the Labour Party, 149; qualities of, 267; recruitment, 20–28, 89–125; roles, 31–3; social & educational characteristics, 171–98; socialisation, 28–9; study of, 9–10, 41–4; theories of, 43–4; visibility of, 16–18
embourgeoisement, 173; of conservative parties, 101; of the labour party, 116; of the N.E.C., 128–58 *passim*; of the S.P.D., 107
empirical evidence, 278
employers' organisations, 57
employment, full, 56, 73
entrepreneur, 251
Epstein, L., 284, 298, 307
equality distinguished from equity, 63, 74
equity and pay claims, 62, 74
Erikson, C., 166
establishment, 200
étatiste corporation, 79, 80
ethics and income distribution, 63–4
exit concept, 292–7

Fabian Society, 133, 146
facts, determination of, 37
false consciousness, 328–44
Farlie, D., 21
Finer, S. E., 117
force, use of, 326
Frey, F., 323, 329
Fulton Committee, 22, 26

Galbraith, J. K., 18–19, 171
Geiger, T., 251
generations, elite, 25
Germany, Federal Republic of, 89–125; cabinet, 110–11, 112–13; civil service, 124n; candidate election, 94–5, 116, 119; constitution, 95; electoral system, 90, 93–7; *Land* lists, 93–4, 98, 121n,; political elites, 89–125; political parties, 91, 120n; political tradition, 90–93
Giddens, A., 173
Glasgow, local councillors, 206, 209–215, 223–5, 233
governments: economic management, 56, 79; intervention, 220–21; patronage, 17; simularity of their policies, 250
grammar schools, 24, 101, 180
Gross, J., 167
Gunn, L. A., 17
Guttsman, W. L., 13, 128

Hacker, A., 20
Hanby, V., 27
Hands, G., 281

356